THE WORKS OF SRI CHINMOY

UNITED NATIONS WORKS

VOLUME I

THE WORKS OF SRI CHINMOY
UNITED NATIONS WORKS

VOLUME I

⋆

THE GARLAND OF NATION-SOULS
THE TEARS OF NATION-HEARTS
THE BICENTENNIAL FLAMES AT THE UNITED NATIONS
REALITY-DREAM
UNION-VISION
TWO GOD-SERVERS AND MAN-LOVERS
U THANT: DIVINITY'S SMILE, HUMANITY'S CRY
THE SEEKER'S MIND
A SOULFUL TRIBUTE TO THE SECRETARY-GENERAL
UNITED NATIONS MEDITATION-FLOWERS AND TO-MORROW'S NOON
PÉREZ DE CUÉLLAR: IMMORTALITY'S RAINBOW-PEACE
A REAL MEMBER OF THE UNITED NATIONS
THE INNER ROLE OF THE UNITED NATIONS

LYON · OXFORD
GANAPATI PRESS
XC

© 2020 THE SRI CHINMOY CENTRE

ISBN 978-1-911319-30-6

See appendix for notice regarding this edition.

FIRST EDITION WENT TO PRESS ON 13 APRIL 2020

UNITED NATIONS WORKS

VOLUME I

PART I

THE GARLAND OF NATION-SOULS

1. *United Nations Meditation Group*

We believe and we hold that each man has the potentiality of reaching the Ultimate Truth. We also believe that man cannot and will not remain imperfect forever. Each man is an instrument of God. When the hour strikes, each individual soul listens to the inner dictates of God. When man listens to God, his imperfections are turned into perfections, his ignorance into knowledge, his searching mind into revealing light and his uncertain reality into all-fulfilling Divinity.

2. The Garland of Nation-Souls

Each nation has five members in its family: inspiration, aspiration, realisation, revelation and manifestation. The body needs inspiration. The vital needs aspiration. The mind needs realisation. The heart needs revelation. The soul needs manifestation.

The body wants to walk. The vital wants to run. The mind wants to fly. The heart wants to dive. The soul wants to be.

Inspiration without aspiration cannot see God. Aspiration without realisation cannot reach God. Realisation without revelation cannot glorify God. Revelation without manifestation cannot fulfil God.

Each nation has a soul of its own. The soul is at once God's illumining Activity and the nation's fulfilling capacity. Each nation is the involution of its highest Light and the evolution of its inmost Power. Immortality is the homeland of the soul. Eternity is the life of the soul. Infinity is the reality of the soul.

The Garland of Nation-Souls: a garland is the embodiment of God's Smile and man's achievement. God's Divine Smile is supremely expansive, and man's divine achievement is eternally impressive. Now, where is the Garland of Nation-Souls? It is here, inside the boat of the United Nations. Who deserves to be garlanded? Undoubtedly the Seeker-Pilot, U Thant. This able, genuine and divine Pilot of ours is blessed with a far-reaching, growing vision, and a wide, expanding, energising reality.

When a nation's outer life listens to the inner dictates of its soul, its earthly desires decrease, its heavenly aspirations increase, its human wants are lessened and its divine needs are heightened. It envisions the Truth Transcendental and grows into God's Pride Supreme.

THE GARLAND OF NATION-SOULS

The great philosopher Arthur Schopenhauer once remarked, "Every nation ridicules other nations, and all are right." It is true that all nations, with no exception, will one day be flooded with God's perfect Perfection, at God's choice Hour. The nations that are aspiring consciously are hastening God's Hour. The nations that are aspiring unconsciously are inwardly valuing God's Hour, and soon their aspiration will increase. The nations that are wallowing in the pleasures of darkening and darkened night are God's so-called failures, but before long even they will open their eyes and, along with their forerunners, will hear God ringing the bell of Inner Victory.

The ascending aspiration of the fully awakened souls and the descending Blessing-Light of God can eventually transform the face of the entire globe.

Imperfection and impossibility we cherished yesterday. Today, imperfection and impossibility are our unwanted guests. Tomorrow, they will be seen nowhere. Perfection and divinity will be our most welcome guests.

The nation that soulfully cries for inner development and devotedly cries for outer growth can alone be in the vanguard of the teeming nations. Why does a nation fail? A nation fails because it does not want the sustaining Truth to be on its side. When does a nation fall? A nation falls when it deliberately and vehemently resists the idea of being on the side of Truth. How can a nation succeed? A nation can succeed by following the Truth within and without. The very pursuit of Truth can make the existence of a nation free, meaningful, purposeful and fruitful. Now, how can a nation flourish? A nation can flourish when it sees no difference between the Creator and the creation. A nation can flourish when it loves the world, not for what the world will give in return, but for the sake of love. Selfless love, true love, never ends, never fails. Love is its own immediate reward.

To me, the real worth of nations lies in their united principles; and it is in the united principles that one can see the fruit of true inner oneness and divine perfection. The united principles must needs have co-operation. If there is no co-operation, then the united principles will bear no fruit whatsoever. The present-day world needs co-operation.

Supremely significant are the words of the Secretary General, U Thant: "I can think of no worthier task for a man or a woman to be engaged in than that of creating the tools for international co-operation and working for the betterment of his fellow human beings." Also, the Secretary-General soulfully affirms: "Our work at the United Nations gives us the privilege of contributing actively from day to day in the ardent process of building peace."

Peace.
Aum. Shanti, Shanti, Shanti.

The World Youth Assembly has been organised here. This is a most momentous task. With our deepest joy and greatest fortune we see here at the United Nations the promising hearts of one hundred and twenty-five nations. Each nation is unique, for in and through each nation the Lord Supreme wants to fulfil Himself. Each nation is chosen by the Supreme, to fulfil Him in an unprecedented, unique manner.

Each nation right now needs peace. We all need peace. To have peace, what we need is the right path, the Path Divine. Four thousand years ago, in the hoary past, the Vedic seers offered a supreme prayer to the Lord Supreme:

O Lord Agni, O Lord,
Lead us, lead us by the right path to well-being.

We can all offer this soulful prayer to our Inner Pilot every day. It is this prayer that can awaken and inspire the length and breadth of the entire world. Peace we need. Man seeks peace because he needs peace desperately. Man welcomes peace because it is in peace alone that he can have his own true achievement and fulfilment. Man needs peace. He has to spread it. The moment he needs peace, he has to feel that sooner or later he will receive it. He has to feel that his inner being will be flooded with peace. But he has to spread this peace. Man spreads peace because he knows that he has to conquer, transcend death.

War and peace. In his outer being and inner being each man has only two words: war and peace. Outer war we all know. Inner war is constant. At every moment a sincere seeker has to fight against his own doubt, imperfections, limitations, bondage and death. This inner war is constant; and when we achieve our victory in the inner life, only then can we claim to be God's children, worthy children of God, divine children of God, the true representatives of God. At that moment God beckons us, and He uses us in His own Way. He takes us for His own Use.

War and peace. Man invents war. Man discovers peace. Man invents war from without. Man discovers peace from within. The smile of war is the flood of human blood. The smile of peace is love, Love Divine, below, above. The animal in man wants war, war to devour the sleeping, snoring world. The divine in man needs peace, peace to feed the hungry world.

3. *The Song Universal*

The Song Universal is freedom. Freedom from what? Freedom from limitations, freedom from imperfections and freedom from ignorance. Man is in stark bondage. Nevertheless, man has the power deep within to cut asunder the teeming ties that have bound him and forced him to launch into the sea of uncertainty.

Four thousand years ago the Vedic seers voiced forth:

> Give freedom for our bodies.
> Give freedom for our dwelling.
> Give freedom for our life.

This soulful prayer of the Vedic seers of yore will echo and re-echo through eternity in humanity's aspiring heart.

Freedom does not mean being away from home. Freedom means accepting and feeling the entire world as one's real home, as one's very own. With a view to achieving and growing into this peerless freedom, man does many things. He simply throws himself into a tornado of blind activities. But man has to learn that he has only one thing to do, and that is to discover and uncover. He has to discover the Divinity within, and uncover the veil of ignorance without. Likewise, man has only one thing to be: God. He has to be God the Infinite, God the Eternal and God the Immortal.

It is said that the quickest way to do many things is to do only one thing at a time. Let us start by thinking of, concentrating and meditating on God, and end, if there is any end, with God-Realisation. This is not only the quickest way, but by far the best.

God is Freedom. In an unparalleled way, the Isha Upanishad speaks of God the Absolute:

> It moves. It moves not.
> Far it is. And it is near.
> Within all this it is.
> It is without all this.

Man's deepest faith in God and man's boundless freedom in himself go together. Sublimely significant is the truth that

James M Barrie offers us: "The reason why birds can fly and we can't is simply that they have perfect faith, for to have faith is to have wings."

"We walk by faith, not by sight." An aspirant, a true seeker of the Infinite Freedom, has to breathe in this life-giving and life-transforming truth that the New Testament endows us with.

Man is sick. His sickness is his ignorance. He has been suffering from this unfathomable ignorance for millennia. There is considerable truth in what Bernard Shaw says: "We have not lost faith, but we have transferred it from God to the medical profession."

It is high time for us to come out of our ignorance-sleep. Let us not play the fool. Let us be wise once again. Let us have back our faith in God, who alone can and will cure our entire life and our earthly existence of this fatal ignorance-sickness.

We are all assembled at the Church Center for the United Nations. The word "United" is hallowed. It can better be felt than described. Rather I should say it can only be felt and cannot be described at all. "United we stand, divided we fall." We are fully aware of this maxim. What we need is to live it.

Now where does this unity come from? It comes from God. It comes from the Brahman, the One without a second. When we walk further along the path of unity, we realise that not only does God have the Consciousness of Unity, but He is Consciousness-Unity itself. When we reach the end of our journey's Goal, we discover that God is both Unity and Multiplicity. In the field of Unity, He is Realisation and Liberation; and in the field of Multiplicity, He is Manifestation and Transformation.

Our inner realisation and outer action must run abreast. Outer achievements should be the conscious and spontaneous revelation of the inner divinity.

Love, harmony, peace and oneness. These are man's divine ideals. On the strength of his inner mounting flame, aspiration, man can easily, unerringly and spontaneously manifest these ideals of his in his human life, in every sphere of his life.

It is quite natural and proper that we should discover our God in and through our own religion. When we go deep within we come to realise that there is only one religion, and that religion is man's inmost cry for God-Realisation. In the hoary past, Asoka, the great Emperor of India, sent missionaries to the corners of the globe with a profound message: "The basis of all religions is the same, wherever they are. Try to help them all you can, teach them all you can, but do not try to injure them."

Let each religion play the role of a flower. Let us make a garland of these divine flowers and offer them at the Feet of God. God will be pleased. We shall be fulfilled.

As there is only one Religion, even so there is only one Song. This Song is man.

> Man is Infinity's Heart.
> Man is Eternity's Breath.
> Man is Immortality's Life.

4. Truth

Truth is God's Treasure and man's property. Truth is God's eternal and constant Progress and man's energising success. Truth is God's Natural History and man's supernatural mystery.

Truth is original and essential when it comes from the soul. Truth is pure and sure when it comes from the heart. Truth is obscure and incomplete when it comes from the mind. Truth is undivinely dynamic and imperfect when it comes from the vital. Truth is weak and insignificant when it comes from the body.

The body is blind. The vital is wild. The mind is ignorant. The heart is aspiration. The soul is realisation. Out of His infinite Bounty, God offers His clearing Sight to the body, His embracing Might to the vital, His illumining Light to the mind, His transcending Height to the heart and His fulfilling Right to the soul. Truth is our inner attitude. Truth is our outer aptitude. Truth is our life's fortitude. When attitude, aptitude and fortitude play together and sing the song of aspiration, Infinitude dawns on them, and soon they bathe in the eternal effulgence of Infinitude.

In the world of desire, Truth is our mind's idea. In the world of aspiration, Truth is our heart's ideal. In the world of realisation, Truth is our soul's Goal.

Idea is the seed. Ideal is the tree. Goal is the fruit.

Idea is self-expression. Ideal is self-expansion. Goal is Self-Union.

5. *God and Truth*

God expresses Himself through Silence. God expands Himself through Light. God unites Himself with His Creation through Delight.

Man's outer life needs God's Silence. Man's inner life needs God's Light. Man's higher life needs God's Delight.

Again, man is God's Hope. Man is God's Smile. Man is God's Pride. Man is God's Hope in his inner life, man is God's Smile in his higher life and man is God's Pride in his outer life.

God's Hope is man's possibility. God's Smile is man's ability. God's Pride is man's necessity.

Truth, the ultimate Truth, plays its role in three different stages of evolution: objective, subjective and absolute. In the objective, Truth is man's searching consciousness; in the subjective, Truth is man's awakening Divinity; and in the absolute, Truth is man's fulfilling Reality.

In Reality man sees the Truth in its universal form. In Divinity man sees the Truth in its theoretical form. In consciousness man sees the Truth in its practical form.

6. *The inner way*

The inner way is the manifestation of the inner creation. The inner creation is the revelation of the inner realisation. The inner realisation is the dynamic expression of the inner will.

Will is power. Realisation is peace. Creation is bliss. Will tells me what I can divinely do for God and humanity. Realisation tells me what God unconditionally does for me and humanity. Creation tells me what humanity and I can devotedly do for God.

The inner way is the origin of the divine intuition. Intuition carries us to revelation. Revelation shows us the real in the ideal, and the ideal in the real. Intuition is the certainty of Divinity. Divinity is the certainty of Immortality. Immortality is the certainty of Reality.

Divinity's child is man. Immortality's child is the soul. Reality's child is Light.

There are two ways: the inner and the outer. To discover the outer way we need outer power, the power of the physical, vital and mental. To discover the inner way we need inner power, the power of the soul.

The outer way always has limited vision. The inner way has the everlasting and ever-transcending Vision. The vision of the outer way culminates in the fast-approaching tomorrow. The vision of the inner way, which marches along the road of Infinity, Eternity and Immortality, has no journey's end. Constantly, spontaneously and soulfully it is marching towards the ever-transcending and ever-fulfilling Beyond.

7. *No chance but God's Concern*

No chance but God's Concern. No golden chance but God's constant Concern.

Before I act, I need to live. Before I live, I need to breathe. Before I breathe, I need to know the purpose of my life, the aim of my earthly existence. If the ultimate aim of my earthly existence is to reach the farthest, feel the deepest and climb the highest, then I have to breathe God's Light in and out from God Himself.

From whom can I have God's Light? God's Light I can have directly from God when the fleeting moment of my unconditionally surrendered life I offer to God.

When can I have God's Light? I can have God's Light when I am consciously aware of the undeniable fact that God loves me infinitely more than I love Him; and I have to feel that God loves me infinitely more than I love myself.

How can I have God's Light? I can have God's Light when I grow into the purest humility of the poor and the mightiest magnanimity of the rich. My humility is my divine brotherhood. My magnanimity is my divine fatherhood.

I have to feel that it is God, God alone, who constantly cares for me. I am not afraid of telling anything to the world, because I feel that God is speaking through me. I am not afraid of doing anything in the world, because I feel that God is acting through me. I am not afraid of transforming the world-nature, because I know that God is doing it for me. Finally, I am not afraid of affirming that God and I are eternally and perpetually one, because God has confided in me that there can be no other Truth than this.

No chance. There is no such thing as chance. There is only God's constant, selfless, unreserved Concern. This Concern is His glowing, flowing and descending Grace.

God is Concern. This Concern enters into the darkening ignorance and darkened humanity to transform the face of the world only when the earth-consciousness is ready to receive God's spontaneous, constant and unreserved Concern soulfully and unreservedly.

No chance but God's Concern. No golden chance but God's constant Concern.

8. *God's brightest Heaven and man's surest haven*

Of all the divine qualities, unfortunately Light is wanted the least, even though it is needed most by all. People want Love, Peace, Joy and Power, but very rarely they want Light. Unconsciously or consciously, they are afraid of Light. They feel that the effulgence of Light will uproot the ignorance-tree that they embody. They feel that the Divine Light will expose their imperfections, limitations and bondage. This is not true.

The Divine Light embraces the world in all its ignorance. Further, the Divine Light feels that it is its bounden duty to elevate the human consciousness into the plenitude of the Life Divine.

If the animal in us, if the human in us, really want a Divine Life on earth, then we have to cry, cry like a child for God's Compassion-Light, which is at once God's brightest Heaven and man's surest Haven.

9. *Meditation: self-transcendence*

Meditation is self-transcendence. Self-transcendence is the message of the Beyond. The message of the Beyond is God, the eternally evolving Soul, and God, the eternally fulfilling Goal.

The animal in man is proud of his self-aggrandisement. The human in man is delighted with his self-awareness. The divine in man is conscious of his self-realisation. The Supreme in man is fulfilled in his self-transcendence.

Man needs material wealth to enjoy a prosperous earthly life. Man needs meditation to live a peaceful heavenly life. Man needs revelation to live as a divine hero, to guide and serve and serve and guide as a divine hero. Heaven does not want a weakling. Earth does not need a weakling.

Life is not empty talk. Life is not the breath of illusion. Life is the action of aspiration. Aspiration is the action of man's Inner Pilot. Let us fight the battle of life within. Let us wake up to the reality of our world consciously and devotedly. Ours will be the victory without. Forget we must not, never. We are of God the Infinite and we are for God the Eternal.

Meditation means the evolution of the body and the soul. The body's ultimate evolution is transformation and perfection.

The soul's ultimate evolution is the highest illumination and complete manifestation.

He who meditates, consciously dedicates his life to God. He who dedicates his life to mankind, soulfully meditates on the real God. His are the eyes that see Heaven on earth. In him divinity and humanity are triumphantly blended.

Temptation and meditation. Temptation: this is precisely what an unaspiring man knows. Meditation: this is what an aspiring man constantly is. An unaspiring man must descend in the scale of life and feel the very breath of ignorance. An aspiring man eternally ascends in the scale of life and lives in the very Heart of God.

We have hundreds of secrets, but meditation has only one: competence is achievement. Competence and achievement are the smiles of God's unconditional Grace.

Sri Krishna meditated. He became God, the Love Divine. The Buddha meditated. He became God, the Light Divine. The Christ meditated. He became God, the Compassion Divine. Now God wants you to meditate. He wants you to become God, the Life Divine.

10. *Is the spiritual life an escape from reality?*

Reality. An unaspiring man thinks that undying pleasure is the only reality. An aspiring man feels that a divine experience is the only reality. A God-Realised man knows that God, the Supreme Lover, alone has the Reality, and that God, the Supreme Beloved, alone is the Reality. Reality is also God, the fulfilling Light, and man, the fulfilled life.

The abode of Transcendental Fulfilment has three doors: Love, Freedom and Delight. The Love-Door is open only to him who serves crying humanity. The Freedom-Door is open only to him who serves struggling humanity. The Delight-Door is open only to him who serves awakening humanity.

The spiritual life is never an escape from reality. On the contrary, the spiritual life is the conscious and spontaneous acceptance of reality in its totality. For a spiritual seeker the idea of an escape from reality is absurdity plus impossibility, for spirituality and reality need each other to be supremely fulfilled. Without reality's soul, spirituality is worse than useless. Without spirituality's breath, reality is more than meaningless. Spirituality with reality means man's inner cry for perfect Perfection. Reality with spirituality means God's omnipotent Will for total and absolute manifestation.

Escape is a base thought. It acts like a thief, the worst possible thief. Into the heart of tenebrous gloom escape gains easy and free access. He who indulges in the idea of an immediate escape unmistakably commits lingering suicide.

Acceptance, the acceptance of life with a divine attitude, is not only a lofty idea, but the very ideal of life. This ideal of life is realised, revealed and manifested through God's soul-elevating inspiration and man's life-building aspiration. Acceptance of life is the divine pride of true spirituality. To live a spiritual life is our only responsibility.

Arnold Bennet said, "You are not in charge of the universe; you are in charge of yourself." I venture to say that if I can be in charge of myself, then God will put me in charge of the universe, His Universe.

Acceptance of the life divine is the transcendence of human ego. The transcendence of ego is man's real dignity and true worth. Momentous are the words of our Secretary-General, U Thant: "The dignity and worth of the human person is not merely a philosophic concept. It is, and should be, a working principle of human existence guiding our daily lives."

There is only one thing that man needs: the inner wisdom. The supreme Pilot of the United Nations' Boat is piloting a countless number of the human family with his wisdom-light to the shores of dream-fulfilled Reality. Inside the heart of learning humanity, his wisdom-tree is growing slowly, steadily, significantly and triumphantly. Him to quote,

> Is the human race so destitute of wisdom, so incapable of tolerance, so blind even to the simple dictates of self-presentation that the last proof of its progress is to be extermination of all life on our small planet? I cannot believe that this is to be the end. I cannot believe that humanity is so bereft of common sense as to launch universal suicide.

Acceptance of life is the assurance of faith. Faith walks along the road of fulfilling and fulfilled immortality. Escape from reality will, in the twinkling of an eye, weaken our resolves, loosen our armour and finally throw us into the very depths of the annihilation-sea.

No, we must never make a cowardly escape. We must always be brave. Divine courage is our birthright. We are the hero-warriors of supreme Reality chosen to fight against the teeming, brooding and threatening ignorance-night.

We are brave. The brave deserve the fair. We are aware. The aware deserve God, the real God.

11. *Does meditation really accomplish anything?*

First of all, let us try to know and understand what meditation actually means. What is meditation? Meditation is man's inner movement and outer progress. Meditation is man's inner soulful promise and outer fruitful manifestation.

A man of no aspiration will dauntlessly ask, "Does meditation really accomplish anything?" A man of sterling faith and aspiration will confidently ask, "Is there anything on earth, in God's Creation, that meditation cannot accomplish? Is there anything that cannot be achieved by meditation?"

God will immediately answer these two questions. To the man who has no aspiration, God will say, "My child, sleep. Sleep. You need rest." To the one who is all aspiration, God will say, "My child, fly. Fly. My highest Height of the Transcendental Beyond is eagerly expecting your arrival."

What is the first and foremost thing we expect from meditation? Peace. Peace and nothing else. Meditation is the embodiment of peace. The present-day world needs only one thing: peace.

The peace-lover, our ex-Secretary-General Dag Hammarskjöld, offers us a sublime message: "No peace which is not peace for all ...." In peace, what looms large is eternal, fulfilling rest. He says, ".... no rest until all has been fulfilled."

Why do we meditate? We meditate just because our life needs inspiration, our life needs aspiration. Aspiration is, to some extent, a form of meditation. It is our meditation that promises to give us our realisation-tree. Today meditation plays the role of aspiration and tomorrow meditation will play the role of realisation. The Inner Pilot, the Pilot Supreme within us, inspires us to act; and it is He who has already kept the fruit of action safe in the life of our aspiration.

The truth-seeker in Dag Hammarskjöld, on the strength of his own inner conviction said, "Somebody placed the shuttle in your hand: somebody who had already arranged the threads."

In our human life two things are of paramount importance: role and Goal. At every moment we have to know what our role is, and then we have to be conscious of our ultimate Goal. At our journey's start we have to be fully aware of our role. At the end of our journey's close we have to be fully conscious of our Goal. Now, there must needs be a connecting link between our role and our Goal. Meditation is this connecting link between our role in the Divine Play, the Divine *Lila,* and our ultimate Goal in God's ever-evolving Universe. Man's role is his conscious self-surrender to the Will of the Absolute Supreme. This is his only role. Man's Goal, the Goal of Goals, is in constant self-surrender to the absolute Will of the Supreme.

Life is conscious ascent and conscious descent. Now, when we say ascent, what do we actually mean? Life's aspiration is ascending towards the Highest. When we say descent, we mean the illumining descent of the soul's all-transforming and all-fulfilling meditation. The human life is an ascending prayer. Again, the divine soul in each human being is a descending meditation. Our ascending cry and the descending Grace are inseparable. Together they move, together they fulfil the Absolute, here on earth. As human beings are countless, even so are their endless prayers. Each human being can doubt the value of spiritual prayer during his short span of life, but no human being on earth can say that he never prayed. Be it for a fleeting second or for hours or for months or for years, each individual has to pray. This prayer has intrinsic value. Again, when it is a matter of the individual, one individual can far excel the rest of mankind; similarly, one individual prayer far excels all prayer.

The profound seeker in Dag Hammarskjöld offers an unparalleled prayer for mankind:

Before Thee in humility;
With Thee in faith;
In Thee in Peace.

Does meditation accomplish anything? Meditation does accomplish something; in fact, it accomplishes everything. God's Divinity meditated and created humanity, humanity in infinite shapes and forms. God's humanity meditates, and before long we shall see the result: the sun of perfect Perfection will shine on the face of aspiring humanity.

Here we are all seekers of the Infinite Truth. None of us has even an iota of doubt about the efficacy of meditation. But we have friends, neighbours, acquaintances, who may ask us, "Does meditation really accomplish anything?" We can tell them, "O unbelievers, O disbelievers, do not sit on the unsure ground of apprehension. Look. Here is the key: meditation. Meditation is the key to unlock the door of God's Plenitude and Infinitude." This is what we can say to the unbelievers. To the disbelievers we can say, "Before you entered into the world arena, yours was the promise to realise Him here in this body, Him to fulfil, Him to manifest here on earth. Now, spread your wings. Spread your wings once for all and catch the first morning breeze with your soul's soulful promise to the Supreme, to the Absolute."

12. *A spiritual Goal for the United Nations: is it practical?*

A spiritual Goal for the United Nations: is it practical? Without the least possible hesitation I venture to say that it is highly practical. It is not only practical, but also practicable. Something more: it is inevitable. We have to know what the spiritual Goal for the United Nations is. Its Goal is to become ultimately the saviour of the world's imperfection, the liberator of the world's destruction and the fulfiller of the world's aspiration.

My heart tells me that the United Nations has a divine Ideal. My soul tells me that this Ideal is going to be transformed into the supreme Reality. Soulful concern is the essence of the United Nations' Ideal. Fruitful patience is the substance of the United Nations' Ideal. Supernal fulfilment will be the essence of the United Nations' Reality. Sempiternal perfection will be the substance of the United Nations' Reality. What is Reality? Reality is the inseparable oneness of Infinity's smile and Eternity's cry.

The great philosopher Aristotle once remarked, "Some men are just as firmly convinced of what they think as others are of what they know." The firm conviction of the United Nations is the confident flight of sublime thought and glowing depth of its knowledge-light.

Today's United Nations sees the nations as its true friends. Tomorrow's United Nations will see the nations as its real sisters and brothers.

Today's United Nations offers hopeful and soulful advice to mankind. Tomorrow's United Nations will offer fruitful and fulfilling peace to mankind.

Today's United Nations feels Truth, Light and Delight in its loving heart. Tomorrow's United Nations will manifest Truth, Light and Delight with its all-embracing soul.

Anatole France said something which is at once interesting and amusing. He said, "It is human nature to think wisely and act foolishly." But in the case of the United Nations it is totally otherwise. The United Nations thinks profoundly and acts selflessly.

My aspiring heart has a soulful message to offer to all the nations that have formed, that have made the Garland of United Nations. The message is:

> There are two stumbling blocks: doubt and insecurity. Doubt in the mind, insecurity in the heart. There are two stepping stones: faith and surrender. Faith in oneself, and surrender to God's Will, conscious surrender to God's constant Will.

True, we have lost and misused thousands of golden opportunities, but we cannot lose or empty God's infinite Compassion. Out of His infinite Compassion, He will make us feel and realise the Transcendental Truth. However, this can be done in two ways. One way is to realise the highest Truth at God's choice Hour; the other way is to realise the Truth when we feel the time is ready, according to our own sweet will. When we open our eyes at God's Will, we fulfil God in His own Way. When we open our eyes at our choice will, at our own selected hour, we fulfil God in our own way. The desire in us fulfils God in its own way. The aspiration in us fulfils God in God's Way. Needless to say, our aspiration is bound to manifest the ultimate, absolute Reality on earth; and in the manifestation of absolute Reality on earth, the face of earth will be transformed into the face of Heaven.

True, the man of the hour need not or cannot be the man of Eternity. But the message that the soul of the United Nations offers to the world at large is for Eternity. Its message is:

> Today's imperfect and unfulfilled man is tomorrow's absolutely fulfilled and supremely manifested God.

13. *Peace is our birthright: how can we have it?*

[Sri Chinmoy sings]

> *O Lord, where is the Truth?*
> *"Where your Beloved is."*
> *Who is my Beloved, who?*
> *"In whom your life is peace."*

Peace. Peace. Peace.

The outer peace and the inner peace: the outer peace is man's compromise; the inner peace is man's fulfilment. The outer peace is man's satisfaction without being satisfied at all. The inner peace is man's satisfaction in being totally and supremely fulfilled.

How can the outer peace have the same capacity as the inner peace? The outer peace can have the same capacity if and when man's creation and God's Creation become inseparably one. What is man's creation? Man's creation is fear. Man's creation is doubt. Man's creation is confusion. What is God's Creation? God's Creation is Love. God's Creation is Compassion. God's Creation is Concern.

Fear is the feeblest ant in man. Doubt is the wildest elephant in man. Confusion is the devouring tiger in man. There is no yawning gulf between man's cherished fear and his forced fear. Doubt God, forgiveness is granted. Doubt yourself, your complete destruction is decreed. Yesterday's confusion was the beginning of your insincerity. Today's confusion is the beginning of your insecurity. Tomorrow's confusion will be the beginning of your futility.

God's Love for man is man's aspiration. God's Compassion for man is man's salvation. God's Concern for man is man's perfection.

Man's fulfilling and fulfilled search for the Real is peace. God the Love is man's eternal Guest in the inmost recesses of his heart. God the Peace is man's eternal Host in the inmost recesses of his heart. That is why we can unfalteringly and unmistakably claim that the loving and fulfilling peace is our birthright.

How can we have peace, even an iota of peace, in our outer life, amid the hustle and bustle of life and our multifarious activities? Easy: we have to choose the inner voice. Easy: we have to control our binding thoughts. Easy: we have to purify our impure emotions.

The inner voice is our guide. The binding thoughts are the dark and unpredictable weather. The impure emotion is the inner storm. We have to listen to the inner voice always. It is our sure protection. We have to be cautious of the binding thoughts. These thoughts have tremendous vitality. We must never allow them to swell into mountains. We have to face them and then dominate them. These thoughts are absolutely non-essential, and we have no time to fret over non-essentials. We have to refrain from the luxury of the emotional storm. Impure emotion is immediate frustration, and frustration is the harbinger of total destruction within and without.

How can we choose the inner voice? To choose the inner voice, we have to meditate early in the morning. To control and dominate our undivine thoughts, we have to meditate at noon. To purify our unlit, impure emotions, we have to meditate in the evening.

What is meditation? Meditation is man's constant awareness and conscious acceptance of God. Meditation is God's unconditional offering to man.

Peace is the beginning of love. Peace is the completion of truth. Peace is the return to the Source. [Sri Chinmoy sings]

There was a time when I stumbled and stumbled,
But now I only climb and climb beyond
And far beyond my Goal's endless Beyond.
And yet my Captain commands: "Go on, go on!"

We have already invoked and received Peace from God. With your kind permission, I wish to invoke more Peace from above. Those who would like to join me are most welcome to come up to the platform and meditate with me for Peace, inner Peace, all-fulfilling Peace.

[The audience responds and meditates with Sri Chinmoy.]

14. *Spirituality: is it only for the chosen few?*

Spirituality: is it only for the chosen few? The answer is at once in the affirmative and in the negative.

The blessed aspirants who cry for the Transcendental Truth, Peace and Bliss are undoubtedly the chosen few. Nevertheless all human beings, with no exception, can easily swim in the infinite sea of spirituality. Those who have lesser goals, those who want to be satisfied with an iota of Peace, Bliss and Truth unfortunately cannot dine with the chosen few in the inner world.

I am afraid the beginners and the budding seekers may, at this point, take me amiss. Truth to tell, I in no way intend to throw cold water on them. On the contrary, I want them to be cognisant of the fact that the highest Goal will never be denied them. It is they who have to cultivate the strongest necessity in the world of their aspiration in order to reach the ultimate Beyond.

What prevents them from reaching the Beyond? Their fear. What else? Their doubt. They must know that fear is the owner only of those who do not believe in God. But they do believe in

God. They do have faith in God. Their love for God is unquestionable. Such being the case, they need not, they must not be afraid of God's Transcendental Height.

Now, about their doubt. When they doubt God it is as if they are playing with a balloon. Their doubt-balloon is bound to burst before long. Their ignorance is bound to be exposed sooner or later. When they doubt themselves they underestimate their own divinity, overestimate their ignorance-reality, belittle their inner potentiality and aggrandise their temporary and fleeting insecurity.

I am sure that the budding seekers have true love for God, and I am sure that they have true love for themselves. Their love for God will eventually transform them into perfect Beauty Supreme, and their divine and fulfilling love for themselves as fully awakened and advanced members of the human family will be manifested on earth by God Himself. Their love is their inseparable oneness with God's Light and with their own inner revealing Reality.

It is high time for me to speak a few words about the chosen few. Theirs is the task sublime to realise God's Universal and Transcendental Consciousness. Theirs is the bounden duty to reveal and fulfil God on earth. And among the chosen few, he is by far the best who unconditionally realises God, reveals God and manifests God at God's choice Hour, in God's own Way.

The chosen few, when they look forward, find themselves already seated in the Dream-Boat of the Supreme. When they look upward, they find themselves already seated in the Life-Boat of the Supreme. When they look inward, they find themselves already seated in the Soul-Boat of the Supreme.

The Supreme blesses a budding seeker. The Supreme caresses a climbing seeker. The Supreme utilises a flowering seeker. The Supreme extols a realised seeker to the skies. The Supreme unreservedly offers Himself to the supremely realised seeker who unconditionally serves Him in the heart of humanity.

15. *Spirituality: the fount of world peace*

Spirituality is aspiration. Spirituality is Yoga. When we have learned what we can expect from aspiration and what we can expect from Yoga, world peace will no longer remain a far cry. Aspiration is an aspirant's conscious longing for the deeper Reality. Yoga is a seeker's conscious oneness with God.

Aspiration leads man to God-Consciousness. Yoga offers God-Consciousness to man. Aspiration takes man back to the Source. Yoga inundates man's consciousness with the Light, Peace, Bliss and Power of the Beyond.

Why do we aspire? We aspire because we love God and want God to love us. Why do we practise Yoga? We practise Yoga in order to feel consciously that God is our very own. We practise Yoga because we feel that our fulfilment on earth can take place only when we have revealed and manifested God's Divinity and Reality here on earth.

When we aspire, we go far beyond the domain of the physical mind and sit at the Feet of God the Light.

When we practise Yoga, we dive deep within, and there we see God and talk to Him face to face.

He who has no aspiration can never free himself from stark ignorance, and he who does not practise Yoga can neither receive nor achieve boundless Light.

Here on earth we have two major instruments: one is the mind, the other is the heart. Very often the mind that we use is the doubtful mind, and the heart we use is the fearful heart. But, unfortunately, the doubtful mind can never aspire, and the fearful heart can never practise Yoga.

True aspiration and teeming human limitations never go together. True Yoga and the life of unlit pleasure cannot go together. Constant aspiration and all-fulfilling Divinity can and must go together. The highest type of Yoga, which is the conscious surrender to God's Will, always goes together with the Life of God.

Aspiration tells man that he will be able to see the Truth of the Beyond. Yoga goes one step ahead. Yoga tells man that the Truth of the Beyond is within him. Finally, God comes and tells man, "My child, you are the Truth of the Beyond. You are My Beyond."

Spirituality is the fount of world peace. Spirituality is the fulfilment of all responsibilities. This is because Divinity is the birthright of spirituality. When an individual touches the foot of a tree, his consciousness enters into the tree; into the branches, into the leaves, into the fruit and into the flowers. In the spiritual sense, God is the tree and the leaves, fruit, branches and flowers are human beings. When you touch the Feet of God, your very consciousness enters into His Universal Consciousness and the infinite beings of His Manifestation.

Each individual has his own way of defining peace. A child finds peace when he is running around outside. That is his fulfilment and in his fulfilment is his peace. An adult finds his peace somewhere else. He finds his peace when he feels that he can lord it over the world. And in the evening of life, an old man thinks that he will get peace if the world recognises his greatness, or if Mother Earth offers Her gratitude to him. He feels that he has done much for humanity and Mother Earth, and he expects something in return. He will have peace only if his expectation is fulfilled.

But peace can never dawn on any individual if it is not properly sought. The child cannot get true peace by running around in the street. He soon finds frustration in his so-called fulfilment. A day will come when he will pray to God for a calm and quiet life. Then he will have peace.

If an adult wants to have peace, real peace, he has to realise that he cannot get it by possessing the world or governing the world. It is only by offering what he has and what he is, consciously and unreservedly, to the world at large, that he will have peace.

The old man who will soon pass behind the curtain of eternity can have peace only if he cherishes the idea that he is not a beggar, but a king. He was a king and he still is a king. He has offered his inner and outer wealth to mankind and Mother Earth. If, in the evening of his life, he doesn't expect anything from the world, then his inner consciousness and outer being will be flooded with peace.

World peace will begin when the so-called human expectation ends. World peace can dawn only when each individual realises the Supreme Truth:

> Love is the revelation of Life and
> Life is the manifestation of Love.

World peace can come into existence when each individual nation consciously feels that the other human beings, the other nations, need not depend on it. No nation is indispensable; but if one nation helps another devotedly and unconditionally, then the world will be inundated with fulfilling peace.

Spirituality is the fulfilment of all responsibility. To love the world is our responsibility. To please the world is our responsibility. We know our own teeming responsibilities; but when we think of the world, unfortunately we do not think of it in a divine or proper way. The world immediately misunderstands us, and we find it impossible to have an inner connection with the world. It is like a mother and her son. In spite of her best intention, the mother finds it difficult to please the son. She thinks of him in her own way and likewise, the son understands the mother in his own way. Because of this lack of communication the mother and the son get no joy in fulfilling their mutual responsibilities.

We love the world. We have to love the world; it is our responsibility. What happens when we try to love the world or when we attempt to fulfil our responsibility to the world? We try to possess and bind the world, and while we are doing this we see that we have already been bound and possessed by the world. We had a sublime opportunity to fulfil our responsibility to the world, but we have badly misused it.

We want to please the world, but how can we please the world if we are not pleased with our own lives? It is sheer absurdity to try to please others if we are not pleased with our inner and outer existence. God has given us big mouths and we try to please others with our mouths, but inside our hearts there is a barren desert. If we have no aspiration, how can we offer the world Peace, Joy and Love? How can we offer anything divine when we don't practise what we preach? Spirituality offers us the capacity to practise what we preach. If we don't follow the path of spirituality, we shall only preach; it will be a one-sided game. But if we really practise Yoga we shall also live the Truth. Our preaching will bear fruit only when it is practised.

How can we fulfil all our responsibilities? We have tried in human ways but we have failed. We think of the world with good thoughts and ideas, but the world remains exactly the same as it was yesterday. We love the world, but the world still remains full of cruelty and hatred. We try to please the world, but the world doesn't want to be pleased. It is as if the world has taken a vow that it won't allow itself to be pleased. And why does all this happen? It is because we have not pleased our Inner Pilot, the One we have to please first. If we have no aspiration to please our Inner Pilot, how can we offer the world Peace, Joy and Love? Unless and until we have pleased the Inner Pilot, the world will always remain a battlefield where the soldiers of fear, doubt, anxiety, worry, imperfection, limitation and bondage will fight; and consciously or unconsciously we will play with these undivine soldiers. Fear, doubt, anxiety, worry and animal propensities can never offer us peace, world peace.

Again, deep within us divinity is crying to come to the fore. There the divine soldiers are our simplicity, sincerity, purity, humility and feeling of oneness. These soldiers are more than ready and eager to fight with fear, doubt, anxiety and worry. Unfortunately, we are not consciously identifying ourselves with the divine soldiers; we are consciously or unconsciously identifying ourselves with the undivine soldiers, and that is why world peace is still a far cry. World peace can be achieved, revealed, offered and manifested on earth when the Divine Power of Love replaces the undivine love of power.

16. *Mediation and meditation*

Two conflicting parties: they need some compromise. A third party, the mediator, is then of paramount importance. His is the task of offering light to the conflicting and strangling parties. When the mediator is successful in his acts of mediation, the two conflicting parties end their mutual enmity and hostility. They live, or at least try to live, peacefully, in their own domain.

Two conflicting parties: one party declares might is right; the other party declares right is might. We observe in the *Mahabharata,* India's greatest epic, that the Kauravas proclaimed that might is right, and the Pandavas maintained, in the light of conscience, that right is might. We all know that the Pandavas won the battle.

The animal in us instigates us by roaring that might is right. The human in us inspires us by feeling deep within that right is might. The divine in us illumines us by offering the supreme Truth that it is God alone who has all Might and who is all Right.

When we look at the unlit consciousness found on the human level, we see something quite disappointing and damaging. We see that this unlit consciousness is very often unthinking, unaspiring and possessing. At this point, we have to invoke the Grace of God. It is the Divine Grace that can transform the unthinking consciousness into the thinking, the unaspiring consciousness into the aspiring and the possessing consciousness into the renouncing.

Here on earth, since everything is fleeting, if we can derive a little joy, a little peace, a little harmony from mediation, our mental wisdom, we should be proud of our achievement. At a certain stage in human development, when most of the people are not aspiring to be perfect, mediation is of great importance. Therefore we must pay attention, reverential attention to mediation. It is a temporary mental relief, a pause, a rest in the life of the vital. It is a clever compromise. But to expect abiding peace and illumining fulfilment from mediation is simply absurd. We cannot expect lasting peace and we must not expect everlasting, illumining fulfilment from mediation. For that we need meditation.

We are now at the United Nations. The United Nations is the mediator unmatched and unparalleled in today's world:

> The Secretary-General and his special representatives have assisted in finding solutions to problems in a number of areas. The Secretary-General's efforts assisted the Government of the Soviet Union and the United States to avert a serious threat to

the peace which arose at the end of 1963 in the Caribbean. In the Dominican Republic crisis in 1965 a representative of the Secretary-General, appointed at the request of the Security Council, helped in securing a cease-fire. The fighting between Israel and the Arab States that followed the eruptions of the Palestine partition – the partition plan in the establishment of the State of Israel – was halted by a United Nations cease-fire. Then following negotiations carried out with a United Nations mediator, armistice agreements were signed in 1949. Peace Corps observers have been in the area ever since, supervising the armistice agreements.

These achievements are unique in the physical world, in the vital world, in the mental world and in the psychic world. Unfortunately these achievements may not, or do not or cannot last. We have seen the First World War, the Second World War. There should not be, at least for God's sake, a Third World War!

Very often animal aggression gives birth to human aggrandisement. This human aggrandisement is chased by bitter frustration. Then, later on, human aggrandisement is devoured by utter destruction.

In the spiritual life, in our inner life, we also see two conflicting parties: fear and doubt on one side; and inner courage and faith on the other side. Meditation plays three distinctive roles in the inner life. Meditation is the medicine; meditation is the doctor; meditation is the cure, the ultimate cure. Meditation cures our fear. It transforms our fear into strength, adamantine will. It transforms our doubt into constant, unmistakable and inevitable certainty. Again, we see that meditation is the road, meditation is the guide and meditation is the Goal. He who is surcharged with inner courage and faith will get constant help and illumination from meditation. Further, let us not forget that meditation is the only road, the only guide and the only Goal.

In the outer world, the blind human body needs constant mediation. The wild human vital needs striking mediation. The unclear human mind needs illumining mediation. The weak human heart needs lasting mediation.

In the inner world, the fleeting, unaspiring human body needs constant meditation. The running, struggling vital needs striking meditation. The searching and climbing human mind needs illumining meditation. The crying and aspiring human heart needs everlasting meditation.

In the outer world, in this world of turmoil, mediation is necessary. In the inner world, in the world of frustration and despair, meditation is necessary. If we can bring the result of meditation to the fore, mediation will have a life, a different life, a new life that will be flooded with everlasting Peace, Light and Bliss.

In the fleeting, in the finite, we shall hear the message of the Eternal and the Infinite.

I wish all of us to stand up and pray to God most sincerely and soulfully for our dear Secretary-General U Thant's quickest recovery.

[Everyone stands up and prays with Sri Chinmoy for five minutes.]

17. God's power of love in today's world

God's Power of Love has three gifts to offer man: aspiration, liberation and perfection. Man's power of love also has three gifts to offer: possession, frustration and destruction.

God's Power of Love in today's world can be felt only by the special few who have discovered the inner truth that Love is the beauty of our aspiring life and the duty of our manifesting soul.

The body of today's world is a filthy pig. The vital of today's world is a mad elephant. The mind of today's world is a devouring tiger. The heart of today's world is a timid deer. The soul of today's world is a helpless lamb.

In supreme silence, God's Power of Love is performing its eternal Divine Duty. Slowly, steadily and unerringly, it is transforming the body, the filthy pig, into a clean and pure child; the vital, the mad elephant, into a one-pointed dynamic runner; the mind, the devouring tiger, into a seeker of the highest Truth; the heart, the timid deer, into a brother of boundless confidence and concern; and the soul, the helpless lamb, into a chosen instrument of Divinity's Eternity.

Marguerite Blessington said, "Love in France is a comedy, in England a tragedy, in Italy an *opera seria* and in Germany a melodrama." Now I wish to add that love in America is at once a frightening and enchanting experience of a green life's red adventure.

The master philosopher Plato remarked, "Love: a great mental disease." When our physical consciousness lives in the doubting, suspecting and unaspiring mind, this great utterance of Plato's is, to some extent, undeniable. But if our awakened consciousness lives in the illumining soul, love is nectar, the very breath of Immortality.

Napoleon Bonaparte has given us an amusing and interesting piece of advice: "The only victory over love is flight." When our human emotions run riot, the necessity of flying away is perhaps indispensable; but when our divine emotion, the all-loving emotion, reigns supreme, we have to know that we do not need victory over love, but the victory of Love. This victory of Love is self-expansion in God-Manifestation.

India's matchless leader, Mahatma Gandhi, has a special message, an inner message, which runs, "Love is the reverse of the coin of which the obverse is Truth." In the life of aspiration we come to realise that Love is Truth embodied and that Truth is Love revealed.

Man's obtrusive ignorance of Divine Love results in a most damaging failure in the battlefield of life. Man's power of love is constantly wanting in perspicuity and lucidity. Man's love of power knows not how to procrastinate. Fast, faster and fastest it runs; and when it finally reaches the goal, it is compelled to shake hands with bitter frustration.

Earthly experience, frustrated and shattered, convinces a lover that there is no such thing as love. It is all chicanery. Heavenly experience, illumined and fulfilled, reveals to a God-Lover the truth that Love alone is here on earth, there in Heaven.

Here at this august hall, the Dag Hammarskjöld Auditorium, we are trying to throw light on love in today's world. My heart tells me that the love that the United Nations has is not a guarded and limited concern, but a soulful dedication to the Supreme Cause.

An unaspiring man loves God in a perfunctory manner. An aspiring man loves God in a soulful and ebullient manner. A God-Realised man loves God in an unconditionally surrendered manner. It is through him that God, the Inner Pilot Supreme, reveals His Power of Love in today's world.

18. *Western dynamism and Eastern spirituality*

Western dynamism lives in its searching mind and manifesting vital. Eastern spirituality lives in its crying heart and illumining soul.

Spirituality is the inner urge of an Eastern seeker to see God face to face and realise God in His totality. Dynamism is the vital urge of a hero Westerner to reveal God and manifest God here on earth. Dynamism serves God. Spirituality loves God.

The body's dynamism is regularity. The vital's dynamism is punctuality. The mind's dynamism is clarity. The heart's dynamism is purity. The soul's dynamism is certainty.

The body's spirituality is simplicity. The vital's spirituality is sincerity. The mind's spirituality is humility. The heart's spirituality is spontaneity. The soul's spirituality is Reality.

A dynamic man is quick on his feet to reach his destined Goal, the Goal of the Beyond. A spiritual man is quick with his answers and pleases God, the Inner Pilot, in His own Way.

Dynamism is the life's capacity. Spirituality is the soul's necessity. The aura of outer success surrounds a dynamic man. The aura of inner progress surrounds a spiritual man.

A dynamic man is a karma yogi. He devotes himself to the path of action, disinterested action, with implicit devotion and surrendered service to God. A spiritual man is a jnana yogi. He tries to live in the knowledge of God with his awakened and illumined mind and heart. Dynamism invites God. Spirituality receives God. Yoga achieves God.

Western dynamism wants to shoulder the responsibility of the entire world. Eastern spirituality tries and cries to know what God's Will is and what God wants.

Western dynamism needs the aspiration of Eastern spirituality in order to please God in the inner world. Eastern spirituality needs the inspiration of Western dynamism in order to please God in the outer world.

Western dynamism has to learn the secret of Eastern spirituality: Love is God, God the Supreme Lover. Eastern spirituality has to learn the secret of Western dynamism: God is the Supreme Warrior, the Supreme Victor over teeming ignorance and darkening death.

God needs Western dynamism to offer His Omnipotence-Light to the world at large. God needs Eastern spirituality to offer His Ocean of Love and Peace to the world at large.

Western dynamism and Eastern spirituality are the two wings of God the Eternal Bird, who will carry the message of earth's aspiration to the highest Abode of the Supreme, and who will bring down the message of infinite Compassion from the highest Abode of the Supreme to the aching, crying consciousness of Mother Earth.

When Western dynamism and Eastern spirituality become inseparably one, God will be known as a fulfilled Man, and man will be known as a perfect God.

19. *The Court of Divine Justice*

The court of human justice tells me that as I sow, so I reap. The Court of Divine Justice assures me that when I devotedly think of God, He smilingly and blessingfully appears before my heart's eye.

The human justice wishes to offer me protection. The Divine Justice offers me protection, illumination and perfection. The human justice is fairness. The human justice is a threatening force. The human justice is a binding law. The Divine Justice is Love. The Divine Justice is self-giving. The Divine Justice is fulfilling.

The human judge is the problem-shooter. The human plaintiff is the problem-bringer. The defendant is the problem-maker and creator. The pleader is either the problem-lover or problem-nourisher; he cannot be otherwise, for that is how he remains on earth.

The Divine Judge is the Liberator. In the divine sense the plaintiff is the hungry seeker. The defendant is the devouring doubter in us, and the pleader is conscience. This pleader is the common friend, mutual friend of the plaintiff and the defendant. Under the threat of wild ignorance the pleader yields to the whims of doubt but inwardly in silence, it loves, cherishes and adores the heart of the seeker. In the physical and vital worlds conscience is helpless. In our inner world, conscience is constantly supported by the adamantine Will of the Lord Supreme. The Supreme Liberator liberates both the hungry seeker and the doubter.

Justice is impartiality. Impartiality is wisdom. Wisdom is the Divine Grace. The Divine Grace is the illumining Vision and fulfilling Manifestation of God.

A transformed and perfected human being is the duty of Divine Justice. A fulfilled and manifested God in man is the duty of Divine Justice. Duty performed on any level of consciousness is beauty blossomed forthwith. God's Consciousness abides in the duty of His Divine Justice.

Here on earth we see that liberty and justice are two different things. They are like North Pole and South Pole. If one enjoys the joy of liberty, we feel that person has violated all the laws of justice. He is acting like a wild elephant. He is enjoying liberty, especially on the vital plane, and therefore he does not care for justice at all. But if one cares only for justice, then we feel that his life has no pleasure; there is no warmth, there is no feeling of enthusiasm in his life. This is all on the human level.

In the inner world, liberty and justice always go together. They are like the obverse and the reverse of the same coin. Only he who has inner liberty can hear the message of Divine Justice. Only he who has known what the Divine Justice is can be free and independent. There is no other way. Liberty and justice in the inner world are inseparable.

The Divine Justice is not a mere human idea. It is the divine ideal in each human being. When a nation is not awakened, when a nation is unaspiring, unillumined, it feels that might is right. This is human justice. But when a nation is illumined, all-loving and all-embracing, it feels that right is might. It feels that justice lies only in the divine right.

Now, what is this divine right? Divine right is the conscious feeling of universal oneness. God's Justice can be seen and felt only when we have the feeling of universal oneness. If not, God will disappoint us and fail us at every moment. Our human mind will never be able to fathom God's Justice. It will always be baffled by God's Justice because of its limited knowledge and limited concern for humanity.

The Divine Justice is ready at every moment to be of help to us; to inspire us, guide us, mould us and shape us. But we are equally afraid of the Divine Justice and the human justice. When we do something wrong, we feel that we will be exposed. This is true in the case of human justice. But the Divine Justice will never, never expose us. The first time we do something wrong the Divine Justice will forgive us with its compassion. The second time we do something wrong it will offer us more compassion. The third time we do something wrong it will offer us infinite compassion. And then, when God sees that even His infinite Compassion is not solving the human problem, He will use His loving Divine Authority, Divine Power.

This Power is not the destructive power. This Power is not the threatening power. This Power is the Power that awakens the dormant lion in each human being. This Power does not dominate. It only arouses the spiritually hungry lion in each human being. The lion can roar, but the lion is fast asleep. This lion embodies our inner cry to see the ultimate Truth, to grow into the Absolute Reality.

Each individual seeker can claim, can feel God's Justice if the seeker feels the necessity of loving humanity more than he expects humanity to love him. If he does not expect humanity to love him at all, yet he goes on loving humanity, then he is bound to feel God's Justice in him, through him. Why? While he is offering his love to mankind, God will not remain silent. God will not remain asleep. God will immediately give him His boundless Peace, Joy, Light and Delight. God will empty His Infinite Consciousness into him.

What we have, we can give to mankind if we want to. But in God's case, He gives to us not only what He has, but what He is. He feels that He is just only when He can give us what He has and what He is. We can also act like God and offer to mankind not only what we have, but what we are.

When we make an inner search, we come to learn that what we have is a dedicated heart; and if we ask what we are, we come to learn that we are the chosen instruments of God. We are the leaves and He is the Tree. Look at a tree from a distance or from any place. If you look at a leaf, a branch or the trunk, you can immediately recognise it is a tree. When we look at an individual leaf, we can immediately enter into its source, the tree, and feel that this individual leaf is the tree itself. When we look at the tree, we see that its manifestations are the leaves. The manifestation itself can be as important as the Creator Himself.

The Divine Justice is the breath of Reality. In the human court we see all kinds of crime; but in the Court of Divine Justice we notice only one crime every day, and that is human ungratefulness. Here the punishment is forgiveness. Constantly the game is being played between God's Forgiveness and man's ungratefulness. In the human way, human beings are justifying their cause by saying, "We are unconscious. Hence we commit crimes. We are not yet illumined. Hence we are ungrateful." In the divine way, God is justifying His cause: He is Love. Hence He is all-Loving. He is Compassion. Hence He is all-Forgiving.

20. *God: the Supreme Actor. World: the divine audience.*

God: The Supreme Actor. World: The divine audience. The Supreme Actor reveals His Love. The Supreme Actor fulfils His Truth. The divine audience believes. The divine audience achieves. Self-awakening is the belief of the divine audience. God-discovery is the achievement of the divine audience.

The Supreme Actor acts three times a day. In the morning, while acting, the Supreme Actor offers inspiration-light to us. In the afternoon, while acting, the Supreme Actor offers aspiration-height to us. In the evening, while acting, the Supreme Actor offers realisation-might to us.

In the inspiration-light of the Supreme Actor, the divine audience sees that the attainment of the ultimate Truth is quite possible. In the aspiration-height of the Supreme Actor, the divine audience feels that the attainment of the ultimate Truth is not only possible, but practical. In the realisation-might of the Supreme Actor, the divine audience realises that the attainment of the ultimate Truth is not only possible and practical, but also natural and inevitable.

The divine audience looks at the Feet of the Supreme Actor and longs for the liberation of mankind from ignorance. The divine audience looks at the Eyes of the Supreme Actor and longs for the perfect Perfection of aspiring humanity.

The Supreme Actor looks at the head of the divine audience, and then enters into its head to fondle its lofty heights. The

Supreme Actor looks at the heart of the divine audience, and then enters into its heart to glorify its Divinity's Light and Reality's Delight.

Believable: the human audience is afraid of darkness. Unbelievable, but true: the human audience is afraid of Light, illumining Light.

The divine audience is always proud of seeing the Light of God's Beauty. The divine audience is always proud of feeling the Delight of God's Beauty. The soul is an actor. The soul participates in the Cosmic *Lila,* the Divine Game. The soul enters into the abyss of ignorance. The soul enters into the chasm of inconscience in order to participate in the Cosmic Lila. For millennia the soul abides there, fast asleep. All of a sudden, a spark of consciousness enters into the soul and awakens it. The soul makes a little movement. At that very moment a question arises from within: "Who am I?" And the immediate answer also is given from within: *Tat Twam Asi,* "That Thou Art."

The soul opens its eyes, looks upward and enters into the mineral world. There again, for thousands and thousands of years the soul abides. Then the soul again gets a message from within, a question: "Who am I?" The answer is again, *Tat Twam Asi,* "That Thou Art." The soul makes another upward movement. From stone, from the mineral, the soul enters into the plant life. From there it enters into the animal kingdom. Again, for hundreds of years, the soul is not fully active or dynamic. Very often it is fast asleep, enjoying the Game in its own particular fashion.

But there comes a time, after hundreds of years, when the soul wants to go one step ahead in the evolving wheel of manifestation. The soul enters into human life. Here the soul becomes either unconsciously active or consciously dynamic. Here the soul gets more opportunity, develops more capacity to look up high into the Beyond. Here the soul quite often remembers its Source, the Ultimate Truth, the Transcendental Reality.

The soul entered into inconscience to begin the Game; and the soul, from the human incarnation, enters into the divine life so that it can eventually go back to its Source: *Sat-Chit-Ananda*, Existence-Consciousness-Bliss.

Each soul is employed by humanity and Divinity. In God's Cosmic Drama, humanity employs the soul to carry its untold suffering and excruciating pangs to a world far beyond the domain of the mind. Divinity employs the soul to bring the message of Light and Delight down into the very heart of the earth-consciousness. Divinity employs the soul, asks the soul to be the boatman so that Divinity can manifest its Infinity in the heart of the finite. Humanity employs the soul to be its boat so that it can carry the load, the burden of humanity, to the world beyond.

The Supreme Actor is the Beloved Sovereign. The divine audience is the eternal lover. Both the Actor and the audience are indispensable, one fulfilling the other.

The audience is receiving and achieving the Ultimate Truth. The Actor is revealing and manifesting the Ultimate Truth.

The Supreme Actor is also the Supreme Dancer. Nataraj, Lord Shiva, the Supreme Dancer, dances. Lo and behold, humanity's aspiration is being awakened, humanity's unlit consciousness is being illumined, Divinity's life-breath is being manifested on earth. Lord Krishna, the Supreme Dancer, dances. Lo and behold, humanity's passion is being transformed into Divinity's rapture.

The Supreme Actor wants each individual soul to be the Supreme Actor in the play of cosmic evolution, for it is only when He allows and wants each individual soul to act the Supreme Act of the Supreme Actor, that unity in multiplicity can be offered to mankind. The Unity of the Supreme can be realised and manifested only when each individual soul is given the chance in the cosmic evolution to rise up high, higher, highest into the ever-transcending Beyond. Then only will God, the Supreme Actor, be totally fulfilled and supremely manifested here on earth.

The human actor tells the human audience, "Take me. You need me."

The human audience tells the human actor, "We do not need you. We appreciate your capacity, but we do not need your life's reality."

The Supreme Actor tells the divine audience, "Take Me, I am for you. Take Me, I am eternally yours."

The divine audience tells the Supreme Actor, "Our devoted oneness, our surrendered oneness with You, O Supreme Actor, has made us feel the significance of Your Transcendental Reality. O Supreme Actor, to You we bow and bow. Our life of aspiration is eternally Yours. Your Life of manifestation is eternally ours."

21. *God's Compassion and the United Nations' dedication*

Unlimited and unconditional is God's Compassion. Thoughtful and fruitful is the dedication of the United Nations.

God's Compassion is ignored by humanity. The dedication of the United Nations is quite often misunderstood and at times suspected by humanity. Why does this happen? It happens precisely because ignorance still lords it over us.

God's Compassion is inner Protection unseen. God's Protection is illumination visible everywhere. Dedication is the soul's promise to God and to mankind. These promises the soul has made to humanity and to Divinity perhaps hundreds or thousands of years; but the promise the soul has made to humanity and to Divinity must be fulfilled.

The promise the soul has made to humanity is very simple: it will kindle the flame of aspiration in the heart of humanity. It will make the earth-consciousness a perfect instrument so that it can receive God's Light from above in infinite measure. It will make the heart of earth feel Heaven's Light, Heaven's Delight and Heaven's Existence. Finally, it will make of earth the divine clarion: Light, the Voice of Heaven.

The soul has also made a promise to Divinity that it will manifest God the Absolute, God the Omniscient, God the Omnipotent and God the Omnipresent on earth. The soul has promised God that, with the help of the physical, the vital and the mental – in short, with the help of the entire being – it will manifest Him here on earth. Here on earth the soul will offer the perfection of dedication to God.

Dedication is delight, the delight of the heart. When we dedicate ourselves to something or to someone, our very dedication expands our consciousness, and we feel that our inseparable oneness with God is something real and fulfilling. Each time we dedicate something of ours, we expand our love for God and our love for mankind. Our very reality, our earthbound reality, is then transformed into a heavenward journey.

Dedication to the Self is union. It is in union that life becomes meaningful and fruitful. A life without the feeling of union is confusion and frustration. Today's dedication is bound to be transformed into tomorrow's Perfection. When Perfection dawns we can foresee clearly all our divine wishes, we can feed all our divine aspiration and finally, we can fulfil all our divine needs. Human dedication has the key to open God's Palace. God's Compassion shows man where his infinite Treasure lies within himself.

A child of God was blessed with a vision. This child was our President Wilson. He had the vision of the League of Nations; now we see the United Nations. There was once a tiny plant;

now the plant has grown into a big Banyan Tree: the United Nations.

Needless to say, the world is still not perfect. Since the world is not perfect, the world opinion cannot be perfect. Since we are imperfect, we consciously or unconsciously, willingly or unwillingly, indulge in criticism, and we see too much conflict in our thoughts, ideas, plans, ideals and missions. There are many on earth who find fault with the activities and the dedicated services of the United Nations. But from the spiritual point of view, I wish to say that each action and each dedicated service is not a mere experiment, but an experience of God in and through the United Nations. Each nation may for its own reasons want to be united with the rest of the nations; but the United Nations means the usefulness of the united notions, united thoughts and united feelings, and the expansion of oneness. In the United Nations unity can be fulfilled through manifested multiplicity. This is what we see and feel in the heart of the United Nations. We have been seeing the desire for supremacy in man since the dawn of civilization. Each human being wants to be an inch higher than the rest; each human being wants to surpass the rest. But from the spiritual point of view, we can surpass only when we become one: one nation, one soul. One nation can surpass all the other nations only by becoming one with them in their suffering, in their joy and in their achievements. When we become one, we really surpass. What do we surpass? We surpass not only the capacity of our *own* achievements and of *others'* achievements, but also the capacity of limited feelings. Real supremacy comes when we grow into vastness. If we become the vastness of Self, then who or what can be superior to us?

From the spiritual point of view, the United Nations is struggling and striving for something meaningful and fruitful. What it needs, it has: the Divine Compassion. The Compassion of God has been unceasingly descending upon the United Nations.

THE GARLAND OF NATION-SOULS

It is not in vain or without any purpose that the United Nations has come into existence. God's Vision has to be manifested here on earth. The suffering nations need a place for consolation; the sacrificing nations need a place for appreciation. Here in the United Nations we see the message of fulfilment. Now it is up to the world. The world, the sleeping, unaspiring, unawakened world is not yet receiving the Light of the United Nations. There are many things that the world could get from the dedication of the United Nations; but if the world is not receptive, it is not the fault of the United Nations. God is all Compassion, He is all-giving; but if we don't want to receive His Light the way He wants to offer it, that is not His fault. The heart of this place is dedication, the soul of this place is concern, the body of this place is for the illumining expansion of human consciousness.

We sow the seed; the seed germinates. First we see a tiny plant, then we see a huge tree. When we go deep within, we see that a seed was sown here in the earth-consciousness, and that seed had boundless potentiality. God's Light is *here* for humanity to receive on a practical level, in an earthly manner. God's Light is *here* to illumine us. Consciously and unconsciously the world is receiving this Light from the United Nations; but the United Nations is not being recognized, and this fact is deplorable. The human beings who have become instruments to offer the Light that the soul of the United Nations has, may not be fully aware of what they are doing. When they see imperfections in others, when they see their limited capacity, at times they feel frustrated. But the Divine in each individual, in each delegate, in each representative from each individual nation, is all-wise. It has chosen the right place, the right instrument: the United Nations.

Here we meet, not for mere consolation when the world is in conflict, when two parties are at daggers drawn. No. Here we meet, not for mere justification, not for mere glorification, but for the feeling of universal oneness and for the manifestation of God's Perfection on earth in a practical manner.

At the United Nations we see the oneness of mental philosophy and psychic religion. All philosophies and all religions are running towards the same Goal. Each religion teaches us to be nice, kind, honest and devoted. Philosophy teaches us how to see the Truth, and religion helps us in applying the Truth in our outer life. Here at the United Nations all major religions meet. Here the outer wealth of desire and the inner wealth of aspiration meet. Each one is offering its might. From the spiritual point of view, in the soul's region, the contribution of each nation is sublime.

The United Nations is the chosen instrument of God. To be a chosen instrument of God means to be a divine messenger carrying the Banner of God's Inner Vision and Outer Manifestation. One day the world will not only treasure and cherish the soul of the United Nations, but also claim the soul of the United Nations as its very own with enormous pride, for this soul is all-loving, all-nourishing and all-fulfilling.

22. *Is the right to happiness a human right?*

Is the right to happiness a human right? First of all, we have to know what happiness is. Happiness is something that feeds our heart, inspires our mind, energises our vital and illumines our body.

When the heart is happy it embraces the whole world. When the mind is happy it accepts the world as its very own. When the vital is happy it offers its very existence to the world. And when the body is happy it serves the world the way the world wants to be served.

Our happiness-moon smiles sweetly, charmingly and soulfully when our hope-kite flies in the skies of Divinity's Heights. Our happiness-sun shines brightly when our dream-boat touches the Reality Shore.

Possession gives birth to human happiness. Renunciation gives birth to divine happiness. Acceptance of God's Will in God's own Way gives birth to supremely divine happiness.

In the domain of lifeless hope, happiness is theoretical and fruitless. In the sea of selfless love, happiness is practical and fruitful. In the domain of teeming fear, happiness bitterly cries. In the sea of brooding doubt, happiness instantly dies.

An aspiring man spreads happiness wherever he goes. An unaspiring man strangles happiness wherever he roams.

> The life of happiness is aspiration.
> The soul of happiness is realisation.
> The goal of happiness is perfection.

Is the right to happiness a human right? Without the least possible hesitation I venture to answer this question in the affirmative. Each man has a soul. Each man has a goal. His soul silently tells him that his perennial Source is all happiness. His goal lovingly tells him that in his constant God-manifestation is his own happiness.

Happiness is in God. Happiness is of God. Happiness is for God. A life of dedication knows that happiness is in God. A life of transformation knows that happiness is of God. A life of liberation knows that happiness is for God.

God's Invention is happiness. Man's discovery is happiness. God's Possession is happiness. Man's achievement is happiness. Man has every right to achieve God's Possession, for that is precisely what God wants man to do. Man has every right to discover God's invention, for that is precisely what God wants man to grow into. What is God's supreme Possession? Peace. What is God's supreme Invention? Love.

A Peace-loving man is a quarter God. A Peace-achieved man is a half God. And a Peace-revealing and Peace-spreading man is a full God. A Peace-loving man is the serving God. A Peace-achieved man is the glowing God. A Peace-revealing and Peace-spreading man is the fulfilling God in earthbound time.

God's supreme Invention is Love. He who consciously loves God radiates the highest Divinity. He who soulfully loves God manifests the inmost Divinity. He who unconditionally loves God lives in the ever-radiating, ever-manifesting and ever-transcending Divinity of the Beyond.

A human God-lover achieves God's constant Happiness. A divine God-lover embodies God the Happiness. A human God-lover still has a sense of separativity, so he achieves God's Happiness according to his capacity and according to his receptivity. But a divine God-lover, on the strength of his inseparable and constant oneness with God, embodies God, the Infinite Happiness.

23. *Why is it easier to disbelieve than to believe?*

Why is it easier to disbelieve than to believe? It is easier to disbelieve than to believe because disbelief is an act of descent, whereas belief is an act of ascent. Descending is easier than ascending.

It is easier to disbelieve than to believe because disbelief is an act of breaking, and belief is an act of building. Building is more difficult than breaking.

It is easier to disbelieve than to believe because disbelief is an act of our self-centred mind, whereas belief is an act of our self-giving heart.

Disbelief begins its journey in the doubting mind and ends in the destructive vital. Belief begins its journey in the illumining soul and continues to march in the vast kingdom of the aspiring heart.

A man of disbelief, with his eyes firmly closed, tells us what others are, what the world is and what he himself can do for the entire world if he wants to. A man of belief, with his heart's door wide open, tells us what God has done for him, what God is doing for him and what God will do for him.

Disbelief has a perfection of its own. Disbelief finds its perfection in the cyclone of separation. Belief has a perfection of its own. Belief finds its perfection in the music of the universal Oneness.

Disbelief tells the world, "Be careful, be careful. If not, I shall devour you." Belief tells the world, "Come in, come in please. I have been eagerly waiting for you."

The human eyes most often believe only themselves; they do not believe others. The human ears most often believe others, even if it is the worst possible gossip. But the divine heart believes in God, in mankind and in its own aspiration.

Disbelief hates the world. Why? It feels that the world is never of it and can never be for it. A man of disbelief always feels that this world does not belong to him and that he can never lord it over the world. This is precisely why a man of disbelief dares to hate the world.

A man of belief loves the world. Why? He believes that this world of ours is verily the aspiring Body of God, the glowing Dream of God and the fulfilling Reality of God.

In the spiritual life, if one cherishes disbelief, one is simply lengthening the distance of the ultimate Goal. But if a seeker has abundant belief in his spiritual life, in his own quest for the ultimate Truth, then undoubtedly he is shortening the distance. Finally, if his inner being is surcharged with boundless faith, then he feels that the Goal itself, the Goal of the Beyond, is running towards him, and not that he is trying to reach the Goal.

There comes a time when a man of disbelief, being totally frustrated, wants to kill the world around him out of exasperation. But to his wide surprise he sees that the wild ignorance of the world has already stabbed him. With his proud knowledge he wanted to kill the world; but before he could kill the world, the world, his own wild ignorance, has killed him.

A man of belief wants to love the world. To his wide surprise he sees that his entire existence is in the very heart of the world. The world has already placed a throne in the inmost recesses of its heart for the man of belief to sit upon.

In our spiritual life, disbelief is nothing short of a crime. When we disbelieve, we pour slow poison into our system. It is we who kill our possibility and potentiality. It is we who wallow consciously and deliberately in the pleasures of ignorance.

Unfortunately, in the cases of some spiritual Masters, disbelief firmly and powerfully knocked at the door before their highest illumination dawned. But by God's Grace they overcame this disbelief. Again, there are other spiritual giants who were blessed with belief right from the beginning of their spiritual journey.

Why do we disbelieve? We disbelieve because we are afraid of oneness, afraid of the vast. We feel that when we enter into the vast, we lose our identity, we lose our individuality, we lose our very existence. But we forget the undeniable Truth that when we enter into the vastness it is not merely entering; it is nothing short of the enlargement of our divinised consciousness.

A seeker finds it infinitely easier to believe the Truth, the Reality, for his is the life of conscious awareness. For an ordinary person, an unaspiring human being, it is extremely difficult not to disbelieve. An aspiring person, an aspiring seeker, knows that there is something within that is pushing him forward to the Light, to the Reality. An unaspiring person feels that something from without is pulling him backwards, pulling him to something unknown, something that will bind him.

When we consciously disbelieve someone, we do not realise the fact that the inner magnet within us pulls the undivine qualities of that particular person into us. What happens when a person has achieved something, but we do not believe it? The person and his achievement remain the same whether we believe it or not. But the person also has imperfections, limited capacity, impurity; and our disbelief is a magnet that pulls only the imperfections of the human being in question. If we have belief and if we offer our belief, then we have to feel we have a magnet that draws the good qualities, the divine qualities, the illumining qualities, of the other person.

When we disbelieve God, when we disbelieve the Reality, God remains the same for the seekers, for the lovers of Truth. But what happens is this: ignorance, the teeming vast, gets the opportunity to envelop the disbeliever more powerfully and more completely. And when we believe in God, God's Compassion gets the utmost opportunity to work in and through us most powerfully.

The deeper we enter into the spiritual life, the more we become aware of the capacity of disbelief and belief. Disbelief is nothing short of destruction. Belief is nothing short of a new creation. Each time we believe in something, we see the face of a new creation within and without us. And when we go one step ahead, when our inner faith looms large, then we see in us a perfected man and a liberated soul.

Again, when we dive deep within, we see that the so-called man of disbelief will also have a time to knock at the proper door of realisation. Let him disbelieve to his heart's content; let him run with his disbelief towards his self-chosen destruction. When he is about to reach the door of destruction, God's Omnipotent Compassion will send him back to the starting point to start his march towards the real Goal once again. Even if the man of disbelief is going on the wrong path, let him march, let him not sit inert. Let the world judge him, let the world offer its comment. A day will dawn when the man of disbelief will come to the right path.

In disbelief the question arises. In belief the answer dawns.

In the spiritual life, in the life of aspiration, in the life of inner awakening, even if one does not have abundant belief or faith in oneself, one need not and must not be doomed to disappointment. Let the person feel that he is sick, he is weak, he needs treatment, he needs hospitalisation. Let him feel that there are people who are physically strong, vitally strong, mentally strong, psychically strong, and let him mix with these people. If he sincerely wants to see the Face, the real Face of the real Goal, then let him mix with a man of belief even for a fleeting hour daily, and he will see the power of belief, the power of inner faith.

We start our life's journey with belief; but when the mind starts functioning, disbelief, secretly, like a thief, enters into our system. A child always believes his parents. To him everything that his parents say is true, unquestionable. But when he enters into his adolescence, the questioning mind, the doubting mind, begins to work. Always he says, "Why? How?" *Why* and *how, it is not possible, it is impossible,* enter into his mind. At that time it is easier for him to believe even the impossible, than to believe something that is possible, natural and quite obvious. This is what we see in the adolescent life.

But again opportunity knocks at our door when we see that the mind has not given us any real satisfaction. When we enter into full-blooded youth, when we see that the mind with its suspecting and doubting has not given us a moment's satisfaction, we want to walk along another road; and that is the road of the heart, the aspiring heart, the self-giving heart. Here we enter into the realm of spirituality. Here the lotus within our heart begins to bloom, petal by petal. Each time a petal blooms, we see that our inner divinity is being manifested more and more.

Then there comes a time when we see a thousand-petaled lotus fully bloomed within us, and we see consciously our Divine Pilot, our Divine Comrade, our Eternal Friend, the Supreme, right in front of us; and He makes us see and feel that through Eternity we shall be not only with Him, but also for Him. In our conscious awareness, in our conscious seeing of His Presence, in our conscious feeling of inseparable oneness with Him, we shall establish here on earth, here and nowhere else, the Kingdom of Light, Truth, Peace and Delight.

24. *Does belief come spontaneously or by effort?*

Belief comes spontaneously. Belief comes by effort. In the spiritual life a sincere seeker, an advanced seeker and a surrendered seeker can and will have spontaneous belief. Belief by effort, personal effort, without the divine Grace, without God's unconditional Protection, cannot be as effective as spontaneous belief.

Spontaneous belief is a gift of God for the human in us to see, to feel and to grow into the very image of God. Belief by personal effort is a human earthly discovery, although to some extent it also is necessary.

Believing is seeing. Seeing is believing. When believing is seeing, a seeker becomes a perfect instrument for the Supreme to use in His own Way. When seeing is believing, a seeker makes a solemn promise both to God and to himself that he will realise God and he will fulfil God on earth. But there is no certainty, no guarantee; he may, but he may not. He may not fulfil his divine promise, for at any moment during his long journey he may be assailed by teeming doubts, fears, worries, anxieties and ignorance-night. Belief by effort is the acceptance, the mere acceptance, of Truth and Light; and this belief is usually mental and intellectual. But spontaneous belief is the conscious and constant oneness with Truth and Light. It is not that belief by personal effort is of no use; personal effort has its own value, but it is not as strong and sure as spontaneous belief.

Not only ordinary human beings but also many spiritual giants have suffered from doubts and other undivine qualities in their human nature before devotedly and wholeheartedly launching onto the spiritual path. So we must not be doomed to disappointment when we are assailed by doubts in our spiritual life. Belief that comes from within is at the head of the divine spiritual army, and this army destroys our doubts, or rather, let us say it illumines our doubts, perfects our imperfections and transforms our limited bondage into divine plenitude.

We have two principal organs: the eye and the ear. Our eyes quite often, if not always, believe themselves. Our ears very often believe others. These are our human eyes and our human ears. But the divine eye, the third eye, will believe only in the vision of Divinity, and the divine ears will believe only in the truth of Reality. When we listen to the inner command, when we have the capacity to grow into constant obedience to our Inner Pilot, we feel within and without the presence of spontaneous belief. Belief is the reality of our inner obedience. This is divine belief, spontaneous belief. Belief by effort is a restricted, disciplined human understanding.

Belief is power. A real seeker of the infinite Truth knows this. An insincere and unaspiring seeker is aware of the truth that belief is power, but he cannot go beyond understanding or awareness; whereas a sincere, genuine, devoted and surrendered seeker knows that belief is dynamic power, and he has this power as his very own.

We see a tree. The tree bears flowers, and soon afterwards we see fruits. The flower is the harbinger of the fruit. In the spiritual life, belief is the flower. Belief is a divine angel which enters into us as the harbinger of the Lord Supreme.

We can cultivate belief. If we do not have belief we *can* develop belief. How? We can do it by mixing with sincere spiritual people who care more for God than for pleasure. There are also people who care only for God in human beings, and if we mix with those people we can cultivate belief. When we have belief we can walk with God in His Garden of Light and Delight.

But in the spiritual life, spontaneous belief need not be and cannot be the last word. There is something infinitely higher and deeper than belief, and that is faith. When we have belief we can make tremendous progress for a day or for a month or for a year. But then, if we unconsciously or consciously become a victim to undivine forces, our belief loses its strength and we cannot make fast progress in the spiritual life in spite of having belief.

The strength of belief, even spontaneous belief is not enough to take us to the ultimate Goal. Belief is like a child's instrument that you can play upon for a limited number of hours or years. But when you have faith you come to realise that you are an eternal player and at the same time you are an eternal instrument. And when you go farther and deeper you come to realise that the player is somebody else, the Lord Supreme, and you are His instrument. He is the eternal Player and you are eternally His chosen instrument.

Spontaneous belief will make you feel what you eternally are: God's chosen child. But if you do not have faith you will not have the abiding satisfaction and the abiding feeling that you and He are eternally one, that you represent the One and that your very presence on earth is the manifestation of the One, the Absolute Supreme. It is only when your outer being and your inner being are surcharged with faith that you can manifest God here on earth. Faith in oneself and faith in God must run together.

If you say that you have no faith in yourself but you have all faith in God, then I wish to say you cannot go very far. You have to have faith, constant faith and abundant faith, not only in God, but also in yourself since you are God's son or God's daughter. When you truly feel that you are God's child, you will find that it is beneath your dignity to make friends with ignorance. Reality, Eternity, Immortality and Infinity are not vague terms; these are your birthright. When you have that kind of faith, God will shower His choicest Blessings upon your devoted head and surrendered heart.

But faith in oneself must not exceed its own boundary. I said before that you have to have faith, constant faith in abundant measure. But you have to remember the source of your faith as well; you have to remember where it comes from. At some time you may think: "Oh, I am working so hard for my realisation of the absolute Truth, for my perfection. It is all my effort, my effort. One per cent of the work will be done by the Grace of the Supreme, and ninety-nine per cent will be my personal effort." But when that most auspicious day dawns and you realise the Absolute, you will see that just the opposite is true: your faith enabled you to contribute one per cent in personal effort towards your realisation, and God supplied the other ninety-nine per cent as His divine Grace, unconditional Grace. And when you are about to manifest your realisation, another truth, a higher and more profound truth, will dawn on you. You will realise that the one per cent of faith you had, which was absolutely necessary, was also God's gift to you.

You were chosen from among countless people to run towards the Light. Others are still fast asleep. It was sheer Grace, God's unconditional Grace, that inspired you to come out of ignorance and look towards the Light. Since it was He who inspired and invited you to join consciously in His cosmic Game, you have to feel that the one per cent of faith you had in the beginning also came directly from God, the Absolute Supreme.

Some people do not have belief; they want to follow the negative path. No matter how far they go, their minds tell them that there is no God. But I wish to tell you, on the strength of my own oneness with God and with humanity, that they will not have even temporary satisfaction on this earth, not to speak of abiding satisfaction. A day will dawn when they will feel that their lack of belief, their denial of God, is not giving them what they want. They will be compelled to look for a fulfilling belief.

We who have started walking along the spiritual path are the forerunners. All will eventually run towards the same Transcendental Goal. The majority of mankind will not always lag behind. All children of God, no matter how unconscious and unaspiring, will one day run towards the common Goal. This Goal is the supreme discovery of one's Divinity and the constant and perfect manifestation of one's everlasting Reality.

III – MEDITATIONS FROM THE UNITED NATIONS

25.

Today's United Nations was yesterday's perfecting Vision.
Tomorrow's United Nations is today's fulfilling Realisation.
Unity is not oneness. A bud is not a flower.
Unity is the temple. Oneness is the shrine.
The absence of unity is imminent confusion.
The absence of oneness is the ultimate destruction.
The presence of unity is the immediate end of human imperfection and limitation.
The presence of oneness is the glorious beginning of man's perfect Perfection.

26.

I am God's child. I embody the Truth.
God is my Child. I reveal the Truth.

I am the child of God's endless Concern.
God is the Child of my breathless meditation.

27.

I imitate God because He alone constantly grows.
I quote God because He alone instantly knows.

28.

A conscious self-dedicated oneness with mankind for mankind can alone make the aspirant feel that he is not only with God, in God and for God, but of God.

29.

The universal oneness is our God-Aspiration within to see the Truth, feel the Truth and become the Truth.
The universal oneness is our God-Realisation without, embodied, revealed and manifested.

30.

The universal oneness is the Father of Eternity. This is what we learn from God's all-embracing Vision.
The universal oneness is the Son of Immortality. This is what we learn from God's all-fulfilling Will.

31.

The universal oneness is the silent language of man's eternal freedom.
Man's eternal freedom is God's eternal Concern.
God's eternal Concern fulfils man the evolving soul and God the Transcendental Self.

32.

I hasten to speak to God because I feel that God is my very own.
I hesitate to speak to the world because I think the world is a stranger to me.

33.

When a seeker meditates on himself, he feels his inner potentiality and sees his outer possibility.
When a seeker meditates on God, he feels his inner divinity and sees his outer reality.

34.

God wants me. How can I sleep?
God needs me. How can I wander?
God demands my life. How can I deny Him His eternal Right?

35.

The body loves the sleeping God.
The vital loves the energising God.
The mind loves the running God.
The heart loves the flowering God.
The soul loves the fulfilling God.

36.

To realise God is to immortalise human aspiration.
To immortalise human aspiration is to feed God, soulfully and supremely.

NOTES TO THE GARLAND OF NATION-SOULS

2. *(p. 4)* United Nations World Youth Congress, United Nations, New York, 15 July 1970.
3. *(p. 7)* United Nations Church Center, 26 November 1968.
4. *(p. 11)* Peace Room, United Nations Church Center, 12 May 1970.
5. *(p. 12)* Peace Room, United Nations Church Center, 19 May 1970.
6. *(p. 12)* Peace Room, United Nations Church Center, 26 May 1970.
7. *(p. 13)* Peace Room, United Nations Church Center, 2 June 1970.
8. *(p. 14)* Peace Room, United Nations Church Center, 9 June 1970.
9. *(p. 15)* Dag Hammarskjöld Auditorium, United Nations, New York, 12 February 1971.
10. *(p. 16)* Dag Hammarskjöld Auditorium, United Nations, New York, 4 March 1971.
11. *(p. 19)* Dag Hammarskjöld Auditorium, United Nations, New York, 1 April 1971.
12. *(p. 21)* Dag Hammarskjöld Auditorium, United Nations, New York, 5 August 1971.
13. *(p. 24)* Dag Hammarskjöld Auditorium, United Nations, New York, 13 May 1971.
14. *(p. 26)* Dag Hammarskjöld Auditorium, United Nations, New York, 4 June 1971.
15. *(p. 28)* Dag Hammarskjöld Auditorium, United Nations, New York, 1 July 1971.
16. *(p. 32)* Dag Hammarskjöld Auditorium, United Nations, New York, 4 November 1971.

16,7. *(p.33)* Excerpt taken from the *United Nations Office of Public Information* booklet.

16,15. *(p.35)* Secretary-General U Thant was in the hospital at the time this talk was given.

17. *(p.36)* Dag Hammarskjöld Auditorium, United Nations, New York, 7 October 1971.

18. *(p.38)* Dag Hammarskjöld Auditorium, United Nations, New York, 2 December 1971.

19. *(p.39)* Dag Hammarskjöld Auditorium, United Nations, New York, 4 January 1972.

20. *(p.43)* Dag Hammarskjöld Auditorium, United Nations, New York, 3 February 1972.

21. *(p.46)* Dag Hammarskjöld Auditorium, United Nations, New York, 2 March 1972.

22. *(p.50)* Dag Hammarskjöld Auditorium, United Nations, New York, 10 May 1972.

23. *(p.52)* Dag Hammarskjöld Auditorium, United Nations, New York, 1 June 1972.

24. *(p.57)* Dag Hammarskjöld Auditorium, United Nations, New York, 2 October 1972.

25. *(p.62)* Inauguration Meditation, 14 April 1970.

26. *(p.62)* 21 April 1970.

27. *(p.62)* 28 April 1970.

28. *(p.63)* 5 May 1970.

29. *(p.63)* 12 May 1970.

30. *(p.63)* 19 May 1970.

31. *(p.63)* 26 May 1970.

32. *(p.64)* 2 June 1970.

33. *(p.64)* 9 June 1970.

34. *(p.64)* 16 June 1970.

35. *(p.64)* 23 June 1970.

36. *(p.65)* 30 June 1970.

PART II

THE TEARS OF NATION-HEARTS

1. *The inner message of the United Nations*

The outer message of the United Nations is Peace. The inner message of the United Nations is Love. The inmost message of the United Nations is Oneness. Peace we feel. Love we become. Oneness we manifest.

The United Nations has a mind, a heart and a soul. Its mind tries to offer flowing Peace. Its heart tries to offer glowing Love. Its soul tries to offer fulfilling Oneness. In the near future, a day will dawn when the message of the United Nations will be absorbing to the child, elevating to the common man, thought provoking to the highly educated and inspiring to the seeker.

Each delegate is a force. Each representative is a force. Each nation is a force. The source of this force is a particular will. This will can be either the Divine Will or the human will. The human will wants to be with the world and in the world only on one condition: that it will be able to gain supremacy over others and maintain this supremacy. The Divine Will wants to be in the world, with the world and for the world without expecting anything from the world. The human will, at most, tolerates the world. The Divine Will constantly wants to liberate and fulfil the world. The human will wants to control and lead the world. The Divine Will wants to transform, glorify and immortalise the world. The human will in us needs the soul's expanding and illumining purity. The Divine Will in us wants the Goal's blossoming divinity.

The League of Nations was a dream-seed. The United Nations is a reality-plant. The aspiring and serving life of man's universal oneness will be the eternity-tree.

In his address to the United Nations in October 1965, Pope Paul VI said:

No more war: war never again! Peace. It is peace which must guide the destinies of people and of all mankind.

The goal of the United Nations lies not only in thinking together, but in thinking alike. Each individual has every right to love his nation; but he must also dedicate himself in order to immortalise his nation's relationships, inner and outer, with the rest of mankind, so that all can run together for the universal good of humanity.

In the words of Pope John XXIII:

> It is our earnest wish that the United Nations organisation may become ever more equal to the magnitude and nobility of its tasks, and that the day may come when every human being will find therein an effective safeguard for the rights which derive directly from his dignity as a person, and which are therefore universal, inviolable and inalienable rights.

All nations together can build a temple. All nations together can make a shrine. All nations together can worship a Deity. At the entrance of the temple, the Divine Protection shall smile. Upon the shrine in the temple, the Supreme illumination shall smile. Within the heart of the Deity, the Absolute Perfection shall smile.

Here at the United Nations, what I feel is an inner voyage. In its inner voyage, the United Nations has to brave many temptations and setbacks. As we all know, defeats and failures are mere steppingstones in our onward march to perfection. At the end of its voyage, there is every possibility that the United Nations will be the last word in human perfection. And then the United Nations can easily bloom in excellence and stand at the pinnacle of Divine Enlightenment.

2. *Salvation, liberation and realisation*

I wish to give a very short talk on salvation, liberation and realisation.

Salvation is God-discovery. Liberation is God-achievement. Realisation is God-fulfilment.

A man with salvation, a man with liberation, a man with realisation: what they are and what they are not. What they are is Reality's smile; what they are not is unreality's cry.

God's pure Compassion gives the seeker salvation. God's sweet Love grants the seeker liberation. God's proud, divine Oneness with the seeker gives him realisation.

In the Western world, salvation is everything. In the Eastern world, especially in India, liberation is really something, but realisation is everything. Many a seeker, before he achieves salvation, feels that his father in Heaven is all for him. This is his hope; this is his dream. But after he has achieved salvation, he knows this as a reality. A seeker, before he achieves liberation, feels that the Truth abides somewhere – not in front of him, but in an unknowable place. After he has achieved liberation, he feels that God the Light was only unknown, and now He has become fully known. Before the seeker attains realisation, he feels that God is here, there, in everything. He feels God's Presence everywhere, but he does not see God face-to-face. After he has realised God, his feeling is transformed into seeing. He sees God face-to-face as he would see any individual he meets.

When a man gains salvation, God tells him to feel at every moment that he is the instrument and God is the Doer. At this time, the man feels extremely happy and grateful that God has chosen him to be His instrument. A man who has achieved liberation hears something else from God. God says, "My son, you have worked hard, very hard, to free yourself from the meshes of ignorance. Perhaps you are tired. If you want to take rest, you may take rest. Don't work if you don't want to. If you work, so much the better; but if you don't work, no harm. I am still very pleased with you." A man who has realised God hears still something else from God. God tells him, "Before, I worked alone for you, for the world, for the universe. Now I give you the key to open up My universal Consciousness. I give you My treasure, My entire wealth. I want you to feel that My wealth is your wealth, and to distribute My wealth as your very own. Your work and My work are the same: the manifestation of Divinity, the manifestation of Immortality on earth. Together we shall work, together we shall liberate the earth consciousness. Together we shall transform our Vision into Reality."

He who has achieved salvation, in God's Eye is very good. He who has achieved liberation, in God's Eye is very great. He who has achieved realisation, in God's Eye is both very good and very great. A man with salvation feels that God is his Father. A man with liberation feels that God is his Friend. And a man with God-Realisation feels that God is his Everything.

3. *Silence*

> Silence, Silence.
> Silence is the soul's preparation.
> Silence is the heart's perfection.
> Silence is the mind's illumination.
> Silence is the vital's determination.
> Silence is the body's inspiration.
> Silence, Silence.
>
> When we are in silence, we grow.
> We grow into our Divinity.
> When we are of silence, we flow.
> We flow into Infinity.
> When we are for silence, we glow.
> We glow in the heart of Immortality.

Man's silence pleases God. God's Silence displeases man. Man's silence touches the very heart, the very life-breath of God's boundless Gratitude. God's Silence touches the mind of man's ever-increasing ingratitude.

The outer silence endures. The inner silence cures. The outer silence is the lamb of God. The inner silence is the lion of God.

We become the lamb of God when we offer ourselves unconditionally to God's Will, and when God unconditionally and constantly makes us feel that we are not only His chosen instruments, but also His eternal friends. Him to realise, Him to fulfil and Him to manifest on earth: for this we came into the world. When we entered into the world, God offered us His inner Promise to unveil our Reality and manifest our Divinity. And when we go back to Heaven, God shall tell us that we have played our role, we have fulfilled His Promise here on earth.

When God's Will becomes our will, when we offer to God not only the possessions and achievements of the outer world, but also the awareness, the aspiration and the realisation of the inner world, then we become the lion of God. When we do not aspire, God in us is a sleeping lion. When we aspire, pray and meditate, God in us becomes a roaring lion. This roaring lion devours our teeming darkness and ignorance.

To see God roaring in us, roaring for our inner victory, our divine victory, we have to make a conscious effort. This conscious effort is our constant self-giving according to the Will of God. The Will of God we come to know when we feel the necessity of inner silence. We develop the power of inner silence when we see that the world without God is illusion, imagination, unreality, and that the world with God is divine Vision, fulfilling Reality and everlasting Divinity.

Silence is the seed of God in man.
Silence is the eternal traveller in us.
Silence is the ever-transcending Goal in us, with us and for us.

4. *Problems*

Problems do not indicate man's incapacity. Problems do not indicate man's inadequacy. Problems do not indicate man's insufficiency. Problems indicate man's conscious need for self-transcendence in the inner world, and his conscious need for self-perfection in the outer world.

You have a problem. He has a problem. She has a problem. Your problem is that the world does not touch your feet. His problem is that the world does not love him. Her problem is that she feels that she does not adequately help God in the world. To solve your problem, you have to conquer your pride. To solve his problem, he has to conquer his greed. To solve her problem, she has to conquer her self-styled and self-aggrandised desiring ego.

Each problem is a force. But when we see the problem, we feel deep within us a greater force. And when we face the problem, we prove to the problem that we not only *have* the greatest force, but actually we *are* the greatest force on earth.

A problem increases when the heart hesitates and the mind calculates. A problem decreases when the heart braves the problem and the mind supports the heart. A problem diminishes when the mind uses its search-light and the heart uses its illumination-light.

Self-denial cannot solve any problem. Self-assertion cannot solve any problem. It is God-manifestation through self-existence that can solve all problems of the present and the future. Our sincere approach to a problem will eventually lead us to a satisfactory solution. Our sincere approach to God will carry our teeming problems in God's Will-chariot into the infinite, eternal Smile.

If fear is our problem, then we have to feel that we are the chosen soldiers of God the Almighty. If doubt is our problem, then we have to feel that we have deep within us the Sea of God's Light. If jealousy is our problem, then we have to feel that we are the oneness of God's Light and Truth. If insecurity is our problem, then we have to feel that God is nothing and can be nothing other than constant and ceaseless assurance to us that He will claim us as His very own. If the body is the problem, our constant alertness and attention can solve this problem. If the vital is the problem, our soaring imagination can solve this problem. If the mind is the problem, our illumining inspiration can solve this problem. If the heart is the problem, our perfecting aspiration can solve this problem. If life is the problem, our fulfilling self-discovery can solve this problem.

The individual problem arises when we want to possess infinite humanity. The universal problem arises when the Infinite wants to mould, guide, shape, transform and divinely and supremely fulfil the finite, but the finite does not want to listen to the dictates of the Infinite.

A problem is not the harbinger of defeat or failure. A problem can be transformed into the beckoning Hands of the Supreme that can take us to our destined Goal, the Goal of the ever-transcending, ever-fulfilling Beyond.

5. *Idea and ideal; the Real and the Eternal*

Idea is man's preparation. Ideal is man's progression. The Real is man's illumination. The Eternal is man's realisation.

Idea is in the mind. Ideal is in the central being. The Real is in the life of existence. The Eternal is in the Soul.

Idea imagines the Truth. Ideal gets a glimpse of the Truth. The Real possesses the Truth. The Eternal *is* the Truth.

The idea of an unaspiring man is weak, very weak. His ideal is low, very low. His reality is obscure, quite obscure. His eternity is uncertain, quite uncertain.

The idea of an aspiring man is strong, very strong. His ideal is high, very high. His reality is clear, quite clear. His eternity is certain, quite certain. His idea is as strong as a giant. His ideal is as high as Mount Everest. His reality is as clear as daylight. His eternity is as certain as his present living breath.

An idea knows how to rush forward. An ideal knows how to soar above. The Real knows how to evolve without, from within. The Eternal knows how to glow in the finite and in the Infinite.

Idea tells us, "Awake, arise! You have slept for a long time. It is high time for you to get up." Ideal tells us, "Go and wash yourself, purify yourself. Get ready to study, you have to study." The Real tells us, "Study, cultivate your inner life. Discover the

Divine within you, the immortal within you, the Infinite within you." The Eternal tells us, "I have a short message for you, my children. You have come from me, the Ever-Unknowable, and you are for me. The unknowable in me you will transform into the unknown; the unknown in me you will transform into the knowable; and the knowable in me you will transform into the known for the earth-aspiration and earth-consciousness.

6. *The soul-love of the United Nations*

The soul-love of the United Nations is life-examination, life-improvement and life-perfection.

Life-examination makes our life on earth meaningful.

Life-improvement makes our rest in Heaven blissful.

Life-perfection makes our rest in Heaven and on earth fruitful.

The soul-love of the United Nations has the fragrance of Divinity's rose on the physical plane and the benediction of Immortality's bird on the spiritual plane.

Mind-love, heart-love and soul-love. Mind-love is just an opinion. Heart-love is a firm conviction. Soul-love is an everlasting illumination. Opinions at times confuse us. Convictions at times disappoint us. But illumination always makes us see the Feet of God and the height of Truth. It also makes us see that it has silenced the roaring lion of darkness in the outer world and that it has fed the soaring flame-bird in the inner world.

The soul-love of the United Nations teaches us three most important things: patience, expansion and oneness. Patience is not peace. But patience eventually shows us the way to peace, world peace. Expansion is not an act of self-aggrandisement. But expansion can easily be a life-offering and love-building reality. Oneness does not indicate a lack of opportunity for revealing and manifesting individual uniqueness. Oneness is like the essence and fragrance of a lotus. It does not prevent each petal of the lotus from revealing and manifesting its own uniqueness.

The soul-love of the United Nations has a philosophy of its own. It says that each nation has its own significant truth. One nation will not and cannot overthrow the realisation and revelation of another nation. On the contrary, the realisation and revelation of one nation can easily complement the realisation and revelation of another nation. The soul-love of the United Nations has a religion of its own. This religion is a silently unified wisdom. In this silently unified wisdom looms large a supremely unifying life.

Voltaire said something quite interesting and illumining: "Four thousand volumes of metaphysics cannot teach us what the soul is." It is the soul alone that can teach us what the soul is. But before the soul teaches us about itself, we have to unlearn the teachings of the obscure, uncertain and doubting mind and, at the same time, we have to learn the teachings of the loving, uniting and illumining heart.

I wish to quote a most significant thought of Emerson: "We can't describe the natural history of the soul, but it is divine." No matter how sincerely, how soulfully, how devotedly and how unconditionally we try to describe the natural history of the soul, we are bound to underestimate its capacity. For the soul is the child of both Infinity's Dream and Eternity's Reality.

In order to know the soul-love of the United Nations, we have to choose to be free, and we have to be free to choose. When we are within the confines of history, we have to choose to be free. When we are in the sky of evolving spirituality, we have to be free to choose. Soul-love is free will. Soul-love is free choice. When a nation's free will chooses self-giving, its free choice expedites God-becoming. In self-giving and God-becoming is the confluence of the outer lustre of the United Nations and the inner effulgence of the United Nations. This confluence will, without fail, be a glorious vision for both mortals and immortals.

From the spiritual point of view, the soul-love of the United Nations will always remain resourceful in all problematical situations, untiring in the discharge of its national and international duties, sagacious in its pursuit of inner knowledge and inner wealth, and spontaneous in its willingness to add to the peace, love and joy of searching and ascending humanity.

7. Freedom

Freedom. Freedom is the creative force within us. Freedom is the sustaining life within us. Human freedom is an experience of the body, in the vital and for the mind. Divine freedom is an experience of the soul, in the heart and for the mind, the vital and the body. There is practically no difference between animal freedom and human slavery. In the domain of the destructive vital, our animal freedom roars. In the abyss of our sleeping inconscient body, our human slavery snores.

God's Freedom lies in His constant Service to mankind, in His unconditional Self-giving. Man's freedom lies in his God-achievement, life-perfection and life-fulfilment.

The freedom of the doubting mind is undoubtedly a reality. But this reality is fleeting, flimsy. The freedom of the loving and aspiring heart is an everlasting reality and an ultimate sublimity.

Freedom of earthly thought is good, but quite often it opens itself to false freedom. Freedom that comes from following the heavenly Will invokes God's Presence in us. It invokes His divine Promise in and through us and His supreme Self-assertion and Self-manifestation in and through us.

What is false freedom? False freedom is our constant and deliberate acceptance of ignorance and our conscious existence in ignorance. What is real freedom? Real freedom is our conscious awareness of our inner divinity, and our constant inseparable oneness with the Inner Pilot.

What can false freedom do? False freedom can do much. It can totally destroy us. It can destroy our inner possibilities and potentialities. It can destroy our inner wealth. What can real freedom do? Real freedom also can do much. Real freedom can make us grow into the very image of our Supreme Pilot.

We have two types of freedom: outer freedom and inner freedom. Outer freedom constantly wants to prove its capacity. It wants to prove its sovereignty. Inner freedom wants to prove that it belongs to God and God alone.

Outer freedom has a new goal every day. It wants to discover this goal only in pleasure. But inner freedom has only one eternal Goal, and that Goal is to achieve the conscious awareness of God and the conscious manifestation of God in and through itself.

Outer freedom is satisfied only when it is in a position to say, "I have no superiors. I am my only master." Inner freedom is satisfied only when it can soulfully say, "I don't want to be superior to anyone, but I want God to be my superior, my only superior."

Forgetfulness takes away our freedom, but God's Forgiveness brings it back. Teeming desires take away our freedom, but God's Compassion brings it back. Self-importance and self-assertion take away our freedom, but God's Light brings it back.

It is our self-awareness that retains our freedom and God's divine Pride in us that perfects our freedom. In the perfection of our earthly freedom we grow, and we sow the Heaven-seed within us. And in the fulfilment of our inner freedom we see Heaven and earth as complementary souls. For earth offers its wealth and capacity, which is receptivity, and Heaven offers its wealth and capacity, which is Divinity and Immortality.

8. *The Divine Mission*

The Divine Mission is not a self-imposition or a world-proposition. The Divine Mission is at once a love-offering and a self-giving.

The world needs attention. The Divine Mission is always willing to offer its one-pointed attention to the world. The world needs concern. The Divine Mission is always ready to offer its soulful, meaningful and fruitful concern to the world. The world needs love. The Divine Mission is always ready to offer its love, inner and outer, to the world. The outer love is constant sacrifice. The inner love is inseparable oneness.

There are two types of seekers: the human seeker and the divine seeker. The human seeker wants to add to his glory, increase his possessions and gain supremacy over others. The divine seeker wants to enter into a spiritual process, a divine progress and a supreme success.

There are two types of nations: the unaspiring nation and the aspiring nation. The unaspiring nation enjoys sleep, ignorance and death. The aspiring nation enjoys self-protection, self-illumination and self-perfection. The unaspiring nation does not know what the Goal is or where the Goal is. The aspiring nation knows what the Goal is and where the Goal is. The Goal is perfect Perfection. The Goal can be found in self-discovery.

The mission of an unaspiring religion is arrogantly to exclude or find fault with all other religions. The mission of an aspiring religion is to proclaim once and for all that Truth is universal, Light is omnipresent and Love is omnipotent.

There are three significant roads that lead us to our destination and then make us aware of our Divine Mission. One road is the road of knowledge and wisdom. Another road is the road of love and devotion. The third road is the road of dedicated action.

If we want to discover our Mission while walking along the road of knowledge and wisdom, then we will come to learn who God is and what God is. We will learn that God is all Love and all Compassion.

If we want to discover our Mission while walking along the road of love and devotion, then we will feel where God is. God is in our living and flaming faith.

If we want to discover our Mission while walking along the path of dedicated action, then we will discover the truth that in revealing our selfless capacity, which is dedication, we are manifesting God's Action on earth.

The spiritual Master comes into the world with a Mission. His Mission is to tell the world that he is of God's illumination but always for man's aspiration. Sri Krishna came into the world with a Mission, and his Mission was the manifestation of Universal Harmony. The Buddha came into the world with a Mission, and his Mission was the manifestation of Universal Peace. The Christ came into the world with a Mission, and his Mission was the manifestation of Universal Compassion.

Here at the United Nations there are many missions representing different countries. To me each mission is like a river flowing into the ocean, and the ocean is the United Nations. Each mission is a flowing river entering into the ocean with hope, with eagerness and with a willingness to become part and parcel of the ocean. At the United Nations the Divine Mission flows not only in the ocean but also through each of the rivers. The Divine Mission of Light exists not only in the infinite Vast, but also in the tiniest drop of consciousness. In the perfection and fulfilment of the Divine Mission in the Infinite, and in the perfection and fulfilment of the Divine Mission in the finite, the Supreme Satisfaction will dawn.

In each of the rivers the Supreme Satisfaction has to dawn, for it is the constant flow of the rivers entering into the ocean that makes the ocean a living reality. And when the ocean flows back into the rivers, it offers them its abundant inner wealth so they can fulfil themselves through it.

The Mission of God in each permanent mission to the United Nations is as important as it is in the United Nations itself. The United Nations is the entire body and each mission is like a limb. The body is perfect only when all the limbs are perfect. If one limb remains imperfect, the body remains imperfect.

When we are really great we care for the small, for the poor, for the invalid. The mission of the great is to become one with those who are less great than they, and to lift them up to a higher standard through self-giving. The mission of those who are not yet great is to feel that the great ones are only the more evolved extensions of their own aspiring consciousness.

9. *Who are we?*

Who are we? We are doubters. We are believers. We are discoverers. We are knowers. We are transformers. We are lovers. We are fulfillers.

We are doubters. We doubt our inner dream. We doubt our outer reality. God says to us, "Attention, you doubters! Don't doubt. Your blue-gold dreams are coming from Me. Your green-red realities are running towards Me."

We are believers. We believe that we are helpless and fruitless. God says to us, "Attention, you believers! Your belief is wrong. You are not helpless and fruitless. My Concern is there for you, to help you all the time. My Compassion cares for you, to make your life fruitful at every moment."

We are discoverers. We have discovered that Truth and Light are far beyond our reach. God says to us, "Attention, you discoverers! Your discoveries are all wrong. I have discovered Truth and Light on your behalf. Truth is what you have. Light is what you are."

We are knowers. We know much about things. We know little about ourselves. We know least about God. God says to us, "Attention, you knowers! You know that it is I who have created all things. You know that it is you who create Me every day in you. You know that it is I who am the perfect slave of your constant desires."

We are transformers. We want to transform doubt into belief, fear into strength, bondage into freedom. God says to us, "Attention, you transformers! I am so glad that you want to transform doubt into belief, fear into strength, bondage into freedom. I wish you also to try to transform the life of the finite into the Life of the Infinite."

We are lovers. We love beauty's body, beauty's soul and beauty's goal. God says to us, "Attention, you lovers! Beauty's body is good. Beauty's soul is better. Beauty's goal is by far the best. Beauty's body is an aspiring child. Beauty's soul is the illumining Father. Beauty's goal is the fulfilling Mother."

We are fulfillers. We want to fulfil Heaven on earth, and earth in Heaven. God says to us, "Attention, you fulfillers! You want to fulfil Heaven and earth. It is a splendid ideal. But I wish to say that until you have fulfilled Me, you cannot fulfil Heaven and earth. In order to fulfil Me, you have to cry in your heart ceaselessly and soar smilingly and everlastingly."

We say to God, "O Father, O Mother, O Friend Eternal, we see that we started our journey as doubters and shall end our journey as fulfillers."

God says to us, "My sweet children, you are mistaken. You started your journey as the distributors of My Light and My Life-Force, and you will complete your journey as the builders of My Body-Consciousness on earth."

10. *The heart-peace of the United Nations*

The heart says to peace, "Peace, I need you."

Peace says to the heart, "Heart, I need you."

Both the heart and peace need each other. Without peace, the heart is fruitless. Without the heart, peace is homeless.

The inner heart of the United Nations is flooded with peace. The outer heart of the United Nations is trying to spread peace all over the world.

The outer existence of the United Nations is a colossal hope. The inner existence of the United Nations is a fulfilling reality.

The heart of the United Nations has peace. The mind of the United Nations seeks peace. The vital of the United Nations needs peace. The body of the United Nations is for peace.

The presence of peace in the heart is divine oneness. The presence of peace in the mind is divine illumination. The presence of peace in the vital is divine dynamism. The presence of peace in the body is divine satisfaction.

The goal of the United Nations is peace, world peace. The secret of the United Nations is sacrifice.

There are two types of people: one wants peace, the other does not. Many nations have formed the outer body of the United Nations. Peace is expected from each nation in abundant measure. The Supreme loves all nations, because all are marching towards the same Goal. But if any nation wants to surpass other nations ruthlessly, then that particular nation will never be claimed by God's Pride, Heaven's Delight and earth's gratitude as their own. When all nations work together devotedly and untiringly, then only can they embody universal oneness and reveal universal love.

11. *Why?*

Why do we think of God? Why do we pray to God? Why do we meditate on God?

We may think of God, pray to God and meditate on God because the world around us has disappointed us or failed us. Our near and dear ones may have deserted us, and we need consolation. If these are the reasons why we think of God, pray to God and meditate on God, then God gives us fifty out of one hundred.

We may think of God, pray to God and meditate on God because we feel that we have made thousands of mistakes in this life. We either want to rectify these mistakes or at least not make any more mistakes, since each mistake undoubtedly creates pain and a sense of frustration and failure in us. Or we may think of God, pray to God and meditate on God because we have missed countless opportunities in life and we want to avail ourselves of all the opportunities that we are going to get in the future. If we think of God, pray to God and meditate on God for these reasons, then God gives us sixty out of one hundred.

We may think of God, pray to God and meditate on God because we feel a tremendous sense of fear and doubt in ourselves. We fear the world; we fear even ourselves. We don't know what to say to people or how to behave; we don't know what is going to happen to us. We are always afraid of others or afraid of our own actions. Also, we doubt others and we doubt our own potentialities, possibilities and capacities. Now, for these reasons if we think of God, pray to God and meditate on God, God gives us seventy out of one hundred.

We may pray to God for more love in the world, and for peace of mind. We don't want to remain in anxiety; we don't want to remain in anger and hatred. If we think of God, pray to God and meditate on God for these reasons, then God gives us eighty out of one hundred.

We may think of God, pray to God and meditate on God because we want Divine Love, Divine Concern from the world or from God. We want only the love that will expand us, the love that will fulfil us. We do not expect any outer success or fame or popularity. We wish to receive only God's Divine Love, if we think of God, pray to God and meditate on God for these reasons, then God gives us ninety out of one hundred.

But when we want only to become what God is and what God has, by constant and unconditional self-giving, then God gives us one hundred out of one hundred. At this point we are not asking God for anything. We want only to be what God is, that is to say Infinite Peace, Infinite Light and Infinite Bliss. Nor do we want anything from the world. If the world tortures us, disappoints us or misunderstands us, that is up to the world. We do not expect anything from the world, but we do expect one thing from ourselves, and that one thing is that we will grow into God Himself. If that is our choice, if that is the reason why we think of God, pray to God and meditate on God, then God gives us one hundred out of one hundred. Otherwise, no matter how sincere our motive is, we will not satisfy God fully. If we want to improve the world or improve ourselves, these things all have value, but they do not have the ultimate value. The ultimate value we get only when we are ready and eager to grow into God and become what God is.

Now how can we grow into God? We must be ready every day to change, and not to remain prisoners of the past. When today is over, we have to feel that it is past. It will not be of any help to us in growing into the Highest Supreme. No matter how sweet, how loving or how fulfilling was the past, it cannot give us anything now that we do not already have. We are moving forward towards the goal, so no matter how satisfying the past was, we have to feel that it is only a prison. The seed grows into a plant, then it becomes a huge tree. But if the consciousness of the plant remains in the seed, then there will be no further manifestation. Yes, we shall remain grateful to the seed because it enabled us to grow into a plant. But we will not pay much attention to the seed stage. Once we have become a plant, let our aim be to become a tree. Always we have to look forward towards the goal. Only when we become the tallest tree will our full satisfaction dawn.

We must always remain in the present. This present is constantly ready to bring the golden future into our heart. Today's achievement is most satisfactory, but we have to feel that today's achievement is nothing in comparison to what tomorrow's achievement will be. Each time satisfaction dawns, we have to feel that this satisfaction is nothing in comparison to the satisfaction that is about to dawn. We have to feel that every second brings new life, new growth, new opportunity. If we are ready to allow change into our life every second, every minute, every day, we are bound to grow. How will we know that this change is for the better and not for the worse? We will know it is for the better if we see that new light is entering into us. If new light is not entering into us, then we have to feel that we are doing something wrong or making some mistake, unconsciously if not consciously.

Every time we think of God, we should feel that He is our Ideal, He is our Goal. At the same time, we have to know that to *see* the Goal is not the aim, to *reach* the Goal is not the aim. Our aim is to *become* the Goal itself. God expects nothing short of this from us. He wants us to be what He is. If this is our aim, then when we think of God, when we pray to God, when we meditate on God, God feels that our thought, our prayer and our meditation is absolutely right, absolutely divine.

12. *Where is God?*

"Where is God?"

"There is no God."

If one says that there is no God, that means he is asserting his conception of God in a negative way. A real seeker takes the view of an atheist as sincerely and seriously as he does his own positive conception of God. A real seeker knows and feels that an atheist's conception of nothingness and the non-existence of God contains the seeker's own conception of God.

"Where is God?"

"No God. Even if God exists, who needs Him? Who wants Him? One can get along without God. One can remain satisfied with what he has."

When one is satisfied with what little he has, that means that God the Happiness in him is making him satisfied, even with his little achievement. One can never be happy if one does not consciously or unconsciously meet with God the Happiness in each thing he sees, does and grows into.

"Where is God?"

"I am not even sure that He exists."

If one says that he is doubtful about God's existence, that means he has at least fifty per cent faith in God's existence. Each human being has a friend and an enemy. His enemy, doubt, negates the living inner truth in him. His friend, faith, feeds and strengthens his inner conception of truth. Finally, it immortalises the truth in his heart, mind, vital and body.

"Where is God?"

"I do not know where God is, but I would like to know."

If someone is just curious to know about God, but has no real need for God, from the strict spiritual point of view he is not a seeker. But if one enlarges his spiritual heart, then he embraces even that curious person and includes him in his spiritual life. He feels that today's man of curiosity can become tomorrow's man of genuine spirituality, provided he is given sincere concern, compassion, encouragement and love.

"Where is God?"

"God is all around me. Now I must learn how to see Him."

If the seeker has genuine aspiration and not mere curiosity, he is undoubtedly on the correct path, for this is the only way to reach God. This seeker is like a child who feels his father's presence everywhere. As a human child feels his father's presence when he is in the living room and his father is in some other room, so also a spiritual child feels that no matter where he is, his Father is there somewhere in the same universal house.

At the end of knowing and feeling, we come to seeing and becoming. The spiritual child knows what God is and feels what God is. Then he goes deep within and sees God face-to-face and eventually becomes God Himself. At this point he answers the question, "Where is God?" with the question, "Where is He not?" He also answers another question, "Who is God?" with the question, "Who is not God?"

13. *No nation is unwanted*

No nation is unwanted. Every nation is wanted. Every nation is needed. Every nation is indispensable. Each nation is great. The greatness of each nation lies in its deep love for other nations and in its self-giving to other nations.

Why does an individual love others? An individual loves others because he knows that if he does not love others, then he remains imperfect and incomplete. Why does one give of oneself to others? One gives of oneself to others because he has discovered the undeniable truth that self-giving is truth-loving and God-becoming. And what applies to an individual human being can equally, appropriately and convincingly apply to a nation.

Sir Winston Churchill once made a most significant remark: "When abroad I do not criticise the government of our country, but I make up for it when I come home." Self-criticism is necessary; self-criticism is obligatory. If each nation values self-criticism when it is at home, then perfection-sun will not remain a far cry. Self-criticism is the harbinger of self-enquiry. Self-enquiry is the harbinger of God-discovery. In God-discovery man rises above the ignorance of millennia.

The great German philosopher Schopenhauer said, "Every nation ridicules other nations, and all are right." Who can deny this most deplorable fact? At the same time, who does not have the courage to think and feel that this fact need not and cannot be an abiding truth? Why do we ridicule others? We ridicule others precisely because our jealousy has not yet left us. We ridicule others because they do not have what we have or because we do not have what they have.

Now a nation may have hundreds of good, divine and even astonishing qualities, but if that nation is wanting in the inner quality, the feeling of oneness, then it cannot have true satisfaction. Everlasting satisfaction is out of the question. Again, if a nation is not blessed with many striking qualities and illumining capacities but nonetheless has the inner quality, a sense of inseparable oneness, then that nation is the creator of fulfilling joy, the distributor of fulfilling joy and the fulfiller of fulfilling joy.

Each nation is a petal of a flower, an inner rose, an inner lotus. If one petal is ruined, then the entire flower loses its beauty; and when a flower loses its beauty, it loses everything. Each nation is like a note in a song. If one note is not properly sung, then the entire song is ruined.

Each nation has the capacity to fulfil all nations through self-giving, and this self-giving is nothing other than God-becoming. Here at the United Nations, each nation shall offer its illumining capacities and fulfilling qualities to all the other nations. Together all nations will walk, together all nations will run, together all nations will fly and dive towards the same goal, the goal of everlasting Reality. When we reach and become the everlasting Reality, we shall see that we have transformed the animal in us and immortalised the divine in us.

How can a nation be happy, purposeful and fulfilled? A nation can be happy, purposeful and fulfilled if it thinks less and meditates more. A nation can be happy, purposeful and fulfilled if it plans less and acts more. Thinking is quite often confusing. Planning is quite often frustrating. Too much thinking and too much doubting and suspecting go together. Too much planning and too much worrying go together.

Meditation and action have a different story. Illumining meditation is self-discovery. Illumining action is self-mastery. The more one can meditate soulfully, the sooner he reaches his destination. The more one can act devotedly, the sooner he manifests God-Life, Truth-Love, Light-Delight. A seeker-nation with God-Life sees God's Body, the universe. A seeker-nation with Truth-Love feels God's Heart, the universal Reality. A seeker-nation with Light-Delight becomes God's Soul, the universal Goal.

14. *Each nation in its place is great*

A nation is a limb of the universal body. Each limb is necessary, essential and indispensable. Each nation represents humanity's hope, humanity's promise and humanity's progress. Hope was our yesterday's treasure. Promise is our today's treasure. Progress shall be our tomorrow's treasure.

THE TEARS OF NATION-HEARTS

Each nation can be great by virtue of a few divine qualities. A nation can be great by virtue of its simplicity. A nation can be great by virtue of its sincerity. A nation can be great by virtue of its humility. A nation can be great by virtue of its sense of duty, both national and international. A nation can be great by virtue of its prosperity, both inner and outer. Finally, a nation can be great by virtue of its generosity, constant and supreme generosity.

A great nation is that nation which offers inspiration to other nations. A greater nation is that nation which offers concern to other nations. The greatest nation is that nation which offers heart's love, spontaneous love, to other nations. With inspiration we begin to form our universal family. With concern we strengthen our universal family. With love we feed and fulfil our universal family.

The divine greatness of a nation lies in its self-offering today. The divine greatness of a nation lies in its God-becoming tomorrow. The divine greatness of a nation lies in its God-revelation today. The divine greatness of a nation lies in its God-manifestation tomorrow.

Self-offering, God-becoming, God-revelation and God-manifestation are possible through each individual nation. Each individual nation can be a perfect example of self-offering, God-becoming, God-revelation and God-manifestation. How? If a nation lives in the heart, then self-offering is not only possible but also inevitable. If a nation lives in the soul, then God-becoming is not only possible but also inevitable. If a nation tries and cries for the transformation of the whole universal family of nations, then God-revelation can no longer remain a far cry. God-revelation then is not only possible, but practicable and inevitable as well. Finally, if a nation cares sincerely, devotedly, soulfully and unconditionally for the perfect Perfection not only of its own existence, but also of the entire universe, then God-manifestation is bound to take place.

In size, in capacity, in receptivity, all nations may not have the same status. But each nation is indispensable in its own way. Each nation is like a drop, a tiny drop or a mighty drop, in the vast ocean of divine, fulfilling, fruitful consciousness. It is all the drops combined that make up the ocean. Again, it is the ocean that manifests or fulfils its existence through the different drops, small and big alike.

Each nation is humanity's conscious cry for perfect Perfection. It is in and through each nation that humanity can make the ultimate progress. This ultimate progress is spiritual brotherhood, divine Reality and immortal Life in the life of the mortal and infinite achievement in the heart of the finite.

15. *You or I?*

O God, are You responsible for all the suffering, darkness and ignorance in the world, or am I?

"Son, I am responsible. I am responsible for everything; I am responsible for everyone; I am responsible for My entire creation. It is I who reside in everything as inspiration and as aspiration. It is I who approve of everything or tolerate everything, show compassion for everything or forgive everything. Therefore it is I who am responsible for everything, whether it is good or bad, divine or undivine. It is I who am responsible in everything, in every action, in every human life."

O God, You want to change the face of the world. Do You want to do it alone, all by Yourself, or do You need my help and dedicated service?

"Son, I do not want to change the face of the world all by Myself. I cannot change the face of the world alone. I need your assistance. I am the tree. You, all human beings, are the leaves, flowers and fruits. A tree without leaves, flowers and fruits is worthless. I need assistance from my created human beings. I am the ultimate realisation of your climbing cry. You are the ultimate manifestation of My descending Dream. The transformation of the earth-consciousness can take place only when you and I work together. Dedicated service from both the Creator and the creation is needed to change the face of the world."

Aum.

"You or I?"

When I think of the divine within my heart, when I meditate on the divine within my heart, I see, I feel my "I". This "I" is not a self-centred "I". This "I" is the infinite expansion of my universal oneness.

When I think of the undivine within my being, when I meditate on the undivine within my being, I automatically choose the life of bondage. I become the life of frustration. I become the life of destruction. When I meditate on the undivine or think of the undivine, I choose mental limitation to be my own. I choose vital frustration to accept me as its own. I choose physical imperfection and unconsciousness to take me as their very own. Each moment that I meditate on the undivine, I enjoy, consciously enjoy, despair, frustration, limitation, bondage and death.

Here at the United Nations let us say "You and I", not "You or I?"

You and I. You as a nation – aspiring nation, searching nation, crying nation, illumining nation – can fulfil the Dream of God on earth. As a seeker of the Highest Truth, with your dedication you can fulfil the Dream of God.

When, as a nation, you think only of yourself, I see you as a petal of a rose. But when, on the strength of your dedication to the world at large, you need the Divine in you to think of you and to meditate on you, I see you as a whole, a rose complete. I do not see you as a petal, but as a fully-blossomed rose.

"You or I?" is determined by our actions. The Divine within us gets abundant joy when we act devotedly and soulfully. The undivine in us gets joy when we want to possess and be possessed. We know the secret of joy. When we do the right thing, on the strength of our inner cry, we get joy. But the supreme Joy will not be, cannot be *our* joy unless and until we know how to devote ourselves. The result of our actions may be satisfactory to us, but if we do not get this result by virtue of our devoted and selfless service, we will not get infinite Joy and supreme Joy.

> Our dynamic joy constantly pleases God.
> Our inner silence constantly feeds God.
> Our total and integral surrender devours God.

Each action of ours affects the world at large. A state of mind can affect the entire being. An individual can affect the entire humanity. An iota of God's Concern can illumine all of mankind.

> Joy is in self-transcendence.
> Joy is in self-offering.
> Joy is in self-fulfilment.

Each individual knows that when he was in the animal world he got joy in struggling and fighting. Now he knows that in the human world he gets joy, real joy, abiding joy, in serving and in self-giving. He knows that in the future, in his life divine, he will get joy only in becoming what he is in his transcendental Self: all the Light, the Wisdom, the Perfection of the Supreme.

"You or I?" Each individual, when he separates a portion of himself from his entire existence, feels his you-consciousness. When an individual uses his hands, if he thinks that his hands are the only reality and not his feet, his head, or any other part of himself, then he will hear the song of "you". But while using his hands, if he thinks that this is the time when he has to use his hands but there will be many occasions when he has to use his legs and other parts of his body, and that therefore all his limbs and organs are important, then there can be no "you". It is all "I".

When we meditate on the Absolute Supreme within us, we see how clearly, how fruitfully, both "you" and "I" can work together. We use our legs to go to the office, and then we use our hands to work in the office, and our head to think in the office. Everything has its own place. Everything has its own hour. Each individual has to abide by the inner hour and give due importance to each thing according to God's Will.

God, when am I going to know that You and I are one, or that You and Your entire creation are one?

"The hour has already struck for you to know that I and My creation are one. If you separate Me from My creation and want to achieve joy or grow into joy, I will have no objection. But you will have only limited joy, limited achievement. If you unite both Me and My creation as one, your joy becomes infinite, your achievements become infinite.

"You or I?" cannot solve the age-long problem of humanity. This problem is the sea of ignorance within us and without. But "you and I" can solve this problem. When the unlit consciousness and the lit and illumined consciousness within ourselves become one, that is the end of "you or I". We become all oneness, universal oneness: the song of universal oneness, the life of universal oneness and the breath of universal oneness.

16. *How secure are we?*

[Before commencing his talk, Sri Chinmoy recites the English translation and then chants in Sanskrit the following chants from the Upanishads:]

>Lead me from the unreal to the Real.
>Lead me from darkness to Light.
>Lead me from death to Immortality.

>*Asato ma sad gamaya.*
>*Tamaso ma jyotir gamaya.*
>*Mrityor ma amritam gamaya.*

Infinity is that.
Infinity is this.
From Infinity, Infinity has come into existence.
From Infinity, when Infinity is taken away, Infinity remains the same.

Purnam adah purnam idam purnat purnam udacyate.
Purnasya purnam adaya purnam evavasisyate.

*

When we live in the body, we are constantly insecure. When we live in the vital, we are hopelessly insecure. When we live in the mind, we are surprisingly insecure. When we live in the heart, we are occasionally insecure. When we live in the soul, we are divinely secure. Finally, when we live in God, we are divinely, supremely and sempiternally secure.

Aum.

What is security? Security is the endless smile of our inner self-confidence. What is our self-confidence? Self-confidence is our infinite achievement in the gradual process of our self-transcendence.

In our outer life, in our everyday life, we notice two deplorable things: insecurity and impurity. These two defects loom large in our day-to-day life. Insecurity is of ignorance and for ignorance. Impurity is of darkness and for darkness. Likewise, in our inner life, two divine qualities loom large: security and purity. Security is of Light and for Light. Purity is of Bliss and for Bliss.

How insecure are we? If we can offer an adequate answer to this question, then automatically we are running towards our eternal security. How insecure are we? We are extremely insecure. Both men and women are extremely insecure. Why are we insecure? We are insecure precisely because we do not claim vastness as our birthright. We are insecure because we do not claim oneness as our soul-right. In our outer life, the power of ignorance wants to offer us its security, which is nothing short of absurdity. In our inner life, the power of Light wants to offer us its security, which is nothing short of complete fulfilment. It is only the power of Light that can offer us satisfaction and perfection.

Security does not lie in our material achievements. Security does not lie in our earthly possessions. The richest man on earth is not secure. His constant anxiety about maintaining and increasing his wealth makes him more insecure than the poorest man on earth. A king, a president or dictator is not secure. His hunger for sovereign power in ever-increasing measure and his fear of losing the power he has do not allow him to be secure. He is more insecure than the most insignificant human being on earth.

As an individual cannot be secure by amassing material wealth and by acquiring heights of power, even so a nation cannot be secure by displaying geographical boundaries and by declaring historical achievements. Money-power is no security. Expansion-power is no security. Possession-power is no security. It is the soul-power that is all security. And our love-power, which has free access to the soul-power, is always at our disposal.

A creator creates. Man is a creator; he is an inventor. He invents the atom bomb, a destructive power which annihilates all human security. Here it seems that the creation has more power than the creator. Once the creation comes out of the creator the creation threatens the creator himself. But if the inner being of the creator is surcharged with light, then the creator always remains omnipotent. He will not be at the mercy of his creation. It is the express will of the creator that the creation will have to execute. Man's inner wisdom-light is infinitely superior to his creation. And who created man? God. God's superior power is oneness. This oneness, inseparable oneness, we can achieve, grow into and become only on the strength of our love. Love is oneness. Oneness is the universal life. Self-giving is God-becoming. Only in God-becoming do we become all security.

Aum.

17. *The answer to world-despair*

Before we offer the answer to world-despair, let us first try to know why there is world-despair. For if we do so, we shall be able to offer the most adequate answer to world-despair. Why is there world-despair? World-despair exists because the world desperately needs the life-illumining Light. Why is there world-despair? World-despair exists because the world constantly needs the life-energising Love. Why is there world-despair? World-despair exists because the world immediately needs the life-immortalising Delight.

The answer to world-despair is Light. The answer to world-despair is Love. The answer to world-despair is Delight. We need Light to see the Creator within and the creation without. We need Love to feel the Beloved within and the Lover without. We need Delight to sail God's Boat within and to reach God's Shore without.

World-despair is at once bad and good, undivine and divine. It is bad and undivine because it lives in the darkness-palace of the ignorance-kingdom. It is good and divine because it cries for Light, more Light, abundant Light and infinite Light; Love, more Love, abundant Love and infinite Love; Delight, more Delight, abundant Delight and infinite Delight.

World-despair exists because there is a yawning gulf between our self-giving and the world's receptivity, between the world's self-giving and our receptivity. World-despair exists because there is a yawning gulf between our life-perfection and God's Manifestation, between God's Life-Perfection and our manifestation.

Grace from above can be the only link between our self-giving and the world-receptivity and between the world's self-giving and our receptivity. Aspiration from below can be the only link between our life-perfection and God's Manifestation and between God's Life-Perfection and our manifestation.

The absolute Grace of the Supreme has given birth to the transcendental Reality and the universal Reality. Man's constant inner cry reaches the transcendental Reality, which is the acme of Perfection in the world of the Beyond, and at the same time this inner cry manifests the universal Reality in the core of each aspiring individual on earth.

In the world of yesterday, ignorance guided and moulded us. In the world of today, despair lords it over us. In the world of tomorrow, glowing hope will guide and lead us. And in the world of the day after tomorrow, we shall grow into God's Promise, the Promise of achievement immortal and infinite.

Talking, lecturing and advising the world can never be an adequate answer to world-despair. The most effective answer to world-despair lies in self-giving. But we learn the art of self-giving only after we have learned the art of self-finding. And we learn the art of self-finding only after we have learned the art of meditating, the art of meditating on the Inner Pilot, the Supreme. What we call meditation is nothing other than God-manifestation. And God-manifestation, both within us and without, is always a perfect stranger to human despair.

This short talk of mine can give us only one per cent capacity to offer the answer to world-despair. But the meditation which we are going to do right now is bound to give us ninety-nine per cent capacity to offer the answer to world-despair. Now I wish all of us to meditate only for Light, Love and Delight. Light will open up our eye that sees. Love will open up our heart that feels. Delight will carry us to our Source, the Supreme.

18. *Beyond the world of reason*

The world of reason is self-partition, self-assertion and self-glorification. Beyond the world of reason is the world of Love-realisation, Oneness-manifestation and God perfection.

In the world of reason, the reasoning mind ignores the inner Light and ridicules the higher Light. Beyond the world of reason, the surrendering heart wants to unite itself with the higher Light and the inner Light for the radical transformation of the earth-consciousness.

Here on earth there are three types of satisfaction: the animal satisfaction, the human satisfaction and the divine satisfaction. The animal and the human satisfaction are far, far below the divine satisfaction. A sincere, genuine seeker of the ultimate Truth must needs go far beyond the world of reason to see the face of supreme satisfaction, to feel the heart of supreme satisfaction.

The animal man in us wants to destroy the world for its satisfaction. The human soul in us wants to govern the world for its satisfaction. The divine being in us wants to love and serve the world for its satisfaction.

There are two types of mind: the human, or physical, mind and the spiritual mind. The physical mind is enmeshed in the gross physical consciousness; therefore, it does not and cannot see the proper truth in its own world. The spiritual mind, which is the illumined or illumining mind, has the capacity to stay in the aspiring heart; therefore, it sees the higher Truth, the Truth of the ever-transcending Beyond, and aspires to grow into this Truth.

The human mind does not like to remain in the aggressive and destructive vital consciousness. Yet this human mind, this physical mind, is afraid of the infinite Vast. It wants to achieve the vastness of the Infinite, and at the same time it is afraid of Infinity. The human mind cares for aesthetic beauty, for poise and balance. The human mind is searching for Truth, for Light, for Reality. But unfortunately, it wants to see the highest Truth in its own limited way. It does not want to transcend itself in order to reach the ultimate Truth. Also, the physical mind wants to examine the highest Truth, which is absurd.

The aspiring inner heart, the psychic heart, knows what it is and what it stands for. It knows that its ultimate realisation lies only in its inseparable identification and oneness with Infinity. The heart knows that even though it is like a tiny drop, when it enters into the mighty ocean it will not lose its identity and personality. On the contrary, its personality and individuality will increase in boundless measure and it will be able to claim the vastness of the sea as its very own. The spiritual mind gets illumination from the soul with the help of the heart. And in the process of its own inner illumination, it wants to go far, far beyond the domain of reason in order to see, feel and grow into the ultimate, transcendental Truth.

The paramount importance of the human mind has, until now, been undeniable. The human mind separated us from the animal kingdom through the process of cosmic evolution. Had there been no awakening of the human mind, the conscious human life could not have blossomed out of the animal kingdom. But now the animal in us has played its role. The human in us, the unaspiring human in us, will complete its role soon. The divine in us has begun, or will soon begin, its role.

The soul, the representative of God on earth will not be satisfied unless and until all the members of its immediate family – the body, the vital, the mind and the heart – march together towards the same goal. The body will serve the Inner Pilot with its dedicated service. The vital will serve the Inner Pilot with its spontaneous determination. The mind will serve the Inner Pilot with its constant search for the Truth-Light of the Beyond. The heart will serve the Inner Pilot with its total and inseparable oneness with the Inner Pilot. When this occurs, all the members of the soul's family will reach their destination, the destination of Perfection, perfect Perfection on earth.

The transformation of the physical, the transformation of the vital, the transformation of the mind and the transformation of the heart are taking place every day, every hour, every second in each human being. But when a human being consciously aspires, his transformation is quick, convincing and, at the same time, most fulfilling. Therefore, those who pray and meditate are the pioneers in the world of supreme Truth, Light and Delight. In this world, far, far beyond the domain of the physical mind we can perfectly sing the song of supreme Perfection, or we can bring the world of Perfection down into our aspiring and glowing heart through our regular, sincere and devoted surrender to the ultimate Truth.

At the end of our journey's close we will see that the animal in us has been transformed and the human in us has been transformed and perfected. We will see that the divine in us has carried safely and perfectly the quintessence of our animal and human life and placed it at the Feet of the Supreme. Once we see it placed at the Feet of the Supreme, we can become, here on earth, the direct representatives of the Truth, Light and Delight of the Beyond.

Beyond the world of reason, the Light that we see, feel and want to grow into is the Light of illumination. It is not the light that wants to expose our earthly, limited and deplorable weaknesses. The Upanishads mention that there, in the world beyond reason, the sun shines not. This does not mean that this realm is full of darkness and chaos. No, there the star sun shines not, because that world is self-effulgent. There the perfection of the inner Light, the higher Light the transcendental Light reigns supreme. Seekers of the ultimate Truth eventually enter into that world, the world of transcendental Bliss. When a seeker can establish a free access to that particular world, his heart sings the glory of that world's supreme secret:

"No mind, no form, I only exist...."

This "I" is not the earthbound "I", the ego. This "I" is the universal Self, which is birthless and deathless. This is the "I" that comes to the fore when the Divine Lover in us realises the supreme Beloved.

In this world, far beyond the domain of reason, God's Vision and God's Reality together live. God's Vision is the cosmic seed, and God's Reality is the universal tree.

19. *The voice of silence*

Today I am going to talk on the Voice of Silence. Dear seekers, with all sincerity I wish to tell you that no matter how long I speak about the Voice of Silence, I shall not be able to make you hear the Voice of Silence. But I wish to assure you that if you meditate with me for a few minutes before I speak, if you can dive deep within as I shall dive deep within for a few minutes, then either you will hear the Voice of Silence or your prayer and meditation will expedite your journey towards receiving the message of Silence.

It is true that it takes years for a seeker to hear the message of the Voice of Silence. But, with all my soul's love for each seeker present here today, I wish to say that on the strength of our inner aspiration and outer dedication to the life divine, we can and must hear the Voice of Silence which sempiternally is guiding our life. Our outer life – the life of hustle and bustle – either does not hear this voice or, when it does hear it, pays no attention to it. The life of temptation is what our outer life wants, and not the life of true fulfilment and satisfaction.

The Voice of Silence is the answer when we want divine satisfaction from our day-to-day existence.

The Voice of Silence is the dream of God's ever-climbing Aspiration-dawn.

The Voice of Silence is the reality of God's ever-illumining Revelation-light.

The Voice of Silence is the Immortality of God's ever-fulfilling Perfection-height.

What is voice?

Voice is our inner and outer choice.

Hunger for life-destruction is our animal choice.

Hunger for supremacy-satisfaction is our human choice.

Hunger for perfection-manifestation is our divine choice.

We wish to hear the Voice of Silence, but how can we hear it? There are two principal ways. One way is to silence the human mind totally. From the gross physical mind we enter into the intellectual mind. From the intellectual mind we enter into the intuitive mind. From the intuitive mind we enter into the illumined mind. And from the illumined mind we enter into the overmind. It is only from this highest mind that we can expect to hear the message of the Voice of Silence.

The other way is to feel that the heart-vessel has to be filled with divine Peace, Light, Bliss and Power. When we want to hear the Voice of Silence through the mind, we empty the mind. But when we want to hear the Voice of Silence through the heart, we fill up the heart. When we empty the mind, we have to know that we do so precisely because we want to receive God the Guest or God the infinite Peace. And when we fill up the heart, we feel that God the immortal Light and infinite Delight is entering into our earthly home. The light of the soul precedes the Voice of Silence. The Voice of Silence can never come to the fore unless and until the light of the soul brings it forward consciously, compassionately and lovingly.

What else must we do to hear the Voice of Silence? When we pray, when we meditate, we have to do something quite specific. When we breathe in, we have to imagine consciously that inside that breath, within us, is a peaceful nest and a bird. After a few minutes we have to feel that the nest is our outer existence and the bird is our inner existence. Now this bird has to come out of its nest. How do we bring the bird out of the nest? There are two ways. One way is to make our concentration, meditation and contemplation as dynamic as possible. Here, dynamism means the constant feeling within you of a speeding train that does not stop. It is an express train, and it does not stop at any station or at any junction. It is a tireless train, an endless train, continuously going on. When we have that inner feeling, from the very starting point we get the Blessing-power of the Supreme. And in dynamism, in the flow of dynamism, we see the bird of our inner being leaving its nest, and the Supreme gives us the experience of the Voice of Silence.

Another way to hear the Voice of Silence is to feel, the moment you enter into your meditation or the moment you start praying, that you are an infinite expanse of ocean. A few minutes later, please feel that you are deep inside the ocean, and from there try to spread the wings of the bird that you were when you followed the dynamic way of hearing the message of Silence.

A seeker may hear the Voice of Silence as something very faint and feeble – a tiny voice like a ripple of calm water. But this feeble voice, this faint voice, can be compared to an atom. When we split the atom we release unbelievable power. Similarly, when we know how to hear the Voice of Silence properly, our inner being immediately is inundated with the Power of thousands of inner suns. The creation and the Creator immediately come to satisfy us. Once we hear the Voice of Silence consciously in our spiritual life, we feel that, like God, we too are responsible for the entire creation. Like God, it is we who are the Creator and we who are the creation itself.

Now, how can we know whether we are hearing the Voice of Silence or something totally different which we are mistakenly calling the Voice of Silence? I wish to tell you that we can easily know if it is the Voice of Silence or not. When we hear a voice from the very depths, from the inmost recesses of our heart, and if that voice gives us a message which our outer mind or physical consciousness is ready to accept with utmost joy and love, then we will know that that is the Voice of Silence. If the physical mind or the outer consciousness does not get immediate joy, then it is not the Voice of Silence. Right now our outer mind gets joy both in the acceptance of reality and in the rejection of reality. But when the Inner Voice enters into the outer mind, then the outer mind has no choice. It immediately accepts the reality as reality. When the Voice of Silence is heard, the outer mind will accept it so wholeheartedly that it will feel that the lofty truth it has discovered is its own achievement.

God expresses Himself through silence and sound. Silence is His Reality's height; silence is His Reality's depth. Sound is His Reality's length; sound is His Reality's breadth. In silence, God is all assurance. In sound God is all confidence. In self-assurance God builds the Kingdom of Light. In self-confidence, God invites His unlit, obscure, unaspiring creation to enter into His Kingdom of Light. A seeker who is a child in the spiritual life finds it quite easy to appreciate, admire and adore God's length and breadth. But a seeker who is advanced in the spiritual life inwardly feels that God's height and God's depth must be appreciated first, and only then can His length and breadth be truly and properly appreciated, admired and adored.

The Voice of Silence is God's conscious preparation in man. The Voice of Silence is God's conscious Dream of Perfection in man. The Voice of Silence finally becomes God's own ever-transcending dream-bound Reality and Reality-freed Dream.

> O Voice of Silence
> Where are you?
> I need your golden wings.
> O Voice of God,
> Where are You?
> Hide not from me.

20. *Why do I have to become spiritual?*

Why do I have to become spiritual? I have to become spiritual precisely because I wish to see something, do something and become something. There are many people on earth who do not feel the necessity of this, and I do not find fault with them. But my inner being tells me that I have to see something, do something and become something.

What I wish to see is perfection in my life and in the life of each and every individual. What I wish to do is to love mankind unreservedly and divinely. What I wish to become is a conscious and chosen instrument of God.

Two lives: a life of aspiration and a life of desire. I have been in the life of desire. In that life I did not have even an iota of Peace and Bliss. Therefore, I entered consciously and soulfully into a new life, the life of aspiration. In my desire-life, my existence was tossing in a shoreless sea, and it found its reality in a goalless shore. In order to swim in the sea of Reality, in order to reach the Golden Shore of the Beyond, I entered into the life of aspiration.

Aum.

It is a mistake to think that a spiritual person is impractical. On the contrary, a spiritual person is really practical. An ordinary, unaspiring person thinks of God as being in Heaven, millions and billions and trillions of miles higher than his own existence. His God is not around him, not in front of him, but in an unknown or unknowable Heaven.

But a spiritual person has a different idea of God. He says, "If God exists, then He has to be inside my heart, all around me, right in front of me." So a seeker is practical. He does not accept the theory that God is in a distant and unattainable Heaven, that God is aloof and uninterested in his life. He says, "Only if my God is right here on earth, will I be able to fulfil my aspiration and my need."

Once he realises that God is right in front of him, he immediately feels that God is everywhere, both in Heaven and on earth. When he thinks of God in Heaven, he immediately feels that God is the dream-fulfilling Reality. And when he thinks of God on earth, he feels that God is the reality-illumining Dream – Divinity's conscious and ever-transcending Dream which illumines reality.

In the ordinary life, there are many needs. But in the spiritual life we come to realise that there is only one need, and that is a love for God. There is also something that is not needed, and that is self-proclamation. When I love God, I feel that I am touching the very root of God-Tree. And if I touch the root, then the dynamic flowing energy in the root will take me to all the branches, leaves and flowers. But when I proclaim myself, I just limit and bind myself; I am not able to taste, to enjoy myself as a universal Reality. My self-proclamation immediately separates me from the Whole, which I once upon a time was, which I want to become and which I eventually will be.

A spiritual person is not only practical but also normal and natural. Everything in his life is orderly. He goes from one to two to three, and not the other way around. For a normal person, first things come first. And what is the first thing? It is God, because God is the Creator, God is the Source. Every day dawns with a new life, a new hope, a new sense of Immortality. Now, when the morning dawns, the seeker does first things first. First he prays to God, then he thinks of mankind, and finally he thinks of himself.

When he prays or meditates on God, the seeker uses the divine instrument called surrender. "Let Thy Will be done," he says. And when he thinks of mankind, he uses the instrument called love. He uses his love-power, his love-instrument to become inseparably one with humanity. Then, when he thinks of himself, he uses his discipline-power, his self-control. If he uses his power of self-control, then at every moment a new dream can be dreamt by the divine within him, the seeker within him. A higher call from above takes him to his reality, which is ever-transcending.

As an individual, I have to know that my physical body is not my only reality. I also have a soul, a heart, a mind and a vital. I have to care for my soul first, because this is the eldest member of my family. The soul is constantly dreaming in and through me, and the dream of the soul is the harbinger of my reality's perfection. So I have to think of the soul or meditate on the soul first.

Next I think of my heart. My heart needs love; it needs to offer love and it needs to receive love. First it gives love, then it receives love and finally it becomes love itself. After giving and receiving love, my heart will feel its inseparable oneness with everything and everyone.

Then I have to think of my mind. If I just think of my mind, that does not solve any problem at all. I have to meditate on the mind with the idea of expanding and illumining it. I think not of the mind that binds me or limits me or separates me; I think of the mind that will gladly listen to the heart and to the soul, the mind that can feel the universal oneness.

Then I have to think of my vital. When I think of my vital, I have to think of dynamic energy. If there is no dynamic energy, I cannot produce or achieve anything. Life is a river that flows constantly and continuously. Vital energy is the current that carries us to the sea, the sea of illumination and perfection.

When we think of the physical, immediately we think of the mind, because we feel that the mind is the most developed member of our family. This is true before we accept the spiritual life. But after we have accepted the spiritual life, we feel that the heart is an older brother superior to the mind. And when we become really spiritual, we can boldly say that we do not need the mind at all; what we need is the heart and soul to guide us through life. Granted, the mind may have everything that the heart has. If we want a diamond, we can find a diamond in the mind-room, and we can find the same diamond in the heart-room. But the moment we enter into the mind-room, we see that that room is full of rubbish, junk and undivine things. The diamond is covered, and it will take us days, months and years to uncover it. But when we enter into the heart-room, we see that there is nothing else but the diamond. The moment we open the door, the diamond is right there before us.

A spiritual person is a man of wisdom. Just by seeing the diamond, he will not be fully satisfied; he will want to grow into the diamond itself. This spiritual diamond is perfect Perfection. The spiritual person enters into the heart-room, sees the diamond, touches the diamond, meditates on the diamond and grows into the diamond. When he grows into the diamond, that means he has become the perfect instrument of God. Then his real satisfaction dawns. A seeker's satisfaction dawns only when he becomes a perfect instrument of the Supreme. At that time, he becomes one with earth-consciousness and one with Heaven-consciousness.

Aum.

A spiritual person wants to realise unity in diversity, harmony in diversity. In the ordinary life, two human beings constantly contradict each other. And even in the spiritual life, two divine qualities in different seekers – if they are not properly guarded or guided – will not become complementary. Let us say one seeker has sincerity and the other seeker has humility. Both these qualities are of paramount importance. But the person who has sincerity feels he is not being admired the way his friend is being admired. He feels that the person who has humility is getting more appreciation from others. So the person with sincerity is not happy. Now, the person who is humble feels that his humility is not giving him total satisfaction either. He feels that the person who is sincere is getting more appreciation and admiration. When we are beginners in the spiritual life, even our divine qualities do not satisfy us.

But when we go deep within, our divine qualities will not oppose one another. On the contrary, each divine quality will complement every other divine quality. When sincerity enters into humility and offers its wealth, immediately humility sees that the only one who is really humble is God. It is God's Humility that makes Him what He is. And when humility enters into sincerity, sincerity feels its own reality.

After I become spiritual, what is expected of me? I have to empty myself before God and I have to empty myself before mankind. When I empty myself before God, I shall empty my teeming ignorance, the ignorance of millennia. And when I empty myself before mankind, I shall empty my love. Love I have to empty before humanity; ignorance I have to empty before God.

The life of a spiritual seeker is not the life of a stagnant pool. His is the life of a fresh spring, a spring of ever-flowing Consciousness-Light. When the seeker feels that his life is ever-flowing Consciousness-Light, he feels that Heaven – which is dream – is being manifested on earth, and that earth – which is cry – is being transformed into the ceaseless Smile of the Supreme.

21. *The United Nations as an instrument of human unification*

The United Nations as an instrument of human unification. This is the subject of our talk, and I am sincerely grateful to Mr Donald Keys, who offered this title. This is a lofty, most significant subject, and time will not allow me to do justice to it. What I wish to speak about is not what I have learned from books or news media, but rather what I feel from within. What I feel in the inmost recesses of my heart as solid experience is what I wish to share with the seekers present here.

The United Nations as an instrument of human unification. What is an instrument? An instrument is the reality of the Creator's Dream. The United Nations is an instrument, a significant instrument, an unprecedented instrument of God for His searching, aspiring and loving humanity. This instrument is the joy of the Creator and at the same time, it is the joy of the creation. The United Nations embodies both Heaven's Vision and earth's reality. There was a time when Heaven's Vision was not manifested as reality. We called it the League of Nations. But then the League of Nations was transformed into reality, and became the United Nations. We are all in the process of evolution. Once upon a time we were in the animal kingdom; now we are in the human world, consciously trying to transcend our earth-bound realities. While we were in the animal kingdom, the message of unification did not exist. There was only the message of destruction. In the human world, the message of unification is something real and significant; but, at the same time, unification is still a far cry.

Unification and perfection go together. They complement and fulfil each other. Unification and satisfaction go together. They, too complement and fulfil each other. Unification is the song of the many for the One. Perfection is the song of One for the many. Satisfaction is the song of the One in the many and the song of many in the One.

When we think of the United Nations, the first and foremost thing that comes to our human mind is reliance. Self-reliance is good; inter-reliance is better. But oneness in multiplicity and multiplicity in oneness is by far the best. There is a great difference between self reliance and independence. When we rely on ourselves, on our inner being, our own divinity acts in and through us. At that time, we are relying on the inner Pilot, who is in all and who is *our* All. But when we advocate independence, our uncontrolled, undisciplined, undivine and autocratic nature comes to the fore. Independence we experienced in the animal world. When we exercised our independence, what did we do? We quarrelled, we fought, we killed and we destroyed one another. The message of unification can never breathe in this type of independence. The forest of independence is full of conflicts and contests that nobody actually wins. But in self-reliance, the divine and the soul-light come forward from within us and show us the way and the goal.

The United Nations is not a thing to appreciate, admire or adore. Rather, it is the way, the way of oneness, that leads us to the Supreme Oneness. It is like a river flowing towards the source, the Ultimate Source. The United Nations is the way that wants to lead the world to the destined Goal, where Light and Delight reign supreme.

In this world we see that some people just talk, others talk and then act, others talk and act simultaneously, and still others only act and then let others talk for them. Finally there is a type of person who just acts for the sake of action divine. This is the supreme category. Without the least possible hesitation I would like to say that the United Nations belongs to this category. Outwardly I will not be able to prove this, for as I said before, I do not know about the United Nations' outer achievements.

But, being a seeker of the highest Truth who lives in the inner world, who sees and feels and knows what the United Nations is doing, I am perfectly familiar with the inner achievements of the United Nations.

The United Nations is a real mother, and the world is like a child in front of it. Now you may say that the world is so vast, whereas the United Nations is just a small building. But you have to know who is playing what role on earth. The United Nations is playing the role of the mother. The mother offers her very existence to feed and nourish the child and give the child the message of Light, the message of Truth, the message of Reality. We notice that the child very often ignores the mother's offering or takes it for granted. It is true that the child accepts, but when it is a matter of offering gratitude to the mother, the child consciously or unconsciously forgets.

Now, when the mother does everything for the child, it is not news. But if the child offers a glass of water to the mother, then that becomes news. The mother will work for twenty-four hours like a slave to please the child, but when the child does something most insignificant for the mother, the world takes note of it. The United Nations receives help from the four corners of the globe – financial help, all kinds of help – and that becomes news in the world. But what the United Nations at every second inwardly and outwardly is offering or trying to offer is not news; this the world does not recognise.

The world is blind; it needs God-Vision. And the United Nations has God-Vision in abundant measure. The world is weak; it needs soul-power. And the United Nations has soul-power in abundant measure. The world is suffering; it needs heart-consolation. And the United Nations has heart-consolation in abundant measure.

With utmost love and humility, the seeker in me tells the world to talk less and listen more. Listen to whom? Not to me, but to the United Nations. The United Nations has much to offer in every field, so the world needs its constant, conscious, unfailing and unceasing advice. If the world does not believe in the soul-peace of the United Nations, how will the world believe in the heart-dedication of the United Nations?

The Creator is at once the Silence-seed and the Sound-tree. As the Silence-seed, as the Silence of the Transcendental Height, He embodies His own highest height and deepest depth. And as the Sound-tree, He offers to His creation His own achievement. Silence prepares; Sound reveals. Sound offers what Silence is. Silence tells us who God is and Sound tells us where God is. Who is God? God is man's eternal cry for the highest Transcendental Supreme. And where is God? God is in man's soulful smile. God is all the time visible in our heart's smile and our soul's smile. Where smile looms large in our existence, there alone we see God's very presence. Silence-life is embodied in the soul of the United Nations, and Sound-life is embodied in the body of the United Nations. If the world does not believe in the Silence-life of the United Nations, how will the world believe in the Sound-life of the United Nations?

The outer reality is not always the real reality. The outer reality sometimes, if not always, deceives us. The outer reality very often comes to us in the form of temptation, whereas the inner reality comes to us in the form of emancipation, liberation and salvation. If from the outer reality we go to the inner reality to challenge and fight against it, then we are acting like a fool. The inner reality will never surrender to the outer reality. But if we become one with the inner reality, which is our Silence-life, which is God's Vision, then we can bring it to the fore and transform the outer reality. The outer reality is the reality created by the human mind, the mind which right now is imperfection incarnate. Again, this very mind will one day be transformed, perfected, divinised and immortalised. By whom? By the Inner Pilot and by the divine forces of the inner world.

Critics are of the opinion that the United Nations sometimes is not brave enough or quick enough. Now it is very easy to criticise an organisation. But we have to know what precisely an organisation is. An organisation is composed of human beings, and human beings are far, far from perfection. It is the human in us that criticises, not the divine in us. The divine in us sees the perfection in ourselves and in others. Who is our brother? He is our brother who sees the divine in us and the perfection in us. A real seeker feels that he is growing from perfection, to greater perfection, to infinite Perfection; from light, to more light, to abundant, infinite and immortal Light. Similarly the achievement of the United Nations in the outer world is the achievement of a perfection that is always becoming more perfect; and a day will come when it will be totally perfect.

There are many ways to serve the United Nations: with the physical body, physical mind, the inner heart and the soul's good will. I wish to say that all the services rendered by each individual are necessary, for through them we all offer our perfection to the soul of the United Nations. Each individual not only *has* the message of perfection, but actually *is* the message of perfection. And if we can offer this message of perfection to the soul of the United Nations, then the capacity of the United Nations multiplies itself into infinity.

Let us not ask the United Nations what it has done. Let us not even ask ourselves what we have done. But let us only ask ourselves whether we are *of* the United Nations and *for* the United Nations. If we say we are of the United Nations, then our source is peace, infinite Peace. And if we say we are for the United Nations, then our manifestation is delight, eternal Delight. Our source is Peace and our manifestation is Bliss on earth. So if we know what we are and what we stand for, then the

United Nations becomes for us the answer to world suffering, world darkness and world ignorance.

The inner vision of the United Nations is the gift supreme. This vision the world can deny for ten, twenty, thirty, forty, one hundred years. But a day will dawn when the vision of the United Nations will save the world. And when the reality of the United Nations starts bearing fruit, then the breath of Immortality will be a living reality on earth.

22. *What is the United Nations really doing for humanity?*

What is the United Nations really doing for humanity? This is a most challenging question. Each person is competent to answer this lofty question according to his soul's light. First, I wish to tell you what the United Nations is, according to my own inner light. The United Nations is humanity's colossal hope. The United Nations is Divinity's lofty promise. Hope needs assurance from Heaven's soul. Promise needs receptivity from earth's heart.

Let us take the United Nations as human being. Naturally, this human being has a body, a vital, a mind, a heart and a soul. The body of the United Nations is trying to serve humanity. The vital of the United Nations is striving to energise humanity. The mind of the United Nations is longing to inspire humanity. The heart of the United Nations is crying to love humanity. Finally, the soul of the United Nations is flying to embrace humanity.

The United Nations as a whole wants to offer peace. Peace and the United Nations are inseparable. Now what is peace? Peace is a very, very complicated word when we live in the physical world or in the mental world. In the physical world, we see children all the time quarrelling and fighting. They derive satisfaction from their fighting. This satisfaction is their peace. In the mental world, people are always doubting, suspecting, arguing and doing quite a few things that the spiritual world may not appreciate. Nevertheless, the mental world gets satisfaction from using its intellectual capacities, its doubt-weapons. This doubt and suspicion is the peace of the mental world. But there is also an inner world. In the inner world is self-giving, and self-giving is immediately followed by love-becoming, truth-becoming and perfection-becoming.

Peace does not mean the absence of war. Outwardly two countries may not wage war, but if they inwardly treasure aggressive thoughts, hostile thoughts, that is as good as war. Peace means the presence of harmony, love, satisfaction and oneness. Peace means a flood of love in the world family. Peace means the unity of the universal heart and the oneness of the universal soul.

To me, the United Nations is great. Why? Because it has high principles. To me, the United Nations is good. Why? Because it leaves no stone unturned to transform these principles into living realities. To me, the United Nations is divine. Why? Because it is the fond child of the Supreme dedicated to promoting world peace.

The world may notice a yawning gulf between the principles of the United Nations and the realities of the world. But the world must remember that in the transformation of principles into realities, time is a great factor. The world is old, and it has old ideas, old idiosyncrasies, old propensities. The United Nations is young, very young. Nevertheless, if we go deep within we can easily observe how many things have been accomplished in the brief twenty-nine years of the United Nations' existence. For the first thirteen years of our human life, we consciously or unconsciously wallowed in the pleasures of ignorance without even trying to live a better life, a higher life, a more fulfilling life. In order to live a higher life, an illumining life, a life that perfects and fulfils us, we need a great length of time.

We expect everything from the United Nations child, but we forget that the child has to grow. If we nourish the child, encourage the child and appreciate him for what he already has offered, only then will the progress of the child be satisfactory. If we place a very heavy load on the child's shoulders while he is still small and weak, whose fault is it if he cannot carry it? It is our fault. The child may think that he can carry the entire world on his shoulders, but the parents know that the child's wish will be fulfilled and manifested only in the course of time.

Unfortunately, the world is a bad parent. The world's pressures are attacking the United Nations, but the world's appreciation is rarely seen or heard. The way the United Nations has become a victim to the world's criticism is most deplorable. The world knows how to criticise, but the world does not know how to become one with the soul of the United Nations and see how hard its light is trying to come to the fore to establish a kingdom of Peace and Light on earth. The United Nations is trying to ameliorate the teeming afflictions that weigh so heavily on the world's shoulders. It is trying so hard to cancel the world's inequalities. The United Nations sings one song: the song that says it is love-power that will conquer the world. No other power can conquer the world. From this song we realise something more: when love-power conquers, the conquest is not for the expansion of influence, but for the illumination of existence.

The United Nations is the meeting place for the big brothers and the small brothers of the world. The big brothers are at times reluctant to share with the small brothers their capacities, their wisdom and their achievements. The little brothers at times want to grab the capacities, wisdom-light and achievements of the big brothers without working for them. When the younger brother sees that his older brother has got his Master's degree, he too wants to get a Master's degree. His wishful thinking far transcends his reality's capacity. But if the big brother offers a little bit of light from his abundant light to the little brother, the little brother feels that he has gained world-knowledge all at once.

The big brother wants only one thing: satisfaction. The little brother also wants only one thing: satisfaction. Complete satisfaction dawns only when elder brother and younger brother smile simultaneously. If I smile because of my possession and you cannot smile because of your lack of achievement, I will have no real satisfaction. The smiles must be reciprocal, universal. The need of the younger brother and the abundant capacity of the older brother can be amalgamated. When they are united, both can together smile.

The younger brother wants nothing but acceptance; the older brother wants nothing but self-transcendence. Acceptance and self-transcendence are the prerequisites of action and perfection. Action means acceptance of the world, no matter how weak or insufficient it is, for its present and future transformation. Perfection means constant transcendence of today's achievement by means of self-giving. Self-giving is immediately followed by self-transcendence, and in self-transcendence only do we get the message of perfection.

People say the United Nations is imperfect. I wish to ask them what organisation on earth *is* perfect. They say the United Nations has not fulfilled human needs. I say we have not given full opportunity, not to speak of full authority, to the United Nations to do the needful. Imperfection is the fate of human organisations until divinity reigns supreme within them. There is no organisation which is totally perfect. But there are organisations which, knowing perfectly well they are imperfect, still pretend to be perfect. There are also human beings who know perfectly well that they are imperfect, but do not want to lift one finger to achieve perfection. Again, there are organisations and human beings that cry for perfection and work for perfection, for they know it is only perfection that can bring satisfaction. Without the least possible hesitation we can say that the heart of the United Nations is crying for perfection. In the inner world, the entire being of the United Nations is crying for perfection. But perfection is not a one-man game. It is a collective game that is played by all men. The capacities of all human beings have to be offered, as well as the capacities of all those who work for the United Nations.

Fifty-four years ago Woodrow Wilson and others had a lofty, sublime, supernal vision: a world united and at peace. The United Nations is trying to transform that vision into reality. Let us consider the vision as the height of Mount Everest, while the present reality is the foot of Mount Everest. We are now still at the foot of the mountain, but if we go deep within we will see that we have definitely climbed up a few metres, although we know how difficult it is to climb all the way to the top. Slowly and steadily the soul of the United Nations is offering its light to the body of the United Nations, which is the world, so that it can reach the height of the lofty vision seen fifty-four years ago. This vision cannot and will not always remain a vision, because inside the vision itself is reality. We can see the face of reality in four hundred years or in one hundred years or in fifty years or in ten years, depending on what the world sees and feels in the heart of the United Nations on the strength of its identification. And this identification can be achieved only if we live inside the soul.

Peace, freedom, progress, perfection – these are the four rungs of the cosmic ladder which the United Nations has perfectly housed in the unseen recesses of its heart. Peace we achieve when we do not expect anything from the world, but only give, give and give unconditionally what we have and what we are. Freedom we achieve only when we live in the soul's light. If we live in the light of the soul, if we can swim in the light of the soul's sea, immediately we grow into and achieve the true inner freedom. Progress we achieve by our self-expansion. How do we expand ourselves? We expand ourselves only by offering our inner concern, which comes directly from the very depths of our heart. Perfection we achieve only when we see the One in the many and the many in the One. When we see the One in the many, we have to feel that Silence-reality is holding the entire cosmos. When we see the many in the One, we have to feel that Sound-reality is nourishing the entire cosmos. Silence-reality is the soul and Sound-reality is the body of the United Nations. From the body of the United Nations we get the message of union. From the soul of the United Nations we get the message of perfection.

If we want to know what the United Nations is really doing for humanity, each one of us has to ask himself or herself the same questions, for each of us represents humanity. Are we really seeing the bright side of the United Nations? Are we sincerely working for the fulfilment of the vision of the United Nations? Are we wholeheartedly trying to become one with the struggles of the United Nations? Are we deeply concerned about the United Nations and its role in the world community? If we can answer all these questions in the affirmative, then the soul of the United Nations is bound to reveal to us what it has already done for mankind, what it is doing for mankind and what it will be doing for mankind. What has it done? It has brought down the message of promise from the highest in Heaven. What is it doing? It is proclaiming this promise to the length and breadth of the world. What will it be doing? It will be manifesting this promise not only in and through the seekers after truth, light and perfection, but also in those who deliberately deny the potentialities, the capacities and the soul-realities of the United Nations.

The United Nations has a big heart. Irrespective of human attainment, irrespective of human assessment, it will offer its nectar-drink to each human being on earth. Its soul's offering will be felt first in the soul's world, the inner world. Then it will be seen in the outer world. Finally, it will be accepted wholeheartedly by the entire world. And in its acceptance of this undeniable truth-reality, humanity will move one step higher on the ladder of divine manifestation and divine earthly perfection.

23. *The United Nations can teach us how to share*

There are a number of things that the United Nations can teach us how to share, but I would like to mention four principal things: the message of trust, the message of concern, the message of unity in diversity and, finally, the message of universal peace.

Each nation is unique in its own way. Each nation has achieved something special, at least for itself. When a nation is ready to feel that other nations are an extension of its own being, when a nation becomes aware that all nations belong to one family, one source, and have one common goal, then that particular nation can easily teach or share its lofty achievements. Each nation knows inwardly that satisfaction and perfection lie only in self-giving, not in displaying its grandiose achievements or in hoarding its capacities.

All nations are pilgrims, eternal pilgrims, walking along the same road, the road of Eternity. On the way, some become tired and want to take rest. They do not have the energy to walk any farther. At that moment, if the nations that are ahead can feed and energise those that have fallen back, then the lagging ones can easily keep pace with the nations that are marching speedily.

If a strong nation feels that its progress will be slow if it helps a weak one, I wish to say that this is not true. If one nation encourages, inspires, feeds and energises the nations that are behind, then the gratitude-flower of those particular nations will blossom inside the strong nation's heart, and the fragrance of the gratitude-flower is bound to accelerate the strong nation's progress towards its destined goal. The fragrance of the flower will inspire it, and from this inspiration it will get abundant life, abundant light and an abundant sense of achievement and perfection.

The great mystic thinker Kahlil Gibran once said something most soulfully true: "The significance of man is not in his attainment but in what he longs to attain." The present-day world has achieved quite a few significant things. It has acquired money-power, technology-power, machine-power, but unfortunately it has not acquired soul-power. It has acquired the power to destroy humanity, but this has not brought it any satisfaction. It longs for world peace, world harmony and world unity. It has the inner cry to love the world, to feel the heart of the world and to become one, inseparably one, with the world at large.

The past has not given us what we really need. Granted, the past was something significant, but right now it pales into insignificance when we measure it against our dream: not against what we are, but against what we want to become. What we are now is a semi-animal, but what we want to become is a full, complete and total God.

Dream and reality are two different things. Right now reality is most deplorable, and man's dream is a far cry. The reality that the United Nations can offer to the world at large is not quite satisfactory. But for that we cannot blame the United Nations: for that we must blame each individual person. Unless each human being cooperates most soulfully with the will of the United Nations, reality will remain a painful accident in life and dream will remain a chimerical castle in the air. Unless and until we become inseparably one with the ideals of the United Nations, we can never be happy and fulfilled. The United Nations can teach us how to share. If we do not share with others what we have and what we are, we are bound to feel unsatisfied, no matter what we achieve and what we grow into.

Millions of people know about the United Nations and admire its capacities, its willingness, its eagerness, its good will. But how many people are ready to become one with the soul of the United Nations? Millions of people can meet together, but if there is no soul's bond, no soul's unity, then all nations will prove to be veritable beggars. In the matter of inner strength, inner power and real achievement, thousands of minds, thousands of bodies, thousands of vital beings or emotional feelings can join together, but if the soul's bond is not established, there will always be loneliness. The soul of the United Nations has to be accepted by all nations, and only then will a sense of completeness, perfection and satisfaction be attained.

Each individual being, each man and woman, should feel that he belongs not to his own nation, but to all nations. That does not mean that he will neglect his own nation and devote all his attention to other nations. But each human being who has the energy and willingness to be of service to other nations will also have the willingness to serve his own country in ample measure. While serving his own country, he has to feel that it is becoming one with other nations. He has to feel that his own arms are becoming one with his eyes. His arms are his power of work, and his eyes are his power of vision. His vision carries him to the length and breadth of the world, whereas his arms remain where he himself is. With his vision he sees the needs of his brothers and sisters of the world. Then with his arms he has to work to fulfil those needs. He can do this only when he feels that he has gone far beyond his little family and has accepted the world-family as his very own.

The greatest wise man of the past, Socrates, taught us something very profound when he said, "I am not an Athenian, nor am I a Greek. I am a citizen of the world." If each individual in each nation can proclaim this message, if each individual in each nation can consciously and devotedly feel that he does not belong to a little family called "I and mine" but to a larger family called "We and ours", then the message of the United Nations, the message of love, of brotherhood, of peace, of soulful sharing, can easily be received, embraced and executed by the entire world.

24. *Does meditation encourage us to escape from reality?*

Meditation is self-perfection. If we have the message of perfection deep within, we cannot neglect anything within or without. If we have doubt within us, we have to transform this doubt into certainty. If we have insecurity within us, we have to transform this insecurity into security. Anything undivine within us must be transformed into something divine. If our eyes see well but our arms and legs are very weak, then we are not perfect. We have to strengthen all our limbs and organs and make ourselves integrally perfect.

Some people are afraid of meditation; they feel that it is something strange or abnormal. They feel that since everyone does not meditate, that means meditation is something unnatural or useless. But we have to know that just because many people are not doing something, it does not mean that the thing is wrong. Numbers have no value; what matters is our awareness of Truth, Light, Divinity, Infinity, Eternity and Immortality within us.

Just the other day an amusing incident took place in front of my house. A neighbour came up to me in a very friendly way and said, "I saw a light in your room at around five o'clock this morning. Usually I don't get up at that time, but today I had to visit a friend. What were you doing at that hour?" I said to him, "I was meditating. As a matter of fact, I get up every morning at two o'clock to meditate." As soon as I said that, he immediately became disturbed. "Meditation! What is that?" he said. "I don't understand all that. I don't care for it! I don't need it!" And then he quickly left. He was quite upset when he heard that I had been meditating. The very word made him shudder. But if I had told him I was reading some interesting novel or doing something else, then our conversation would have continued for a long time.

In this world there are many, many people who, like my neighbour, are afraid of meditation. They feel that meditation is something that will take them away from the reality-world. For them the only reality is the desire-world. If desire goes away, then they have nothing to cling to, nothing to possess and claim as their very own. If they are not playing the game of temptation and becoming victims to temptation, if they are not wallowing in the pleasures of ignorance, then they feel that there is no life in what they are doing. For them, life is conscious participation in ignorance, but they call it knowledge, experience, enjoyment.

Meditation does not encourage us to escape from reality. Who escapes? He who has done something wrong or he who does not claim reality as his very own. Our divine Father has two homes: one is in Heaven one is here on earth. In our Heaven-home we enjoy divine rest, and in our earth-home we work and accomplish our multifarious tasks. We have as much right to stay in one home as in the other. When we are in our earth-home, if we act like a stranger and feel that we have come to a place which does not belong to us, then naturally we will want to escape. But why should we have to escape from our own home? Even if we quarrel and fight with the members of our family, still we remain in our home and do not go elsewhere, because that home belongs to us.

In the ordinary life, there are some people who are fond of watching baseball, volleyball, basketball and other sports, but they do not want to participate. They feel that if they participate they may not do well or they may be injured, but they do enjoy seeing others play. There are also people who both appreciate sports and participate in them. These people feel that they can feed their cheerfulness and enthusiasm, bring cosmic energy into their system and, at the same time, discard all their undivine qualities by participating. In the spiritual life also, there are seekers who want to enjoy the cosmic game from a distance, but do not want to participate actively in this game. They want to enter into the Himalayan caves or go off to some secluded place to meditate. From the strict spiritual point of view, they are not liberated. They are afraid that if they mix with the world they will lose everything or will not be able to make any progress. But real spirituality is for those who are brave divine soldiers. Thousands of years ago, the Upanishadic seers and the Vedic seers declared: *Nayam atma balahinena labhya:* "This soul cannot be won by the weakling." Only the strong can and will realise the soul.

Also, we have to know that the world is not our only enemy. Even if we enter into the Himalayan caves, we still have to deal with the mind. When we go off by ourselves, the mind plays its role most powerfully. All the world's activities enter into our mind and prevent us from meditating. The mind will start thinking of friends, enemies and various incidents that occurred in our life. So who is the real enemy? We thought our enemy was someone or something outside of us which was disturbing our meditation. But even when we isolate ourselves, we still have to face the mind with all its undivine qualities, and we find that our real enemy is inside us. If we do not conquer the mind and discipline it here amidst the teeming activities of life, there is no guarantee that we will be free from earthly disturbances when we withdraw from the world.

India's greatest poet, Tagore, once made up his mind to go to a lonely forest to compose some songs. He said to himself, "Here I have so much to do, and so many people are constantly bothering me. Yet in spite of this I have written quite a few most significant poems. Now, if I enter into the forest, where I will be all alone, I will be able to write a great many most beautiful poems, many more than I write usually." But after a fortnight in the forest he came back with very little to show for his time, for his mind had been constantly thinking of Shantiniketan, his school, and of his students, his friends and his relatives. He could hardly write at all.

What is reality? Reality is something divine. Reality and divinity are synonymous, and divinity and immortality are synonymous. If something is divine, then it has an immortal life. Here on earth we are crying to be immortal. If we can live on earth for five minutes more, we try to stay. It is very easy for us to say we are not afraid of death, but when we are hurt or when some calamity has taken place, immediately we are afraid that we will die. But those who follow the spiritual life try to conquer death – not in order to live for two hundred, three hundred or four hundred years, but in order to have time to accomplish quite a few significant things for Mother Earth.

While in the soul's world, before entering into a physical body, each person's soul consciously, devotedly and unconditionally makes a solemn promise to the Supreme that here on earth it will manifest its divinity in boundless measure. But in order for the soul that is inside the physical to manifest the Supreme on earth, time is necessary. We have to pray, we have to meditate, we have to discipline our life for a long time, and only then will we achieve something significant and fulfil our promise to the Almighty Supreme.

If we are able to meditate for only ten years and gain only an iota of Peace, Light and Bliss, with this insignificant quantity of Peace, Light and Bliss, what will we be able to offer to mankind? But if we continue to pray and meditate most soulfully for many years, one day our inner being will be inundated with these divine qualities, and then we will be able to share them abundantly with all and sundry. We accept earth as reality, as divine Reality. With our naked eyes we see tremendous aggression, hostility, brutality and other undivine things on earth, but with our inner heart we can feel that this is not the ultimate aim of God. On the contrary, the Vision of God is Peace, Light and Bliss.

We have to know that the creator is always superior to the creation. It is human beings who have created atom bombs and hydrogen bombs. In these people the human brain has reached a high level of development. If the soul's will can now come to the fore and operate in the brain, it will ask the person who has created the atom bomb what he really wants. Immediately his vital will say he wants to conquer. But his soul will reply, "You will not get any satisfaction if you conquer by force, for you will conquer only the body of the world and not the soul. And if you do not conquer the soul, then you have conquered nothing. If you really want to establish your victory permanently, then use your other power, your soul-power, your love-power, your heart-power."

Reality means the acceptance of life. Reality can never be found in destruction or in lording it over others. Reality is to be found in equality. Reality is in the sense of inseparable oneness. Does meditation encourage us to escape from reality? No! On the contrary, meditation inspires us to accept God's creation as an unmistakable reality that still awaits transformation and perfection. When the earth-consciousness is transformed, and our body-consciousness is transformed, only then can we be true receptacles of the infinite Truth and infinite Light.

Earth and each individual on earth must co-operate; otherwise, God's Peace, Light and Bliss will not be received here. Right now human beings are not able to receive God's Blessings because there is a constant sense of separation between the earth-consciousness and the individual consciousness. But when the earth-consciousness and the individual consciousness unite, earth will play the role of a home and the human being will play the role of the dweller in the home. What is the use of having a home if there is no dweller? And again, what is the use of having a dweller if there is no home for him to live in? The earth-home and the individual beings are complementary. When we as individuals are ready to live in our earth-home and when earth is fully ready to receive us and welcome us as members of its family, then God's choicest Blessings are bound to shower on our devoted heads and on earth's devoted heart.

25. *Are spiritual people somewhat abnormal?*

The title of my talk, "Are spiritual people somewhat abnormal?" is rather amusing. If we answer the question in the affirmative, then all of us in this room are abnormal. But the truth is otherwise. We are not abnormal in the least. We are normal, natural, soulful, devoted, dedicated and God-loving.

In this world, when someone does not see eye-to-eye with us, we immediately say that he is abnormal and unnatural. We even go to the length of saying that he is undivine or hostile. This is the experience that we unfortunately treasure. But if each day we pray and meditate soulfully, then we come to realise that the most important thing in each person's life is the freedom of his inner life, the freedom to follow his own Inner Pilot. Everyone is being motivated and guided by his Inner Pilot. Just because you do not have the same realisation that I have, we cannot call each other abnormal.

Here in God's creation countless beings are consciously or unconsciously fulfilling God in their own way. But a seeker tries to please and fulfil God in God's own Way. This is the difference between those who aspire and those who do not aspire. Non-seekers try to possess God and utilise God in their own way, whereas seekers try to achieve God's Light to please Him, fulfil Him and manifest Him here on earth in His own Way.

Those who are not crying for God, for Truth or for Light, according to strict inner philosophy, are dead soldiers. One need not be dead on the physical plane, but one is inwardly dead if he does not aspire. If he is wallowing in the pleasures of ignorance, he is already dead. When there is no Light, when there is no divine satisfaction, we feel that life is nothing short of death.

Earth's understanding of Light is very limited. When we try to judge others or examine others, we immediately lose our sense of identification. But if we focus our attention on all things with the same amount of sympathy, love and concern, then we feel inside all things their basic oneness with everything else and with ourselves. In the matter of strength, my thumb has considerably more than my little finger. But there is a oneness between my little finger and my thumb; so when I concentrate on these two portions of my being, I do not consider one abnormal just because it is weaker or stronger than the other.

Here we are a small group; let us say a family. Right now we are treasuring a spiritual feeling, a feeling of brotherhood and oneness. Now, if someone here happens to have a large fruit, his feeling of oneness will compel him to share the fruit with the rest of us. But if he is miserly, if he has a sense of separativity, he will try to eat it all himself. It is in this separativity that real abnormality looms large. When we see others in ourselves and feel our oneness with them, then there can be no abnormal feeling in us.

Anything that is contrary to our experience seems abnormal to us. But we have to know that the world is singing the song of oneness. God's Unity and God's Multiplicity we have to see as one. God the Creator, God the Preserver and God the Transformer are all one. In each seeker God is playing the distinctive roles of Creator, Preserver and Transformer. When we see them separately in a limited consciousness, we become a victim to our own limited understanding. If this moment we identify ourselves only with God the Creator, then without the least hesitation we shall say that God the Transformer is abnormal.

God started His creation with His Silence-Light. From His Silence-Light, Sound-Might came into existence. He wanted to experience Himself in a million, billion, trillion forms, countless forms, like the seed that eventually grows into a Banyan Tree. When the seed grows into a huge tree, we see millions of leaves and thousands of fruits and flowers. But it started its journey as one single seed.

The first thing we have to do in our life is pray and meditate. Early in the morning, if we pray to God, we enter into the world of the Source. Then we try to offer the Light that we have received from our prayer and meditation to the world around us. First we achieve and then we give. If I do not have any Light, then what am I going to give?

We have to go from one to two to three. Our first realisation is one, our second realisation is two, our third realisation is three, the Ultimate. When we start with one, we have to know that we are going to the Root, the Source, the Unity. But the Source needs manifestation; otherwise it will remain unfulfilled. For manifestation we have to enter into the world of multiplicity.

And finally we have to transform the world and bring Heaven's Perfection into the world. Only in this way can we have true satisfaction, and true satisfaction is God's Perfection-Love.

In unity there must be the song of multiplicity. When we enter into the spiritual life, if we ignore the world around us, if we feel the world around us is dirty and undivine and can never be transformed, then we are mistaken. This attitude is unhealthy, abnormal. We have to accept the world around us as our very own, and inside the world we have to see and feel the living Breath and living Presence of God. Then our realisation will tell us that the world is absolutely normal, that God is evolving in His own Way in and through the world. You may be flying to your destination on a jet plane, and somebody else may be travelling at the speed of an Indian bullock cart. But who is the driver of the bullock cart and who is the pilot of the plane? In both cases it is God. According to His own Will, according to the seeker's evolution, God is using the bullock cart or the modern jet plane. And it is also He who is proceeding towards the destined Goal, His own ever-transcending Height.

There is a significant anecdote I wish to tell you. An atheist once said to one of his friends, who was a God-believer, "My friend, you constantly pray to that Fellow, but He ignores you. You have given up everything for Him, but He has done nothing for you and He will do nothing for you. Yet even so, you feel that you can live without all worldly pleasures and enjoyments, but not without God. You must be really great." Immediately the believer replied, "You are infinitely greater than I am, for you need only the fleeting earthly pleasures and you have given up God for them."

Now, who is normal and who is abnormal in this story? If we have a limited consciousness, then we will say that the one who believes in God is normal, and he who does not believe in God is abnormal. But if we go deep within, into our heart of love and oneness, we see that the atheist is none other than God Himself in the process of evolution. This is not our first nor our last incarnation. We were once in the mineral world, then in the plant world and then in the animal kingdom. Now we are human beings, half animal and half divine. When we enter into the desire-world, we enter into temptation. From temptation we enter into frustration, and in frustration destruction looms large. But since we are all seekers, we are entering into the aspiration-world. And in the aspiration-world we go from Light, to more Light, to abundant and infinite Light.

Now, some seekers who are weak feel that if they remain in the world they will be devoured by earth-ignorance. This kind of seeker feels that the best thing for him to do is to enter into the Himalayan caves where he will be safe. But this is not the answer. Human beings who have undivine, ferocious qualities may not follow him to the Himalayan caves, but whatever is inside him will follow, including his unillumined mind, his earthbound desires and his own animal qualities. These things will play the role of the undivine human beings whom he has left behind him. They will torture him. He will be in the Himalayan caves, but his mind and his vital will be all the time roaming. He will meditate there for five minutes or half an hour, and then if he does not see an iota of Light or if he does not feel any certainty in his inner life, immediately he will say, "I have come here to the Himalayan caves, but I am only fooling myself. There is no truth, there is no reality here. This is all self-deception."

If we are real seekers of truth, like divine warriors we will face the world and brave the world here and now. Who escapes? He who has done something wrong, he who is a culprit. But we have not done anything wrong, so we need not and must not try to escape. We have to feel that the members of society are like the limbs of our body. If even one part of our being is not transformed, then we are not perfect. We have to strike a balance. Spirit will give us realisation, but matter will offer us the message of manifestation. We have to try to combine the messages of spirit and matter. Only then will we be able to establish the Kingdom of Heaven here on earth.

How can we combine these two? By uniting Heaven-Vision with earth-aspiration. When earth-aspiration climbs up high, higher, highest and Heaven-Vision descends, there is a place where the two meet. And that meeting place is inside our heart of acceptance, in our conscious acceptance of both the Vision of Heaven and the aspiration of earth.

When we separate earth-consciousness, which is manifestation, from Heaven-consciousness, which is realisation, we are totally lost. But when the aspiration of earth and the Vision of Heaven are amalgamated, we become chosen instruments of the Absolute Supreme. At that time, our Heaven-free consciousness and earth's aspiring consciousness make us complete, whole and perfect. The idea of abnormality is absurd then. We become normal, natural, spiritual, divine and perfect, for we consciously, devotedly, soulfully and unconditionally unite the vision of our height with the aspiration of our depth.

26. God and Goal

I wish to speak today on God and Goal. We all know that God and the transcendental Goal are one. But in this talk, I would like to show that, in spite of their oneness, each has a distinctive role to play. The Goal is the House, and God is the Inhabitant or Owner of the House. Since I wish to enter the House, I need permission from the Inhabitant or the Owner. In the spiritual life, I pray and meditate and God, out of His infinite Bounty, allows me to enter His House. If I am all appreciation and admiration for the House, if I am all adoration for the House, then the Owner will allow me to come inside.

If we appreciate God's creation, the House, then God feels that He Himself is being appreciated, for He and His creation are eternally one. The creation that God has revealed is His own manifestation of His Silence. If we appreciate His creation-manifestation, if we appreciate what the Creator has already revealed, then the Creator will show us that this creation of His is not and cannot be His ultimate achievement. He will elevate our consciousness and show us His unmanifested Capacity, His infinite Capacity, His Eternity and His Immortality. And He will not only show us His Infinity's Treasure, but will also share it with us.

But we have to know that when we appreciate the creation, we have less of a chance to reach the Highest than if we appreciate the Creator. For if we appreciate the Creator, He gives us not only what He has already revealed, but also what He inwardly has kept aside or what He inwardly is. So although Creator and creation are inseparable, if we are wise we shall appreciate the Creator more than the creation, for He is the Supreme Artist who reveals through His creation the Reality of His unlimited Infinity.

God is evolving. God is transcending. When He evolves, we call Him man, man in the process of his cosmic evolution. When He transcends, we call Him God. Matter is aspiring and evolving. The dance of Spirit is smiling. The smile of Spirit is what we call transcendence. When Spirit smiles, immediately we see that the earth-bound consciousness is freed from its limitations and becomes the Heaven-free Reality.

The Goal is satisfaction and perfection. Satisfaction is what we have in our achievement. But perfection is not found in our achievement; perfection is in our becoming. This becoming is founded upon our self-giving, and self-giving is the constant, conscious and all-fulfilling reality in us and for God.

We are all seekers and we shall always remain seekers, even after we have realised God. Before we realise God, we seek God-realisation; after we realise God, we seek God-manifestation. So we always remain seekers. There are three principal stages in our seeking. At first we are all beginner-seekers. We feel that God is inside our hearts, but we feel that the Goal is high above us, hiding in the sky somewhere, and not inside us, not in ourselves. When we pray and meditate, we feel that God is listening to our prayer. Where is He? Inside our heart. Inside the body is the heart, and inside the heart is the soul. The soul is a spark of God's Consciousness. God is inside the building, but there is a particular room where we can see Him and always feel His Presence, and that is inside the soul.

But we do not remain always beginners in our spiritual life. If we study for a few years, we do not remain in kindergarten, but go on to primary school, high school and college and complete our course. In the spiritual life also, we someday become advanced seekers. When we become advanced seekers, we feel that God is inside our heart and that the Goal is also inside our heart. We feel that God and Goal are inside our inner being and are inseparable. If we reach the House, our destination, definitely we will find the Owner there. And if we reach the Owner, and He sees that we have tremendous love and devotion for Him, then He will certainly be gracious enough to take us into His House.

Eventually we reach the third stage: we become realised. When we become realised, it means that we have seen God and have been in His House. Now it is up to us, after seeing the House and the Owner, to become something. After seeing God, we become God-lovers. At every moment we try to love God and please Him in His own Way. And after seeing the Goal, we feel that it is our bounden duty to share the Goal with others. At that time we become God-distributors. We have got the fruit, and now we feel it is our duty to share the fruit with others, for only in this way can we become totally satisfied.

In the seeker's life there is an inner urge constantly trying to come to the fore. But there is also a constant battle going on between the divine forces and the undivine forces. A seeker observes that his days have wings and just fly away. He cannot catch the time-bird or keep it inside him; it flees inexorably. There is much to do, but so little is done and perhaps so little will be done. If one is a sincere seeker, he feels that there is so much he can achieve and so much he has to achieve, and for everything he needs time. He prays and meditates, but feels that this is not enough. He feels he has to do more, that he has to be more devoted and dedicated. This is what happens when he looks at his days.

Now, when a seeker thinks of his hours, he has a different experience. He feels that slowly and steadily his hours are passing away. The days fly away very fast, but the hours pass slowly and steadily, giving him constant opportunity. If even then the seeker is not achieving what he is supposed to achieve, he becomes sad and miserable. He feels that there is something lacking in him which keeps him from making fast progress. Why is he not achieving? Because his inner cry is not intense; because he does not need God at every second. He needs God, true, but *every* second of his time he does not need God. When he is engrossed in earthly matters, he forgets God. But if he can remember God in all his actions, in all his multifarious activities, then earth-time will fly away, but God-experience, which is eternal Life, will remain with him.

An individual moment, when observed with the human mind, looks fleeting. It seems to have lightning speed. But when the seeker observes the moment with his sincere aspiring life, he sees that each moment is loaded with many undivine thoughts, ideas and worlds which linger in him. These unhealthy thoughts, these unaspiring, undivine ideas and destructive worlds are in the life of each second. He finds that he cannot get rid of these undivine experiences that are housed in the life of each second. This happens precisely because the seeker is not in touch with the eternal Time. If he goes deep within, he sees that Infinity and Eternity are within him. He sees that he cannot have a fleeting moment separated from Infinity, he cannot have a fleeting second separated from Eternity.

The experience of earth-life is only a flow in the eternal Life. It is the flow of separativity. But this earth-flow is not the product of earthbound time. It is the creation of infinite Time, eternal Time. If the seeker is aware of infinite and eternal Time, then he realises that these are nothing other than the eternal Now. God's Body, creation, is growing in the eternal Now. God's Spirit is glowing in the eternal Now.

A sincere seeker longs for God-realisation. For him, God-realisation means the transcendental Height, which is the height of Silence, the height of Light and Delight. One may reach the highest pinnacle of Truth, Light, Beauty and Delight, but that does not necessarily mean that one is near the highest Height. No! In order to achieve the highest, loftiest Height, one has to enter into the oneness-life. If one neglects or rejects God's oneness-life, God's Universal Life, then no matter how many times he reaches the highest pinnacle, he cannot be closest or dearest to God, the Highest Absolute. The height has to be scaled, but we have to know that while climbing up the mountain we are carrying within us the Universal Life, the life of multiplicity which we are carrying to the Source, the transcendental Reality.

We speak about God, but why is it that we do not realise God as our supreme necessity, as the fulfilment of our reality? The main reason is that the earth-thoughts we treasure are composed of conscious or unconscious temptations. When temptation is fulfilled, we see nothing but futility; we see a barren desert. Since our earth-thoughts right now are nothing but futility, we do not realise God. But there are also Heaven-thoughts. Heaven-thoughts right now are nothing short of curiosity. We are curious to know what is happening in Heaven, what it looks like, how many angels are there, what the cosmic gods are doing. It is all curiosity. When we live on earth and think of Heaven with a curious mind, we do not realise God and accomplish our supreme task. But when we love or treasure God-thoughts at every moment in all our activities, God becomes the living Reality in our life. At every moment God's Divinity and God's Reality loom large when we feel the God-necessity in ourselves. At that time God cannot hide from us. As a matter of fact, He does not hide at all. He is nearer to us than our nose, our eyes, but we are wanting in the cosmic vision. How can we be endowed with the cosmic vision? We can be endowed with the cosmic vision only when our necessity for God is immediate and constant. If we have come to the realisation that without food, without air, without water, without everything we can exist, but not without God, then God-realisation does not remain a far cry.

But we have to know that this God-realisation cannot be achieved by hook or by crook, by adopting foul means or by torturing the body or the physical consciousness. No, no, no! If we just torture our body or fast most rigorously, if we threaten God, saying, "God, if You don't come to me I shall commit suicide, I shall destroy my life," God will simply laugh at our stupidity. There are seekers who have fixed a date at which they have to realise God and who say they will put an end to their life if they fail. But God-realisation cannot be achieved in that way.

The right method is prayer and meditation. When we pray and meditate, God observes whether our prayer and meditation is sincere or not. When He sees that we are sincere, slowly and steadily He appears before our vision. Right now He is within us, but our vision does not see Him. But when we pray and meditate, He improves our vision, and then we see and feel Him as our very own.

Besides prayer and meditation, there is another important method. We have to cry inwardly. It is through our inner tears, our intense inner cry, that we can immediately see God face-to-face and have Him as our own. When we pray sincerely, when we meditate sincerely, we realise God slowly and steadily. But if inside the prayer and meditation there is an intense inner cry, then God stands before us immediately – and not only immediately, but also unreservedly. And if He sees that our inner cry is flooded with sincerity, then He grants us something else. He becomes unconditional. First He stands in front of us, as a momentary blessing and boon, then He becomes ours unreservedly and continuously and finally, He becomes ours unconditionally.

NOTES TO THE TEARS OF NATION-HEARTS

1. *(p. 71)* Dag Hammarskjöld Lecture Series, Dag Hammarskjöld Auditorium, 4 January 1973.
2. *(p. 73)* Conference Room 10, 5 January 1973.
3. *(p. 75)* Conference Room 6, 12 January 1973.
4. *(p. 76)* Conference Room 9, 19 January 1973.
5. *(p. 78)* Conference Room 9, 26 January 1974.
6. *(p. 79)* Dag Hammarskjöld Lecture Series, Dag Hammarskjöld Auditorium, 1 February 1973.
7. *(p. 81)* Conference Room 9, 2 February 1973.
8. *(p. 83)* Conference Room 9, 9 February 1973.
9. *(p. 85)* Conference Room 10, 23 February 1973.
10. *(p. 87)* Dag Hammarskjöld Lecture Series, Dag Hammarskjöld Auditorium, 1 March 1973.
11. *(p. 88)* Conference Room 9, 2 March 1973.
12. *(p. 91)* Conference Room 8, 16 March 1973.
13. *(p. 92)* Dag Hammarskjöld Lecture Series, Dag Hammarskjöld Auditorium, 5 April 1973.
14. *(p. 94)* Dag Hammarskjöld Lecture Series, Conference Room 9, 3 May 1973.
15. *(p. 96)* Dag Hammarskjöld Lecture Series, Dag Hammarskjöld Auditorium, 2 August 1973.
16. *(p. 100)* Dag Hammarskjöld Lecture Series, Dag Hammarskjöld Auditorium, 13 September 1973.
17. *(p. 102)* Dag Hammarskjöld Lecture Series, Dag Hammarskjöld Auditorium, 11 October 1973.
18. *(p. 104)* Dag Hammarskjöld Lecture Series, Dag Hammarskjöld Auditorium, 9 November 1973.
19. *(p. 108)* Dag Hammarskjöld Lecture Series, Dag Hammarskjöld Auditorium, 1 February 1974.

20. *(p. 112)* Dag Hammarskjöld Lecture Series, Dag Hammarskjöld Auditorium, 15 March 1974.
21. *(p. 117)* Dag Hammarskjöld Lecture Series, Dag Hammarskjöld Auditorium, 9 May 1974.
22. *(p. 122)* Conference Room 14, 31 May 1974.
23. *(p. 128)* Dag Hammarskjöld Lecture Series, Dag Hammarskjöld Auditorium, 6 June 1974.
24. *(p. 131)* Conference Room 14, 7 June 1974.
25. *(p. 136)* Conference Room 14, 26 July 1974.
26. *(p. 141)* Dag Hammarskjöld Lecture Series, Dag Hammarskjöld Auditorium, 1 August 1974.

PART III

THE BICENTENNIAL FLAMES
AT THE UNITED NATIONS

1. *Preface*

This is the most significant year for America, the Bicentennial year. It is my sincere wish to answer a few questions on the Bicentennial offered by the United Nations Meditation Group from the spiritual point of view. If each of you can kindly meditate for a couple of minutes and then give me a question, I shall be very grateful. This will help all the members of the Meditation Group considerably. If the questions are meaningful and soulful and the answers also are soulful, then it will be a great service not only to the soul of the United Nations but also to the soul of America. Something more: it will be a great service to the Universal Soul, for America's independence is something most meaningful and fruitful in God's entire creation.

2. What could America's contribution be to the family of nations in the next two hundred years?

Sri Chinmoy: In the next two hundred years America's contribution to the family of nations will be equality's universal birthright and reality's transcendental height. America is great. America is good. America's greatness is going to increase in infinite measure in the next two hundred years because America knows what greatness is and where it comes from. Greatness is self-giving and its source is love in peace and peace in love. America's goodness lies in this: God for God's sake, man for God's sake. Aspiration for a higher life is for God's sake. Truth-discovery is for God's sake. Peace-distribution is for God's sake. Delight-manifestation is for God's sake.

America's matchless contribution shall be her supreme universal friendship in which the family of nations will see beckoning hands, oneness-satisfaction and perfection-manifestation. America means contribution. Right now this contribution at times is conditional, at times unconditional. But either in the near or distant future, America's contribution will always be unconditional in the outer life because America is undoubtedly going to make tireless efforts to become a supremely unconditional instrument of the Pilot Supreme.

3. How can we rekindle the significance of America in our hearts and in the hearts of others?

Sri Chinmoy: We can rekindle the significance of America in our hearts and in the hearts of others by becoming glowing sacrifice in the inner life and growing service in the outer life.

THE BICENTENNIAL FLAMES AT THE UNITED NATIONS

4. What is the difference between political independence and spiritual independence?

Sri Chinmoy: The difference between political independence and spiritual independence is this: political independence is the individuality of a particular party whereas spiritual independence is the independence of a seeker from darkness, bondage and ignorance.

5. What is the most important thing America has learned in her first two hundred years and what is the most important thing she has to learn now in order to make the fastest progress?

Sri Chinmoy: In her first two hundred years America has learned the momentous necessity of the childlike heart. Now, in order to make the fastest progress, the most important thing is for her to have a life of conscious and continuous self-giving.

6. How can other nations of the world feel their oneness with the United States in celebrating our Bicentennial?

Sri Chinmoy: Other nations of the world can feel their oneness with the United States in celebrating the Bicentennial if they feel that they have one goal and that goal is to love God and practise truth unconditionally.

7. Do the Bicentennial celebrations add strength to the soul of America?

Sri Chinmoy: The Bicentennial celebrations without fail add strength to the soul of America, for a Bicentennial is not a mere celebration but a genuine invocation of the soul of America that liberated the body of America from a foreign yoke.

8. *Has the character of America changed significantly since the nation was born two hundred years ago?*

Sri Chinmoy: Yes, the character of America has changed significantly since the nation was born two hundred years ago. Previously a soulful promise reigned supreme; now a fruitful hope reigns supreme.

9. *As our souls come forward on our birthday, does the soul of America also come forward during this Bicentennial year?*

Sri Chinmoy: The soul of America comes forward during this Bicentennial year to bless America's Heaven-climbing aspiration and America's earth-transforming service.

10. *Is there any special significance to the outer events which will occur this year?*

Sri Chinmoy: The outer events will bear special significance only if the inner awareness is conscious and complete. If not, the outer events in this year will have no special significance.

11. *Is there any special quality that Americans can especially work on now to help bring forward all their potential divinity?*

Sri Chinmoy: There are two special qualities that Americans can work on to help bring forward all their potential divinity. These two divine qualities are the feeling of universal oneness and constant and cheerful self-giving to the Supreme Pilot, who is man's own highest Reality.

12. *How can American politics return to the spiritual values that they had during the time of the Founding Fathers and some of our earlier presidents?*

Sri Chinmoy: American politics can return to the spiritual values that they had during the time of the Founding Fathers and some of the previous presidents only if the political leaders and other leaders feel the supreme necessity of an inner life that has the capacity to bring about outer success, outer achievements, outer perfection and outer satisfaction.

13. *How can we regain the nobility and wisdom of the Founding Fathers in America today?*

Sri Chinmoy: You can regain the nobility and wisdom of the Founding Fathers in America best by meditating on the independence-spirit of America, which was treasured not only by earth's aspiration but also by Heaven's illumination.

14. *Is the soul of America like a child that keeps on growing and developing?*

Sri Chinmoy: The soul of America, like a child, is growing, glowing, developing, illumining and fulfilling. It is a soul that is most progressive and most striking.

15. *When the soul of America and the soul of the world discuss things, what suggestions and advice do they have to mankind?*

Sri Chinmoy: When the soul of America and the soul of the world discuss things, they have many suggestions to make, much advice to offer to mankind. But primarily they have one suggestion, one piece of advice to offer and that is, "Move on, move on! The Goal, the ever-transcending Goal, is ahead and not behind."

16. *What is the spiritual significance of being two hundred years old?*

Sri Chinmoy: The spiritual significance of being two hundred years old is that the journey of America will continue eternally towards the establishment of a better, more illumining and more fulfilling human family on earth.

17. *How can America make the most spiritual progress and how can America be of most service to the world?*

Sri Chinmoy: America can make more spiritual progress if it can feel that it has been selected as a choice instrument of the Supreme, for the Supreme. America can serve the world most provided America feels that the service it renders to the community of nations is nothing but its own illumining and self-fulfilling expansion.

18. *What does the soul of America always try to teach its American children?*

Sri Chinmoy: The soul of America always tries to teach its American children to be divinely brave and remain so eternally in order to fight against humanity's outer darkness and inner ignorance. Humanity's outer darkness is the sense of division; humanity's inner ignorance is the life of doubt.

THE BICENTENNIAL FLAMES AT THE UNITED NATIONS

19. *In the next two hundred years will the spiritual forces tend to manifest more than they have in the first two hundred years?*

Sri Chinmoy: Undoubtedly the spiritual forces will be able to manifest in the next two hundred years much more than they did in the past two hundred years, for not only America's but also humanity's aspiration is continuously proceeding forward, upward and inward.

20. *As citizens of the United States, what can we do to help our development in the next century?*

Sri Chinmoy: In the next two hundred years, as citizens of the United States you can help yourselves develop just by clearing the mind of the thick forest of doubt and by liberating the heart from its insecurity-cave.

21. *When America emerged as a nation two hundred years ago, she stood forth as a symbol of hope, promise and freedom for the peoples of the world. How can she transmit these qualities to the world-body today?*

Sri Chinmoy: America's hope, America's promise and America's freedom – these America can transmit to the world-body today provided America does not claim them as her own personal achievements, but as compassionate boons from above, from the Almighty Father.

22. *Is independence as spiritually significant for other nations as it was for the United States?*

Sri Chinmoy: Yes. The spiritual significance of independence is always the same for each nation. But one nation can receive much more Light from above and offer much more sacrifice to God than other nations, on the strength of its inner cry to become one with the universal Reality and the transcendental Vision.

23. *How can the American people realise their love for the soul of America?*

Sri Chinmoy: The American people can better realise their love for the soul of America if they discover that the real and immortal reality in each human being, in each nation, is only the soul-reality. Everything else is transitory.

24. *How can we incorporate the spirit and the outer activities of the Bicentennial?*

Sri Chinmoy: You can incorporate the spirit and the outer activities of the Bicentennial by becoming consciously aware that the spirit of the Bicentennial is carrying the outer activities along with their results to the most illumining and fulfilling Goal.

25. *Is there an art form that is intimately tied to the soul of America, such as music is associated with Germany?*

Sri Chinmoy: Yes. There is an art form that is intimately tied to the soul of America, and that is America's untiring inner and outer efforts to grow into a supreme God-seeker, a supreme peace-lover and a supreme satisfaction-distributor to humanity.

26. How can American citizens best further America's role in the world in the next two hundred years?

Sri Chinmoy: American citizens can best further America's role in the world in the next two hundred years by claiming the rest of the world as their very own. This feeling of oneness can alone bring to America an unprecedented leadership and a unique friendship.

27. We celebrate the spirit of 1776. What exactly was that spirit, and also what is the spirit of the United States today?

Sri Chinmoy: Previously a soulful promise reigned supreme; now a fruitful hope reigns supreme. The spirit at that time was promise; now it has become hope. The spirit of the past was the discovery of inner adamantine will to fight against bondage. The present spirit is the aspiration for God-manifestation plus the aspiration to become humanity's brother, humanity's selfless lover and divinity's constant server.

28. What birthday gift would the Supreme want the soul of America to place at His Feet on this Bicentennial?

Sri Chinmoy: The Supreme would like to have a gratitude-heart from each and every American placed at His Feet as the birthday gift.

29. *How can American citizens learn to love their country more?*

Sri Chinmoy: American citizens can learn to love their country more by realising the supreme fact that there is no difference between true love of one's country and true love of God. One's country is nothing short of God's concentrated creation.

30. *Will the next two hundred years see the manifestation of the soul's qualities of America and, if so, how will it take place?*

Sri Chinmoy: Yes. The next two hundred years will see the manifestation of the soul's qualities of America. This manifestation will take place in America's conscious and unconditional leadership of humanity and America's constant and self-giving friendship with humanity.

31. *What gift will the United Nations give to the United States on its Bicentennial?*

Sri Chinmoy: There are two gifts the United Nations may give to the United States on its Bicentennial. One gift is gratitude, for the United Nations is housed in the United States. The other gift is its promise to help and fulfil America the way America's soul wants to be helped and fulfilled.

32. *When the government of America was young, it seemed to have a greater spiritual aspiration. How can that be regained in the government today?*

Sri Chinmoy: Today's government can regain the same spiritual aspiration if it feels that there is only one thing both on earth and in Heaven that will satisfy and fulfil the real in it, and that is aspiration.

33. *How will the degree of unity in the spiritual community affect the spiritual progress of America?*

Sri Chinmoy: The degree of unity in the spiritual community automatically reflects the spiritual progress of America. Spiritual unity is not and cannot be a stagnant pool. It is a flowing, glowing and running river which is going to enter into the universal sea of humanity's perfection.

34. *Is the soul of America satisfied with America's outer and inner progress?*

Sri Chinmoy: The soul of America is satisfied, but since there is no end to outer and inner progress, the soul of America could be more satisfied if America cared more devotedly for its outer and inner progress.

35. *Does the United Nations have a role to play in the celebration of America's Bicentennial?*

Sri Chinmoy: Yes, the United Nations has a significant role to play in the celebration of America's Bicentennial. America's dynamism, America's speed, America's willingness to help mankind towards world success and world progress can be brought to the fore by the conscious appreciation of the United Nations.

36. *What role can gratitude play in America and the world at large during the Bicentennial?*

Sri Chinmoy: Gratitude during the Bicentennial can easily expedite America's dream for fulfilling satisfaction, and this dream will be seen in the transformed face of the world at large.

37. *America gained her independence two hundred years ago. What will the spiritual independence of America be like?*

Sri Chinmoy: America gained her independence two hundred years ago by virtue of determined will-power. Now her spiritual independence will be founded upon her conscious oneness with God, and this can be established only on the strength of her implicit surrender to God's divine Dispensation and Will.

38. *We know that the United States is very powerful militarily and politically on the world horizon. In God's scheme of things, what is the role of the United States in the evolution of mankind's spiritual development?*

Sri Chinmoy: Militarily and politically the United States is very powerful. Your statement is perfectly true. In the Supreme Pilot's scheme of things, the United States is going to play the role not so much of leadership as of friendship, nay, brotherhood, in mankind's evolution. And evolution is another name for mankind's spiritual development.

39. *After two hundred years, has America accomplished much of her main goals?*

Sri Chinmoy: America's goal, like the goal of all the nations and human beings, is always in the process of self-transcendence. There is no fixed goal. America's main goal is a flood of satisfaction, inner and outer. This satisfaction has undoubtedly been achieved to a certain extent. But since everything is progressing and evolving, America's goal is an ever-loving and ever-illumining and fulfilling goal of continuous self-transcendence.

40. *What is the relationship between the American Declaration of Independence and the United Nations Charter?*

Sri Chinmoy: The American Declaration of Independence had the pioneer vision of faith, dignity and humanity's basic needs: equal rights, justice and freedom. Basically, the same things are found in the Charter of the United Nations. Therefore we can safely say that the Declaration of Independence and the UN Charter are two close friends walking along the same road. One came and joined the other later on the road, and now both are walking together to reach the self-same goal, the goal of world peace and satisfaction.

41. *Is America's Bicentennial inwardly significant in any special way?*

Sri Chinmoy: America's Bicentennial is inwardly significant in a special way because it is bringing to the fore once again the all-illumining faith of the soul and the all-fulfilling promise of the heart.

42. *How can the United Nations body derive benefit from the Bicentennial and take part in its activities?*

Sri Chinmoy: If the United Nations body feels that America's Bicentennial is the birthday of its own brother, then naturally it will want to congratulate the brother. This act of congratulation demands cheerful participation in the Bicentennial activities. Needless to say, in doing so the United Nations body will derive not only much joy but also great benefit.

43. *I would be grateful if I could love America much more sincerely and soulfully. What can I do to make this a practicality, especially on America's Bicentennial?*

Sri Chinmoy: You can love America much more sincerely and soulfully provided you feel that America is not a vast piece of land and a machine-driven country, but a life-illumining, love-fulfilling, peace-spreading country.

44. *Does America have anything special to offer to the United Nations during its Bicentennial year?*

Sri Chinmoy: Yes, America has something special to offer to the United Nations during the Bicentennial year. America is not going to intimidate her weak, small brother and sister nations, even unconsciously. America will offer her unprecedented capacity to the community of nations and make all nations feel that her height and depth and speed and power are for them to claim as their very own, and thus create a satisfying and satisfied world-family.

45. *How should the American Indians celebrate the Bicentennial?*

Sri Chinmoy: The American Indians are always looked down upon as inferior. Therefore, they have some inner resistance to throwing themselves heart and soul into pleasing, satisfying and fulfilling other Americans. But in this Bicentennial period, they should forget their sad dispute in the one-family reality. The weaker one should come to the fore and offer his present capacity to the stronger one, for the stronger one badly needs the capacity of the weaker one. It is like a tug-of-war. The stronger one needs the help of the weaker, since the combined strength of the stronger and the weaker naturally surpasses the strength that the stronger one would have if he were alone. So the American Indians should celebrate the American Bicentennial. If they do so, the American heart quality, which is nothing short of oneness, will grant them material wealth as well as spiritual help. The American Indians would be wise if they cared for quick progress in the inner life and success in the outer life by becoming one with the other Americans.

46. Will this year of the Bicentennial help us to feel the same patriotism Americans used to feel?

Sri Chinmoy: To be very frank with you, the patriotism you are seeing in the Bicentennial is no match for the genuine sentiment that the pioneer American leaders had. The divine feelings, divine sacrifice, divine vision that they had will remain unparalleled. When I think of what took place in 1776, I feel that in those days there was no difference between theory and practice. Now there is a yawning gulf between theory and practice. The genuine enthusiasm of this year should have been infinitely more than what it is. What God wants in the Bicentennial is our determined will-power to dive deeper than the deepest, run farther than the farthest, fly higher than the highest. He does not want us to remain self-enamoured by the grandiose achievements of the past but to aspire for higher ideals and higher goals that will promote in a significant way the cause of world-peace, world-perfection and world-satisfaction.

47. *What does the soul of America feel about the different nations eventually making decisions rather than the individual will of America?*

Sri Chinmoy: The soul of America can play the role of the mother and feel that all the other nations are her children. The children mix together, play together, sing together, dance together. Then, when it is time to achieve something, if all the members meet together and jointly do something, it is like children coming to a conclusion on the strength of their genuine effort. So, America's children play in her heart's garden and come to a conclusion together. Naturally, the soul of America will be highly pleased, for she feels that it is a harmonious family. Together they achieve, together they accomplish, together they fulfil.

NOTES TO THE BICENTENNIAL FLAMES AT THE UNITED NATION

1. *(p. 153)* United Nations Headquarters, 21 May 1976.

PART IV

REALITY-DREAM

I – TALKS

1. *United Nations Meditation Group*

We believe and we hold that each man has the potentiality of reaching the Ultimate Truth. We also believe that man cannot and will not remain imperfect forever. Each man is an instrument of God. When the hour strikes, each individual soul listens to the inner dictates of God. When man listens to God, his imperfections are turned into perfections, his ignorance into knowledge, his searching mind into revealing light and his uncertain reality into all-fulfilling Divinity.

2. *Spirituality*

Dear friends, esteemed brothers and sisters, before I give a talk I wish to sing a devotional song. "Lord Supreme, I do not know who You are. I do not know who You are to me in my inner life of aspiration and in my outer life of dedication. But I know that You are my Beloved Supreme."

[Sri Chinmoy sings *Tumi je amar devata eka*.]

Once more I wish to tell you that I am extremely glad and grateful that you have given me this opportunity to be of service to each of you.

I wish to give a very short talk on my most favourite subject, spirituality. Spirituality is at once a simple and a complicated word, a simple and, at the same time, complicated concept. Each individual has a special approach to spirituality. Whatever I know with regard to spirituality, in a few words I wish to offer to the aspiring hearts in you.

Spirituality is truth-awareness. Spirituality is life-emancipation. Spirituality is oneness-manifestation. Spirituality is perfection-satisfaction.

There are two types of spirituality. One is false, totally false. The other is true, absolutely true. False spirituality tells us that we have to negate and reject life in order to reach Heaven or in order to achieve Peace, Light and Bliss in our human life. False spirituality tells us that we have to renounce everything if we really want Joy, Peace and Bliss in life and from life. True spirituality tells us that we must not reject anything, we must not negate anything, we must not renounce anything. True spirituality tells us that we have to accept everything. We have to accept the world as such and then we have to transform our inner world and our outer world for God-realisation, God-revelation and God-manifestation. It is only in God-realisation, God-revelation and God-manifestation that we can have boundless Peace, boundless Light, boundless Delight.

False spirituality is the dance of teeming desires. Desire is something that binds us to our possessions. There comes a time when we realise that although we are the possessor, we are actually slaves to our possessions. True spirituality is the song of aspiration. Aspiration liberates us from our binding and blinding possessions – material possessions, earthly possessions, possessions that do not help elevate our consciousness to our life's true inner and outer goals.

False spirituality is desire. The acme of desire is this: "I came, I saw and I conquered. I came into the world, I saw the world and I have conquered the world. Now I am in a position to lord it over the world." The strangling vital, the demanding vital, the authoritarian vital wants this world for its enjoyment. But aspiration tells us something quite different. The teachings of aspiration are soulful, meaningful and fruitful. Aspiration tells us that each individual has come into the world to see, to love and to become inseparably one, to become fully aware of his universal existence. Mere individual existence is of no avail. One has to have a free access to the universal life within him.

Desire-life is the life of success; aspiration-life is the life of progress. The life of desire constantly demands, whereas the life of aspiration soulfully expects. The life of desire demands constantly from the world around us. The life of aspiration expects everything from the world within.

Success is short-lived satisfaction. Most of the time this short-lived satisfaction is followed by bitter dissatisfaction. In dissatisfaction what actually looms large is frustration; and frustration is the harbinger of total destruction. Progress is our continuous, illumining and increasing satisfaction within and without. Those who follow the spiritual life know and feel the supreme necessity of progress each day, each hour, each minute, each second. A seeker has to feel that he is making progress. He is running fast, very fast, towards his destined Goal. He is climbing high, speedily, towards his transcendental Goal. He is diving deep within extremely fast to reach the Absolute Lord in the inmost recesses of his heart.

In order to make progress each seeker has to have two satisfactory friends. These friends are always reliable, most reliable. Prayer and meditation are two most intimate friends of a seeker of the Absolute Truth. When the seeker prays to the Almighty Lord, he feels his Lord's presence high up in the skies above his head. He feels his Lord's existence above, far above, his mental vision – let us say in Heaven. In Heaven is his Lord Supreme. But when he meditates, he feels that his Lord Supreme is nowhere else except in his heart – in his loving, aspiring heart. His prayer tells him that his God is above. His meditation tells him that his God is within. When he reaches his Beloved on the highest plane of consciousness on the strength of his prayer, he enjoys the sweetest intimacy. He claims his Lord as his eternal

Friend, his beginningless and endless Friend. And when he reaches his Friend inside the very depth of his heart, he enjoys boundless ecstasy and delight in his Beloved Supreme.

Spirituality is the simplification of life. Spirituality is the glorification of life. When we are in the ordinary human life, there are countless problems. Every day we encounter these countless problems, and we find that there is no way to solve these problems or to simplify our complicated human life. But spirituality is our saviour. It comes to solve our problems, to simplify our complicated life; and again, it glorifies the divine in us. The divine in us is that very thing that wants to expand, illumine and fulfil the Immortal in us.

How do we simplify our life? Is there any specific way to simplify our complicated life? Yes, there is a way which enables us to simplify our most complicated life; and that is our concentration, our power of concentration. When we concentrate on our problems we come to notice that our power of concentration has actually come from a Source which is infinitely more powerful than all our problems put together. And this Source shows us how to simplify our problems. If we can concentrate on our problems even for five fleeting minutes, I wish to tell you from my own experience that this complicated world of ours will not remain complicated.

Once our complicated life is over, once our life of confusion and complication is over, we expect satisfaction from our lives. We naturally expect a life of peace and harmony. This world of ours has everything except one thing: peace of mind. If we have peace of mind, we do not need anything more from this world, from any individual or from ourselves. Now, how do we get peace of mind? The answer is the same: through spirituality, through meditation.

Spirituality has a most powerful hero-soldier. The name of that hero-soldier is meditation. If we know how to meditate for five minutes early in the morning before the day dawns, before the hustle and bustle of life begins, then we enter into a world of serenity, clarity, purity and finally peace – a world which is flooded with peace. Each individual seeker has the potentiality, the capacity to meditate soulfully. Some may not know how to meditate immediately. It may take a few days or a few weeks or a few months. But no individual will forever remain unknowledgeable in the art of meditation. The art of meditation is something inherent in each individual.

So, meditation is the way to acquire peace of mind. Once we have established peace of mind, then in our day-to-day multifarious activities we shall enjoy boundless satisfaction. And in this satisfaction we shall notice progress – gradual, continuous, illumining and fulfilling progress. When we walk along the road of Eternity, what we need is progress. And inside our progress is God the ever-transcending Reality, which is the birthright of each individual seeker here and everywhere.

3. Punishment

To be on my own side and not on God's side is not only an unpardonable crime, but also an unbearable punishment.

My Lord's punishment-dog cannot change me and my life. It is only the constant increase of my love for my Lord that can and will change me and my human life totally.

The punishment that I get from my Supreme Pilot when I disobey Him is next to nothing in comparison to the punishment that I inflict upon myself by separating myself from my sweetest and closest oneness with Him, in Him and for Him.

When I do something wrong, no matter how trivial and insignificant it is, my Lord Supreme, do punish me immediately, for that is what I richly deserve. But do love me even when You punish me, for Your Love is my aspiration-life's only soul and my dedication-life's only goal.

4. *The role of humility in the spiritual life*

In our spiritual life, in our life of aspiration and in our life of dedication, humility is the root, divinity is the tree and immortality is the fruit. Only when I am soulfully humble does God allow me to make a perfect estimate of His Universal Reality, His Transcendental Reality and my own life.

The perfect man is he whose inner being is flooded with humility. And it is he who eventually becomes God's Transcendental Choice and God's Universal Voice.

Humility and self-conceit are two real strangers to each other. Humility and God-awareness are two eternal friends. Humility and divinity's reality-expansion are eternally inseparable, inseparably one.

When I am humble to my inferiors, they adore me. When I am humble to my equals, they love me. When I am humble to my superiors, they appreciate me. When I am humble to God, He claims me as His best instrument on earth.

To climb up God's Vision-tree I need only one thing: humility's beauty. To climb down God's Reality-tree I need only one thing: humility's magnanimity.

There are many roads that lead to God. There is one road which is undoubtedly by far the shortest and, at the same time, most illumining and that road is the humility-road.

5. Self-giving and happiness

Dear seekers, I hope at the very beginning I can make you feel what we mean by the term "seeker". A seeker need not be an individual who only cries and tries to realise God. A seeker can be someone who sees something that he does not have right now. He wants something that will give him joy and satisfaction in life, but he does not have that very thing.

Here we are in the company of some distinguished individuals of various professions. In order to become proficient in a particular profession, deep inside us we have to have an inner cry. We want to do something, to grow into something, to become something. This means we are seekers. In your case, this seeking eventually bore fruit and you have now become men and women of profession.

Each profession is like a quality that we offer to the world at large, a quality that satisfies and fulfils us. We have a human family and in that family one member is a doctor, another member is a professor, a third is a lawyer and a fourth can be a soldier. All feel an illumining and fulfilling bond among them. Each one plays his respective role in the family, and by playing that role he brings peace, light and delight into the family. The help of each one is needed. The help of each one is of paramount importance.

Each profession is a signal capacity of God. If we are afraid of using the term "God", let us use the term "happiness". Each capacity offers us happiness. If someone is endowed with a special capacity, that means he has happiness and this happiness makes him go forward. In his life he embodies capacity, he represents capacity and he manifests capacity for the satisfaction of human life on earth.

In this world we notice only two things: quality and quantity. Let us take quantity as ignorance-sea and quality as wisdom-light. We observe an overwhelming quantity of ignorance in us and around us, within us and without. Again, in the inmost recesses of our being we observe quality, divine quality, which wants to illumine us and, at the same time, illumine the rest of the world. So let us take quality as something illumining and quantity as something that has kept us under the jurisdiction of ignorance-night.

Each individual has some special quality. That means he has capacity in abundant measure, in boundless measure. Yet, as individuals, we are not perfectly happy, in spite of having capacity in one particular field. How can we be happy? We can be happy only if we believe in the theory of change. We have to change ourselves. We have to change what we have and what we are.

What do we have? We have the physical body, the vital, the mind and the heart. The body is right now unconscious. The vital is aggressive. The mind is doubtful. The heart is insecure. The body is unconscious like a solid wall. The vital is aggressive like a hungry wolf. The mind is doubtful like a doubting Thomas. The heart is insecure like a child in the woods. Again, this can all be changed, transformed. We can have a conscious body, a dynamic vital, a believing mind and a secure heart. When we cry like a child, in silence, and our prayer is sanctioned, we get a conscious body, a dynamic vital, a believing mind and a secure heart.

What are we? We are followers of the neutral life. In this world very often we try to compromise as a last resort. We feel that we are not in a position to know right from wrong, that we are not in a position to judge; or we feel that the only way to remain in peace is to surrender or compromise. But this is a deplorable mistake. Compromise can never give us abiding joy. He who compromises is consciously surrendering to a neutral life. Someone who is neutral is not sure of what the truth is or what the truth should look like. We know we are in between ignorance-night and knowledge-light. It is up to us to accept knowledge, which is wisdom, and to free ourselves totally from the snares of ignorance.

We want happiness – happiness from life and happiness in life – and we want to offer this happiness to our near and dear ones. In order to achieve happiness in life, we have to give unreservedly what we have and what we are. What we have is the body, vital, mind, heart and soul. And what are we? We are God's constant Concern, constant Compassion and constant Manifestation. Again, if you don't want to use the term "God", you can use the term "happiness" or "truth".

We feel that everything in life disappoints us and deserts us with the exception of one thing, and that thing is truth. To live in truth is to live in happiness. There are various ways to achieve this truth in life. But only one way is most effective and that way is the way of self-giving – unreserved and unconditional self-giving to our own extended, expanded, enlarged, boundless, unlimited existence.

When we enter into our unlimited existence, we feel that we are of the One and for the many. At the same time we feel that we are in the many, for the One. This moment we are the tree; next moment we are the branches. The tree needs the branches, the flowers, the leaves and the fruits in order to prove to the world that it is actually a tree. And the branches need the trunk, the tree as such, to prove to the world that it is part and parcel of the tree.

Each profession here is a branch of the life-tree. And again, each profession knows that there is a root to the tree, to the capacity-tree. For if there is no root, then there can be no branches, fruits, leaves and so forth. We have to live in the root and this root is happiness. How can we live in the root all the time? We can live in the root only by self-giving: giving what we have and what we are. What we have is love and what we are is oneness. By offering love in any form to mankind – to our so-called superiors and so-called inferiors, or to our brothers and sisters of the world – we come to know what we ultimately and eternally are: oneness inseparable.

Some of you may wonder why we have invited today only the professionals and not ordinary people. On other occasions we always invite people irrespective of mental capacity or vital capacity, but today we wanted to observe something special here. We feel that each profession represents a special quality of the everlasting reality. And sometimes we do feel like being in a group where each member is well understood by the others. Birds of a feather flock together at times in order to add beauty, joy, light and delight to one another. It is with this understanding that today we have invited people of profession. Each one has something special to offer to the rest of the members. As a matter of fact, each individual has a special quality, a special capacity of the Source, and that Source is delight, happiness. Happiness is seeing what has to be seen, happiness is feeling what is actually to be felt, happiness is self-giving, happiness is becoming one with the eternal Source.

6. 25th anniversary of Unicef's "Trick-Or-Treat"

[Sri Chinmoy opens the programme with a short song and then speaks to the children.]

Sweet children, dear young friends, my heart is all joy and pride to be in your loving company. I wish to tell you that I have hundreds of friends. Most of them are grown-up people. But I treasure the company of the children much more than I treasure the company of my grown-up friends. Why? Because you are all heart; you are all joy.

My young friends, do you know that there is a person who loves you infinitely more than your best friend loves you? Do you want to know his name? His name is God.

Do you know there is a person who loves you infinitely more than your dear parents love you? Do you want to know his name? His name is God.

Do you know there is a person who loves you infinitely more than you love yourselves? Do you want to know his name? His name is God.

Do you want me to prove it? It is very easy to prove. Your best friend never feels that you are as great as God. But God always feels that you are as great as He is.

Your parents never feel that you are as good as God. But God always feels that you are as good as He is.

You never knew that you are another God. But God knows that you are another God and He all the time tells you that very thing. But in order to hear His Voice, you have to pray lovingly every morning and every evening. Please ask your parents to teach you how to pray. If you pray daily, I assure you one day you will hear God's Voice. And then what I have just told you, you yourselves will be able to hear directly from God.

7. Prayer-Life, Meditation-Life, Contemplation-Life

Dear seekers, here we are in a prayer room. This prayer room is dedicated to the United Nations to serve the spiritual life of the United Nations. In this prayer room I wish to give a very short talk on Prayer-Life, Meditation-Life and Contemplation-Life.

Why do we pray? We pray because we want to become great. We pray because we want to become good. When we become great, we feel that the entire world is at our feet, that the entire world is at our command. When we become good, we feel that the entire world is in us and that the entire world is for us.

By praying we can either become another Julius Caesar and Napoleon, or a Christ and a Krishna. When we become a Caesar or Napoleon, we will try to conquer the world to serve ourselves. But when we become another Christ or Krishna, we plead with the world to grant us the opportunity to elevate and illumine the world-consciousness and make other human beings feel that ours is the task to serve and fulfil them the way the Eternal Beloved Supreme wants us to fulfil them.

A life of prayer is a life of simplicity. Simplicity is a very simple word, but it houses the highest truth. It houses God, who is all simplicity. When we are simple, we come to realise that there are very few things that we actually need. Each time we can eliminate one need from our list of necessities, we derive an iota of peace of mind. And it is peace of mind that is of paramount importance in our earthly life.

Right after simplicity we see that there is something else. This is a friend, a real friend, who is waiting for us and welcoming us. The name of that friend is sincerity. When we become sincere, we are bound to feel that our goal can be reached, that the goal need not and cannot remain always a far cry. The life of sincerity makes us feel that we are eternal travellers along the road of Eternity, and are constantly reaching a certain goal. Today's goal, as we reach it, becomes the starting point for tomorrow's new adventure. We are in the process of an ever-transcending goal, an ever-transcending reality.

Then comes the life of purity. Each time we pray, we feel that something within us is coming to the fore, and that something is purity. This purity-friend of ours is liked most by our Eternal Father, our Beloved Supreme. Our Eternal Father feels that His Vision, His Dream, His Reality – whatever He has and whatever He is – can be expressed, revealed and manifested most soulfully, divinely and supremely through purity. A breath of purity holds God the Infinite, God the Eternal, God the Immortal.

Each prayer leads us to an experience. This experience can at times make us feel how helpless we are in comparison with infinite Light and Delight. And again, this experience can make us feel that Infinity, Eternity and Immortality are not vague terms but real realities within our easy reach.

After we have had the experience of the reality, we go one step ahead: we knock at the door of realisation. When we enter into the room of realisation, we see that the things we wanted to achieve, the things we have spent years or even incarnations trying to achieve, are already within us. From Eternity they have been within us, only we did not have the vision to see them. Now, we not only see them but claim them as our very own.

Each individual here is a seeker. That means each of us has a prayer within us and also something else within, which is called meditation. When we are in the prayer-world, each time we think of our body, our physical consciousness, we are reminded of something else, something more fulfilling. When we think of our physical consciousness, our earthly frame, we feel that we need something else to satisfy ourselves and to satisfy the needs of the rest of the world. But when we dive deep within and establish a free access to our life of meditation, we see that we have everything; only we have to offer it and distribute it to others. When we consider ourselves as the soul, as the divine representative of God, the highest absolute Truth, then we see, we feel, we know clearly that we have everything within us; only we have to reveal it and offer it to the world at large.

Here we are at the United Nations Chapel. When we look at the United Nations Secretariat building from the outside, when we look at the body of the United Nations, we feel that the United Nations is like a beggar: it needs everything, everything in God's creation. A beggar needs everything for himself, not for anybody else. His is an unquenchable thirst. Once we are inside the Secretariat building, we feel the infinite Light, Peace and Harmony that is inside the soul of the United Nations. This soul is crying at every moment to be of service to mankind. If we can become one with the soul of the United Nations, then we see that it has everything: world peace, world harmony, world union, world oneness.

But if we look at the body of the United Nations, then we feel that it is infinitely worse than a street beggar. A street beggar feels in the inmost recesses of his heart that some generous persons will give him alms. If we think of the United Nations as begging from country to country for support, then we feel that there is no certainty that the United Nations can last even a day beyond its present existence.

This is the case, not only with the United Nations, but also with each human being. Each time we pray with the body, in the body, for the body, we have to feel that we are acting like beggars. We feel that there is something else that we need in order to satisfy ourselves. But if we remain in the soul-consciousness, in our inner life, then we become the real emperors: we have everything.

There is a slight difference between a human emperor and a divine emperor. When a human emperor gives something to his subjects, he feels a sense of gratification. He feels that his subjects are at his mercy. They depend on his boundless compassion. But the divine emperor has a different story to offer. He feels that each human being on earth is part and parcel of his own existence. He is composed, like the ocean, of thousands of drops. Each drop is equally necessary. When he does something for an individual being, for the individual drop, he feels that he is only pleasing, satisfying, fulfilling his own dream, which is blossoming like a lotus, petal by petal.

REALITY-DREAM

The body reminds us of the necessity of prayer. The soul reminds us of the necessity of meditation. Each time we pray, we feel that the finite consciously or unconsciously is trying to enter into the infinite. And each time we meditate, we feel that we are cheerfully, devotedly and soulfully welcoming the Infinite to manifest itself in and through us. Then comes something else, a living reality which we call contemplation. In our prayer-life we go up to see, to feel, to bring down something. In our meditation-life we just become the recipient. In and through us the high, higher, highest Reality is manifesting itself. But when we contemplate, we feel that the finite and the Infinite are interdependent. The finite needs the Infinite; the Infinite needs the finite. Earth needs Heaven; Heaven needs earth. The divine lover needs the Supreme Beloved; the Beloved Supreme needs the lover divine. In contemplation we embody both earth-consciousness and Heaven-consciousness. We embody the divine lover and the Eternal Beloved. We embody the finite; we embody the Infinite.

Now, when we want to sing the song of the many in the One, we play the role of the Heaven-consciousness, the Infinite and the Supreme Beloved. And when we want to play the role of the One in the many, then we embody the earth-consciousness, the finite consciousness and the divine-lover consciousness. Each individual has to feel that this moment he is the tree of the one absolute Reality and the next moment he is the branches and the countless leaves, flowers and fruits. God the Creator and God the creation each seeker embodies and each seeker at every moment has the boundless duty to fulfil. And this duty he fulfils only when he feels that he is of the One for the many and he is of the many for the One.

When the seeker identifies himself inseparably and eternally with earth-consciousness, he feels that there is a constant hunger in him, a hunger that constantly mounts high, higher, highest.

Then, when he identifies himself with Heaven-consciousness, he feels there is constant nourishment, boundless energy, infinite nectar-delight in him; he feels that Immortality is growing in and through him. He is at once infinite hunger and infinite Delight and immortal Life. In the body-consciousness he needs. In the soul-consciousness he not only *has,* but also he eternally *is.*

8. *Success and progress*

Meditation defines success and progress in life. Success is the body-dance of self-gratification. Progress is the heart-song of self-perfection.

Success says, "I am above you. You are below me." Progress says, "I only want to be ahead of myself."

Success is my temporary achievement on earth. Progress is my lasting achievement in God and God's lasting achievement in me.

Success thinks that it only needs confidence and perseverance. Progress thinks that it needs not only confidence and perseverance but also something infinitely more, and that thing is God's infinite Grace and God the infinite Grace.

The difference between God's infinite Grace and God the infinite Grace is this: God's infinite Grace paves the way for the Hour of God to strike before God grants us what He wants to grant us. But God the infinite Grace not only wants to expedite the Hour, but He also does everything unconditionally, in the twinkling of an eye.

Experience is the pioneer-runner of success. Illumination is the pioneer-runner of progress. Success is the measure of man in earth-bound time. Progress is the measure of man in Heaven-free time.

REALITY-DREAM

Success fights against teeming opposition and destroys it. Progress fights against teeming opposition too, but instead of destroying it, progress transforms opposition into perfection for God's greatest satisfaction in and through man on earth.

Success is an idea well-proclaimed and well-acclaimed. Progress is an ideal well-distributed and well-accepted.

Success is the preserver of today's strong arms. Progress is the preserver of yesterday's searching mind, today's aspiring heart and tomorrow's totally consecrated life.

Success is my promise to humanity's curious eye. Progress is my promise to humanity's loving heart, to divinity's unifying soul and to God's all-sheltering and all-loving Feet.

II – SERIES ON GREAT MEN AND WOMEN

9. Introduction

Here we are at the United Nations. If we say that the United Nations is the result of the twentieth century awakening, then we are mistaken. The United Nations is the outgrowth of the inner awakening of human beings from time immemorial. I do hope that you do not misunderstand me, as I have made it very clear to you all that it is the joint aspiration of the hoary past, the immediate past, the present and the fast-approaching future that will bring about the union of the world-soul and the world-goal. The human beings who are now here on earth can tangibly see and feel what the United Nations on the outer plane can do.

Each individual nation has aspiration of its own. Again, each individual nation has been blessed with seekers. Each nation has human beings who aspire for a better, more illumining and more fulfilling world. These seekers have expressed their aspiration in and through various fields: spirituality, religion, philosophy, science, music, art, poetry and so forth. The United Nations is not only for the delegates and the representatives of the various nations. It is for all those who have aspired and do aspire and will always aspire.

Many souls came and presently are coming and eventually will come into the world for the world-aim and the world-goal. That aim and that goal is to see a beautiful, fruitful, unifying and united oneness-world. It is my wish to speak on those souls who have undoubtedly contributed in their respective fields to world-transformation, world-illumination and perfection-oneness. I wish to start this series with William Blake, the English poet.

10. *William Blake*

William Blake, English poet. Imagination he had; vision he had. Needless to say, he had these two supernal qualities in abundant measure. To him, imagination was reality's all-illumining beauty and vision was beauty's all-fulfilling reality. To him, imagination was a true man and vision was a true and perfection-inspiring man.

Insane he was – so thought some of his contemporaries, even some of his own friends. But he was not insane. Unfortunately, his reality-worlds most people were not and are not wont to see. Most people have no access to these worlds. An inner cry is needed, a true love of the unknown is needed and a brave heart is needed to go beyond the fact-world, beyond the reality-world already seen and already acquired.

Blake's immortal poem *The Tyger* is humanity's invaluable treasure.

> Tyger, Tyger, burning bright
> In the forests of the night,
> What immortal hand or eye
> Could frame thy fearful symmetry?

Here we see that ignorance-energy, which threatens to devour the entire world, finally discovers its transformation-salvation in the realisation of the absolute One. This absolute One embodies both ignorance-energy and knowledge-energy and, at the same time, far transcends them both.

The soul's soulful originality was Blake's gift to mankind. Blake the art-painting-lover and the thought-progress-lover was the puissant and incessant flow of originality-creativity.

Blake's friend and disciple, Samuel Palmer, realised him and made it easy for the world to realise him. Blake was a man without a mask: his aim single, his path straightforward, his words few. So he was free, noble and happy. Something more: Blake was humanity's challenge to go beyond the achievements of the earthbound life and divinity's challenge to grow and glow in the ever-transcending Beyond's reality-existence.

Blake's life-boat sailed between the soul-essence-purity and the body-substance-impurity. Indeed, this experience each human life encounters. Then there comes a time when the unlit and undivine part in us cheerfully and devotedly surrenders to the lit and divine part in us. Here surrender means conscious awareness, inseparable oneness. In the realisation of its inseparable oneness with the divine, the undivine in us receives illumination, satisfaction and perfection.

In his lifetime Blake was obscure; recognition was a stranger to him. Now, a century after his departure from the world-scene, the world has discovered and recognised in him a world-lover who had the message of transformation – the transformation of hell-torture into Heaven-rapture and the transformation of the body's ignorance-sea into the soul's wisdom-sky.

Today is Blake's birthday. On 28 November, over two hundred years ago, Blake was born; but his soul is still aspiring, still illumining the world and still trying to manifest the divinity that it embodies for earth-awakening, earth-illumination and earth-fulfilment. The poet has the vision of tomorrow, the artist has the vision of tomorrow; the scientist, the singer and the musician all have the vision of tomorrow. All the human beings who are awakened and who are more than ready to contribute something of their own, their very own, in the world at large are really blessed souls and the invaluable, immortal treasures of Mother Earth.

11. *Thomas Carlyle*

Last time I mentioned the importance of the great figures who have illumined our world. Today I shall speak about Carlyle.

Carlyle. The colossal pride of his country he was. A thinker he was. A philosopher he was. A historian he was. Most of his life-experiences were founded upon his inner awakening and inner illumination. He stirred quite powerfully and significantly not only the Scottish consciousness and the British consciousness, but also the entire European consciousness.

According to his philosophy, materialism and the machine-world cannot and will not illumine and fulfil mankind. It is the message of the spirit that can and will transform the face of mankind. In unmistakable terms he declared that only the life-disciplined and ideal heroes can steer humanity's boat to the shores of satisfaction-fulfilment.

Something more: in Carlyle's philosophy, all human beings are in essence one, because they are of the same Source. But if one individual is more awakened and more illumined than the others, naturally he has to lead and guide the rest. Carlyle maintained that this individual has to play the role of a pioneer precisely because he himself was one of the pioneer world-thinkers and world-transformers. Dauntless he was. Nothing could cow him. He hoisted high his lofty banner of life-awakening and life-illumining reality.

He spoke in clear and emphatic terms with regard to the inner resource, and it was here that he was badly misunderstood. His critics saw in him an unbearable autocrat and not an apostle of a new dawn. To his admirers' sorrow, impatience and irritation plagued his mind. Nevertheless, he made his mighty contribution to the world's life-code. Especially his work for the world of German literature and for the French revolution made him a most significant member of the human family. His enthusiasm for German life in his early years added considerably to the German contribution to the world community. And his book on the French revolution is an immortal book. There he offers a most significant idea: an inner guidance, an unseen hand guides and shapes the destiny of mankind. In all human actions, in all activities, in all worldly, earthly affairs there is a spirit that moves, guides and shapes the world-destiny; there is an inner purpose for outer action.

His father wanted him to be a priest. But he became something else: a world teacher. In fact, his father's desire was fulfilled in an infinitely wider and more profound way. Had he become a priest, perhaps only a few Scottish religion-lovers and truth-seekers would have received his light. But by becoming an illumining thinker and writer, a historian and finally a philosopher-saint in the purest sense of the term, he offered to this world of ours his world of light, abundant light. Thus, he has become the property of the world and he belongs to the world-treasure.

Yesterday was Carlyle's birthday. For a second let us offer to his soul our gratitude-heart for what he has done to create a better world, a better mankind.

12. *Emily Dickinson*

The day before yesterday was the birthday of Emily Dickinson: the unparalleled American woman poet and the universally celebrated world poet. Emily and her family formed an inseparable and unique reality. Her family's need was all to her. Her family saw in her reality's intensity, which is a portion of her future-building, illumining divinity's fulfilling touch in the heart of humanity.

Emily's heart carried her physical consciousness and her vital consciousness to her soul's world. Her soul, in a sublime yet subtle manner, carried three other members – the body, vital and heart – to the soul's own source, Immortality-Land. When they returned, the body, vital and heart were convinced of the reality of this divine Immortality-Land.

Just because the mind was not invited to take the trip either by Emily or by her soul, heart, vital or body, her mind violently refused to believe in the authenticity of Emily's illumining, fulfilling and immortalising experiences. The mind stood adamant between the finite and the infinite, between the body and vital and the heart and soul, between the consciously known world and the unconsciously known world. And what is worse, at times the mind was so successful in convincing her, that her previously intoxicating reality-world became nothing more than a visionary hallucination-conception-world in her human life. This formidable and blightful doubt resulted in an indulgence of self-mockery, truth-mockery and world-mockery in her life. Naturally, therefore, her heart's illumination-sky could not grant her the boon of a free access to her inner vastness and her outer plenitude.

Emily learned very little from her association with her outer life. But she learned much from her inner association with her world-seclusion. Indeed, the outer world was an experience devoid of integral reality to her. Therefore, what she knew of earth and thought of earth could not become an encouraging, sustaining, inspiring, illumining and fulfilling experience leading to her own existence-reality.

Emily's love of God and her love of nature made her inwardly beautiful. All her life Emily lived the life of an introvert. A self-imposed seclusion-life she embraced. God's Compassion-Beauty was her reward. In God's Compassion-Beauty, her world and those who wanted to live in her world became preparation-instruments for the transformation and perfection of the frustration-experiences of life.

Her aspiration was in seclusion. Her aspiration was not only in seclusion, but seclusion itself became her aspiration. Inside seclusion-aspiration she did get a few striking glimpses of the inner illumination-sun. Life's buffets gave her two or three times intolerable frustration-experiences, which commanded her to dive deep, deeper within to discover the wealth of the inner life.

Obscurity was her name when she was on earth. Only seven poems were published while Mother Earth nourished her. But when Father Heaven started nourishing her, earth lovingly acknowledged Emily's great achievement and felt considerable pride in her soul-stirring gifts to mankind.

About eighteen hundred flower-poems formed her entire garland. Some of the petals of the flowers offered by her were childish beauty, while others were childlike duty and still others the mature wisdom of a Christian saint. It was her realisation that the Unknown and the Beyond always remain an uncertain and unknown reality. Just because she felt that it would remain unknown forever, the real Reality-Source could not quench her thirst-reality and satisfy her.

Some disproportionately foul critic found in her nothing but a lunatic of the superlative degree. If so, why? Is not this world of ours responsible for not being able to give her the heart's satisfaction which she so richly deserved? Is not the other world responsible for not granting her the life-perfection which she so desperately needed? Her heart-experience says to earth, "Earth, I understand your dilemma. You want and, at the same time, you do not want a transformation-face; a transformation-face, according to you, either is not real or may not satisfy you at all. Therefore, your inner cry is not intense enough, it is not genuine or abiding."

Earth says to the poet, "You are right, you are right. You are more than right. I wish to tell you that what I have is not satisfying me and what I may get is not satisfying me at all. But I do feel that if, in God's creation, satisfaction never dawns, then God will have to remain incomplete. To cherish the idea that God is or will remain incomplete leaves my own existence-reality incomplete for all Eternity. Question I have; answer I do not have. But I am sure my patience-life will be inundated by answer-light in the bosom of Eternity's choice hour."

To Heaven, the poet's life-experience says, "Heaven, if you are really soulful, then you must please me powerfully too. And if you are really powerful, then you cannot endure a yawning gulf between your own ecstasy-reality and my depression, frustration and destruction-reality. True reality exists in self-expansion founded on illumination-distribution.

Heaven says to her soul, "O seeker-poet, you have to dive infinitely deeper. I am not exactly what you have seen of me. I am not in the least what you think of me. I am far beyond your desire-discovery-aspiration. Within your aspiration-discovery-realisation, you will find me, my universality's oneness."

13. Margaret Wilson

We all know about your President Woodrow Wilson. He had a daughter named Margaret Wilson. Here we have someone who happened to be her childhood friend, Mrs Pearce K Drake. Mrs Drake, today I wish to speak about your friend, Margaret Wilson.

Many years ago she read a book written by the great spiritual Master, Sri Aurobindo. The book, *Essays on the Gita,* is about Sri Krishna's conversations with Arjuna in the Bhagavad-Gita. Sri Krishna was the divine soul and Arjuna was the aspiring human soul. We have many, many scriptures in India, but the Bhagavad-Gita is our matchless scripture. The quintessence of all our other scriptures can be found in the Bhagavad-Gita;

it is India's Bible. Sri Aurobindo wrote some most beautiful, luminous essays on the Bhagavad-Gita. Once Margaret Wilson happened to find and read the book. She was extremely moved and wanted to meet the author. But in those days the author of the book was in complete seclusion; he never left his room. But nevertheless, Margaret Wilson went to the Sri Aurobindo Ashram and stayed there permanently. Four times a year she used to see the Master, as others did, for two or three seconds each time. But she was deeply moved by Sri Aurobindo's books, by Sri Aurobindo's philosophy, by Sri Aurobindo's yoga. So she stayed in his ashram.

Sri Aurobindo eventually gave her the name Nishtha, which means faith – divine faith, intense faith. One who has total faith in the Divine, in God, in the Supreme, is Nishtha. Nishtha became the perfect embodiment of divine faith. She led an exemplary life full of devotion and had a surrendering attitude towards the inner, spiritual life.

Unfortunately, we are all susceptible to disease. In her later years Nishtha developed a serious illness. The Indian doctors, in spite of their best efforts, could not cure her. So one of the doctors suggested to her: "Why don't you go back to America? American doctors are far more advanced than we are in the medical field. If you go back to America, the doctors there will take care of you and cure you." But Nishtha's immediate answer was: "True, the doctors in America can take care of my body, but who will take care of my soul? My soul is infinitely more important to me than my physical body. I shall stay here." So she stayed in Pondicherry. She delayed death for a few years more while leading a most dedicated, most spiritual life. Then she passed away.

What do we learn from Margaret Wilson? The soul is infinitely more important than the physical body. But again, in the physical is the soul. We have to give the necessary importance to the physical, but when it is a matter of comparison, when it is a matter of choice, the soul is far more important. If we care for the body all the time, then we shall lead a most ordinary human life. We shall live on earth to no avail. In Indian villages there are farmers who are more than one hundred and fifty years old. But they have no aspiration. Just to live here on earth and count the years on the calendar is of no avail. But if we can stay on earth for even forty or fifty years and can bring the soul's light and divine qualities to the fore and try to manifest them here on earth, then life is meaningful. But for that, we have to live in the soul, not in the body. If we live in the body, we become constant victims to teeming desires.

Today's meditation said that God works in our teeming desires. But again, we have entered into the spiritual life, so for us God is in our climbing aspiration. And tomorrow, in the future, we all shall realise God, and at that time God will be in our glowing realisation. Margaret Wilson knew what desire is. She was brought up in America, so desire was not foreign to her. But she left America for India, and there she lived the spiritual life, the life of aspiration. And what she wanted was realisation and liberation, the third and last step. We can all learn from her. We started our journey with desire. Now all of us here live at least sometimes in the world of aspiration. And in the future, near or distant, we all are bound to enter into the world of realisation.

Nishtha had a Corona typewriter. She typed on that machine for many, many years. But when she passed away, after a few years I was given that typewriter to use. It is not a coincidence that out of two thousand or so disciples, admirers and followers of Sri Aurobindo in the ashram, it was I who was given that particular machine, Nishtha's type writer, to use. Thousands and thousands of times I have typed on Nishtha's machine. And whenever I typed, my soul used to show loving concern and sweet gratitude. From my highest concern, I used to bless her soul.

Thrice I visited her home in the cemetery; three times I paid my soulful homage to her soul there. The cemetery was three and a half miles from the place where I lived. According to our Indian tradition, one has to go to the cemetery with utmost love, concern, purity, simplicity; and finally, if one has real concern for the person's soul, then one has to go barefoot. One cannot carry an umbrella, one cannot wear shoes or sandals and one has to walk. So I walked all the way barefoot. And you can well imagine the scorching heat of South India! Three times I paid my deepest homage to Margaret Wilson. "Faith" in its purest, simplest and highest form, this is Nishtha. I wish to say that all of us can have this kind of faith. It is already within us. We do not have to invent or create faith in ourselves. We have just to discover it. It is not something unknown or foreign or inconceivable or unimaginable to us. No, it is deep inside us. We have only to search, and then we will be able to discover our own treasure. If we have faith in God, then there is no such thing as impossibility.

If one does not have faith in oneself, then one can never, never have real faith in God. This faith in oneself is not arrogance or a showing off of what one can do or say. This faith is the conviction of one's inseparable oneness with the highest Absolute: "I can do this, I can say this, I can go into this, I can become this precisely because deep inside me is my Supreme Lord. It is on the strength of my identification with the Highest Supreme, the Inner Pilot, that I can do this, I can say this, I can become this, I can help the world because God has made me His conscious instrument."

Faith in oneself and faith in God must run together. Otherwise, if one has faith in God and not in oneself or if one has faith in oneself and not in God, then progress will always be unsatisfactory and transient. But if we have faith in ourselves, if we can feel that God has chosen us and we are His chosen instruments, if we can feel that He is with us, in us, of us and for us, then here on earth we can achieve the message of Immortality in our consciousness and the message of universal Perfection in our day-to-day lives. Let us try. We shall succeed.

III – TALKS

14. 1976: *The new year, new opportunities, new challenges*

A new year means a new experience. The new year experiences a new aspiration from human beings. Aspiration is a climbing cry that becomes an illumining smile.

Human beings expect a new satisfaction from the new year. Satisfaction is the embodiment and manifestation of happiness. When we embody happiness, each little individual world of ours becomes a big and vast world. When we manifest happiness, the mortal in us becomes immortal.

What is happiness? Happiness is what God eternally has and what God supremely is. Happiness is not something inside the heart of self-giving. No! It is our unconditional self-giving itself. Self-giving is God-becoming, slowly in reality, steadily in divinity and unerringly in immortality.

Each new year reminds us of the ideal and the real in us. The ideal in us is to see the Truth. The real in us is to become the Truth. Truth is the Eye of God in Heaven; Truth is the Heart of God on earth. God's Eye guides us and leads us. God's Heart feeds us and immortalises us.

Each new year is a new responsibility. A new responsibility is a new opportunity. What is the message of opportunity? Opportunity tells us that a goal, even our ultimate goal, does not have to remain always a far cry. The goal can be reached by transforming animal hunger into divine hunger. The goal can be reached by transforming human thirst into divine thirst. Animal hunger devours the divine vision in us. Human thirst dominates the divine reality in us. Divine hunger is for self-transcendence. Divine thirst is for self-perfection.

This new year of 1976 is the year of either destruction or satisfaction. If we please ourselves in our own human way, then we will undoubtedly meet with destruction. If we please God in God's own Way, then we shall without fail meet with satisfaction. To doubt the divine in us and to indulge the human in us is to please ourselves in our own human way. To perfect the human in us and to fulfil the divine in us is to please God in God's own Way.

15. *Concentration, meditation, contemplation*

I have offered to each of you a flower. A flower signifies purity. Let us feel that our hearts have become as pure as the flower.

Concentration, meditation and contemplation are of utmost importance in the spiritual life. Therefore, let us try to concentrate, meditate and contemplate. We shall now concentrate. Try to look at the entire flower for a few seconds. While you are concentrating on the entire flower, please feel that you are the flower and also that this flower is growing inside your heart, in the inmost recesses of your heart. You are the flower and, at the same time, you are growing inside your heart. Then, gradually try to concentrate on one particular petal, any petal that you select. At this time feel that that petal is the seed form of your reality-existence. Again, in a few minutes' time, please concentrate on the entire flower. At that time feel that it is the universal reality. So right now concentrate on the flower itself and then a few minutes later on one petal. In this way you go back and forth. And please do not allow any thought to enter into your mind. Try to make your mind absolutely calm, quiet, tranquil, and kindly keep your eyes half open.

*

Now kindly close your eyes and try to see the flower that you have concentrated upon inside your heart. Then, in the same way, kindly concentrate on the flower inside your heart with your eyes closed.

*

Now we shall meditate. Kindly keep your eyes half open and imagine the vast sky. Either try to see or feel the vast sky right in front of you. In the beginning try to feel that the sky is in front of you; then later please try to feel that you are as vast as the sky, or that you are the vast sky itself.

*

Now kindly close your eyes and try to see and feel the sky inside your heart. That is to say, please feel that you are now the Universal Heart, which you truly are. You are now the Universal Heart, and inside you is the sky that you meditated upon and identified yourself with. Your heart is infinitely, infinitely vaster than the sky, so you can easily house the sky within yourself.

*

Concentration we have done. Meditation we have done. Now we shall contemplate.

Kindly try to imagine a golden being or figure. Try to feel that this golden being is infinitely more beautiful than the most beautiful child that you have ever seen on earth. This being is our beloved Lord Supreme. We are divine lovers, supreme lovers, and the golden being is our beloved Lord Supreme.

Now we shall try to imagine the presence of our Beloved on the top of a mountain in the Himalayas or at the very bottom of the Pacific Ocean, whichever is easier for us. Please try to feel your existence and the Presence of your Supreme Beloved

Lord at the top of the highest mountain or at the very bottom of the ocean. Once you feel this, then in silence you smile.

Then, after a few seconds, please feel that you are the Beloved Supreme and that the golden being is the Supreme Lover. It is like divine hide-and-seek. When you become the Supreme Beloved, the divine lover seeks you. When you become the divine lover, you seek the Supreme Beloved. When you are the Supreme Beloved, the divine lover searches for you; and when you are the divine lover, you search for the Beloved Supreme. So one moment you are the supreme lover and the next moment you are the Supreme Beloved Lord. Kindly do this with your eyes half open in the beginning.

16. *Payments*

What must I pay? I must pay my earth-body's regular earthly rent. What should I pay? I should pay my Heaven-soul's regular heavenly telephone bill for my conversation with the cosmic gods and with the Absolute Lord Supreme. What am I paying now? I am paying for my former love-friendship with my ignorance-night.

17. *Three soulful prayers*

Lord Supreme, I have all along treasured three most soulful prayers. Today I offer them to You.

Lord Supreme, may I always remain awake to see Your Universal Face.

Lord Supreme, may I always remain conscious to feel your boundless Grace.

Lord Supreme, may I always remain surrendered, unconditionally surrendered, to become a member of Your earth-perfecting, earth-illumining, Heaven-satisfying, Heaven-manifesting race.

18. *Humanity's promise*

Humanity's promise to humanity is a life of service. Humanity's promise to divinity is a life of oneness. Humanity's promise to God is a life of perfection. But this perfection is preceded and followed by service and oneness. Oneness has to be found in perfection and service has to be found in oneness. So we can safely say that humanity's promise to God is a life of service, oneness and perfection.

Service is Eternity's meaningful achievement. Oneness is Infinity's soulful achievement. Perfection is Immortality's fruitful achievement. Service is the transformation of the human within us. Oneness is the realisation of the divine within us. Perfection is the satisfaction of the Supreme within us.

God says to the body, "Body, promise Me that you will not always sleep." The body says to God, "Father, I promise You that I shall listen to You. Now, do accept a promise of my own. My promise to You is that I shall try to be always wakeful, alert and vigilant."

God says to the vital, "Vital, promise Me that you will no longer be aggressive." The vital says to God, "Father, I shall abide by Your Command. In addition, I wish to offer You a promise of my own. From now on I shall be divinely dynamic always."

God says to the mind, "Mind, promise Me that you will no longer cherish your friendship with doubt. Doubt can no longer be your friend." The mind says to God, "Father, I shall definitely listen to You. I also have a promise of my own, and that promise is that I shall make friends only with faith. I will have faith only as my friend. I shall live with faith and I shall fulfil my existence on earth only in faith, for faith – soulful, fruitful, all-offering, all-embracing faith."

God says to the heart, "Heart, promise Me that from now on you will not feel insecure under any circumstances." The heart says to God, "Father, I give You my word of honour that I shall not in any way feel insecure. I shall listen to Your Command. Now, my promise to You is that I shall establish my oneness-existence with each human being in Your entire creation. I shall feel and cherish my oneness with all throughout the length and breadth of the world."

The divine in us promises; the human in us forgets. Again, the Supreme in us revives all our countless promises and fulfils them. Our promise and our aspiration – the inner cry, the mounting flame – are two intimate friends. Promise says to aspiration: "Friend, I do know what to do. I have to establish a life of divinity here on earth. Then there will be no ignorance, no darkness, no limitations, no bondage. I know that this is what I have to accomplish." Aspiration says to promise: "Friend, let me tell you how you can do it. You can do it only on the strength of your self-giving. Give what you have, give what you are at every moment. Then only your goal will not remain a far cry. What do you have? A soulful cry. This is what you can give to mankind. And what are you? You are God's eternal Dream, the Dream that every moment is in the process of blossoming."

Humanity's promise is a movement forward, upward and inward. Humanity's forward movement leads us to the universal Reality and helps us claim the entire creation of God as our very own. Humanity's upward movement carries us to the transcendental Height and helps us claim the transcendental Reality as our very own. Humanity's inward movement leads us to God Himself: God the Dream, God the Reality, God the Silence, God the Sound, God the Omniscient, Omnipotent and Omnipresent. It is within our aspiration's abode that God's Presence looms large.

Our forward movement is for the recognition of the universal Reality. Our upward movement is for the recognition of the transcendental Reality. Our inward movement is for the recognition of the eternally Real in us: God the Supreme.

Humanity has a promise. This promise is self-discovery. Self-discovery comes from self-mastery, and again, self-mastery comes from self-discovery. When we dive deep within we discover our reality-existence, and when we spread our vision-light around us we achieve self-mastery. The most effective way to attain self-mastery is to spread our heart's light, which is the Vision of the Supreme within us. If we spread our vision-light, then the darkness around us surrenders and becomes transformed.

Humanity itself is a promise: a promise of God to Himself, for each individual is a portion of God's Reality-Existence and God's Vision-Existence. Each individual is a representative of God's ultimate Height on earth. In and through each individual God fulfils something unique in Himself. God's promise to Himself is His Aspiration, His Realisation, His Revelation and His Manifestation in and through each individual being.

Each individual has already made an inner promise to humanity. Again, humanity also has made an inner promise to each individual. Each individual, when he prays and meditates and enters into his highest transcendental Height, looks around and sees countless beings around him. At that time he feels it is his bounden duty to carry all and sundry – all human beings, all his brothers and sisters – to the highest Height. This is his promise. And humanity, as a collective soul, promises to each individual that it will offer him the universal Light and Delight. Mere height is not all. The vision and reality have to embrace the entire creation. Length and breadth as well as height are equally needed. The individual will carry the collective soul to the height and humanity, the collective soul, will carry the individual to the universal Reality within all of us.

We have to know whether we shall always remain with mere promise or whether we shall go one step ahead. That step is commitment. There is a great difference between promise and commitment. Promise can be a mere word, a meaningless, fruitless and lifeless gift. But when it is commitment, the soul's commitment to mankind, inside the commitment itself the illumining reality and the fulfilling reality abide.

The promises that we have made to God, to mankind, to ourselves must be transformed into conscious, constant and unconditional commitments. It is inside the heart of commitment that all the promises of the past, present and future can blossom into fulfilling reality. Humanity's promise to God: "Take me." God's promise to humanity: "I am accepting you."

Each soul offers a solemn promise to mankind when it enters into the earth-arena. Ordinary souls and special souls both make promises. In the case of ordinary souls, because of countless weaknesses and the teeming ignorance all around, it is difficult for them to fulfil their promises. But great souls quite often fulfil their promises because they have an indomitable will. Souls of the superlative degree, who are constantly one with the Will of the Supreme who are absolutely direct representatives of the Supreme, come into the world with the loftiest promise. Now, unlike ordinary souls or even great souls, they deal with the entire humanity. Their promise is most sublime and, at the same time, most difficult to execute. But they are not earth-bound. They are Heaven-free. They live on earth for a few years – thirty, forty, fifty, eighty – and then go back to their heavenly abode.

Three souls of the highest calibre, the highest magnitude the highest order have come into the world. Sri Krishna came into the world to establish the divine code of life: righteousness must reign supreme; wickedness must give way to righteousness and a life of light. But his promise has not yet been fulfilled. There are still wicked people on earth wickedness still looms large and reigns supreme. But he has not given up his promise. In and through you and me and each individual he is trying to conquer humanity's wickedness and replace it with the divine code of life, which is justice-light all around.

The Buddha came and promised to make the world at large a world without suffering. There will not remain an iota of suffering here on earth, he said. He tried his best, but the world is still suffering like anything. Yet he has not given up his promise. His promise is now being executed in and through us, in and through each individual seeker here on earth. Each seeker wants to free himself and also the entire world from suffering. So the loftiest promise of the Buddha is now being executed in and through each individual seeker on earth.

The third soul of the highest magnitude is the Christ, the Son, the Saviour. His promise to mankind was the establishment of the Kingdom of Heaven. We all know what the Kingdom of Heaven will look like. There will be no ignorance, no darkness, no bondage, no limitation, but only boundless light, boundless delight, boundless harmony, boundless peace. All divine qualities in boundless measure will comprise the Kingdom of Heaven. Right now, when we look around we see anything but the Kingdom of Heaven. Does it mean that the Christ has given up his promise to mankind? No, not in the least. His promise is now percolating, his promise is now flowing like a river in and through each individual seeker on earth. The Kingdom of Heaven must come into existence – either today or tomorrow or in the near future or in the distant future. The promise of the Saviour Christ will definitely be fulfilled in the course of human evolution. No God-Promise can remain unfulfilled. The promise that God made to mankind through Sri Krishna, the promise that God made to mankind through the Buddha, the promise that God made to mankind through the Christ, the promises that God is offering to mankind through you, through me, through each individual seeker, will all be fulfilled.

19. The Buddha

> *Buddham saranam gacchami*
> *Dhammam saranam gacchami*
> *Sangham saranam gacchami*

When I go to the Buddha for refuge, he blesses me.
When I go to the inner Law for refuge, he illumines me.
When I go to the Order for refuge, he utilises me.

Siddhartha did. He flew from his household life into the state of homelessness. The Supreme did. He placed the Buddha in the adoring heart of humanity, in the lap of universal Love. Temptation Siddhartha saw and shunned; austerity he felt and lived; the Middle Path he realised and offered. The Omnipotent did two things through Siddhartha. He revealed the ideal of perfection in a human being. He revealed His Enlightenment and Compassion in a divine being. The Buddha cast aside caste. The fallen learned from him the value of self-respect. The unbending learned from him the necessity of humility.

Nirvana is a miraculous power. Negatively, it pleases the souls who want extinction. Positively, it pleases the souls who long for the ultimate and transcendental Bliss. The Buddha stood not against the Hindu religion. He stood against the perversions and corruptions of Hinduism. He was never ashamed of the Hindu religion, but he was utterly ashamed of some of its ways and methods.

The Buddha had Divinity in its fullest measure. With His Heart, the Unfathomable came to the Buddha; with His Mind, the Unknowable came to the Buddha; with His Bliss, the Transcendental came to the Buddha. Hinduism is the tree; Buddhism is its largest branch. The son discovered that his mother was not perfect, so he decided to live alone.

Buddhism gave birth to two schools of thought: *Hinayana* and *Mahayana*. Hinayana depends on self-reliance. Mahayana depends on Grace. Hinayana longs for individual salvation. Mahayana longs for collective salvation. Hinayana feels that the monks alone are entitled to pray for the ultimate Truth. Mahayana feels that not only monks but also laymen are entitled to pray for the ultimate Truth.

Meditation gives enlightenment, feels a Hinayanist. Meditation, prayer and invocation – all these give enlightenment, feels a Mahayanist. A Hinayanist sits at the feet of Buddha's teachings, following the advice that one must work out one's own salvation. A Mahayanist sits at the feet of Buddha's earthly personality, following the advice that one should not cross the Gate of Transcendental Bliss until each and every soul has been liberated.

True, Buddhism is no longer alive in the land of its birth, but Mother India is abundantly proud of her spiritual prince, and she ever cherishes her world-illumining teacher. Her fondest feeling is: My Buddha is a rebel child. My Buddha is a great contributor. My Buddha is a great reformer.

20. *A new teacher: heart*

Here we are all seekers. We are consciously seeking God's Light; but there was a time when we did not seek God's Light, even unconsciously. Now we consciously seek, but yesterday we did not seek at all. We are all students. Previously we also were students; at that time we had a teacher and the name of that teacher was mind. Now we have a new teacher, and the name of that teacher is heart. Our previous teacher asked us to walk along the desire-road. As we were students, we walked along the desire-road in order to get the satisfaction which the teacher promised us. For it is satisfaction that makes life meaningful and fruitful. But to our surprise, the mind could not offer us satisfaction. Each time we took a step ahead, instead of satisfaction it was all frustration; instead of real happiness, it was false, totally false pleasure. We were totally dissatisfied and we changed teachers.

We previously tried to please the mind, so that we could derive happiness from life, but there was no happiness. Now we have a new teacher, the heart. The new teacher tells us that we can and shall get happiness only if we please God in God's own Way. The new teacher tells us we can never achieve happiness unless we become one with happiness itself. Happiness itself is the soul in us.

The mind does not have happiness. If I do not have something, how can I give you that very thing? Because the mind has no happiness, it can't teach us. The heart says, "I cannot give you happiness, but I know someone who has happiness and who is all happiness, and this person is eager to grant you happiness. I shall take you to that particular happiness-reality and you can achieve and receive as much as you want." So the heart takes us to the soul, which is all Light and Delight. The heart says it does not have joy of its own, but only when it becomes inseparably one with the soul does it become really happy.

The heart says, "O human being, O seeker, you have not an iota of happiness. And I have only limited happiness, limited joy. But I know someone who has boundless happiness, and I am more than eager to take you to him. As your teacher, I am telling you, O seeker, walk along with me. I am leading you to the Source. I am guiding you, I am leading you; but it is up to you if you want to find it. Stay in the soul and you will get unlimited joy, happiness and satisfaction. I cannot give you happiness in my own way, but I am being guided by the soul.

"The mind, your previous teacher, wanted to guide you in its own way. But the mind is not aware of the destination, so how can you expect the mind to give you the message of the destination, let alone take you there? I am not the destination, but I have seen the destination, and I will take you there. Like you, I will try to develop capacity, O seeker, and from the destination receive infinite joy and happiness. Our destination is eager to give us constant satisfaction, joy and Delight."

21. *My captain commands, "Go on!"*

My captain commands, "Go on! Go on! Go on!" The captain is the Lord Supreme within us. The captain has commanded, "Children, go on, go on." But right now we have become inseparably one with the body, the vital, the mind and the heart.

The human body tells the seeker in us, "Look, we have become one. Let us tell God that we wish to sleep for some time and then we shall accept Him, we shall accept His command." So the human body and the seeker tell God that they will enjoy sleep for a short while and then they will listen to God's dictates.

God immediately says to the human body and the seeker in us that they can do so. If they want to sleep, they can sleep. But after some time they have to wake up; they have to accept God and walk along the road of Light and Delight. So the body and the seeker start to sleep and sleep and sleep. They do not want to wake up. Sometimes they forget to get up; sometimes they deliberately do not get up. Therefore, they do not proceed along the road of Light and Delight to the Golden Shores of the Beyond.

The vital and the seeker within us say to God, "Lord, we shall listen to Your command. But before that, allow us to fight, struggle and win. That is to say, before we proceed, before we march on towards the ultimate Goal, let us dominate and lord it over the world for a few days, a few months, a few years. After that, we shall definitely abide by Your command; we shall walk, march and run towards the destined Goal."

God says to the vital and the seeker, "Granted. But don't forget that after you have fought with the world and won your supremacy, after you have dominated the world in your own way, you have to walk along the road of Eternity to reach perfection in life."

Both the seeker in us and the vital in us then fight against the world and bring the world under their feet. They dominate the world and they are satisfied. But then they don't want to walk along the road any farther. They don't want to reach the destined Goal. They are satisfied. They have forgotten the promise they made to God that after they enjoyed their supremacy they would walk along the road to reach the highest Truth and Light.

When the mind and the seeker become one, they say to God, "Lord, we shall definitely listen to You. You want us to march on along the road, and we shall do so. But before that, please allow us to think, to judge, to see if the world deserves our faith or our doubt. Let us spend some time either in doubting the world or in having faith in the world, in thinking of ourselves or in thinking of the world. When all this is done, we shall without fail proceed along Eternity's road. To please You, to fulfil Your command, we shall without fail reach the highest Height."

God, out of His infinite Bounty, says to the mind and the seeker in us, "Children, all right, I wish to fulfil your desire. But don't forget to fulfil My desire after you have fulfilled your own desire. You have to walk far, farther, farthest. You have to walk along Eternity's road in order to reach the highest Goal."

So the mind and the seeker within us start thinking of the world, thinking about the world within them and the world without. Then day and night they start doubting the world, or occasionally they exercise their faith in the world. That is enough for them. They become satisfied and totally forget their promise to God. They don't want to walk any more. They don't want the highest Truth, the highest Light, the highest Reality, the illumining Perfection and fulfilling Satisfaction.

So the body, the vital and the mind fail.

But the seeker in us also has the heart, and the heart has the seeker. They become friends. They are doubtful in the beginning whether they will be able to walk along this eternal road. They see that their brothers, the body, the vital and the mind, have totally failed. They had good intentions – they just wanted to sleep a little, they just wanted to dominate a little, they just wanted to doubt a little and then they were ready to please God in His own Way. But they failed. They did not keep their promises to God.

So the heart in us and the seeker in us are confused and worried when they start. They say to God, "We want to please You in Your own Way, in spite of knowing that the rest of the members of our family have failed You. We would also like to come to You by doing something."

God says, "What is it?"

The seeker and the heart say, "We wish to identify ourselves with the achievements of the body, vital and mind."

God says, "Their achievements are nothing but frustration and destruction."

The heart says, "We know, but we are tempted to feel their frustration and destruction first, then immediately come to You for satisfaction. We will definitely start walking along Eternity's road, for we desperately need abiding satisfaction."

God says to the heart and the seeker, "Yes, My children. You can try."

So the heart becomes one with the body, the vital and the mind. Then the quality of the body, lethargy, the quality of the vital, aggression or supremacy, the quality of the mind, suspicion and division, all immediately enter into the heart! On the one hand, it was more than eager to please God in His own Way when it saw the confusion that the body, vital and mind had created by not doing so. But temptation arose in the aspiring human heart, and because of this temptation the heart became one, inseparably one, with the rest of the members of the family before it was in a position to offer its existence totally to the Supreme Pilot, the Captain Supreme.

So the heart and the seeker become helplessly and hopelessly one with the body, vital and mind for some time. Then, after having known and felt their suffering, torture and ignorance-night, the heart starts to cry out for Light and Truth. The body is satisfied with its achievements. The vital is satisfied with its achievements. The mind is satisfied with its achievements. But the heart, fortunately, is not satisfied with its achievements. The heart wants to achieve something else, something higher, something deeper, something more fulfilling and illumining. So the heart leaves the body, vital and mind and approaches God.

It says to God, "Lord, I am entirely Yours. Now tell me, shall I stay with You and receive Your Light while walking along the road, or shall I stay inside the body, the vital and the mind to cry for Your Light? Which do You want? Shall I give up my body-consciousness, shall I give up my vital-consciousness, shall I give up my mind-consciousness in order to please You? Or shall I remain inside them and invoke Your Light? Please tell me."

God says to the heart-seeker, "If you are really brave, if you feel that you can pray and meditate inside the lethargic body, the aggressive vital, the doubtful and suspicious mind, then I have no objection. But it is an almost impossible task. You have to come out of the body-consciousness. You have to come out of the vital-consciousness. You have to come out of the mental consciousness. First you have to be inundated with boundless Light, and then only can you enter the body-consciousness and change its lethargy into alertness and dynamism; then only can you change the aggression of the vital into a positive will for God-manifestation; then only can you change the mind's doubt and lack of faith into constant faith. If you want to please the young members of your family – your body, vital and mind – you have to first become strong and please Me. Heart, if you please Me in My own Way, only then will the rest of the members of your family be pleased."

The heart fully accepts God's Command and wholeheartedly tries to fulfil God's Will; therefore, the heart becomes inseparably one with God's Will, and receives and achieves Light in abundant measure. Then God tells the heart to enter into the mind, to enter into the vital, to enter into the physical body for their illumination, and the heart enters. It suffers a lot because the body-consciousness does not want to accept the heart's light, the vital-consciousness does not want to accept the heart's light and the mental consciousness does not want to accept the heart's light.

But the heart in the meantime has developed boundless patience, and this patience is the lengthening of time itself. Patience is the constant expansion of time within us. So now the seeker and his heart are inundating the seeker's physical body, inundating his vital and inundating his mind, with the Light of the Supreme. They are not being compelled to do this by any outer forces or by the members of their family, but they are acting out of their inseparable inner oneness with the Lord Supreme who wants them to illumine the younger members of their family.

Here we are all seekers. Individually we seek, collectively we seek. We seek for Truth, we seek for Light, we seek for perfection within and without. In order to discover perfection in life, what we need is a flood of Light and Delight within us.

We have to know that what we have principally is the heart and the mind: the mind that is constantly bringing us the message of subtraction and division, and the heart that is constantly bringing us the message of addition and multiplication. It is through addition and multiplication that illumination, salvation, liberation, realisation and perfection evolve.

We are all seekers of the infinite Truth. Let us feel from now on that what we have is only the heart. The heart can not only fulfil the divine in us, but it can awaken the stone consciousness and the plant consciousness in us and transform the animal in us. It is the divine qualities of our heart that can awaken the stone life and plant life in us and at the same time, transform the animal in us, illumine the human in us and fulfil the divine in us. So let us try to become this heart which has the inner longing to fulfil God in all the members of our family.

[Sri Chinmoy sings *My Captain commands, go on, go on*.]

22. *The inner call*

The inner call is not everything, but on the basis of the inner call we make a choice. Sometimes the inner call is a tempting one. Sometimes the inner call is an illumining one. For those who are not sincere, the inner call is temptation. But for those who are sincere, the inner call is always illumination.

When we get the inner call, very often we notice a few conflicting forces. These forces are from the desire life and from the aspiration life. The forces of the desire life tell us that we are under obligation to remain with them, since for many, many years they have fed us, nourished us and fulfilled us according to their capacity. But the forces of aspiration tell us that only a new life, a new nourishment, can give us happiness and satisfaction. If we properly accept the call of aspiration, then we begin walking along the path of illumination. But if we do not properly accept the call of aspiration, we feel that the forces of aspiration are nothing but temptation forces. We feel that we are being invited by the unknown and that we may be totally swallowed by the unknown.

As I said before, based on the inner call we make a choice. Sometimes we make a choice to become good. Then we have to decide how far we want to go with the call. In order to become good, we have to give up quite a few things, and we have to accept and adopt quite a few things. But we have to know that the things that we are giving up are not worth having. At the same time, anything that is worth keeping from our previous life – from our life of desire – anything that can be transformed, illumined and perfected, that we shall not give up.

The day after tomorrow we shall observe the fourth of July, a day which is most significant in the firmament not only of America but also of the entire world. What do we notice here? We notice that two hundred years ago there was a significant call that came directly from the Absolute Supreme. This call reached a considerable height, and the inner beauty, the inner light and the inner perfection from that height were received by awakened Americans and by the world at large.

Always there will be a call, and the call will come to each individual on a different plane. It can come on the political plane, on the spiritual plane, or on any other plane. When we hear that call we have to know how far we should go with it on the physical plane, on the vital plane, on the mental plane, on the psychic plane. Each plane is limitless, and it is we who have to decide how far to go according to our capacity and receptivity. Some people want only to start their journey, while others want to walk a considerable distance and still others want to reach the destination. Again, there will be a few who will not be satisfied even when they reach the destination. They want to come back to the starting point again to teach others how to walk properly and how to reach the goal.

Seekers who follow the inner call ultimately reach God. Some do so on the strength of a mutual agreement with this inner call. They feel that they will give what they can give, and they will get from the call, from the choice, from God, what God can give. Again, there are some higher seekers who reach God on the strength of their conscious, constant surrender to their inner call. They tell God that they will do everything unconditionally right from the beginning to the end. These seekers God is extremely pleased with, both in Heaven and on earth. But sometimes they break their unconditional surrender to God's Will. Some of them fail to keep their promise on earth. And some of them, while they are on earth, do become unconditionally surrendered to God's Will; but then, when they go to Heaven, they may not keep their promise, keep their surrender to God's Will. In spite of being fully illumined, they make an emotional demand of God. It is not a human emotional demand, but it is a kind of charming, illumined emotional demand. Those seekers tell the Absolute Supreme, "Look how much we have suffered on earth. We saw that people were hungry and we wanted to help and serve them. But almost all of them misunderstood us and kicked us. Why go back again, when we see that earth is unwilling to accept light? Now that we are in Heaven, please allow us to remain in perfect peace. On earth we helped according to our capacity, our aspiration. Here we wish to acquire another capacity, the capacity to stay in peace and watch. Watching is also a capacity."

In some cases, the Absolute Supreme grants their request. "My children, you have worked so hard. If you don't want to go back, since you feel there is no hope, then you can stay. I never lose hope, but if you want to take an indefinite rest, I will allow you. But if you don't go back to earth, it will make Me sad." When God says this, some of the seekers and Masters in the soul's world feel sad. They immediately change their attitude; they become brave, and they do come back. And when they come back, they feel inwardly that this time they will have a better environment, they will have better students, they will have a better spiritual Master. It may happen, however, that they get a worse environment, worse students, a worse spiritual Master. But if they are really brave, even then they struggle to the end. They may win or lose, but they take everything as an experience, and they keep coming back.

No matter which plane the inner call comes on, whether it is on the physical plane, the vital plane, the mental plane or the psychic plane, once we start our journey, we should not go back. If we want to go back, then we may be on the physical plane, but our consciousness will be on the inconscient plane, at the stone level, the plant level or animal level.

Even those who are very bad students in the aspiration world are far better than those who are still living in the desire world. If we totally give up the world of aspiration and go back to the ordinary world, to the desire life, then we are going back to the plane where there is no satisfaction. Just because the inner plane is not giving us satisfaction in our own way, we cannot go back to the plane where we have seen that there is no satisfaction at all. We have to continue from where we are. Today I am not getting anything to drink. Shall I then drink filthy, dirty water?

Since my goal is to drink Nectar, I shall not go back and be satisfied with dirty, filthy water, even if I cannot drink Nectar today. No, I will go on, go on.

It is not that no one has ever drunk Nectar. There *are* people who have drunk Nectar. Sri Krishna, Lord Buddha, the Christ, Sri Ramakrishna and others have drunk Nectar. And they started their journey like us.

Take the Buddha, for example. The Buddha received a call. The Buddha had everything; he was the prince. He had a most beautiful wife, a child, a kingdom. He had money-power, he had world-enjoyment, everything. But he gave all this up when he got the inner call.

In the Buddha's case, the world of desire was all around him. When the call came, he gave up everything. But in Sri Ramakrishna's case, he did not enter into the desire world at all.

For Sri Aurobindo, the call came when he was serving as a professor. And from that call he entered into politics. Then another call came, and he gave up politics and entered into seclusion for God-realisation and manifestation.

In Vivekananda's case, in spite of being well-educated according to Western standards, when the call came he went and fell at the feet of someone who did not care for earthly knowledge or education at all. In order to fulfil the call, he just placed himself at the feet of someone who could nourish him spiritually. Again, there was considerable conflict in his life. When he was going through conflict, at times he would go back to the ordinary life. But his inner call was so powerful that in spite of this conflict, he was able to maintain the intensity of his inner call.

When we get an inner call, no matter where we are, we have to go forward. Even if we are standing at the head of the line, we have to go forward. When we go forward because of an inner call, it means a special blessing has descended upon us. But if we do not avail ourselves of this opportunity, it may take a number of years, a whole lifetime, or quite a few incarnations before we get another call.

To receive a call is not like receiving an earthly meal. If we have missed a meal, then in a few hours' time we will be able to eat again. If we have missed lunch, we know we will get supper in three or four hours. But once we miss an inner call, we may have to wait for centuries before we can get inner nourishment again. An earthly meal lasts two or three hours. But the meal that we get from the inner call may last for centuries. We can live for Eternity on the inner meal which we get when we listen to the inner call.

Once we accept the spiritual life, the inner life, and listen to the inner call, we totally change the course of our development. Here we are all seekers. True, we have all kinds of weaknesses and defects, but from the strict spiritual point of view, we are not human beings. God tells us that once we accept the spiritual life we should never think of ourselves as human beings. The moment we start aspiring, we become divine beings. Again, there are grades of divinity. In the world of divinity, somebody can be more divine than somebody else. There will be some who do not yet take God seriously, who do not take Truth seriously, who do not take Light seriously. And there will be others who do take God seriously, but their seriousness does not always last. When we are in the spiritual life, we have to take ourselves seriously and we have to take God seriously at every moment. When we take God seriously, we do everything for God. At first we say, "I am doing this because I want to see God." Then we see that it is not we, but God Himself who is doing everything in and through us. God will do everything for us, but before He does something, since God is a Gentleman, in silence He asks us, "Can I do this for you?" If we say "Yes, I would be very happy if You would," then He will do it.

Each individual has God inside him; each individual has Divinity, Truth and Light. When he has realised the Highest, each individual will realise that God's Vision is nothing but Wisdom-Light. God created the world with His inner Vision and this Vision is all Wisdom. Wisdom is not mere talk, Wisdom is not cleverness; Wisdom is something else. Believe it or not, Wisdom is Compassion. God's Wisdom and God's Compassion are the same thing. Because of His Compassion, today God is using His Wisdom for us. And because of His Wisdom, today God is using His Compassion for us. When we listen to the inner call, we receive God's Compassion and grow into God's Wisdom.

Here we are all at the United Nations. The United Nations is the offspring of the League of Nations, President Wilson got an inner call, and from his inner call he tried and cried, cried and tried to have world union, union of the world forces. Now this League of Nations has become a world body. We call it the United Nations. The United Nations also has a call, an inner call. The outer call we see when something happens. The United Nations gets a call from a suffering country, from a country that needs help, or a call from the strong countries that want to be of help in creating a peaceful world.

But the inner call the UN has already got. That inner call is from the soul and not from the body. It does not come from the geography of the world or the history of the world; it comes from the cry, the inner cry of the world. The geography of the world will say one thing about the UN, history will say something else about the UN and the inner cry will say something else. The living inner cry says that the role of the UN is to serve, not men as such, not the world as such, but the cry that is inside the world, the cry that is inside each human being, inside each individual on earth.

An inner call comes to awaken us, to illumine us. It tells us that just because God the infinite Truth and God the infinite Light is inside us, for that reason we are trying and crying and hoping to become inseparably one with God. We use the term "hoping" because we do not know how much faith we have: faith not only in Peace, Light and Bliss, but also faith in ourselves. When we have sincere faith in ourselves, we come to see the Source of that faith. We see that faith comes from the Supreme, from the highest Absolute. If we know that we have a Source which has boundless Peace, Light and Bliss for us, then we can go forward always. But we have to have faith that we can and shall move forward, precisely because we have a Source that is more than willing to lead us forward to the ever-transcending Vision-World and Reality-World.

If it is from the inner call that we make a choice, then it is from the inner call that we move forward, and it is from the inner call that we eventually realise the Highest. Then after we realise the Highest, we feel that if anything remains unillumined anywhere on earth, then the main purpose of realisation, which is satisfaction, we can never achieve. Everything must be illumined and perfected. Only then can we have real satisfaction. So we go from call to choice, from choice to destination and from the destination to more inner aspiration for the ever-transcending Goal. And this happens only when we do not turn back. The road is a one-way road.

Again and again, I wish to tell you that here we are all seekers. A seeker is not a human being who is half animal. He is more than that. A seeker is one who has glimpsed the light. Otherwise, he could not have become a seeker. This light is more than eager to expand itself into boundless, infinite Light provided we follow the inner call. If we don't follow it, if we don't have faith in it, then our inner light gets hidden or extinguished by the desire forces, the suspicion forces, the doubt forces, the temptation forces, the frustration forces and all the other negative forces.

23. *On a birthday*

Each birthday is a new awakening. Each birthday is a new hope. Each birthday is a new promise. Each birthday is a new fulfilment.

The new awakening takes place in our physical, earth-bound consciousness. The new hope dawns in our frustrated, disappointed and unaspiring vital. The new promise comes inside our doubtful human mind. This new promise challenges the doubting, doubtful mind and reminds the mind of its origin: consciousness-flood. The new fulfilment occurs inside the entire being: in the earth-bound being and the Heaven-free being.

When the soul descends to earth, the soul takes responsibility not only for the earth-consciousness but also for the Heaven-consciousness. The earth-consciousness cries for light, cries for peace, cries for love, cries for delight. The soul promises the earth-consciousness that it will help it achieve peace, light, love, delight, joy, harmony and everything that the earth-consciousness needs. Again, it is the same soul that promises the Heaven-consciousness that it will manifest Heaven's joy, satisfaction and perfection here on earth.

Each birthday is a tune, a melody of the universal music. Each individual is also a melody of the universal music. The seeker grows and glows in this music, which he can hear with his soulful ears. The very presence of the soul-child inside us is what grants us a taste of the universal music. The soul needs to climb like music, soulful music. The soul, when it climbs, knows no boundaries, no religious barriers, no political boundaries. It is all freedom, freedom within and freedom without.

Each birthday is a petal of a flower. The flower, petal by petal, blossoms and then it is ready to be placed at the inner shrine in the aspiring heart.

A thought indicates a new birthday. An iota of will indicates a new birthday. An upward movement indicates a new birthday. At every moment, whether we look within or without, we celebrate the birthday of our oneness with God, the Creator of the entire universe. When we look at something, we become one with it. On a birthday we feel our inseparable oneness with the expansion of a new light, a light that will ultimately cover the length and breadth of the world.

The real birthday does not come only once a year. The real birthday is the birth of each second in a seeker's life. An aspiring second in the seeker's heart is the real birthday. At every moment, God the Author of all good celebrates the seeker's birthday.

As seekers we have to be consciously aware of something divine and supreme within us. What this divine and supreme thing is is our promise to humanity and our promise to divinity. The transformation of humanity's face is our soul's promise to humanity and the manifestation of divinity's light here on earth is our soul's promise to divinity.

It is our Devadip's birthday. As I have spoken about the soul in connection with music, I wish to dedicate this very short talk to the sublimely great musician-soul inside Devadip. Some of you know him as Carlos Santana, while others know him as Devadip, the Lamp of God, the Vision, the Light of the Supreme.

[To Devadip Carlos Santana:] The United Nations is an international body. You play music all over the world with your soul's love for mankind. May the soul of the United Nations bless you. May the soul of the United Nations grant you its inner peace, inner love, inner joy, inner oneness with the rest of the world. Your dedicated service of joy, love and peace you offer to the world. The soul of the United Nations, therefore, offers its most blessingful love to you.

24. Tribute to Dag Hammarskjöld

We wish to offer our soulful homage to this great soul and also we invoke this great soul to bless us in our life of inner aspiration and our life of outer dedication.

[A short meditation follows.]

Dag Hammarskjöld was a great man, a good heart, a soulful life, a possessor of perfect vision-light. Something more, he became a fulfilling bridge between humanity's excruciating pangs and divinity's illumining Compassion.

They say that the mind's brilliance and the heart's oneness do not and cannot go together, because the mind tends to enjoy a sense of separativity. But Dag Hammarskjöld's life amply proved that the mind's brilliance and the heart's oneness can and do go together.

They say that the selfless purity of the body and the bold dynamism of the vital usually do not run abreast. Indeed, Dag Hammarskjöld was a rare exception.

They say that there is a yawning gulf between earth's practical reality-body and Heaven's theoretical vision-soul. If what they say is true, then it is also unmistakably true that Dag Hammarskjöld bridged that yawning gulf in his own life's short span

The practical man in Dag Hammarskjöld teaches us, "Do not look back, and do not dream about the future, either. Your duty, your reward, your destiny, are *here* and *now*."

The theoretical soul in Dag Hammarskjöld teaches us,

The moon was caught in the branches.
Bound by its vow,
My heart was heavy.

Naked against the night
The tree slept.
Nevertheless,
Not as I will...

The burden remained mine:
They could not hear my call
And all was silence.

Religion-blood Dag Hammarskjöld inherited from his sweet mother. Manifestation-flood he inherited from his dear father. Something more he inherited from his father: loneliness. Both father and son were assailed by loneliness.

The divine seeker in the Secretary-General left a special message for those who are married to inescapable loneliness: "Didst Thou give me this inescapable loneliness so that it would be easier for me to give Thee all?"

A great man is, indeed, a great power. Human power cleverly avoids justification. Divine power does not avoid justification for there is no need on its part to do so. It knows that justification is only another name for its selfsame reality. The Secretary-General's wisdom-light reveals to us, "Only he deserves power who everyday justifies it."

We desire many things. Sometimes we do not know what we desire and why we desire. Unlike us, God has only one desire: independence. And that independence, too, is only for us. The seeker in Dag Hammarskjöld not only tells us about God's desire for us, but also tells us when we can attain it: "God desires our independence, which we attain when, ceasing to strive for it ourselves, we 'fall' back into God."

Dag Hammarskjöld was a man of unparallelled duty. Duty demands capacity. He perfectly mastered the art of duty. Out of his heart's magnanimity, he shares with us its quintessence: "Somebody placed the shuttle in your hand. Somebody who had already arranged the threads."

The seeker's life need not always be a bed of roses. Sometimes it can ruthlessly be a bed of thorns. When the seeker Dag Hammarskjöld's inner crisis loomed large, his frustration-life voiced forth: "What I ask for is unreasonable – that life shall have a meaning. What I strive for is impossible – that my life shall acquire a meaning."

Again, when the same seeker's life-tree blossomed into a glorious satisfaction, he immediately and unreservedly voiced forth,

> *That chapter is closed.*
> *Nothing binds me.*
>
> *Beauty, goodness,*
> *In the wonders here and now*
> *Become suddenly real.*

Every time I go to the Secretary-General's birth-place, Uppsala, Sweden, I make it a special point to offer my soulful homage to his Long Home. His life's sterling simplicity illumines my life of aspiration and his soul's ever-glowing luminosity fulfils my life of dedication.

A flying earth-plane killed his body, only to help his soul fly to reach the highest height. But his Heaven-bound flying soul got the immediate opportunity to see the Face of the Beloved Supreme.

25. *Emotion: is it our enemy or our friend?*

Emotion is both our foe and our friend. There are many planes of consciousness, but usually we deal with two planes of consciousness: the physical and the spiritual. On the physical plane, emotion at the very outset is sweet, sweeter, sweetest. Then there comes a time when this emotion is followed by frustration and frustration is followed by destruction. Why does it happen so? It happens so precisely because the emotion that is in play in the physical proper is still unlit, unillumined and impure. On the physical plane emotion is nothing short of self-exposition, either consciously or unconsciously, either under compulsion or at one's own sweet will.

There is also a kind of emotion in the spiritual plane, in our heart or psychic existence. Here the emotion is constantly self-illumining and God-fulfilling. In the spiritual world, in the inner world emotion is truth-expansion, divinity-expansion and perfection-manifestation. Naturally we can also add "God-satisfaction", for God-satisfaction can loom large only in truth-expansion and divinity-expansion and perfection-manifestation.

On the human plane there are quite a few undivine forces that attack us and eventually compel us to surrender or resort to anger, anxiety, worries, attachment, self-pity and self-immolation.

Anger: what is it, after all? Anger is a force that does not permit us to be consciously aware of our oneness-reality with others, who are our extended, expanded reality. When anger assails us we not only forget our existence-reality, our oneness-reality with others, but we try to destroy or we actually do destroy our oneness-reality.

Now, how do we conquer anger? A spiritual Master will tell us to make our mind calm and quiet and to pray and meditate on God. Then we will be able to free ourselves from the wild anger in us.

The advice of the spiritual Master is absolutely correct. But if we want to conquer anger on the spot, then the easiest and the most effective way is to repeat God's Name as fast as possible each time we breathe in. The first time we breathe in we can repeat ten times, "God, God, God." And the second time we breathe in, if inside each time we say "God" we can mentally visualise or count God's Name twenty times more, then the power of anger almost totally vanishes.

Lack of poise, lack of mental equanimity, is anger. How do we attain poise? How do we achieve mental equanimity? We achieve mental equanimity when we live not in the mind but somewhere else. And where is that place? It is in the heart.

The mind that doubts, the mind that is subject to anxiety, worries, suspicion and attachment cannot give us poise, cannot give us clarity and vision. It is the heart, the aspiring heart that has already established its constant and conscious oneness with the soul that can give us poise. And this poise that we get from the heart can easily be brought into the suspicious, doubtful, arrogant, unlit, unillumined mind. And once the poise of the heart, which is founded upon the soul's light, is brought into the human mind, which is immersed in the gross physical, the mind is bound to be illumined slowly, steadily and unerringly.

What is poise? Poise is a kind of divine emotion in us. But it is anything but excitement. This poise we get when we identify ourselves with the Infinite, the Eternal, the Immortal.

Fear is another kind of emotion which plays its role only in separating us from our vast oneness-reality. Doubt also practically does the same. When fear plays its role, we either unconsciously or consciously separate our existence from the Vastness itself. When doubt plays its role, we unconsciously shorten our own reality-existence. We minimise our consciousness, our own experience and realisation of reality.

Attachment is a form of emotion. As attachment is a form of emotion, so also is detachment a form of emotion. When there is attachment, we immediately notice that there is a constant tug-of-war between two armies.

Attachment binds us for our own gratification. Attachment makes us feel that no individual is complete. It makes us feel that only in the unification of two individuals – no matter whether it is on the physical plane, vital plane or mental plane – will the two individuals derive satisfaction. But this feeling is incorrect. The human in us is right now half-animal. The animal consciousness in us quite often plays its role most powerfully. So when two people use attachment as a magnet or pull each other, quite often destruction plays its role.

Detachment is also a form of emotion. On the outer plane we may feel there is no emotion involved. Unfortunately this conception of ours is built on air. No, detachment is also a form of emotion. Detachment is not indifference; detachment is our true existence, the existence that lives in reality proper – either in Heaven-reality or in earth-reality. Detachment is emotion, only it is not affected by the happenings, incidents and experiences of the reality that it is seeing; it is always an inch higher in consciousness. Although it may remain on the earth plane, in earth's multifarious activities, it keeps its consciousness higher than the reality where the experiences or incidents are taking place.

Although a seeker is detached, that doesn't mean he is indifferent. He sees and experiences the reality that is apt to threaten him and frighten him, the reality that quite often belittles his capacity, his potentiality and even his own existence and immortality. But the seeker does not let this affect him. He feels there is only one reality in him and that reality is God-Reality. This

God-Reality he can feel, he can experience no matter where he is, provided he knows the supreme art of focusing all his attention on one object or subject: God.

Sincerity and insincerity: these are also emotions. With sincerity we fly, fly in the vast, uncharted sky. With insincerity we enter into a tiny cave in order to escape. With sincerity we try to spread our wings and give to the world what we have and what we are. With insincerity we hide our reality-world which we claim to be only ours.

Purity and impurity. Purity is our self-expansion and impurity is our self-immolation. With each purity-breath we breathe in, we increase our God-Reality. And with each impurity-breath we breathe in, we surrender our very existence to the jaws of death.

Sincerity and purity are the two divine attributes that all the seekers can apply to their day-to-day activities. Emotion has to be disciplined sincerely in the mind proper. When the mind becomes sincere, then the mind opens itself consciously, devotedly and soulfully to the Vastness. At that time, the multiple encouraging, inspiring experiences of the world descend from above through the mind and prepare for the universal opening to the transcendental heights.

Purity is of the heart and in the heart, but for the soul. The soul is the conscious representative of God within us. The heart of purity is the heart that consciously discovers God. The heart of purity is conscious God-revelation and God-manifestation.

Ultimately all our emotions give way to tears, either to earthly tears or to heavenly tears. Earthly tears are the outcome of depression, frustration and lack of fulfilment. Heavenly tears are the tears of gratitude offered to the Source, to the Supreme Beloved, the Inner Pilot, the Eternal Friend.

We start our journey with earthly tears because this is what we get when we walk along the road of desire. But there comes a time when we discover that the road we are walking upon will never lead us to our destination. Then we change our road. We start walking along another road, the road of realisation. When we walk along this road, each day, each hour, each minute, each second we feel we are approaching our cherished destination. Here the tears that we experience are divine tears composed of our unalloyed love for God and flowing from our heart-flower of gratitude.

With earthly tears we start our journey. But this journey does not satisfy us; it cannot lead us to our destination. So we resort to heavenly tears, which come from our heart's gratitude and true love of God. When we become heavenly tears, we not only start our journey properly but also we hasten our true Truth-realisation and God-revelation which is Beauty-revelation, God-manifestation and Bliss-manifestation for earth.

Emotion that says, "I came, I saw, I conquered," is a destructive emotion, an animal emotion in us. Emotion that says, "I came, I loved, I became," is divine emotion, illumined emotion, fulfilled emotion – perfect, all-illumining, all-fulfilling emotion.

"I am for myself" is either the animal emotion in me or the human emotion in me. "I am for my Reality-Source, for my Reality-God" is a divine emotion. I see the Truth just because the Truth wants to see in and through me. I become the Truth just because the Truth reveals itself in and through me. Then I am inundated with divine emotion, which is conscious and constant love of God and awareness of God: Truth-expansion, God-manifestation and man-and-God-satisfaction.

NOTES TO REALITY-DREAM

2. *(p. 173)* Conference Room 14, 6 October 1975.
4. *(p. 178)* Chapel of the Church Center for the United Nations, 7 October 1975.
5. *(p. 179)* United Nations Development Programme – Alcoa Building, 29 October 1975.
6. *(p. 182)* Dag Hammarskjöld Library Auditorium, 30 October 1975.
7. *(p. 183)* Dag Hammarskjöld Lecture Series, Chapel of the Church Center for the United Nations, 7 November 1975.
8. *(p. 188)* Dag Hammarskjöld Lecture Series, Dag Hammarskjöld Library Auditorium, 4 December 1975.
9–13. *(p. 190)* During meetings of the United Nations Meditation Group, Sri Chinmoy gave these lectures on great men and women.
10. *(p. 191)* Room 550, 28 November 1975.
11. *(p. 193)* Room 550, 5 December 1975.
12. *(p. 194)* Room 550, 12 December 1975.
13. *(p. 197)* Peace Room, Church Center for the United Nations, 8 September 1970.
14. *(p. 202)* Dag Hammarskjöld Lecture Series, Dag Hammarskjöld Library Auditorium, 8 January 1976.
15. *(p. 203)* At a meeting of the United Nations Meditation Group in February 1976, these instructions by Sri Chinmoy on concentration, meditation and contemplation were read out. Dag Hammarskjöld Library Auditorium, 3 February 1976.
16. *(p. 205)* Peace Room, Church Center for the United Nations, January 1976.
17. *(p. 205)* Peace Room, Church Center for the United Nations, January 1976.

18. *(p. 206)* Dag Hammarskjöld Lecture Series, Dag Hammarskjöld Library Auditorium, 6 February 1976.
19. *(p. 211)* Dag Hammarskjöld Lecture Series, Dag Hammarskjöld Library Auditorium, 21 April 1976.
20. *(p. 213)* Room 550, 30 April 1976.
21. *(p. 214)* Dag Hammarskjöld Lecture Series, Dag Hammarskjöld Library Auditorium, 6 May 1976.
22. *(p. 219)* Dag Hammarskjöld Lecture Series, Dag Hammarskjöld Library Auditorium, 2 July 1976.
23. *(p. 227)* Room 550, 20 July 1976.
24. *(p. 229)* Dag Hammarskjöld Library Auditorium, 29 July 1976. On the anniversary of Dag Hammarskjöld's birth, 29 July 1976, the United Nations Meditation Group dedicated a programme to the late Secretary-General, held in the Dag Hammarskjöld Auditorium.
24,8. *(p. 229)* Excerpt from *Markings* by Dag Hammarskjöld.
24,16. *(p. 231)* Excerpt from *Markings* by Dag Hammarskjöld.
25. *(p. 232)* Dag Hammarskjöld Lecture Series, Dag Hammarskjöld Library Auditorium, 2 October 1976.

PART V

UNION-VISION

1. *United Nations Meditation Group*

> We believe and we hold that each man has the potentiality of reaching the Ultimate Truth. We also believe that man cannot and will not remain imperfect forever. Each man is an instrument of God. When the hour strikes, each individual soul listens to the inner dictates of God. When man listens to God, his imperfections are turned into perfections, his ignorance into knowledge, his searching mind into revealing light and his uncertain reality into all-fulfilling Divinity.

I – TALKS

2. *Joy*

Joy within is always a rarity.

Joy without is almost an impossibility.

Joy in oneness with God is a constant certainty and an eternal reality.

Joy within is always a rarity. Most of us are living in the world of desire. We have no time to go deep within. There are people who feel that they do not have even one minute, one single minute out of twenty-four hours, to go deep within. Then, there are those who have the time to go deep within for a minute during the day. But when they go within for a minute during the twenty four hours, they may not get joy. Inside us is a vast field and we have to cultivate it like a farmer. We have to plough the inner field and, after we have ploughed, we have to sow the seed – the seed of our aspiration, the seed of our concern for the inner life. Then, after a few months or after a year or so, we may get a real glimpse of inner joy. Inner joy is always something rare. We think no matter how we meditate we get immediate joy. But this is not true. What we may get at times is only a kind of vital pleasure. Real joy we get only from our silent and profound meditation. In the outer life also, when we talk and mix with people, or exchange ideas with others, we may get a kind of satisfaction. But this is not real joy. It is only vital pleasure. Joy is something very deep, illumining and fulfilling.

When I say joy is always a rarity in the inner life, it means first of all that we are not crying for this inner joy. Once a day we don't have the time to go deep within even for a minute. And even if we do go deep within for a minute or two, we have to know that one has to meditate for hours, for months, for years in order to get real inner joy. If one tastes this inner joy even once, one is immediately transported into Heaven for a while. When one has real inner joy, one sees that Heaven is all around him. He is in Heaven or he has become Heaven itself. This is inner joy.

In Sanskrit we use the term *amrita,* which means "nectar". The gods drink this nectar and that is why they are immortal. When we go deep within, we also drink this divine nectar. When we drink this nectar just for a fleeting second, we feel that our consciousness is immortalised. But it is a very rare thing. Seekers don't get this amrita unless they are on the verge of realisation. Swamis, even yogis who are not absolutely realised or not of the highest calibre, may drink this nectar only once in their lifetime. Others say, "Oh, when you go deep within, you get tremendous joy." But real joy, amrita, is something else. This joy is pure. On those very rare occasions when we get real inner joy even for a fleeting second, it immediately expands our consciousness and makes us feel that we are really divine, that expansion is our birthright, liberation is our birthright.

In the outer world, what gives us joy is the fulfilment of desire. This moment I have a desire to have one house. Then, when God grants my desire, immediately I become a victim to the desire to have two houses. And when God grants this, the next moment I become a victim to still more desires. In the outer life we want only to grab – from one car to two cars, from one dollar to two dollars. All the time we are trying to increase our possessions. Each time a desire is fulfilled in the outer life, we become victims to a greater and more destructive desire, because in desire itself there is no end. A fulfilled desire gives us pleasure for a second, but the next moment another desire comes with tenfold power and puts us into the frying pan again. In the life of desire we are never satisfied.

The very nature of desire is to possess. If desire sees a flower, it will try to possess it. If desire sees something beautiful, immediately it wants to grab it, and the ultimate result is that the beautiful thing is destroyed. Even when we see some spiritual person with light, we try to possess that spiritual person with our desire. We don't want that spiritual person to act in the divine way with his inner light, with his inner joy, with his inner compassion. No, we want to possess him and try to regulate his outer life and inner life.

The difference between man and God is this: man is possessed by his little possessions and God is released by His infinite possessions.

When we remain in the outer world, we are taking conscious or unconscious part in the game of desire. Each moment we are opening ourselves to desire. Desire, the thief, is entering into our heart to steal away our faith in God, our love for God, our concern for God, our dedication to God, our surrender to God. When our own will is one with desire, it eventually ends in destruction. But when our will becomes one with our aspiration – which is desire purified and transformed, desire which has gone through a fire-pure change – at that time we can sit at the Feet of God. When we sit at the Feet of God and become one with God, our own will is one with God's Will. What is God's Will? God's Will is His Concern for humanity, His Love for humanity, His inner Cry for the perfection of humanity. When we establish our oneness with God's Will, we enter into a constant flow of joy. There we see that God the creator, God the creation and God the reality are all one.

When we have established our oneness with God's Will we get joy, but humanity as a whole is still separated from God's Will. Every person wants something different. God has created millions and millions of people, and each one has a new idea, a new aim, a new ideal. When all the ideas and ideals become one and are still given the opportunity to flourish, to fulfil themselves in multiple form, then, too, we will get joy. The

UNION-VISION

highest joy comes from oneness with God. When humanity as a whole enters into this oneness of God, we will feel that the multiplicity of God is also getting the same joy as the unity of God. We do not lose our joy if we also realise our oneness with God's creation. The joy of multiplicity and the joy of unity we must have. When we become one with humanity and go to God together, then we get the joy of multiplicity. And when we go directly to God alone, then we get the joy of unity. Again, from unity, if we want to come to God's infinite multiplicity, we also get true joy. Either by taking everyone to God with us or by going to God alone and then bringing God to the rest of humanity, we get this boundless inner and outer joy.

Right now the outer life and the inner life are like the North Pole and the South Pole. They will never meet together. The inner life has more light than the outer life, but this light is not enough to satisfy us. Right now the inner life is not strong enough to transform the outer life, which is like a stubborn child or even like a mad elephant. In spite of knowing that the inner life has more light, the outer life does not surrender to it. The outer life does not want to abide by the dictates of the inner life; it does not even want to co-operate with the inner life. The inner life has almost unlimited light and joy and the outer life has practically none. But a day will come when we *can* get joy from the outer life. When the inner life and the outer life have become one and are ready to be consciously dedicated at the Feet of God, at that time we will find joy within, joy without.

The outer life and the inner life have to become one. They have to feel the necessity of their oneness with God. The younger brother is the outer life and the elder brother is the inner life, because inside the inner life is the soul. If the inner life listens to the dictates of the soul and the outer life listens to the dictates of the inner life, then the inner life and the outer life will go together. At that time we will have abiding joy, everlasting joy, here on earth and there in Heaven – here in our outer life, which will be totally transformed, and there in our inner life, which will be constantly aspiring to be one with the infinite and ever-transcending Joy of God.

3. *Confidence*

We are all God's chosen children. God has perfect faith in us. Let us try to have an iota of divine confidence in ourselves.

If we want to have confidence, we have to be true to ourselves. If we want to hear from God that we are good, great and divine, then we must always be true to ourselves.

Temptation, depression, frustration and destruction go together. Man's confidence and God's acceptance go together. Man's confidence is man's joy and God's divine Pride.

Confidence is growth. It is the flowering of our human aspiration and divine liberation. Aspiration is what man has and offers to God. Liberation is what God eternally is, and He offers Himself to mankind. He scatters liberation all around us.

Confidence is the illumining conscience deep within us and our fulfilling inheritance.

God says to man, "My son, I have all confidence in you because you are of Me." Man says to God, "Father, I have full confidence in myself because You are for me."

God says to man, "My son, I have all confidence in you because you want the Truth and the Truth alone." Man says to God, "Father, I have full confidence in myself because I know that You are not only *the* Truth but You are also *my* Truth."

God says to man, "My son, I have all confidence in you because of our present divine conversation." Man says to God, "Father, Father, Father, I have full confidence in myself because of Your present and eternal Compassion for me.

4. A living shrine

I see a few new seekers today. I wish to tell all the new seekers that your presence definitely adds to our aspiration.

We are the most fortunate people on earth, for God has chosen us to be His instruments to serve Him in mankind. Please try to feel that the United Nations is not a mere building, but a place of worship, a place where all human beings can worship and pray to God. This place is a living shrine for the Supreme.

If we do not do what we are expected to do now, if we do not offer our soulful meditation and soulful dedication now, in days to come we shall feel sorry. But if we do the right thing now, in the near or distant future the Supreme will entrust us with higher tasks. Each time we do something for Him, He is pleased with us and He gives us the responsibility to do something higher and more fulfilling in His cosmic Game.

God is pleased with us if we try every day, every hour of our inner and outer existence at the United Nations to be soulful and self-giving. If we are soulful and self-giving, then our Goal can never remain a far cry. On the contrary, instead of seeing ourselves running alone towards the Goal, we shall see that our Goal is also running towards us.

Run always very fast. In the month of March let us try to run the fastest towards our destined Goal.

5. Invitation to meditate

Dear seekers, every Friday we meditate in one of the conference rooms here, and offer our aspiration to the soul of the United Nations. I wish to invite the United Nations members who are present today to come and meditate with us. This meditation is not only for the United Nations but for the world at large.

This meditation is for the God-lover and the man-lover. If we really love God, and if we really love mankind and consciously believe that we are responsible for mankind, then we feel that our aspiration and dedication to the soul of the United Nations and our Inner Pilot is of paramount importance.

Please feel that it is your own aspiration that will expedite the vision for the United Nations. And when the vision is transformed into reality, the Inner Pilot will know our contribution whether or not the world ever recognises it. Our contribution, which is our aspiration, cannot be measured by money-power or any kind of world-power. It can be measured only by God's Love-Power, His Concern-Power, His Confidence-Power.

6. *Can meditation enhance leadership?*

Can meditation enhance leadership? The answer is in the affirmative. Meditation can and does enhance leadership. But we have to know what we mean by meditation. If meditation means a secluded life, if meditation means only an individual triumph over oneself, this type of meditation can never enhance leadership. If meditation means that I exist only for myself, if it means that my own self-mastery is my only goal and that I alone am important on earth, then leadership cannot be enhanced, for there is no necessity of leadership. If meditation means a secluded life, a life of individuality, then the necessity for leadership does not and cannot arise at all. If I alone exist on earth, who am I to lead? I am all in all. Only when there are two persons is leadership necessary or important. Either I take the lead or somebody else takes the lead.

But if meditation means an expansion of our consciousness, if meditation means that we are of all and for all – that we are of our inner divinity and for aspiring humanity – then our qualities of leadership are bound to increase. If we take leadership as something qualitative, then we have to feel that the light of meditation will make the quality go from bright to brighter and from brighter to brightest. If we take leadership as something quantitative, then we can say that the light of meditation will enable us to transform much into more and more into most.

When we encounter leadership, immediately the physical in us surrenders because it is perfectly aware of its teeming limitations. It knows how weak and frail it is, how insignificant its capacity is. But the vital in us immediately sees leadership as a kind of challenge either from the inner world or from the outer world. After accepting the challenge, the vital wants to conquer and dominate the world around it. The vital immediately wants to dominate others and kick the world around like a football for its own pleasure. This kind of leadership our vital enjoys.

Mental leadership is somewhat different. In mental leadership we notice that the world around us is all imperfection and we feel that only our own mental world is perfect. You as an individual feel that you are perfect, but that the world around you is imperfect. He feels that he is perfect, while the rest of the world is all imperfection. Since he feels that he is perfect and everybody else is imperfect, he accepts his self-styled leadership to perfect us. God has not entrusted him with leadership. As long as he sees only imperfection around him and feels that his being alone is flooded with perfection and light, then he is not the right instrument to lead others.

There is another type of leadership. We call it psychic leadership, the leadership of the heart. This leadership is totally different from the vital and mental leadership. Psychic leadership is founded upon the heart's inner awareness and oneness with reality as a whole. Whoever leads in the heart is a real leader. This is not the leadership of a self-styled leader. This leadership is the recognition of one's inseparable oneness with the rest of humanity. The one is for the many and the many are for the one. When we think of ourselves as the one, we feel that the many are our branches, leaves, fruits and flowers. When we think of ourselves as the many, immediately we, as the branches, leaves, fruits and flowers, feel that we are the trunk. Here oneness, real oneness, makes us feel that all are equally responsible for embodying the highest Truth, revealing the highest Truth and manifesting the highest Truth.

Meditation is a dynamic active power; it is movement. Movement itself is progress. Movement itself is the growth and expansion of our reality. Whenever we meditate, no matter what plane of consciousness we are on, at that time we are moving towards some destination which we are bound to reach. While progressing towards the destination, this movement increases its potentiality, its capacity, its reality, its vision, its identity with its Source. And once it reaches the Source, all its capacities increase in boundless measure.

In the outer world, a leader is he who has more capacity than some other individual or two other individuals or many other individuals. If his capacity far surpasses theirs, then he becomes the leader. But in the spiritual life it is not like that. In the spiritual life, real leadership depends on one's awareness of reality and one's conscious and constant acceptance of this reality as one's very own. If one can accept the reality around him as his very own despite all its imperfection, limitation and bondage, then he is the real leader – and not he who has a little more capacity than another individual or the rest of the group. He who claims his brothers and sisters as his very own, he who accepts the challenge of ignorance and who stands in front of ignorance-night determined to conquer it and transform it into the flood of Light – he is the real leader. In the spiritual life, leadership means our conscious wish to be a chosen instrument of the Supreme. The moment we become His chosen instrument, we feel that we have become real leaders. A divine instrument is he who has the capacity to lead and guide humanity.

According to Indian scripture, when a devotee worships the cosmic gods and goddesses, the capacity of the gods and goddesses increases. You may ask how this can be. The cosmic gods and goddesses already have tremendous Peace, Light and Bliss. Just from the worship of a devotee, how can these qualities increase? It is like saying that if you stand in front of the ocean and worship the ocean, immediately the length and breadth of the ocean will increase. Your physical mind will immediately laugh at the idea, but the Indian scriptures were not an inch away from the truth.

What actually increases in the cosmic gods and goddesses when they are worshipped is their conscious awareness of humanity's need for them. When the gods feel that they are consciously needed by humanity as a whole, then they feel that they have a task to perform on earth. They think, "The children of earth need us. Let us help them, let us guide them, let us mould them, let us shape them into divine beings." When the cosmic gods and goddesses feel earth's need, immediately they shower their choicest blessings on earth. The satisfaction that dawns in them because of earth's need is the increase of their capacity. Previously earth did not need them, humanity did not need them; so their capacities were kept dormant. But when they are pleased and satisfied with humanity, they deliberately bring forward and increase all their capacities.

We are spiritual people; we need Peace, Light and Bliss in abundant measure. That is why we invoke the presence of the cosmic gods. But there are people who want the divine help in order to achieve something which will not be a creative force but a destructive force. Indian mythology offers us hundreds of stories about seekers who meditate for years and years and, at the end of their journey's close, when their chosen deity is satisfied and agrees to grant them a boon, they ask for something destructive. One very well-known story is about a devotee of Lord Shiva who meditated for years and years to satisfy Lord Shiva. Then the boon he asked for was this: that any person whose head he touched would immediately be burned to ashes. When Shiva granted him this boon, he wanted to test it on Shiva's head. But Shiva ran away and took shelter with Vishnu, and Vishnu's clever wisdom saved Shiva. Vishnu said to the aspirant, "You are a fool. Why have you to chase Shiva in order to know whether the boon is genuine. You could easily place your hand on your own head and see its efficacy." The foolish aspirant did this and was destroyed.

What do we learn from this story? When we want something undivine or destructive, God may give it to us; but there is a divine force which is infinitely more powerful than our undivine force, and this will come to God's aid. If the ignorance in us wants something and cries for it, the boon may be granted; but if God does not fulfil our ignorance-prayer, it is a real blessing. And when He does fulfil our ignorance-prayer in order to give us an experience, then we have to know that this experience is necessary so that later we will cry for real Truth and Light. After giving us the necessary experience of ignorance, God will try to pull us towards His Height. At that time He does not actually destroy the capacity of our prayer; He only shows us that the capacity of our prayer should be directed towards some reality which is divine and immortal.

In India, when thieves enter into the temple to commit a theft, first they pray to Mother Kali that they will not be caught red-handed. Mother Kali may listen to them a few times, but after a while they are caught. When they pray, Mother Kali says, "All right, you want a life of ignorance; I will fulfil your ignorance." But there comes a time when her higher wisdom, which is compassion, starts to operate. She wants these desire-bound souls to be liberated from ignorance, so she exposes them to earthly justice.

If we want to achieve leadership through the fulfilment of ignorance, God grants us that boon. But when we have the inner cry, God immediately removes from us the leadership which is based on ignorance, and He kindles the flame of aspiration in us so that we can become endowed with divine leadership and be the torch-bearers of His Light and Truth.

On the physical plane we have a human body. When the physical in us listens to the inner voice or has a free access to the inner being, even the physical can become a real leader. One striking instance I can tell you. All of you know about India's great political leader, the father of the Indian renaissance, Mahatma Gandhi. His physical frame was very frail and weak, but his physical frame embodied inner light in abundant measure. His mental capacity was not on the same level with that of Nehru and others, but his soul's light guided India's fate and the leaders who were mental giants sat at his feet. Why? Just because he saw a higher light, a higher truth, which he wanted to express through his philosophy of *ahimsa,* or non-violence. Ahimsa does not mean that one will not strike someone or fight with someone. Gandhi's non-violence was the vision of universal and transcendental Light in humanity. This is the vision that he had and embodied and wanted to reveal. That is why he became India's unparalleled and supreme leader. A real leader is he who has inner light in boundless measure; it is he who represents the soul inside the physical, outside the physical and everywhere. He who wants to convey the message of the soul is the real leader.

It is said that a poet is born, not made. There is much truth in this. But I have seen that by the grace of spiritual Masters, or by the grace of inner awakening, many people have become poets. I am using the word in its largest sense – as an artist in any plane of consciousness or in any form of art. If one has not brought with him at birth a particular capacity, that does not mean that he will not be able to acquire or develop that capacity in this lifetime. One can! If one has not come into the world with a quality of leadership, it does not mean that that person will never have leadership in this incarnation. No! If one accepts the spiritual life, it means one is beginning a new life. If one has an inner guide, a spiritual Master, he enters into a new life and is awakened to the highest Truth. A new life means a new hope, a new promise, a new prophesy, a new dream which is about to be blossomed into reality. This new life is bound to offer the seeker what he wants, whether it be leadership or anything else.

So an individual can become a divine instrument even though he did not bring down on his own the capacity to be a divine instrument. To become a chosen instrument of God is to become a divine leader, a supreme leader. This can be done by mutual acceptance. If light accepts darkness as its very own, and if night accepts light as its very own – that is to say, if the higher part in us is accepted by the lower part and vice versa – only then can the light act in and through the darkness which needs guidance and constant assurance. If he who needs and he who has can consciously become one, then one sees through the other. The lowest needs the highest for its realisation. The highest needs the lowest for its manifestation.

Divine leadership either one has or one is going to have. It is not the sole monopoly of any individual. It is granted to all. But each individual has to be aware that this capacity and reality abide in him. He has to exercise his inner capacity; he has to feel the need of this reality. Then automatically, spontaneously, divine leadership comes forward and increases in boundless measure. This leadership must come to the fore. How does it come to the fore? When one consciously and constantly feels that he is of one Source and he is for all mankind. This moment he is the Creator; the next moment he is the creation. When he thinks of himself as the Creator, he is one. When he thinks of himself as the creation, he is many. He has to see and become the Dream; he has to see and become the Reality; and finally he has to see the Dream and the Reality in his being as one, each complementing the other. Dream we need to fly in the sky of the ever-transcending Beyond. Reality we need to manifest the transcendental Height and to give value to the universality in and around us. The song of the Transcendental we sing through our Dream. The song of the Universal we sing through our Reality. Both Transcendental and Universal, both Dream and Reality, make us whole, complete and perfect.

7. The past, the present and the future

The past is important. The future is more important. The present is most important. The present is infinitely more important than the past and the future put together.

The past is a promise, an unfulfilled promise. The future is a hope, an uncertain hope. The present is necessity's reality and reality's necessity. The present is the eternal Now. The "eternal" is God the Name. The "Now" is God the Form. When God the Form enters into God the Name, God the Form becomes the transcendental Vision. When God the Name enters into God the Form, God the Name becomes the universal Reality.

Transcendence and universality, Vision and Reality, are inseparable and invaluable. When we want to become members of the world of Vision-Dream, transcendence is invaluable. When we want to become members of the world of Reality-manifestation, immanence is invaluable. Transcendence is the seed. Immanence is the fruit. A seed is no seed if it does not reveal the fruit. A fruit is no fruit if it does not embody the seed. So the seed and the fruit are at once inseparable and invaluable. In Heaven we are all seeds of God's Dream. On earth we are all fruits of God's Reality.

8. *The United Nations and world union*

The United Nations is the seed. World union is the fruit. Both are equally important; both are of supreme importance. God-Vision embodies the seed. God-Reality reveals the fruit.

The United Nations is the morning. World union is the day. When the heart of the morning is flooded with inner light, divine light, the Light of God, then it is not only possible but almost certain that the entire day will be flooded with light. On very, very rare occasions we see otherwise. But most of the time morning shows the day.

The United Nations tells us where truth is. World union tells us what truth is. Where is truth? Truth is in self-giving. What is truth? Truth is man's transformation of his earth-bound nature.

The United Nations is a group of pilgrims on a journey. As the pilgrims walk along the path of light towards the same destination, they feel mutual appreciation. From appreciation they go one step ahead to love. From appreciation comes love and from love comes oneness. Oneness is the perfection of man in God and the satisfaction of God in man. He who is a true member of the United Nations treasures a shared life in a shared world.

A divided mind and a separated heart cannot quench the inner thirst either of the United Nations or of the world. We must cultivate a new type of reality, a new type of truth. This truth is creative, illumining and fulfilling. This truth must awaken the dormant physical in us, marshal the unruly vital in us, illumine the doubtful and suspicious mind in us and strengthen and immortalise the insecure heart in us. This truth is world union.

Each individual must dive deep within and discover his pent-up reservoir of dynamic energy. This energy has to be released so that the human mind can enter into the universal Mind, so that the human heart can enter into the eternal Heart and so that the human life can enter into the Life immortal.

Both the United Nations and the world have a special type of faith. This faith is evolutionary. It evolves from within to without, it evolves from unity to multiplicity and it evolves from multiplicity into the transcendental Reality.

The United Nations and world union have an evolutionary faith and a revolutionary life. This revolutionary life wants to challenge the untold poverty and teeming ignorance of the world. The golden day is bound to dawn when this world of ours will be totally freed from poverty. But the outer poverty can be transformed only when the inner poverty is removed. Inner poverty is our lack of faith in our divine reality, our lack of faith in our capacity to realise the ultimate Truth. Unless and until we have put an end to our inner poverty, the problem of the outer poverty cannot be solved.

Inner poverty is disharmony and restlessness; inner plenitude is peace, harmony and love. For the lover of the United Nations and world union, the watchword must needs always be peace. Peace is found in self-giving and in our recognition of others' good and divine qualities. The more we see the divine qualities in others, the sooner we will establish world peace.

Each nation has the strength and will-power of the Absolute. Each nation has the golden opportunity in the inner world to offer to the outer world a living hope and a living promise. This hope and this promise are not a mental hallucination or a false aggrandisement of ego. They are an inner reality that the nation can easily bring to the fore. In the inner world all the nations are equally important, for in the inner world each nation has a free access to world peace, world light, world harmony and world perfection. But in the outer life the nations that consciously aspire and cry for light are in a position to help the less advanced nations that are walking behind.

In the evolutionary process of human life, the first rung of the ladder is the United Nations, the second rung is world union and the third rung is man's total and perfect Perfection. But if we do not place our foot on the first rung and then on the second, it will be simply impossible for us to climb up to the Highest.

Each nation is a promise of God for God Himself. What we call world union today has to be surpassed tomorrow by something else, and that something else is world perfection. Union as such is not enough; the perfection of union is what we actually want. We may stay in a family even if we quarrel, fight and kill one another. But only if we can establish the sweetest feeling of oneness, does our union reach the acme of perfection.

9. *Simplicity, sincerity and purity*

I wish to give a very short talk on simplicity, sincerity and purity. All we need is simplicity. A child is simple; therefore everybody loves the child. All we need is sincerity. A child is sincere; therefore everybody loves the child. All we need is purity. A child is pure; therefore everybody loves the child.

Simplicity, sincerity and purity. On the one hand, these three things we are able to use at any moment in our day-to-day life. On the other hand, they are the most difficult things that we have to achieve. It takes only a few seconds to spell "simplicity", "sincerity" and "purity". Again, these are not mere words. These are not mere ideas or conceptions. They represent three illumining and fulfilling worlds: a world of simplicity, a world of sincerity and a world of purity.

UNION-VISION

Each individual on earth is running towards his destination. If the runner is simple, he will wear only the basic garments that are necessary. He will not wear something very heavy or expensive to draw the attention of the spectators. If the runner is sincere, then he will run in his own lane. He will not enter into the lanes of others and thus disturb them and create confusion in them. If the runner is pure, then in silence he will conquer the spectators' hearts. So by being simple, sincere and pure he will run the fastest. Not only will he run the fastest, but while he is running there will come a time when he will feel that the goal itself has been within his easy reach right from the beginning.

Each time an individual becomes simple, he feels an extra amount of peace and joy inside his restless mind. Each time an individual is sincere, he feels that he has gained a considerable portion of the world, of the length and breadth of the world. And each time an individual is pure, he feels that the whole world is not only *in* him but also *for* him.

Each human being – no matter how old he is, how mature he is, how developed he is, how intelligent he is – if he wants to have an iota of peace, abiding peace, then he must needs have simplicity, sincerity and purity. These are the three things that are most essential in each individual life and in the collective life.

There are people who are of the opinion that simplicity is almost tantamount to stupidity. A child is simple, yet inside the child's simplicity some people are apt to see stupidity. But I wish to say that simplicity and stupidity are like North Pole and South Pole. One can be as simple as a child and, at the same time, one can have boundless knowledge, light and wisdom. The great philosopher Socrates is a striking example. He was at once simplicity and wisdom. And, in his case, we can see something more. He was not only a man of simplicity, but also a man of inner sincerity and inner purity.

It happened once that a friend of his invited a palmist to read Socrates' palm. While examining Socrates' hand the palmist said, "I have never seen such a bad man! He is full of such undivine qualities. This man has impurity flowing through him like anything."

Socrates' friend became furious and said, "It can never be!" But Socrates replied, "Wait, my friend. I am sure the palmist has something more to say." The palmist said, "Yes, I have something more to say. All these undivine things that I am seeing are under his perfect control. The evil forces that I noticed have not manifested and will not be able to manifest in and through him. Socrates has the wisdom-power to keep them under perfect control like an animal that is tamed by the master."

Each human being wants satisfaction. Satisfaction in life can come only by acquiring some knowledge, more knowledge, abundant knowledge, infinite knowledge. In order to achieve infinite knowledge, we have to become students. Socrates, a great philosopher, a man of boundless wisdom, said, "I would like to become an eternal student." A child is a student. A child's life is the life of a student. A child feels at every moment that he has something new to learn and to become. A child grows; he opens his heart's door to the world-knowledge. And each time he learns something he feels there is something more he has to learn. A new sun has to dawn in his life.

All those who are working at the United Nations or working for the United Nations are serving the United Nations individually and collectively according to their capacities. But if we want to increase this capacity, either in the physical world, the vital world, the mental world or the psychic world, then we all have to feel that we are students, that we are children.

The United Nations is at once the body and the soul of God's unique Vision. Those of us who serve the body and the soul of God's Vision will be blessed divinely, supremely, unreservedly and infinitely – but only when we feel the necessity of seeing in ourselves a child's heart, feeling in ourselves a child's life. The dreamer in us is a child. He dreams of God's infinite Peace, Light and Bliss. And today's dream-life of his will tomorrow grow into reality-experience and reality-satisfaction.

The more we feel the necessity of simplicity, sincerity and purity, the more we become perfect instruments – not only of the nations that we represent, but also of the Almighty, whom we represent here on earth. Let us become simple. Let us become sincere. Let us become pure. If we can become simple, sincere and pure, then not only will the dreams that we treasure for our own countries soon be fulfilled, but also all the dreams that the Almighty has for His own Manifestation will be manifested in and through us. Not only our dreams for our own countries, but also the dreams for Manifestation that God has, in and through us will be manifested. At that time we shall grow into His Reality-Satisfaction and Reality-Perfection.

Simplicity, sincerity, purity: right now they are our most faithful, devoted instruments which will help us reach the ultimate Goal. There will come a day when we see that the Goal of the transcendental Heights is smiling in and through these three faithful and devoted friends of ours. And in this transcendental Smile we will see and feel that we are not mere mortals subjected to ignorance-life, but rather we are part and parcel of Infinity's Light, Eternity's Love and Immortality's all-embracing, all-illumining and all-fulfilling Oneness.

10. *The chosen instrument of God*

U Thant was a chosen instrument of God. U Thant was a chosen instrument of man.

God gave him His Compassion-sky to offer to man. Man gave him his suffering-sea to offer to God.

U Thant started his earthly sojourn as a Rangoon, Burma Buddha-son. The Absolute Supreme gradually made him into a universal Wisdom-son and a universal Blessing-gift.

To us, peace is something that belongs in a dream-land. Since it belongs to dream-land we talk about it. To U Thant, peace is something that belongs to the reality-world. Therefore he lived in the reality-world of peace and was a solid and treasured member of the reality-peace-world.

To us, oneness is something that we seem to want but do not actually feel the need for. To U Thant, oneness was something of constant need, something indispensable. His heart cried for this oneness and the Lord Supreme, the Author of all good, fulfilled his heart's burning desire.

The United Nations gave U Thant the opportunity to speak to the world-body as a supreme leader of mankind. In return, U Thant gave to the United Nations the message of the world-mind-illumination, of the world-heart-perfection and of the world-life-satisfaction.

U Thant was the supreme choice of the United Nations, and God was pleased. But God wanted U Thant to please Him more. Therefore, he made U Thant a pioneer voice of light from the higher worlds.

Simplicity, purity and integrity he was. He was a child's simplicity. He was a saint's purity. He was a God-lover's integrity.

He struggled calmly. He suffered ceaselessly. He hoped sleeplessly. Again, he knew how to dream of success. He knew how to become the river of progress.

We feel that man is bad, imperfect and undivine. His conviction was that man is good, perfect and divine, for that is what each individual in the inner world eternally is.

U Thant's life of humility was the result of his heart's nobility. His heart of nobility was the result of his soul's unparalleled divinity.

Sincerity spoke through him, integrity breathed in him, spirituality walked with him. He knew the world-problem: ignorance. He knew the world-answer: meditation, and this he practised in silence.

God practised His silence-meditation in and through U Thant. God practised His sound-dedication in and through U Thant.

U Thant was at once God-Humility and man-dignity. He was at once man-frustration and God-Illumination. He was at once the soulful son of God and the faithful slave of man.

Self-demonstration he ruthlessly shunned. Self-perfection he practised. God-Perfection he sought to embrace and treasure. Before him the United Nations was great, divinely great. With him, after him, the United Nations has become supremely good.

In the inner world he was God's Promise, God's Promise to the outer world. In the outer world he was man's confidence, man's confidence in becoming a dedicated instrument of the inner world.

Earth gave him the responsibility. Heaven knew it and saw it. Heaven gave him the authority but, unfortunately, earth did not know it or did not care to know it. His heart of brotherhood was misunderstood. His life of sacrifice was not valued. But his vision of oneness-goal will eternally be pursued by aspiring humanity.

An Asian seed he was. A world-fruit he has become and forever and forever he shall remain.

11. The New Year, 1975

Today we are holding a special meeting to commemorate the arrival of the new year. Each new year is an important chapter in our book of life. We know that if a book has seven chapters, all seven chapters will not be of the same importance. Similarly, although every year has great importance, one year may be more important than another year.

The New Year's Message

The year 1975 will be the year of the seeker's outer success and inner progress. With his outer success, he will love and serve the Supreme Pilot. With his inner progress, he will manifest and fulfil the Supreme Pilot.

This year is a most significant year, for it will affect both the inner life and the outer life at the same time. There have been years when we have noticed outer success without inner progress. Again, there have been quite a few years when we have experienced inner progress but no outer success. The success we are referring to is not the success of an unaspiring human being, not the success of an earthbound man who wants to achieve success by hook or by crook. Our success is not of that type. Ours is the outer success that is the manifestation of our inner progress.

Inner progress and outer success we shall observe simultaneously this year in our life of aspiration and dedication. Aspiration symbolises our inner progress and dedication symbolises our outer success. We need inner progress for the full realisation of the aspiring immortality within us. We need outer success for the full manifestation of the Divinity within us.

When we think of our outer success, we have to know that success means offering to the Lord Supreme what we have: love, concern and the feeling of universal oneness. When we think of our inner progress, we have to realise that inner progress means our constant, conscious, glowing and undying gratitude to the Absolute Supreme.

By offering to the Transcendental Supreme what we have, we shall achieve divine outer success. By offering to the Transcendental Supreme what we eternally are, we shall achieve ever-increasing, ever-transcending inner progress.

Here we are all sincere seekers. We are sincere according to our capacity and receptivity, but undoubtedly we are sincere. A sincere seeker makes an inner commitment to his inner Pilot. His commitment is that he shall not be satisfied unless and until he has grown into the very image of the Supreme.

We travel along the road of sincerity and humility in order to run fastest towards our goal. When we run fastest, at that time our very existence shall be an offering of unconditional surrender and all-surrendering gratitude to our inner Pilot, the Supreme.

Most of the seekers here belong to the United Nations Meditation Group. Each member must feel that it is a great honour to be part and parcel of this Meditation Group, for it is through the Meditation Group that we enter into the heart and soul of the United Nations. Inside the heart and soul of the United Nations we feel the real hunger and real thirst of bleeding, crying, desiring and aspiring humanity. Since we are all members of the Meditation Group, it is our bounden duty to be of totally dedicated, devoted inner service to the loftiest ideals of the United Nations. Each member of this Meditation Group is trying to be a real instrument of Truth, Light, Love and Peace. Each member of the United Nations Meditation Group is aspiring to serve humanity's divine cause and longing for the fulfilment of humanity's divine cause.

The League of Nations was a tiny plant, but now it has grown into a huge tree, the United Nations. The time will come when the whole world will take rest at the foot of this tree – this tree of patience, this tree of compassion, this tree of love, this tree of universal oneness. And one day we shall have to climb up the tree, pluck its most energising fruits and offer them to hungry humanity.

To each member of the United Nations Meditation Group, I offer my blessingful gratitude and pride. Especially to Sumedha do I offer my most sincere blessingful gratitude for her constant loving service to the supreme cause that we have undertaken here. Now I wish to invite the members of the Meditation Group to come up and meditate for a few minutes.

12. *Human will-power and divine will-power*

We are all seekers, and what we all need is divine will-power. What do we mean by will or will-power? Human will is an experience of the body in the material plane, in the human consciousness. Divine will is an experience of the soul in the body, vital, mind and heart.

In the hoary past, human beings used will in order to remain simple. They thought and felt that God was all simplicity; therefore, they too wanted to be simple. But in the modern day world, human beings think and feel that God is not at all simple. They think that He is complicated and difficult to understand; therefore, the modern day world looks for truth in a very complex and sophisticated manner. In the hoary past, humans wanted to realise what they eternally are. Now we try to become what we can ultimately claim as our very own.

Will is an experience. This experience we utilise to cultivate and manifest the truth in us. When we utilise the soul's will, we feel that God the Truth and God the Light are infinite and immortal. But when we utilise the will of the physical consciousness, the earth-consciousness, we feel that God is only a little better, only an inch higher, only a little more perfect than we are.

When we use the human will, we make a comparison between God's Height, Capacity and Reality and our own height, capacity and reality. But when we use the divine will, at that time we make no comparison. We know God is infinite, God is eternal, God is immortal. We also know that what God is, we inherently are. God is manifesting Himself – what He eternally is. We are trying to realise ourselves – what we eternally are. Right after our realisation, we shall also act like God; we shall also sing the song of manifestation.

The world is progressing towards a specific goal. But the seeker in us is progressing towards the highest transcendental Goal. In the course of its progress, the world has succeeded in reaching the moon, it can travel down to the bottom of the ocean. But the world does not have the capacity to cover the distance between its eyes and its nose. Our eyes are closed shut, or, even if they are open, they are unable to see the truth. The nose is the life-breath; it brings in cosmic energy, cosmic light and power. But the present-day world denies the existence of light or feels that light is far beyond its reach or that, even if it has the capacity to reach and become light, even then it will not gain satisfaction by doing so. The world feels that what it has so far received and achieved has not given it ultimate satisfaction and perfection, so why should it believe that there is something else that *can* give it ultimate perfection? But here the present-day world is making a deplorable mistake.

Will-power makes us see and feel what we are in God's Eye. In God's Eye we are more than perfect. Every conception of perfection is different. Once we attain to our ideal of perfection, we feel that we have played the game; our role is over. But in God's Eye, perfection is something constantly transcending itself, something constantly singing the song of Eternity's transcendence. God's idea of perfection constantly sings the song of self-transcendence.

Human will gave the world its prosperity and glory. The divine will shall give us what we eternally have and what we eternally are. What we eternally have is God's Concern, and what we eternally are is God's Perfection and God's Manifestation.

13. *Education*

Dear seekers, I wish to give a very short talk on education, and then I shall welcome a few spiritual questions.

From the spiritual point of view, what is education? Education is a sacred opportunity to learn and unlearn. What do we learn? We learn God-knowledge. What do we unlearn? We unlearn the teachings of ignorance-night. What is God-knowledge? God-knowledge is self-giving. And what is ignorance-night? Ignorance-night is self-binding.

Education is also a sacred opportunity to achieve. What do we achieve? At the end of our journey's close, we achieve God-perfection. And what is God-perfection? God-perfection is "I am; I eternally am; I universally am."

Education is continuous self-transcendence. This self-transcendence is not a visionary idea. It is not a chimerical mist. It is not a song for tomorrow's dawn. No! Self-transcendence is a divine reality, an all-fulfilling reality in the immediacy of today.

Education human and education divine. Human education is either an unconscious or a conscious desire to gain supremacy and autocracy. Divine education is our devoted willingness to love and serve the Divine in the human, the infinite in the finite and the Heaven-free Reality in the earth-bound reality.

Human education, even when it reaches the ultimate rung of the ladder, quite often can be partial, hurtful, aggressive, unlit, obscure, impure and undivine in the truest sense of these terms.

Divine education is spontaneous, soulful and fruitful. It is an inner urge to perfect one's outer life and bring to the fore the forgotten essence of Eternity, Infinity and Immortality within us.

Human education, at its very best, is greatness. But this greatness quite often fails to mix with goodness. Therefore, we can safely and unmistakably say that human greatness is blind to goodness. But divine education is goodness within, goodness without.

Again, we have to know that there is human goodness and divine goodness. Human goodness is charity-flower and philanthropy-fruit, which satisfies the human in us. Divine goodness is devotion-flower and surrender-fruit, which satisfies the divine in us and pleases the Inner Pilot, the Ultimate Absolute within us.

Human education always means money-power and time-power. Divine education is devoted willingness, which far transcends money-power and time-power. Divine education is something that establishes or will establish its inseparable oneness with something beyond time and space, far beyond the domain of material power, earthly possessions and earthly achievements.

As you all know, today the United Nations is observing Woman's Day. This is a most significant and most auspicious day not only for the United Nations but also for the entire world, for all of aspiring humanity. Sri Ramakrishna, the great Indian spiritual Master of Himalayan height, taught us to see each woman as the mother, the direct representative of the divine Mother.

Today our subject matter is education. It is our mother who gives us our education first and foremost. It is from her that we get not only our first lesson, but also the last transcendental lesson. When we see the light of day she tells us, "Children, look around. The earth is beautiful." As years advance upon us, our mother tells us, "Children, go deep within, dive deep within. There is something which is infinitely more beautiful than the earth." Her final teaching is this: "Children, the beauty of earth and the beauty of Heaven have only one source, and that source is God, our Eternity's beloved Supreme, who is All-Beauty."

From earth we get one kind of education; from Heaven we get another kind of education. We need education both from earth and from Heaven. Thousands of years ago the Vedic Seers offered us a lofty message. Their message was to accept both knowledge and ignorance as one and then finally to transcend both ignorance and knowledge.

> He who knows and understands knowledge and ignorance as one, through ignorance passes beyond the domain of death, through knowledge attains to an eternal Life and drinks deep the Light of Immortality.

Through earth-knowledge we make scientific discoveries and become the masters of our earth-life. Through Heaven-wisdom we learn universal love and the feeling of inseparable oneness; we become the lords of our inner existence.

Since it is Woman's Day, I wish to offer a soulful song which heralds the victory of the Divine Mother, the Mother Supreme. *Tomari hok jai* – Mother, may Thy victory be proclaimed....

14. *Tribute to Mohammed*

The world is celebrating the birthday of Mohammed, the great prophet. On behalf of the United Nations Meditation Group I wish to offer our soulful salutations to this great prophet.

Mohammed was the founder of the world religion, Islam. When he first saw the light of day, he saw the face of poverty too. Poverty dogged him and tortured him practically from the start to the finish of his earth-journey.

He prayed on Mount Hira. Illumination dawned. The angel Gabriel appeared and declared him the prophet of God. In Mohammed and with Mohammed a new and true religion-flower began to blossom. The prophet offered two courses, lower and higher. The lower course ran like this:

> The sword is the answer to the world's problem-question. Conquest is the answer to the world's difference-opinion. No compromise, no compromise. Declare war and conquer once and for all.
> If you really want to keep the world-citizens at your feet, under your feet, to grant them your own illumination in your own way, then fight, fight. Victory-dawn, satisfaction-sun are for the brave.
> O Muslims, O followers of mine, indeed, you are those dauntless soldiers of true Truth.

Mohammed's higher course ran like this:

> Abandon idolatry. Conquer the pleasure-life in yourself. Conquer the sense-world in yourself. Replace them with purity's beauty.

Yes, like other mighty prophets, Mohammed too had a world-illumining message:

There is one God and He is great. *Alahu Illah Akbar.* Worship the One, the one true God. Nothing more. Nothing less. He is everything in everything and everything of everything.

The Koran, the great voice of his good soul, was fed sumptuously and energised considerably by the lighthouse of the Old Testament. To our sorrow, the Cross and the Crescent are not good friends. Blind rivalry reigns supreme. But to our joy, one is serving the Father and illumining mankind according to its height of compassion-salvation. The other is serving Allah and illumining mankind according to its height of dedication-satisfaction.

Mohammed, O world prophet, to you we offer our soul's obeisance.

15. *An inner duty and an outer duty*

I shall be extremely glad and grateful if all the members of the Meditation Group attend the functions that quite often take place here. If you are not actively participating, please do not feel sorry; you will be given ample opportunity to participate. Your very presence is of tremendous importance. Please feel that each of you is of paramount importance. In God's Eye, you are His chosen instrument. Whenever there is any function at the United Nations, I request you most sincerely to be there unless you have something very urgent or important to do. Your presence will give the aspiring soul of the United Nations tremendous joy. It is a great opportunity that all of us here have to serve not only the body and the soul of the United Nations, but also the living breath of humanity and God's constant, glowing, dream-fulfilling Reality.

UNION-VISION

Each member of the United Nations Meditation Group has an inner duty and an outer duty. Your inner duty is to pray and meditate and your outer duty is to serve and dedicate. All of you are working at the United Nations, serving the United Nations and the world according to your capacity. But "capacity" is a very complicated word. Although we know how to spell it, although we know the dictionary meaning of it, we do not know the actual secret or true wealth of our capacity; we do not know how much we can do for the world. Our capacity goes far beyond the flight of our imagination-bird. We have been given the opportunity to serve this world-body and world-soul. For the last five years we have tried, but we could have tried more. We could have tried in a more soulful way. What we have done is nothing in comparison to what we could have done. Political history right now does not value us, and it may not value us even in the future. But there is something called spiritual history. And I wish to say that spiritual history will bear witness to what we are doing. In spiritual history, our love of light, our love of truth, our love of brotherhood, our feeling of loving oneness, will be inscribed in letters of gold.

It is not for world-recognition, but to help bring about a better world and a more fulfilling life that each of us has to do something. We have to give ourselves consciously, constantly, unreservedly and unconditionally. Let us not miss this opportunity. If we miss this opportunity, we shall miss much, for we shall have to live in a poor and blind world, as we have been living up to now. But if we consciously dedicate ourselves to the supreme cause with our aspiration, prayer, meditation and devoted service, then in us and through us will grow a better world, a more illumining world and a more fulfilling world.

16. *Silence*

Silence, silence.
    Silence is our aspiration-plant.
    Silence is our realisation-tree.

    Silence, silence.
Silence transcends our mind-seed.
Silence transcends our thought-fruit.

    Silence, silence.
On earth, silence speaks most eloquently. In Heaven, silence acts most powerfully. In God, silence lives most fruitfully.
    Silence is the illumination of our earth-bound greatness. Silence is the illumination of our Heaven-free goodness.

    Silence, silence.
Silence is the world-teacher yet unappreciated. Silence is the world-student yet unrecognised.

    Silence, silence.
Silence is at once the beauty of the universal creation and the duty of the transcendental Creator.

    Silence, silence.
Silence is man's ascendence in God, for God. Silence is God's transcendence in man, for man.

II — SPIRITUAL WORDS

17. *Spiritual words*

Sri Chinmoy: I wish to invite each seeker to give me a spiritual word, and I shall say a few words on that particular word or concept. I shall be extremely happy and grateful if you would offer me one spiritual word. Please meditate for a minute and then we shall start.

18. *Sincerity*

> A human being
> Does not know
> What sincerity is.
>
> A divine being
> Does not know
> Anything else save
> And
> Except sincerity.

19. *Intensity*

Concentration
Is
Intensity-power.

Meditation
Is
Immensity-power.

Contemplation
Is
Earth's,
Heaven's
And
God's
Utility-power.

20. *Love*

Human love
Tells the world
What it can do for the world,
Although
It does not do it.

Divine love
Tells the world
That it is crying to be accepted
As a real friend
By the world of suffering,
The world of misunderstanding
And
The world of constant miseries,
Frustrations, trials and tribulations.
Love divine
Is begging this world of ours
Only to be accepted
So that it may then serve the world.

21. *Transcendence*

> The human in us
> Ascends for success,
> Greater success
> And
> Greatest success.
>
> The divine in us
> Transcends for self-giving,
> More self-giving,
> And
> Most self-giving.

22. *Will-power*

> Will-power
> Is the light of the soul.
> This light of the soul
> Does not expose
> The darkness of millennia
> Which we embody.
> On the contrary,
> This light of the soul
> Illumines the ignorance-night
> That has captured us
> And wants to strangle us.
> This light frees us,
> This light liberates us
> From ignorance-night
> And
> Then illumines the ignorance-night
> That had enveloped us.

23. *Oneness*

Oneness with the physical world
Teaches us
How to divide,
How to separate,
How to limit
And
How to bind;
It teaches us
How to destroy the thing
That we feel is real in us,
Which is love.

Oneness with the spiritual world
And spiritual life
Shows us
How to give,
How to serve,
How to grow into
And
How to become a divine being,
The Being Supreme
Who embodies the Love of the
World Beyond.

24. *Vastness*

>Vastness
>Is
>The expansion of purity
>In the human being.
>Vastness
>Is
>The song of oneness
>In the life of the seeker.
>It is
>The life of oneness
>With the world of love
>In the life of a genuine seeker.

25. *Light*

>Where is light?
>Is it in the mind?
>Yes, it is.
>When will it come to the fore?
>Nobody knows.
>Only God knows.
>
>Where is light?
>Is it inside the heart?
>Yes, it is.
>When will it come to the fore?
>Now, right now.
>Not only does God know it,
>But we all know it.

26. Purity

Purity
In the mind
Can save the world.
Purity
In the vital
Can build the world for God's use.
Purity
In the body
Can alone create a
Kingdom of Heaven on earth.
Purity
In the heart
Is God-Perfection
In a human being.

27. Courage

With physical courage
We take pride
In breaking the world
In our own way.
With the courage of the spirit
We offer the world to God.
We place the world, our world,
At the Feet of God
So that He may guide and mould
The world, our world,
In His own Way.

28. *Harmony*

If you want to see
The world with your human eyes,
You can never see harmony.
If you want to see
The world with the eyes of the world,
You can never see harmony.
But
If you want to see the world with God's Eye,
Then you will see
That this world
Is nothing but cosmic harmony.
How do you see through God's Eye?
You see only through constant self-giving
To the Source within you.

29. *Delight*

My yesterday's experience was:
Receiving is all delight.
My today's experience is:
Giving is all delight.
My tomorrow's experience will be:
God-becoming in God's own Way
Is all delight.

30. *Compassion*

> Compassion
> Is God's Perfection
> In man
> And
> Man's total, ultimate transformation
> In God.

31. *Heart*

> A seeker's heart
> Cares neither for success
> Nor for failure.
> A seeker's heart
> Longs for the seeker's
> Constant acceptance of God
> And
> God's constant
> Unconditional experience
> In and through the seeker's life.

32. *Charity*

>Charity needs a beggar,
>But who wants to play
>The role of a beggar?
>Nobody.
>
>Oneness-necessity needs reality
>And
>Reality needs oneness-necessity.
>
>Not charity,
>But oneness-necessity
>Is reality's divinity.
>Oneness-necessity
>Is what God wants from us.

33. *Humility*

>Humility is not only
>The swiftest speed to God-destination,
>But something more.
>Humility brings God-destination
>Nearer to our starting point.

34. *Victory*

>The hour of victory strikes within me
>In my aspiring heart
>Only when I offer the reality-second
>To the hour of victory.
>The reality-second
>Which is flooded with aspiration-light
>Has to be offered
>To the hour of victory for its arrival.

35. *Affection*

>Sweet
>Is affection-plant.
>Sweeter
>Is love-tree.
>Sweetest
>Is oneness-fruit.

36. *Speed*

>My aspiration-speed
>Will carry me to God.
>My dedication-speed
>Will carry me to God.
>My surrender-speed
>Will not only bring God to me,
>But it will make God work in and through me
>In a God-illumined way.

37. *Divine Beloved*

> The human beloved
> Is a one-day wonder,
> And then it becomes boring
> And is all gone.
> It is an experience
> Of frustration-night.
> The divine Beloved
> Is He who grows in me,
> Who makes me feel that
> I am eternally of Him
> And
> I am eternally for Him.

38. *Discrimination*

> Discrimination is
> A power of illumination.
> In the mental world,
> Discrimination is the height achieved
> By the aspiring divine in us.

39. *Perfection*

Human appreciation
Of perfection
Is a short-lived proclamation.
Divine appreciation
Of perfection
Is a continuous proclamation
Of perfection
And
A continuous transcendence
Of perfection.

III — TALKS

40. *Philosophy, religion and yoga*

I wish to offer my heart's deepest gratitude to the professor of Eastern philosophy who has so kindly given me the opportunity to be of service to the students and seekers of his school. Nothing gives me greater joy, nothing has greater value in my life than to be of dedicated service to those who love the truth and who need the truth.

I wish to give a very, very short talk on philosophy, religion and Yoga.

Your professor has told me that you are studying Eastern philosophy. Here I think it will be appropriate on my part to invoke the presence of the Lord Buddha, to bring down peace, light and bliss in abundant measure. The main reason is that your teacher is, I understand, a follower of the Lord Buddha. So, with your most kind permission, I would like to recite the most soulful and fruitful chant for the followers of the Lord Buddha. [Sri Chinmoy chants:]

> *Buddham sharanam gacchami*
> *Dhammam sharanam gacchami*
> *Sangham sharanam gacchami*
>
> I go to the Buddha for refuge.
> I go to the *Dharma* for refuge.
> I go to the Order for refuge.

Philosophy sees the truth. Religion feels the Truth. Yoga becomes the Truth. God-Perfection is the Truth.

Philosophy is in the searching mind. Religion is in the loving heart. Yoga is in the aspiring entire being.

UNION-VISION

A real philosophy teacher teaches the outer world. A real religion teacher loves the inner world. A real Yoga teacher discovers his inseparable oneness with both the inner world and the outer world.

> The inner world achieves.
> The outer world reveals.
> The inner world achieves God-Height.
> The outer world reveals God-Depth.
> God-Height is soulfully beautiful.
> God-Depth is beautifully soulful.

When a seeker becomes soulfully beautiful, he embodies the cry of continuous self-transcendence. When a seeker becomes beautifully soulful, he reveals constantly the smile of self-transformation and self-perfection.

The human philosophy ignores the animal in us and belittles the human in us. The divine philosophy accepts the challenges of life, braves the buffets of life and finally, offers life a conscious awareness of the purpose of life.

Human religion is the song of the unfulfilling and unfulfilled many and the marked and isolated many. Divine religion is the dance of the liberating and liberated, fulfilling and fulfilled One in the aspiring many and of the many in the immortalising and immortal One.

The human Yoga needs God because God is great, absolutely great and because He is powerful, eternally powerful. The divine Yoga needs God because God is good, in the sound life of the finite and in the silence-life of the Infinite.

41. *The outer power and the inner power*

Each human being on earth embodies the outer power and the inner power. He is aware of his outer power when he looks without, around himself. He is conscious of his inner power when he dives deep within.

Each human being is the outer power and the inner power. When he calls himself the head and the body-consciousness, nothing more and nothing else, then he is the outer power. When he calls himself the soul, the soul-light, then he is the inner power.

The body-consciousness has light of its own. The soul-consciousness has light of its own. The body-consciousness, because of its limitations, does not see far. For the body-consciousness the future always remains a far cry. The soul-consciousness, because of its unlimited capacity, at one and the same time sees, grows into and becomes the achievements of the past, the realisations of the present and the vision-dreams of the future.

The outer power blinds the human in us. The outer power is devoured by the animal in us. The inner power clears and expands our vision; it shows our vision the way to reach the highest transcendental Goal.

The outer power is competition: conscious and constant competition. The inner power is conscious conception: conception of its own worth, its own reality and divinity. Divinity proceeds and succeeds, succeeds and proceeds. Reality eternally is. Again, in its silence-life, reality is at once the transcendental Height and the immanence-Light.

The outer power is supremacy. The inner power is accuracy: accuracy stating the fact of what it has and what it is. What it has is the source and what it is, is the manifestation of the source.

The outer power sings with imagination, dances with temptation, dies in frustration. The inner power is concentration, meditation and contemplation. Concentration accepts the challenges of life. Meditation purifies and illumines the challenges of life. Contemplation transforms the challenges of life into golden opportunities in life for the inner being, the Inner Pilot in us.

The outer power wants to strike and then immediately wants to escape. The inner power wants not only to embrace the world but also to convince the world that the world's existence and its own existence are eternally inseparable.

The outer power says to the inner power, "Look what I have. I have the capacity to destroy God's entire creation." The inner power says to the outer power, "Look what I have. I have the power to illumine God's entire creation."

The outer power is at times afraid of its own creation: the atom bomb and the hydrogen bomb. The inner power is constantly feeding its creation with love-light, concern-light and perfection-light.

The outer power feels that there is a height which has to be transcended and that if this goal is achieved, then satisfaction will dawn. The inner power feels that height and depth, the foot of the mountain and the top of the mountain, are all at one place. It sees that they are singing the song of one reality, that they are all inside the cosmic Heart in perfect union, enjoying inseparable oneness.

The outer power wants only to ascend. It is afraid of descending. The inner power wants to ascend and descend. It knows perfectly well that when it is descending, it is carrying down to earth the descending God; and when it is ascending, it is carrying up to Heaven the ascending God.

The outer power is the dance of sound. The inner power is the song of silence. The life of sound is the creation of the human in us. The life of silence is the creation of the divine in us. The human in us wants to prove its existence. It feels that unless and until it can prove its existence, the world will have no respect for us, the world will not care for us. The divine in us does not want to prove its existence for world-acceptance, world-appreciation and world-admiration. The divine in us feels that its existence is God's universal existence. God is experiencing His own ascending, descending and transcending Light in the divine in us.

The outer power is the human power. The inner power is the divine power. The outer power says, "I can do. I need no help, no assistance." The inner power says, "I can do nothing and I am nothing. At the same time, I can do everything because there is someone in me, the Inner Pilot, who will do everything for me." Furthermore, it says that the Inner Pilot has already done everything for us and that we only have to be aware of this.

When we live in the desire-world, the outer power lords it over us. The desire-world is the world of possession and frustration. When we live in the aspiration-world, the inner power illumines us and fulfils us.

The desire-world is the world without. The aspiration-world is the world within. Realisation has a free access to the inner world. And what is realisation? Realisation is the acceptance of reality as it is, reality at its present stage of evolution and reality at its ultimate height. Realisation tells us that the animal in us is for transformation, the human in us is for perfection, the divine in us is for manifestation.

42. *Aspiration*

What is aspiration? Aspiration is speed.

What is aspiration? Aspiration is the fastest speed.

What is aspiration? Aspiration is Eternity's fastest speed.

What is aspiration? Aspiration is Eternity's fastest speed-communion between man and God.

What is aspiration? Aspiration is silence-vision. It is God the Supreme Beloved's Silence-Vision.

What is aspiration? Aspiration is sound-mission. It is God the Supreme Lover's Sound-Mission.

What is aspiration? Aspiration is the crying man's duty. Aspiration is the smiling God's Beauty.

Aspiration is God's constant declaration of man's capacity. Aspiration is man's conscious necessity of God's real Reality within and without him.

Aspiration is not and cannot be the destination. Aspiration is the eternal journey. It is man's eternal journey to self-transcendence in the soul-light of perfection.

Aspiration is God's eternal journey of supreme manifestation in the satisfaction-heart of His transcendental Height, universal Length and unfathomable Depth.

With aspiration God started His journey. With aspiration He asks His children, His creation, to continue the journey.

43. *Patience*

Patience is our unrecognised capacity; patience is our unrecognised achievement. Capacity succeeds; achievement proceeds.

Physical power, vital power and mental power are no match for patience-power. When physical power is misused against someone, the patience-power of that person will eventually triumph. In the outer life and the inner life, the victim will eventually succeed.

Human power is nothing short of animal power, destructive power, if we do not aspire, if we do not long for truth, light and beauty. Patience is our soul's light. This light is always unconditional.

Here on the physical plane we notice patience in the mother and in the father. The mother's compassion-light is patience; the mother's concern-light is patience. The father's wisdom-power is patience in his son. The father's wisdom-power, his all-seeing wisdom for his son, is patience.

God created this world. In His creation vast He considers only one person as His friend: Patience. God and His Patience are inseparable.

God's creation is not complete; perfection is still a far cry. God with His infinite Patience-Light aspires in and through each creation of His. God feels that His Patience-Light is a divine, magic power that can undo the past and transform it into the golden future.

There is nothing on earth that can undo the past but patience. If we have patience we can easily undo the past. The past is a morning mist, a meaningless experience in comparison to our future realisation. The past brought us the message of suffering, sorrow, weakness, limitation, bondage and death. Again, the soul's light, which is patience, will eventually conquer delusion, illusion, temptation, limitation, everything undivine. God's Patience-Light will conquer everything in and through us.

Man needs patience in order to discover what he truly is and God needs patience in order to make man feel not only that he is God's son, God's dearest creation, but that he is exactly the same as God. Man has to realise what he eternally is: God Himself. Man is now God veiled; with patience-light man will unveil his inner divinity. Man is God yet to be consciously and constantly realised and God is man yet to be manifested totally, completely and unmistakably here on earth.

Deliberately and consciously man claims something as his own which is not actually his: ignorance. But there is only one thing that man can claim as his own: God, nothing less and nothing else. Unless and until man comes to realise this, he will never know who he is. Man is divinity's reality. This is the only thing that he has to discover: his real reality which is dormant within him.

When he is in the desire-life, each man should realise that in him there is God-seed. That God-seed is going to germinate eventually into a plant, and from a plant it will grow into a Banyan tree. Again, when the same person enters into the spiritual life, he has to feel that the fruit, the eternal fruit, is already there just for him to eat. In the desire-world he has to discover God the seed so that he can grow and grow in aspiration. In the aspiration-world he has to discover God the fruit so that he can recognise what he eternally is.

Patience is our revealing and revealed faith in God, the Supreme Pilot, and our revealed and revealing faith in our own existence. Patience is our faith in our own discovery that we are not only *of* God but also *for* God.

The human cry that climbs up from the inmost recesses of our heart makes friends with patience in order to see the smiling face of Heaven and the Eternal Pilot. Again, the Eternal Pilot makes friends with patience so that one day He can see here in humanity's cry the perfect liberation, everlasting salvation, complete illumination and total transformation of humanity.

44. *As you see yourself*

Every day, early in the morning, stand in front of the mirror. If you dare to stand in front of the mirror, then you can easily stand in front of the whole world. Now, when you stand in front of the mirror, if you see an undivine face looking back at you, then rest assured that the whole world is undivine. But if you are getting joy from your face, if it is pure and divine, then rest assured that the world is also pure and divine. According to the way you see yourself, the rest of the world will present itself to you. If you see aspiration in your face, I assure you this aspiration you are bound to notice in the whole world. If you see aggressive forces, a devouring tiger inside you, then when you leave the house a big tiger will come and devour you. We are exact prototypes of the world. We are like a microcosm and the world is the macrocosm. A saint always sees everyone in the world – even the worst possible thief – as a saint. Similarly, a thief will see even the most divine saint as a thief. We judge others according to our own standard, according to our own realisation. A thief will think a saint is a thief and a saint will think a thief is a saint. Those who have not realised God will always suspect and doubt those who have. Everyone has to judge others according to his own standard of realisation.

45. *Action*

Let us not think before we act, for each thought is a heavy burden, a heavy pressure on our shoulders. This burden and pressure weakens our life-energy considerably.

Let us silence the mind before we act. If we silence the mind, if we know the art of silencing the mind, then we can not only accomplish our tasks faster than otherwise, but we can do hundreds of things at the same time in a fleeting minute.

Let us not talk before we act, for talk does nothing but bind us to action. And I really want to add, we have to be free within and without so that with each action we can breathe in the fresh air of perfecting, perfected and perfect action.

Let us pray before we act. Each prayer is our soulful devotion, and this devotion is our self-illumining life in action.

Let us not decide before we act. Each decision will be challenged and will be devoured by hesitation. Let us act spontaneously, for each spontaneous action is the expression of our expanding consciousness, the result of our heart's preconceived ideals, the result of our life's preconceived light and the result of our soul's preconceived goal. Action is perfect when it is of God-inspiration and for God-manifestation.

Each desire-action makes us feel how weak, how ignorant, how hopeless, how helpless and how useless we are. Each aspiration-action makes us feel how strong, how powerful, how soulful, how meaningful and how fruitful we are. Again, action for action's sake is not and cannot be the right thing. Action has to be for God's sake.

Before the birth of action, inspiration is our guide. During the course of action, aspiration is our guide. At the end of action, our surrendering height and surrendered depth is our satisfaction and God's satisfaction.

Imagination tells action, "Run forward, dive deep within, fly above." Aspiration tells action, "God-Height has not to remain and cannot remain always a far cry. God-Height is our birthright; it is within us. We have only to discover it. And when we discover it, we feel that God-Height does not only belong to us but we belong to it."

Perfection-satisfaction tells us that each individual is not only a direct representative of God on earth, but God Himself in the process of making and shaping His own Vision-Reality yet unfulfilled and His own Reality-Vision yet to be fully manifested.

Each action is God's Song here on earth for God-manifestation and there in Heaven for God-satisfaction. Each action on earth is God's Dance for humanity's eternal progress and eternal self-transcendence. Each action in Heaven is God's satisfaction in divinity's self-awakening and self-illumination for a new universe; each action in Heaven is a new creation and the constant fulfilment of an ever-growing, ever-glowing, ever-satisfying and ever-satisfied God.

46. *Human art, divine art, Supreme Art*

First see it and then do it: this is human art. First feel it and then do it: this is divine art.

First see it and then draw it: this is human art. First feel it and then draw it: this is divine art. First live in the inner world with your capacity-light and then live for the outer world's necessity-life: this is supreme art.

Calculation of earth's beauty is human art. Liberation of earth's beauty is divine art. Perfection of earth's beauty is supreme art.

Human art declares, "Nothing succeeds like success." Divine art affirms, "Nothing proceeds like progress." Supreme art whispers, "Nothing satisfies like service, divine service, soulful service."

The lofty height of human art is the inspiration-moon. The sublime depth of divine art is the aspiration-sun. The illumining goal of supreme art is Eternity's perfection-day.

Beauty's possession is human art, the art of earth. Beauty's distribution is Heaven's art. Beauty's satisfaction is supreme art.

Earth's possession of beauty is earth's art. Heaven's compassion for beauty is Heaven's art. God's Perfection in beauty is supreme art.

Human art looks around while running towards the goal. Divine art looks ahead while running fast, faster, fastest towards the goal. Supreme art does not run, does not fly, does not dive; supreme art becomes what the Inner Pilot, the Supreme Artist, wants it to become.

Human art is the reality that we have, the reality that needs its expression, the reality that needs world-acceptance, world-appreciation, world-admiration, world-adoration. Divine art is the divinity that we see in the inner world and the outer world – in the world of our earthly experiences, earthly realisations, earthly sacrifices and earthly achievements. Supreme art is the divine reality that is constantly transcending its own height for God's ever-new creation, ever-new revelation, ever-new manifestation and ever-new perfection.

Human art is the leaf-experience of our life-tree. Divine art is the flower-realisation of our life-tree. Supreme art is the fruit-perfection of our life-tree.

A leaf inspires us: therefore, we run towards our destination. A flower purifies us; therefore, our speed becomes tremendous and we run fast, faster, fastest. A fruit energises us; therefore, we become chosen instruments to fight against teeming darkness and ignorance, to conquer the undivine forces within us and finally, to establish in ourselves the real, the divine, the eternal silence-life and eternal perfection-beauty.

Each creation of God has the real in it. This real reality is the soul. Now, the soul of a bench or a chair need not and cannot be as developed, as illumining, as fulfilling as the soul of an advanced seeker or a realised Master. So if we want to draw a bench or a chair, we may draw it well; but our inspiration is bound to fail us after a few minutes when we try to draw a chair, a bench or a table. But if we draw something or someone that has contributed considerably to the world of aspiration and light, then naturally our inspiration will last a long, long time. In this case, inspiration is the precursor of aspiration, aspiration is the precursor of revelation and revelation is the precursor of manifestation, which is none other than God-perfection: complete, absolute perfection.

The human artist is great, undoubtedly great. The divine artist is good, unmistakably good. The supreme artist is he who cares neither for greatness nor for goodness, who longs for only one thing: God-satisfaction, the satisfaction of God the Supreme Artist in and through him. He doesn't need greatness, he doesn't need goodness; he only longs for God-satisfaction in his life.

2. *(p. 242)* Peace Room of the Church Center for the United Nations, 28 July 1970.
3. *(p. 246)* Peace Room of the Church Center for the United Nations, Tuesday, 4 August 1970.
4. *(p. 247)* After the meditation on Friday, 1 March, Sri Chinmoy gave this address to the group (Room 550).
5. *(p. 247)* Dag Hammarskjöld Library Auditorium, 9 May 1974.
6. *(p. 248)* Dag Hammarskjöld Library Auditorium, 12 September 1974.
7. *(p. 255)* Room 550, United Nations, 20 September 1974.
8. *(p. 256)* Dag Hammarskjöld Lecture Series, Dag Hammarskjöld Library Auditorium, 18 October 1974.
9. *(p. 258)* United Nations Development Programme, Alcoa Building, 19 November 1974.
10. *(p. 262)* Dag Hammarskjöld Lecture Series, Dag Hammarskjöld Library Auditorium, 12 December 1974.
11. *(p. 264)* Dag Hammarskjöld Lecture Series, Dag Hammarskjöld Library Auditorium, 16 January 1975.
12. *(p. 266)* Room 550, 14 February 1975.
13. *(p. 268)* Dag Hammarskjöld Lecture Series, Dag Hammarskjöld Library Auditorium, 7 March 1975.
14. *(p. 271)* Chapel of the Church Center for the United Nations, 25 March 1975.
15. *(p. 272)* Room 550, 28 March 1975.
16. *(p. 274)* Chapel of the Church Center for the United Nations, Tuesday, 1 April 1975.
17–39. *(p. 275)* Room 550. On 4 April 1975, during a meeting of the United Nations Meditation Group, Sri Chinmoy invited those present to give him spiritual words, on which he then

elaborated. The resulting 22 poems have been published in the book *Beauty-Drops*.

40. *(p. 288)* Talk to Professor Ralph Buuljen's Eastern Religion and Philosophy Class from New York University, Chapel of the Church Center for the United Nations, 12 June 1976.

41. *(p. 290)* Dag Hammarskjöld Lecture Series, Dag Hammarskjöld Library Auditorium, 20 June 1975.

42. *(p. 293)* Chapel of the Church Center for the United Nations, 8 July 1975.

43. *(p. 293)* Chapel of the Church Center for the United Nations, Tuesday, 15 July 1975.

44. *(p. 296)* After the meditation in Room 550 on Friday 18 July 1975, Sri Chinmoy gave this brief talk.

45. *(p. 296)* Chapel of the Church Center for the United Nations, Tuesday, 22 July 1975.

46. *(p. 298)* Dag Hammarskjöld Lecture Series, Dag Hammarskjöld Library Auditorium, 23 July 1975.

PART VI

TWO GOD-SERVERS AND MAN-LOVERS

QUESTIONS BY MR ROBERT MULLER

1. *Mr Robert Muller: The first three of U Thant's four categories of needs, namely physical, intellectual and moral needs, do not create any insuperable problems, but the last and most important one in his view, spirituality, gives me considerable difficulties. There are indeed so many definitions of that term. U Thant described it as "Faith in oneself, the purity of one's inner self". Suppose – as I would ardently wish – that humanity would adopt some day his four broad categories of goals. How would you define the spiritual goals?*

Sri Chinmoy: The seeker in me fully agrees with our beloved brother U Thant's four categories – physical, intellectual, moral and spiritual – which are necessary for an individual to become integrally perfect. The term "spiritual" always creates problems, not only in the minds of seekers who are endowed with few spiritual potentialities but also in the minds of those who are endowed with great spiritual potentialities. Each individual must needs have a way of feeling and describing his own spirituality. To some, it is faith in oneself; to others, the purity of one's inner self; to still others, God for God's sake. Again, there will be no dearth of definitions of the term "spirituality". According to my inner conviction, spirituality is at once self-giving and God-becoming. This self-giving is not an offering to somebody else, to a third party. This self-giving is an offering to one's own higher self. This self-giving is nothing short of an act of self-uncovering. Self-uncovering is another name for self-discovering, and self-discovering blossoms into God-becoming.

Now, what is God-becoming? This question can be answered in billions and trillions of ways. Each individual will have an answer of his own in accordance with his soul's development and his life's needs. Here again, my inner conviction is that God-becoming is the soulful recovery of one's own forgotten self, one's cheerful acceptance of it and one's fruitful discovery of this realisation: "In my yesterday's life, I had; in my today's life, I am. What did I have? God the man as an aspiring seed. What have I become? Man the God as the fulfilling fruit."

2. Mr Robert Muller: I often think that U Thant's four categories of human qualities or needs – physical, intellectual, moral and spiritual – could well form the basis for a world agenda of human goals. From your writings, I notice that these categories are also quite fundamental to you, but you add to it a fifth which you call the "vital". Could you elaborate on it?

Sri Chinmoy: The existence of the vital-reality is in between the physical and intellectual. As there are physical, intellectual, moral and spiritual worlds, even so there is also a vital world. This vital world is situated between the physical and the intellectual worlds. Again, this vital world is divided into two: the human vital and the divine vital. The human vital is nothing short of aggression. It always says, "I know how to become, I know how to become." But the divine vital says, "I know how to spread, I know how to spread. And also I know what to spread, why to spread and where to spread. What to spread? My love-wings. Why to spread? Because that is the only way I can have satisfaction. How to spread? Soulfully and unreservedly. Where to spread? Where there is a need – an urgent need, a sincere need, an undying need."

When Julius Caesar said, *Veni, vidi, vici,* "I came, I saw, I conquered," it was the human vital in him that was speaking. This is the vital that enjoys satisfaction through destruction. Needless to say, this kind of satisfaction is absurd. The other way is the way of the Saviour, the Christ, who said, "Father, forgive them, for they know not what they do." Here the Christ teaches us that true satisfaction comes into existence only through oneness.

This oneness can be discovered in any plane of consciousness. On the physical plane, for example, the head is at a particular place, the arms are at another place and the legs are at a third place. But they have established their oneness, because they are all part and parcel of the body-reality. This same kind of oneness has to be discovered in the development of each individual. The divine statement of the Christ, with its fathomless magnanimity, identifies itself with the unlit reality of humanity as the Christ asks his Father for humanity's redemption. For this, what he needs is his Father's immediate Compassion and express Forgiveness.

The human vital says, "Behold, I have." And when we see what it has, we are disappointed, distraught and disgusted; we curse ourselves for our stupid action. The divine vital says, "I am, because you have made me. And I shall remain always so by offering to you consciously and constantly a portion of what I have. In this way I become my own universal self."

3. *Mr Robert Muller: When I speak to audiences about U Thant's four ways to happiness, I sometimes hear the following criticism: "Life is one and cannot be artificially cut into four. Everything is interdependent and linked. We must concentrate on life as an entity and not on components which are the product of the intellect." I am not over-impressed with this argument, for I have indeed observed that life is richest when I cultivate simultaneously all four categories of needs, namely physical, mental, moral and spiritual. Nevertheless, there is some truth in that criticism and I would be grateful to learn how you would respond to it.*

Sri Chinmoy: I am sorry to say that it is not possible for me to see eye to eye with your critic-friends. Indeed, they are right when they say that life is one, but in the same breath when they say that it cannot be artificially cut into four, I wish to ask them where they got the idea of cutting life or the life-tree into four parts. There is no necessity of artificially cutting life-reality into four; it is absurd.

Let us take life as a ladder that serves us and helps us reach the pinnacles of liberation, illumination, realisation and perfection. This life-ladder has four rungs. The first rung we unmistakably call the body-reality. The second rung is the intellect-reality; the third rung, the morality-reality, and the fourth rung, the spirituality-reality. Once we firmly step on the body-reality-rung, the body casts off the ignorance-cover of millennia. Once we ascend from that rung and step on the intellect-reality-rung, we see the vastness inside smallness and the smallness inside vastness, the infinite Beauty inside the finite duty and the finite duty inside the infinite Beauty. Then we ascend and step on the morality-reality-rung. Here we try to illumine our lower self, which consciously or unconsciously enjoys the song of division and the dance of separativity through self-indulgence and by unreservedly and deliberately embracing the earth-bound goal while ignoring the Heaven-free goal. The earth-bound goal is: "Possess and become." But to our sorrow we see that we possess only to lose; what is worse, to get totally lost. Finally we ascend to the spirituality-reality-rung and reach our Heaven-free goal. What is our Heaven-free goal? Our Heaven-free goal is: "Offer and become."

To quote your singularly momentous and apposite inner depth: "We progress physically, mentally, morally and spiritually towards a higher level of human consciousness, towards that smile of divinity which knows that someday the human race will be able to re-establish paradise on Earth. There is no longer much difference between the political approach and this broader, richer concept of human fulfilment."

I fully agree that these four approaches are not independent; they are interdependent. They are interdependent precisely because they know that they can reach their satisfaction-goal only on the strength of their becoming one, inseparably one. Interdependence is the harbinger of oneness. Human life in itself is an eternal road, eternal journey, eternal soul and eternal goal. While walking along Eternity's road, if the seeker covers some distance and then gives the distance he covered a name, and if he continues to do this, he is perfectly entitled to do so. But in the heart of his heart, he knows that it is only one road, one journey, one crying soul and one smiling goal. These four are Eternity's duty, Infinity's beauty, Divinity's necessity and Reality's immortality.

4. *Mr Robert Muller: Do you think the UN exercises a real influence in the world? What is, in your view, its principal contribution? How does it appear to you in the great stream of history and human evolution?*

Sri Chinmoy: Not only do I think, but I am positive in my soulful statement that the United Nations exercises certain influences in the world. These are the vision of peace, the mission of brotherhood, the sense of perfection in a oneness-world-family and the total satisfaction of complete oneness.

The principal contribution of the United Nations is the hope-sky that it offers to the world at large. This hope-sky is not a product of vital fantasies, mental vagaries or the idiosyncrasies of weaklings. This hope-sky is the all-illumining revelation of the United Nations soul. The seeker-servers at the United Nations – no matter in which capacity they are serving the UN – and the supporter-lovers of the United Nations – no matter in which part of the world they are – are seeing a glimpse of the UN soul's all-illumining revelation. And each glimpse embodies a growing and glowing fulness-satisfaction in man's life of inner hunger and his life of outer feast.

In the great stream of history and human evolution the contribution of the United Nations is not only to be the great and ultimate pathfinder of the ultimate Truth, but also the good and supreme bliss-distributor of humanity's Divinity.

5. Mr Robert Muller: If you were given the task of laying down the basic principles for the education of all the children of this world, what would be your recommendations?

Sri Chinmoy: According to me, education is self-cultivation and self-cultivation is God-perfection in human life. You want to know the basic principles for the education of all the children of this world. Let us divide this world into halves: the Eastern world or, let us say, the Indian world, and the Western world, or the American world. For an Indian child, freedom is a far cry. For an American child, freedom is an act as easy as breathing in and breathing out. In India, even now I see that a child is taught and learns the message of the world through severe discipline and imposed fear. Here in America, as far as I can see and feel, in most of the cases, if not all, parents get satisfaction in fulfilling their own dreams, but they neglect their children's needs. They say to the children, "We don't want to impose anything on you. You find out your truth and you pick out what is best for yourself, for how do we know what is best for you? It is better that you look around and find what you need." Some will say that this is a broad expression of the parents' oneness with their children, while others will say that the parents unconsciously, if not consciously, are unburdening their so-called burdens. The parents will say, "Look, we really love you. Here is the proof that we love you. We have given you a TV set. We have given you a tape recorder, a radio – everything in the material world that you long for. Therefore, we expect you to stay with your friends and let us fulfil our dreams in our own way."

Unfortunately, I can subscribe neither to the Indian method of bringing up a child nor to the American method. Parents should not allow their children to grow up in the Elysian lap of exorbitant luxury; nor should they keep a devouring, intransigent tiger before their children so that at every moment the children will be forced to do the right thing. The parents should tell their children that they are not disciplinary, autocratic parents but unreservedly loving, discerning friends.

The education of the children and the education of the parents must go together. The parents must dream in and fulfil themselves through their creations, their children. As the creation cannot be separated from the creator, even so the creator cannot be separated from the creation. The creation without the creator is helpless. The creator without the creation is meaningless. Therefore, both the creation and the creator must contribute to each other in order to derive oneness-satisfaction and fulness-satisfaction. It is in the parents' right decision that we can find the children's freedom. This freedom is founded on their oneness with their parents' will. Let us consider the children as finite realities and the parents as infinite realities. The children become infinite and enjoy infinite freedom only by becoming consciously, unreservedly and inseparably one with their parents.

The parents must not think of their children as unnecessary projections of their life; for if these projections are unnecessary, then they can go in their own way. On the contrary, they must feel that their children are absolutely necessary projections of their life. The improvement of the projections, perfection of the projections, considerably adds to the source. The beauty of the leaves, flowers and fruits of the tree only adds to the seed-reality of the tree. It does not diminish the beauty-reality, divinity and necessity of the seed.

Here I wish to quote from your most illumining insights about global education: "A child born today will be faced as an adult, almost daily, with problems of a global interdependent nature, be it peace, food, the quality of life, inflation, or scarcity of natural resources. He will be both an actor and a beneficiary or a victim in the total world fabric, and he may rightly ask: 'Why was I not warned? Why was I not better educated? Why did my teachers not tell me about these problems and indicate my behaviour as a member of an interdependent human race?'....

"Global education must transcend material and intellectual achievements and reach also into the moral and spiritual spheres. Man has been able to extend the power of his hands with incredible machines, of his eyes with telescopes and microscopes, of his ears with telephones, radio waves and sonars, of his brain with computers and automation. He must now also extend his heart, his sentiments, his love and his soul to the dimension of the entire human family and to our total beautiful planet circling in the universe."

The parents should bring the presence of God, the presence of love, the presence of truth and the presence of purity into the hearts and eyes of their children as soon as the children can see the light of day. They should tell their children that they themselves and the children are great companions and that they have a good Guide, a good Leader, who will guide them, mould them and shape them into perfect Perfection. They know a little more about that Guide than the children, and He has told them to say certain things about Him to the children. Therefore, they are listening to the Guide's dictates. Right now the parents are asked by the Guide to act as intermediaries between Him and the children. But there shall come a time when the children will not need intermediaries. They will be able to go directly to the Guide, the Source. Until then, the children must listen to their intermediaries, their earthly friends. The acme of the children's

TWO GOD-SERVERS AND MAN-LOVERS

education is their perfection in life and their perfection for God-satisfaction. And to offer their children that, the parents should not impose, nor expose, nor even propose; only they should become the living flame of self-giving in order to realise their own world-satisfying life and to please the Source in its own Way.

6. Mr Robert Muller: Anthropologists have found a gradation of religious beliefs over the history of mankind: ritualism, animism, ancestor worship, polytheism, monotheism. All these forms were associated with changes in the social structure. Recently, the "age of reason" and the scientific and industrial revolution have rendered religion and spirituality obsolete – even harmful – in the eyes of many. What, in your view, is likely to be the "religion" or "spirituality" of humanity tomorrow as a satisfactory answer to man's queries about his relationships with the universe, his fellow men and the mysteries of life? Is this likely to be reflected in the United Nations as a forum where humanity is seeking new ways for its destiny and fulfilment?

Sri Chinmoy: The spirituality of tomorrow will neither be the merciless rejection of life nor the disproportionate imposition of life; the spirituality of tomorrow will be the devoted acceptance of life and the pure dissemination of the seeker's self-giving breath in order that he may become a God-blossoming beauty within and without.

Here at this point I am tempted to share with the rest of the world your most illumining ideas and most nourishing thoughts: "Indeed, how can we reach full consciousness and enlightenment if we do not let the entire world and humanity enter ourselves? Humility and the lowering of one's ego lead in the end to righteousness, happiness and the full mastery over oneself, enriched by the thoughts, dreams and feelings of others. Together with meditation, it is perhaps the clue to serenity in our bewildered, complex world. U Thant was a living proof of it."

The spirituality of tomorrow's dawn will beckon the desire-world to show the desire-world that real satisfaction looms large only in the aspiration-life. The real spirituality of tomorrow's dawn will beckon the aspiration-world to show the aspiration-world that real satisfaction lies only in the seeker's unconditionally surrendered oneness with his Source, his Beloved Supreme.

The blind world can be sceptical of the reality or it can deny the reality when the reality is in the flame stage. But when the reality grows into the sun stage, even the stone blind must admit that the sun does exist, because of its scorching heat and loving warmth. Today's United Nations divinity-flame can be denied or challenged, but tomorrow's United Nations divinity-sun shall give sight to the blind, offer legs to the lame and offer voice to the voiceless to mark the slow, steady and unerring beginning of man's quenchless satisfaction in God and God's breathless satisfaction in man.

7. Mr Robert Muller: U Thant often said that in his view the West was too materialistic and intellectual, and not spiritual enough, whereas the East was too spiritual and fatalistic, and not caring enough for the material and intellectual welfare of the people. Do you see a synthesis developing between the two and how would you envisage a harmonious, happy world society?

Sri Chinmoy: I readily, immediately and unreservedly agree with our beloved Secretary-General U Thant's most illumining assessment of Eastern achievements and Western achievements, Eastern possessions and Western possessions, Eastern contributions and Western contributions, Eastern outlook towards the Reality and Western outlook towards the Reality.

The East is spiritual, the West is material. The East cries for the transcendental Spirit, the West cries for the universal matter.

The East is in the heart and for the heart. The West is in the mind and for the mind. The East from within comes to the fore and flowers. The West from the outer existence goes deep within and flowers.

The East wants silence. The West wants sound. Silence embodies the teeming Vast eventually to proceed. Sound inspires the teeming Vast continuously to succeed.

The East sings the song of God the One. The West sings the song of God the Many. The East loves unity. The West loves multiplicity.

This world of ours is beset with countless problems. The spiritual East thinks that the Beyond is the only answer. The material West thinks that the answer is to be found here on earth; it thinks that the answer is: live and enjoy and enjoy and live.

The East believes in fate because it believes in reincarnation. The West does not believe in reincarnation; therefore, it does not believe in fate.

We can endlessly see and determine the differences between the East and the West. But the real question is whether these differences are being synthesised or not. At the very beginning, if we know what the heart can offer and what the mind can offer, then it will be an easy task to synthesise the two. The heart wants to see the oneness, feel the oneness and become the oneness itself. The mind wants diversity in the vital and multiplicity in the mind proper. The heart knows that there is a road that leads upwards. The mind knows that there is a road that leads forwards. The East wants to walk along the road that leads upwards. The West wants to walk along the road that leads forwards.

The synthesis between East and West starts because of their feelings of insufficiency. The East sees that if it does not accept the material life, then it will not be able to manifest what it inwardly has. The West feels that if it does not accept the spiritual life, then it will not have a solid foundation. Then everything can be easily shattered.

We can clearly see that the East has already gained considerable knowledge and wisdom from the West, especially in the scientific world. The West has gained considerable knowledge and wisdom from the East, especially in the spiritual world. Here we see that the heart and the mind cannot function separately and individually. They have to function together, provided they feel the need of an integral perfection in life. The mind without the heart will not know what the supreme Reality is. The heart without the mind will not know how the supreme Reality can be manifested here on earth. To our great joy, the East and the West are constantly complementing each other to make each other perfect consciously, and more so unconsciously.

The East is like the body of a bird and the West is like the wings of a bird. If the bird does not spread its wings, then how will it fly? And again, when it flies and reaches the highest Height, at that time it has to know that there is another goal and that goal is God-Manifestation on earth. There are two goals: one goal is Heaven-reality and the other goal is earth-reality. When we use the wings to go upward to the heavenly goal, we go with the earth-reality to the Heaven-reality. And when we come down to the earthly goal, we come down with the Heaven-reality to the earth-reality. It is like climbing up and down a tree. We climb up a mango tree and pluck mangoes, and then bring them down and distribute them. The East says, "Gather!" The West says, "Spread!" If we do not gather, then how can we spread? Only if we gather can we spread. Again, if

TWO GOD-SERVERS AND MAN-LOVERS

we spread what we have, then the Source is pleased with us and the Source gives us everything in infinite measure.

For the last quarter of a century, both the East and the West have felt the supreme necessity of receiving light from each other. To quote your own illumining ideas and fulfilling ideals: "Beyond the turmoil, the divisions and perplexities of our time, mankind is slowly but surely finding the ways, limits and new codes of behaviour which will encompass all races, nations and ideologies. It is the formulation of these new ethics which will be the great challenge for the new generation. It will concern not only men's material fate, but also their mental and spiritual lives."

There was a time when the renouncer of life felt that it was beneath his dignity to love the lover of life, and the lover of life felt that it was beneath his dignity to mix with the renouncer of life. Now the lover and the renouncer are modifying their views and becoming one. The renouncer feels that to love life because God the All-Love is inside life is absolutely correct. At the same time, God the Lover of life sees that things need not be renounced; He sees that they can be modified, transformed and perfected. After all, perfection only can give humanity abiding satisfaction. So the East, instead of rejecting, gladly accepts the great possibilities, capacities and realities of the West. The West too does exactly the same. They are combining their possibilities and transforming these possibilities into divine practicabilities with the hope that supreme satisfaction will dawn in the all-embracing and all-illumining common realisation of East and West.

We will have a harmonious, happy world-society only if this synthesis continues, and we can take East and West as the two arms, two eyes, two feet and two legs of the Supreme Pilot within and without. The other human divisions and distinctions – racial, cultural and linguistic – are destined to disappear from the human consciousness when it is flooded with a higher Light. This is the inevitable consequence of the Hour of God that is dawning all over the world. When the Hour of God appears, diversities will be there, but these diversities will be enriched and enhanced in fullest measure. And they will not disturb the general consciousness; on the contrary, they will harmoniously complement the whole. Humanity will be a true human family in every sense of the term and also in a sense that the human mind has yet to discover. And here I wish to say that this discovery will exceed all human expectations.

The awakened consciousness of man is evolving towards the Divine Existence. This is a most hopeful streak of light amidst the obscurities of the present-day world. This is a moment when human beings do not only join hands, but also join minds, hearts and souls. All physical, vital and mental barriers between East and West will dissolve, and high above national standards, above even individual standards, we shall see the supreme banner of divine Oneness.

NOTES TO TWO GOD-SERVERS AND MAN-LOVERS

1–7. *(p. 305)* In the spring of 1977, these profound and soulful questions were submitted by Mr Robert Muller, Director and Deputy to the Under-Secretary-General for Inter-Agency Affairs and Coordination, to Sri Chinmoy, Director of the United Nations Meditation Group. In their interchange, these two luminaries complement each other by becoming soulfully one with humanity's multifarious needs and divinity's gracious gifts.

PART VII

U THANT:
DIVINITY'S SMILE, HUMANITY'S CRY

I – DEDICATION TO U THANT, PART I

1.

> Beloved Brother,
> Man of silence,
> Man of peace,
> May the Supreme grant your soul
> Eternity's Silence,
> Infinity's Peace.
>
> — Sri Chinmoy

2.

U Thant's compassion-philosophy explained and expanded becomes U Thant the forerunner and liberator of mankind.

3. *The chosen instrument of God*

U Thant was a chosen instrument of God. U Thant was a chosen instrument of man.

God gave him His Compassion-sky to offer to man. Man gave him his suffering-sea to offer to God.

U Thant started his earthly sojourn as a Rangoon, Burma Buddha-son. The Absolute Supreme gradually made him into a universal Wisdom-son and a universal Blessing-gift.

To us, peace is something that belongs in a dream-land. Since it belongs to dream-land we talk about it. To U Thant, peace is something that belongs to the reality-world. Therefore he lived in the reality-world of peace and was a solid and treasured member of the reality-peace-world.

To us, oneness is something that we seem to want but we do not actually feel the need for it. To U Thant, oneness was something of constant need, something indispensable. His heart cried for this oneness and the Lord Supreme, the Author of all good, fulfilled his heart's burning desire.

The United Nations gave U Thant the opportunity to speak to the world-body as a supreme leader of mankind. In return, U Thant gave to the United Nations the message of the world-illumination, of the world-heart-perfection and the world-life-satisfaction.

U Thant was the supreme choice of the United Nations, and God was pleased. But God wanted U Thant to please Him more. Therefore, he made U Thant a pioneer voice of light from the higher worlds.

Simplicity, purity and integrity he was. He was a child's simplicity. He was a saint's purity. He was a God-lover's integrity.

He struggled calmly. He suffered ceaselessly. He hoped sleeplessly. Again, he knew how to dream of success. He knew how to become the river of progress.

We feel that man is bad, imperfect and undivine. His conviction was that man is good, perfect and divine, for that is what each individual in the inner world eternally is.

U Thant's life of humility was the result of his heart's nobility. His heart of nobility was the result of his soul's unparalleled divinity.

Sincerity spoke through him, integrity breathed in him, spirituality walked with him. He knew the world-problem: ignorance. He knew the world-answer: meditation, and this he practised in silence.

God practised His silence-meditation in and through U Thant. God practised His sound-dedication in and through U Thant.

U THANT: DIVINITY'S SMILE, HUMANITY'S CRY

U Thant was at once God-Humility and man-dignity. He was at once man-frustration and God-Illumination. He was at once the soulful son of God and the faithful slave of man.

Self-demonstration he ruthlessly shunned. Self-perfection he practised. God-Perfection he sought to embrace and treasure. Before him the United Nations was great, divinely great. With him, after him, the United Nations has become supremely good.

In the inner world he was God's Promise, God's Promise to the outer world. In the outer world he was man's confidence, man's confidence in becoming a dedicated instrument of the inner world.

Earth gave him the responsibility. Heaven knew it and saw it. Heaven gave him the authority but, unfortunately, earth did not know it or did not care to know it. His heart of brotherhood was misunderstood. His life of sacrifice was not valued. But his vision of oneness-goal will eternally be pursued by aspiring humanity.

An Asian seed he was. A world-fruit he has become and forever and forever he shall remain.

4. *Interview between U Thant and Sri Chinmoy*

[The Secretary-General and Sri Chinmoy greet each other with folded hands at the door of the room where the interview is to take place, and then U Thant invites Sri Chinmoy to come in.]
U Thant: Sri Chinmoy, please come in. I have been hearing about you from many, many people. Whoever speaks to me about you is all appreciation and admiration and I personally feel that you have been doing a most significant task for the United Nations. I have been observing it from the very beginning.
Sri Chinmoy: It is most kind of you to tell me all this. I am most grateful to you. Before our short interview, may I invoke the Lord Buddha to bless us? You are a most devoted child of the

Lord Buddha and I have the greatest admiration and adoration for him.
U Thant: Yes, please, please chant.
Sri Chinmoy: [Sri Chinmoy chants three times]

> *Buddham saranam gacchami*
> *Dhammam saranam gacchami*
> *Sangham saranam gacchami*
>
> I go to the Buddha for refuge.
> I go to the *Dharma* for refuge.
> I go to the Order for refuge.

U Thant: [U Thant is silent for some moments, deeply moved.] I have not been able to see you before, please forgive me. Because of my heavy schedule and politics, my inner life was not coming to the fore for me. That is why I hesitated a little to see you. Today I am seeing you and I wish to say that all I have heard from others about you is absolutely true.
Sri Chinmoy: The world knows you as a champion of peace. Being a spiritual man, I wish to tell you that in the inner world too you are something really great. Now that you are physically away from the outer battlefield you will be able to see the world situation with your intuitive light and you will make a contribution in the inner world that will be most effective and most fulfilling.
U Thant: I am so happy to hear that. This is what I wanted. Now I will be writing my memoirs and I need a peaceful life. My memoirs will be different, totally different, from the memoirs that others write. Here I want to show how spirituality and philosophy can lead and guide politics.
Sri Chinmoy: This is the thing that only you can do because in you I see a true seeker of Truth, Peace, Light and Bliss. I

know nothing about politics, but I do feel that politics has to be guided by spirituality and philosophy. What you are saying, most revered Brother, gives me immense delight.
U Thant: I pray to the Lord Buddha for a continuous success in your mission in spreading God's Peace and Light on earth.
Sri Chinmoy: I appreciate and admire you, not only as a great lover of mankind, but as a most devoted, dedicated child of God who wants to bring God's wealth from the inner world and offer it to his brothers and sisters.
U Thant: It has been a great privilege for me to see you. Please feel my sincere respect and sincere concern for what you are doing for mankind.
Sri Chinmoy: Please feel my deepest joy and pride in you and my most soulful gratitude for what you have done for the United Nations and also for the entire world.

[As Sri Chinmoy leaves, he and U Thant salute each other with palms joined together, in *pranam*.]

5. *On the first meeting with Secretary-General U Thant*

With your kind permission I wish to offer two most striking experiences of mine. The first was when I met with Secretary-General U Thant in his office. His simplicity, sincerity, humility, purity and divinity made me immediately feel that I had found in him a true and genuine spiritual brother. In him I also discovered a heart of universal oneness. Then, a few years ago, I had the golden opportunity to pay my most soulful respects to the soul of Secretary-General Dag Hammarskjöld at his grave in Uppsala. While I was offering my most soulful love, appreciation and adoration to this divinely great soul, I discovered immediately the luminosity of his mind. In his mind I found the most illumining and fulfilling vastness. Two supremely giant souls – Dag Hammarskjöld and U Thant, U Thant and Dag

Hammarskjöld. Inside the vastness of Dag Hammarskjöld my heart felt the love of oneness, and inside the oneness of U Thant my soul envisioned the vastness. Their oneness and vastness and vastness and oneness make me feel and realise that this United Nations – their dream-fulfilling reality and reality-transcending dream – will forever and ever be cherished and treasured by the aspiring, self-giving and truth-loving humanity.

6.

During the course of his life, U Thant received these honorary Doctor of Law degrees:

- Carleton University, 1962
- Williams College, 1962
- Princeton University, 1962
- Mount Holyoke College, 1963
- Harvard University, 1963
- Dartmouth College, 1963
- University of California, 1964
- University of Denver, 1964
- Swarthmore College, 1964
- New York University, 1964
- Moscow University, 1964
- Queen's University, 1965
- Colby College, 1965
- Yale University, 1965
- University of Windsor, 1966
- Hamilton College, 1966
- Fordham University, 1966
- Manhattan College, 1966
- The University of Michigan, 1967
- Delhi University, 1967

- The University of Alberta, 1968
- Boston University, 1968
- Rutgers University, 1968

U Thant also received the degree of Doctor Honoris Causa from Louvain University in 1968.

7.

U Thant was a seeker in the purest sense of the term. He reduced his bodily needs to the bare minimum. Sublime was his renunciation. Perfect was his meditation. Satisfied was the mother earth.

II – KIND WORDS FROM WORLD LEADERS

8. Abdelaziz Bouteflika

The past and the present can be united. The past can offer its wisdom-light to the present so the present can be a source of pride, light and delight to the future. It happens that sometimes it is necessary to break asunder the past in order to have a clear and illumining vision of the years to come. But U Thant had the unusual inner strength to do what was nearly impossible and unite the past, the present and the future.

Abdelaziz Bouteflika, President of the UN General Assembly in 1974, has brought to the world's attention something unique with regard to U Thant's unusual capacity and unprecedented achievement: "Who was better qualified than U Thant to preside over such a transformation without breaking with the past while keeping a clear vision of the future, without frustrating the great powers or driving the small ones to despair? The metamorphosis through which our Organization went at that time resulted from a gradual evolution the scope or depth of which, since it took place smoothly, was often unguessed at."

9. Secretary-General Kurt Waldheim

Mortals long for name and fame, for they feel that to have name and fame is to have everything. But U Thant did not see eye to eye with human beings. He felt that only service to mankind, acceptance of the inner light and the manifestation of truth, light and bliss on earth could quench his inner thirst.

He refused world acclaim sincerely and smilingly. Service was his joy. The result of all his actions he offered in silence at the Feet of the Lord Buddha. The supreme pilot of the United Nations-Boat, Kurt Waldheim, who brings about world progress with lightning speed, graciously tells us of U Thant's genuine concern for world problems and his significant contribution to world hope and world peace: "In 1965, when full-scale war erupted between India and Pakistan, U Thant went to the subcontinent to negotiate a cease-fire. At about the same time also, the tragedy of Viet-Nam, in which the United Nations was never directly involved, began to assume its historical momentum. U Thant made a long personal effort to help in ending the Viet-Namese tragedy. In 1967, there was renewed war in the Middle East. In early 1971, the war clouds gathered again in the South Asian subcontinent and the situation dominated U Thant's last months as Secretary-General."

*

His body U Thant sacrificed. Untold suffering he embraced. Wild frustration he endured. The present-day world is extremely grateful to Secretary-General Waldheim for revealing these illumining and fulfilling secrets about his predecessor: "No one will ever know the intense internal struggle which U Thant's discipline and his deep faith concealed from the public gaze. He was occasionally even reproached for his calm. His medical history, which he concealed as far as possible, tells another story – the story of a good and disciplined man doing his best to perform one of the most difficult jobs in the world, and privately enduring the extremes of fatigue, worry and frustration."

10. *Dr Sarvepalli Radhakrishnan*

In presenting the first Jawaharlal Nehru Award for International Understanding to U Thant at a ceremony on 12 April 1967, Dr Sarvepalli Radhakrishnan, India's philosopher-king and former President, expressed his heartfelt congratulations to the esteemed Secretary-General: "We are all happy that U Thant is selected for the first Nehru Award for International Understanding. His outstanding work in this direction as Secretary-General of the United Nations has inspired confidence. All these years he has been engaged in a passionate quest for peace and his selection for the Award has evoked universal acclaim." With these remarks, we see one world teacher appreciating another world teacher.

11. *President John F Kennedy*

Only a man of vision can recognise another man of vision. Only a man of promise can recognise another man of promise. Only a man of concern can recognise another man of concern

President John F Kennedy saw in U Thant a sun of wisdom-light. President Kennedy discovered in U Thant a colossal achievement.

In a telegram, President Kennedy declared: "The election of His Excellency U Thant is a splendid achievement in which the whole world can rejoice.

"Please express the congratulations of the United States Government to the United Nations membership for their action in electing so distinguished a diplomat to succeed the late Dag Hammarskjöld.

"In preserving the integrity of the office of the Secretary-General, they have reaffirmed their dedication to the UN Charter.... As he [U Thant] begins one of the world's most difficult jobs, he has our confidence and also our prayers."

Mr Zenon Rossides, Ambassador of Cyprus to the United Nations, described President Kennedy's response to U Thant's handling of the Cuban missile crisis: "The most dangerous of all crises since the Second World War was resolved in a manner that prompted President Kennedy to say, 'U Thant has put the world deeply in his debt.'"

12. *Prime Minister Jawaharlal Nehru*

Prime Minister Jawaharlal Nehru, India's peerless freedom-fighter and India's matchless nation-transformer, offered these words of welcome and cooperation to U Thant in a speech to the UN General Assembly on 10 November 1961, a few days after U Thant had been appointed Acting Secretary-General: "To you, sir, who occupy now this high seat of the Secretary-General, I offer my warm welcome and regard and greeting. And I can assure you that we, in common with others, not only welcome you here but offer you our full cooperation, for you represent the United Nations, to which all of us must offer cooperation."

13. *Prime Minister Indira Gandhi*

Prime Minister Indira Gandhi, Queen of India's heart and veerless pilot of India, expressed her strong support and admiration for U Thant in an address to the United Nations General Assembly on 14 October 1968. Speaking of U Thant's miraculous perseverance, she said: "I should like to pay a special tribute to the Secretary-General. Where others might have been overwhelmed by heartbreak, U Thant has persevered, undaunted, in his great work with rare faith, devotion and detachment. It is up to all of us to give him our fullest support."

14. *CV Narasimhan*

His confidant and closest associate, CV Narasimhan, U Thant's chef de Cabinet, shares rare insights about U Thant: "U Thant was a Buddhist, but not a fanatic. Indeed one could not conceive of his being fanatical on any subject, except perhaps in respect of his total commitment to the Charter of the United Nations. From his religion derived his modesty and humility. It was these qualities which made him repeatedly assert in the course of 1966 that he would not be available for a second term as Secretary-General. He used to say that no person should aspire to a second term as Secretary-General. His calmness in times of crisis bordered on nonchalance and was in fact sometimes even criticised when it was mistaken for indifference. His total serenity in his personal relations was no doubt the cause of his ulcers; although his doctors advised him to 'explode' now and again, it was inconceivable that he would, even to save his health."

15. *Swaran Singh*

The Indian heart comforted him by presenting him with the first Jawaharlal Nehru Award for International Understanding. By honouring him, India once more reaffirmed its message to the world at large – its motto *Satyam eva jayate:* "Truth alone prevails [triumphs]."

Swaran Singh, Indian Minister of Foreign Affairs, a man who perfectly blended mind and heart, said: "My country recognised his great contribution to world peace by conferring on him the first Jawaharlal Nehru Award for International Understanding on 12 April 1967. We wish him a well-earned rest but we hope his advice will still be available to all of us in the years to come."

16. *TN Kaul*

TN Kaul, former Ambassador of India to the United States, who is highly esteemed around the world, illumines us as to U Thant's success in bearing the burden of the Secretary-Generalship: "U Thant served the world community with rare distinction and understanding of the hopes and aspirations of peoples in different parts of the world. He was a firm believer in human dignity and brotherhood. U Thant realised that, in the words of Jawaharlal Nehru, 'Peace is indivisible; so is Freedom, so is Prosperity now, and so also is Disaster in this one world that can no longer be split into isolated fragments.' He also knew that 'the consequences of acting in a passion are always bad for an individual; but they are indefinitely worse for a nation.' It is not surprising, therefore, that he brought a great vision and a deep sense of compassion to bear on the solution of intricate international problems. These qualities, combined with a deeply felt commitment to social justice and practice of meditation, gave him the inner strength to bear the awesome burden of one of the loneliest jobs in the world and to face with equanimity the many crises which confounded the world community during the ten years of his tenure as Secretary-General of the United Nations. India was one of the first countries to recognise his outstanding contribution to the promotion of peace and international understanding by conferring on him in 1967 the first Jawaharlal Nehru Award for International Understanding. I have no doubt that his life and work will serve for many years to come as a beacon of light and a source of inspiration to increasing numbers of people in our world, which he did so much to bring together in peace and harmony."

17. Ole Algard

Ole Algard, UN Ambassador and Permanent Representative of Norway, with his penetrating insight and life-elevating vision, speaks very highly of the new consciousness that U Thant introduced at the United Nations: "It happened that, during his tenure of power as Secretary-General, we saw a great transformation in the world. And we saw another thing to which U Thant greatly contributed, which was the creation of a new consciousness, a consciousness that went much further than the small, petty political problems we were dealing with in the fifties and sixties. This had to do with a respect for the underdog. Today we are witnessing the results of this new consciousness that Secretary-General U Thant so greatly helped to introduce in his work at the United Nations. We see today a world where the old colonialism is, for all practical purposes, gone, and where the interest and political energy is now geared towards finding a better world where the underdog and the unprivileged will prevail. I think this is the greatest legacy that the great man U Thant has given to the United Nations and to the world at large."

18. Piero Vinci

In speaking about U Thant, Piero Vinci, Italian Ambassador and Permanent Representative to the United Nations, a strikingly genuine thinker and a staunch supporter of U Thant, referred to what he called one of the former Secretary-General's most inspiring statements: "U Thant was one of the most inspiring forces, if not the main force, in drawing the attention of the governments and of the peoples of the world to the ever-present global challenges: outer space, disarmament, environment, law of the sea. At one moment, on 26 May 1970, he came out with one of his most inspiring statements. He stated that, living in the shadow of atomic weapons, it is no longer enough for the member states of the United Nations to pay allegiance to their own country. What is required, he added, is a second allegiance: namely, the allegiance to the international community embodied by the United Nations. Speaking personally, I would say that I and many of my compatriots would give priority to our allegiance to the United Nations and to all it stands for."

19. *Mr Robert Muller*

Mr Robert Muller, Director and Deputy to the Under-Secretary-General for Special Political Affairs and Coordination, treasures unforgettable memories of U Thant. A true seeker endowed with inner wisdom-light, he was deeply connected with U Thant and served the Secretary-General with true dedication. Here he tells us that it was U Thant's spirituality-sea that brought him closer to the Secretary-General: "It was spirituality that brought me closest to the beautiful soul of U Thant. I had learned of the importance of religion in his life through the book *U Thant, the search for Peace* by June Bingham. A neighbour of U Thant, she had written his biography on the basis of interviews while she rode with him from Riverdale to mid-Manhattan. I made a special effort to acquaint myself with Buddhism. After U Thant discovered that I was not the dry, pragmatic, Western economist he first thought I was, but that I had an inclination for humanism and spirituality, he became both a teacher and a second father to me. He would have long conversations with me after office hours. One evening I remember telling him that he had made me aware again that simplicity and kindness were the highest values a man could aim at and that he reminded me greatly of my father, who had always taught me that love and honesty were qualities far superior to intelligence."

20. Leopoldo Benites

The devout U Thant, like his Lord Buddha, discovered that the world is full of suffering. Like the Father, the son's heart cried with humanity's heart and suffered for humanity's life.

Momentous are the words of Leopoldo Benites, the Ambassador of Ecuador to the United Nations: "It may well be that for U Thant, a Buddhist, the world was a painful illusion, as Prince Siddhartha Gautama discovered under the fig tree before he became the Buddha, and that a life of goodness, peace and justice led him to ultimate liberation."

21. Gunapala P Malalasekera

U Thant was and is and always will be in humanity's heart. Him to choose unanimously as Secretary-General was absolutely the right thing to do.

Gunapala P Malalasekera, who was the Permanent Representative of Sri Lanka to the United Nations, said: "A unanimous decision was arrived at to recommend to the General Assembly the nomination of His Excellency U Thant .... for appointment as Acting Secretary-General of this organization. The decision was followed by universal acclaim. This was very largely due to the fact that the qualifications of His Excellency U Thant to the post for which he was nominated were never in doubt."

Mr Malalasekera also told the world that the strength U Thant possessed was unlike the strength that others possess: "In an age where strength is often equated with the booming voice and the bouncing fist .... U Thant displays a strength of a different kind, the strength of quiet dignity. He combines in himself in a remarkable way the strength of the strong man with that of the diplomat who believes in consultation with others."

22. Mr Rachid Driss

U Thant meditated. His meditation was at once soulful and fruitful, as observed by Mr Rachid Driss, Ambassador of Tunisia to the United Nations: "The United Nations will always need the fruits of his meditation and the illumination shed by his free and universal spirit."

23. Governor Rafael Hernandez Colon

The lion-hearted and most illustrious son of Puerto Rico, Governor Rafael Hernandez Colon, voices his strong support for U Thant's cause of peace: "The life and work of U Thant is an example and inspiration for Puerto Ricans and all the world's people.

"His fight for the cause of peace is a fight we all must take up if man is to rise above his historical limitations to build a just and lasting world society."

24. U Khant

Human life is beset with difficulties, anxieties and worries. We are constantly assailed by these destructive forces. But he who practises spiritual discipline can remain far above the snares of these negative forces and enjoy supreme relaxation by virtue of detachment-light. To quote U Thant's brother, U Khant: "He [U Thant] is one of the fortunate men who have the capacity to cast aside care and relax, however anxious the situation. He has that power of detachment in a most remarkable degree."

25. *France Vacher*

France Vacher, who has been devotedly serving the United Nations for the last thirty years, speaks thus about this great soul: "During the last two years of U Thant's service I was able to see a feeling of holiness surrounding him, so even though I was unaware of all his achievements, still I was able to know he was a great soul. And to his great soul, on behalf of all of us – the United Nations staff and the UN Meditation Group – I offer my deepest gratitude."

III – DEDICATION TO U THANT, PART 2

26.

An individual life always bristles with teeming and surmounting problems; more so when the individual has to deal with the comity of nations and the world-body. U Thant tried to solve these problems according to his heart's illumining capacity and his soul's fulfilling divinity. And he did succeed considerably.

27.

Simplicity was U Thant's life. Sincerity was U Thant's mind. Purity was U Thant's heart. His was the approach of serene and illumined dignity.

28.

Trumpet-dynamism U Thant was not. Flute-dynamism he was.
  A stranger was he to sound-life, an eternal friend of silence-life.
  Might is right: that can be the goal of countless individuals. Right is might: that was his only goal, the goal of goals.

29.

U Thant was a man of illumining and fulfilling determination. This determination was born of his disciplined life.
  Some people are apt to distinguish academically between the earth-bound and the Heaven-free realities. Nevertheless, they do not or, rather, cannot come out of the snares of ignorance-life. Indeed, to our deepest joy and pride, U Thant was a very rare exception.

30.

Time and again the soul of the United Nations unreservedly clasped her beloved son, U Thant, to her heart.

31.

Each member of the United Nations basks in the sunshine of U Thant's supreme glory.

32.

What U Thant gave to the United Nations was nothing short of God's bountiful Concern-Light.

33.

U Thant was a perfect stranger to anger and rancour. What he offered was forgiveness. What he was, was a flood of compassion.

34.

U Thant's life of signal service to mankind was illumined because inner aspiration strikingly carried all its appurtenances – belief, simplicity, generosity, sincerity, humility and purity – to the loftiest height.

35.

Some people are afraid of evil in life, others try to avoid evil, while still others do not even think of evil. In U Thant's case, he was not afraid of evil and he did not think of evil. So how can the question of avoiding evil even arise? Absurd!

36.

This world of ours is assailed by injustice and insecurity. To liberate the world from injustice and insecurity, U Thant served tirelessly the heart of mankind. His heart of peace and his heart of oneness he offered to see the appreciable progress of humanity.

IV – PERFORMANCE OF SIDDHARTHA BECOMES THE BUDDHA

37. Speech of welcome by Sri Chinmoy

[Sri Chinmoy opens the programme by singing:]

> *Buddham saranam gacchami*
> *Dhammam saranam gacchami*
> *Sangham saranam gacchami*

★

[Sri Chinmoy then gives a speech of welcome and garlands U Thant. These are Sri Chinmoy's remarks.]
When I go to the Buddha for refuge, He blesses me.
When I go to the Inner Law for refuge, He illumines me.
When I go to the Order for refuge, He utilises me.

A child of Bihar, a son of India, a citizen of the world, a denizen of the higher spheres: Siddhartha, the Buddha.

In the outer world He is known as the Light of Asia. In the inner world He is, indeed, an ever-illumining Light of the universe.

To the world-sorrows He offered His heart of infinite Compassion. To the world-aspiration He offered His soul of transcendental Illumination.

The Omnipotent did two things. Through Siddhartha Gautama, He revealed the ideal of Perfection in a human being. Through the Buddha, He revealed His Enlightenment and Compassion in a Divine Being.

With His Heart, the Unfathomable came to the Buddha.
With His Mind, the Unknowable came to the Buddha.
With His Bliss, the Transcendental came to the Buddha.

U THANT: DIVINITY'S SMILE, HUMANITY'S CRY

★

This evening we are deeply honoured and blessed by the gracious presence of our most esteemed Brother, U Thant. Two thousand five hundred years ago the World-Father, the Buddha, came with the Message of universal Peace. Now, two thousand five hundred years later, He has sent His chosen son, U Thant, to offer the same Message of Peace.

Dear Brother, for ten long years you have served the world-consciousness most devotedly and most significantly through the world body of the United Nations. Mother Earth and Father Heaven have bestowed their choicest blessings on your devoted head, aspiring heart and illumining soul. The outer political world has lost you, but the inner spiritual world has gained you and claims you as its very own. Your silent life of aspiration, dedication and illumination is guiding the outer world and leading it to its destined Goal.

With deepest joy and gratitude I am dedicating this play, *Siddhartha becomes the Buddha,* as a humble token of my treasured feeling towards you. In you I feel the pioneer-pilot of world-peace. In you I see a beacon-light of world-redemption. And in you I discover true love of human life and an utmost reverence for Truth, both in the inner world and in the outer world.

The Absolute Supreme claims you as His very own. The Lord Buddha claims you as His very own. We, your brothers and sisters of this world, claim you as our very own.

38. U Thant's reply

Revered and highly esteemed Sri Chinmoy and brothers and sisters, it is a great privilege to be able to participate in this spiritually rewarding experience. And for this I am most grateful to our esteemed teacher, Sri Chinmoy, for this innovative undertaking. I also feel particularly moved and touched by his very gracious blessing bestowed on me.

Sri Chinmoy very kindly sent me a copy of the play, *Siddhartha becomes the Buddha*. I have read it with great interest and with great admiration and profit. Of course, it is extremely difficult to depict the important episodes of the life of the Buddha in the course of a few minutes or an hour or so. But I found that Sri Chinmoy has done a most remarkable job in presenting the play in simple language understandable even to the uninitiated. His stress on the basic characteristics of Buddhism – on compassion, love, renunciation, peace – should stimulate the thoughts of leaders of men and leaders of thought everywhere. As you all are aware, I was brought up as a Buddhist by tradition, by faith and by practice. And I find myself in complete agreement with Sri Chinmoy in his enunciation of the ethical and moral aspects of Buddhism which in my view should be the basis for each of us in our search for inner light, in our search for truth.

Sri Chinmoy in his play also has drawn a very vivid picture of the identity between God and Truth, soul and inner light, which I very much hope will create an abiding interest in these two great religions – Hinduism and Buddhism – which in many ways constitute the key to all great religions. I feel very strongly, as some of my friends know, that only by the practical application of the teachings of great religious leaders, particularly the development of the moral and spiritual aspects of life as Sri Chinmoy has stressed in the play – love, compassion, tolerance, the philosophy of live-and-let-live, modesty and even humility

— that only with this approach, only with this method, will we all be able to fashion the kind of society we want, a truly moral society, a decent society, a livable society, which is the goal of all great religions.

I want to thank particularly those friends who are participating in this play. I wish all of you peace of mind and eternal joy, and particularly the inner joy. Thank you very much, Sri Chinmoy, thank you. Thank you. Thank you. Thank you.

39. *Remarks on the meeting*

[Sri Chinmoy recalled afterwards:]

U Thant was very pleased with the performance. I was sitting beside him, and I remember that on his own, he went up to the stage to congratulate all the players, especially the young man who performed the role of the Buddha.

PART V – PRAYERS FOR U THANT'S RECOVERY

40.

Let us most fervently pray for the recovery of our most revered brother, U Thant, who is now in the hospital. As long as he is in the hospital, it is my fervent wish that every day we shall pray to the Supreme for his quick recovery. I have sent flowers to the hospital on behalf of our Meditation Group here.

Not because U Thant was once the Secretary-General but because he is a great seeker of Truth and a true lover of mankind, I wish all of us to pray to the Supreme for his quick recovery. He is our real spiritual brother, and it is our bounden duty to pray for him. Even though he is not in the political arena any longer, still his presence on earth is a great blessing for humanity.

While he was in the field of politics there were many things which he could not say or do. Owing to pressure from the world at large, he was unable to enter into the real divine life. Now, since he has freed himself from the United Nations, his inner life has come to the fore and he has become a real divine hero.

When his memoirs are published, we will see the real seeker and the real God-lover in him. May God's transcendental Blessing and God's highest Pride rain on his illumining head and consecrated heart.

Now, for a few minutes, let us most fervently pray for his recovery.

41.

U Thant was a learned man. Therefore, he was honoured everywhere. U Thant was a man of compassion. Therefore, he was loved by everyone.

VI — LETTERS FROM U THANT

42. *29 November 1971*

Dear Sri Chinmoy,

I am most grateful for your kind expression of concern for my indisposition. Thank you so much for your beautiful flowers which have brightened my stay in hospital. I am feeling much better and looking forward to resuming my activities.
With kind regards,
Yours sincerely,

— U Thant

43. *10 April 1972*

Dear Reverend Chinmoy:

I am most appreciative of your kind letter of 3 April 1972 which I received along with a coloured photograph while you were chanting blessings on me. You have indeed instilled in the minds of hundreds of people here the moral and spiritual values which both of us cherish very dearly. I shall always cherish the memorable occasion of our meeting at the United Nations.
Thanking you for your very kind sentiments,
Respectfully,

— U Thant

44. *23 January 1973*

Dear Sri Chinmoy,

I thank you most sincerely for your kind message on the occasion of my birthday. I am deeply touched by your thoughtfulness.

Let me take this opportunity of renewing my very best wishes and warm regards.

With admiration,

— U Thant

45. *19 April 1973*

Dear Sri Chinmoy,

I am most grateful for your kindness in inviting me to attend a stage performance *Siddhartha becomes the Buddha* on Friday, 25 May in White Plains. I wish I could immediately accept your kind invitation, but as of this moment I have a plan to be in Chicago during the last week of May. If I can get out of this commitment, I shall be delighted to be present on that occasion. Let me write to you as soon as my schedule is firm.

I am also most appreciative of your thoughtfulness in sending me a copy of the play, as well as other copies of your collected spiritual statements.

With my warm esteem,

— U Thant

46. *25 April 1973*

Dear Sri Chinmoy,

Thank you very much indeed for your second letter of 21 April.

My schedule for the month of May is now firm, and I am very happy to be able to tell you that I will be present at the performance of *Siddhartha becomes the Buddha* on the evening of Friday, 25 May in White Plains.

I am eagerly looking forward to the occasion.

With my warm esteem,

— U Thant

47. *11 June 1973*

Dear Sri Chinmoy,

I was deeply touched by your kind letter of 6 June 1973, which I received along with a beautiful album of photographs taken on that memorable occasion on the evening of 25 May 1973.

I shall always cherish the happy memories of that delightful occasion.

With my very best wishes and respect,

— U Thant

48. *25 March 1974*

Dear Sri Chinmoy,

I just want you to know how appreciative I am for your kindness in sending me those lovely flowers which cheered me up during my moment of illness in the hospital.

I am now recuperating and hope to recover my health in a few weeks time.

Sincerely,

— U Thant

49. *10 May 1974*

Dear Revered Sri Chinmoy,

I thank you so much indeed for your very kind letter of 3 May 1974, which I received together with a bound volume of the 1973 issues of the UN Meditation Group's monthly bulletin. I look forward to reading it as soon as I am fit enough to do so.

After two major operations I am still receiving chemo-therapy treatment and, of course, I am doing meditation every day. I am confident that I will fully recover my health in a few months time.

Needless to say, I am deeply touched by your prayers, love and concern for my health.

— U Thant

50. *28 June 1974*

Dear Sri Chinmoy,

I was deeply moved by your kind letter of 21 June 1974, which I received together with a copy of *Meditation at the United Nations*. I was particularly touched to know that you and your group have been praying for my health while I was in the hospital, and for this I am most grateful. I am now recovering, although slowly and on doctor's advice I am still not receiving any guests.

I am so glad to know that *Siddhartha becomes the Buddha* was recently performed by a group of young ten-year old students from a school in New Jersey. I wish you continued success in your propagation of the moral and spiritual values which are so essential to everyone.

With my sincere esteem and appreciation.

— U Thant

VII – PRAYERS AND TRIBUTES

51.

The Lord Buddha granted U Thant an illumined mind, a oneness-heart, a liberated soul. He also learned from the compassionate Buddha that war is insanity, war is stupidity, war is futility; that a warless world is a soulful and fruitful world.

52.

Lovingly we all received from U Thant his very own: his life's Vision-Truth. Devotedly we all received from U Thant his very own: his Goal's Reality-Bliss.

53. *Prayerful tribute*

[In silence the Group meditates on a photograph of U Thant which stands surrounded by flowers on the altar of the Chapel. Sri Chinmoy offers his prayerful tribute.]

Beloved Brother, man of silence, man of peace, may the Supreme grant your soul Eternity's Silence, Infinity's Peace.

[Sri Chinmoy then quietly addresses the Group.]

The passing of our beloved Brother U Thant marks the real death of a colossal hope for the twentieth century. Divinely great he was; supremely good he is. The greatness of his earth-height his body-consciousness is carrying. The goodness of his Heaven-Delight his soul has left for us, for Mother Earth to claim as her very own and treasure forever and ever.

We the members of the United Nations Meditation Group, have a special place for him, for our beloved Brother U Thant, in the inmost recesses of our gratitude-heart, for he has helped us unreservedly with his aspiring heart and with his illumining soul, both inwardly and outwardly. We have been extremely fortunate in being blessed by his soul's light. I have received from him quite a few letters of deepest light and profoundest wisdom encouraging us and inspiring us to be of greater service to the soul of the United Nations and to aspiring mankind.

VIII — REMINISCENCES ABOUT U THANT

54. *Kurt Waldheim*

Why does the world remember U Thant? We are extremely fortunate to have the most apposite answer by none other than his great successor Kurt Waldheim: "His integrity and his courage were rooted in his firm Buddhist faith and in an unshakable belief in humanity and in the necessity of improving the quality of lives of all mankind. We remember him for his achievements and for the difficulties he faced in presiding over our Organization for ten tumultuous years."

55. *Consul General Lakhan Mehrotra*

Consul General Lakhan Mehrotra of the Consulate General of India in San Francisco, a man of illumining vision and a rising sun of Tomorrow's Dawn, speaks most soulfully of U Thant's spiritual presence with these significant words: "It was a matter of the greatest privilege for me to have met Mr U Thant, Secretary-General of the United Nations, in 1963 and 1964 when I was myself posted in New York at the Consulate General of India. I was deeply impressed by the spiritual glow which seemed to emanate from the personality of the Secretary-General. I had known him for several years as a devout Buddhist and as one who carried something of the Buddha in him in terms of sympathy for the suffering humanity. But one had to see him to believe what was preserved of the spiritual strength he carried within himself. His passing has been a great loss, particularly to us in Asia who had known him as one sincerely anxious for the liberation of regimes under colonial rule. It was only right and proper that among the many distinctions with which Mr

U Thant was honoured, he should have received the Jawaharlal Nehru Award for International Understanding."

56. Mayor Abraham Beame

New York's untiringly dedicated Mayor Abraham Beame remarks on the former Secretary General's adeptness in piloting the world-boat: "In stormy times, he was an island of calm in a sea of controversy. His meditative ways helped him to maintain the neutrality so necessary to sustaining the confidence of differing nations.

"The people of our own nation always respected his ability to mediate differences among the nations, and we always admired his desire to attain justice for all.

"The City, which is proud to be the home of the United Nations, will always revere the memory of the Burma-born schoolteacher who guided the world through a particularly turbulent decade in its history."

57. Mr Donald Keys

U Thant's service to the United Nations and his dream for mankind will forever flourish, irrevocably affirms Donald Keys, a very good friend and genuine well-wisher of U Thant. Mr Keys, who is UN Representative for the World Association of World Federalists, declares: "U Thant was one with the soul of the United Nations, which is the soul of mankind. He lived and worked for the enlightenment, freedom and unification of mankind in all that he did. Out of his own divinity he created a bridge between humanity and the Supreme – the Father of us all. His service to man is not ended with his passing, because it will persist forever, proceeding out of his own spiritual stature. It is only universalised, transformed to a greater and more powerful dimension. The touch of sadness in his going comes from his own sadness that he was unable to serve more, do more, to be received more fully by mankind. We will all endeavour to take up more effectively the little part that we may play in realising his dream of human enlightenment and liberation."

58. *Jose D Ingles*

Jose D Ingles, Under-Secretary for Foreign Affairs, said, "Although U Thant stepped down from the high position of Secretary-General soon after the silver anniversary of the Organization, he remained its living symbol, and was affectionately called 'Mr United Nations'. His death marks the close of an era in the life of the United Nations."

The world knew U Thant as the Secretary-General. Some devoted friends and admirers called him "Mr United Nations". The seekers called him a giant apostle of peace. God called him His Manifestation-Fulfilment son.

59. *Bradford Morse*

In silence U Thant adhered dauntlessly to his wise principles. It happens that sometimes when one is unyielding and forthright, one loses friends, dear ones and even the world's good will. But in the case of U Thant, the story is otherwise during the ten years that he so successfully piloted the United Nations-Boat.

Bradford Morse, Under-Secretary-General for Political and General Assembly Affairs at the time, has offered us abundant light and convincing assurance on this matter: "Both in the political crises which occurred during his time as Secretary-General and in the development of the economic and social work of the Organization, he displayed courage and total dedication to the United Nations in disregard of any private interests or even of his own physical well-being."

Something more that Mr Morse tells the world is quite soul-stirring: "Many of us here became his devoted friends. We admired, above all, his humanity, his respect for human dignity and his complete integrity. To me, U Thant was a personal friend whose wisdom, kindness and generosity I shall never forget. We shall all remember him as a man who gave himself unstintingly to the cause of peace, progress and justice in the world."

60. *From Mrs Aye Aye Myint-U, 1 April 1975*

Dear Sri Chinmoy,

My mother, my husband and I would like to thank you for the copies of *Meditation at the United Nations.* It was so beautiful, and we are deeply moved by the warmth and affection you have shown towards my father. We will always be grateful for your kind words and will always treasure these issues.

We also want you to know that daddy had great respect for your spiritual leadership, and we send our best wishes for your continued success in helping for a better mankind.

Respectfully,

— Aye Aye Myint-U

PS: We would be very happy to receive a few more issues of the bulletin to send to friends in Burma. Thank you.

IX – DEDICATION TO U THANT, PART 3

61.

U Thant's wisdom-light removed the pall of suspicion-night that had fallen on many unfortunate human beings and certain countries.

62. *U Thant the peace-lover*

U Thant the peace-lover illumines the human mind in us: "There is no peace in the world today because there is no peace in the minds of men."

The human mind needs peace for its transformation and illumination. Peace needs the human mind for its continuous expansion and complete manifestation on earth. Therefore, both divine peace and the human mind need each other and are supposed to work like two complementary souls.

63. *U Thant the peace-educator*

Peace is a universal hunger. Each individual needs peace right from the cradle to the grave. When the young generation acquires peace, the teeming problems of the world will not remain problems any longer. The young generation will unite the old and the new with its dynamic achievement: peace.

Peace spreads, peace flows, peace becomes, peace is. In the domain of the vital, peace spreads. In the domain of the mind, peace flows. In the domain of the heart, peace becomes. In the domain of the soul, peace is.

Peace spreads its illumining beauty. Peace flows with its satisfying delight. Peace becomes perfection. Peace is Immortality's infinite treasure.

U Thant the peace-educator teaches us: "One of the great tasks of education all over the world is to educate the young for peace because, on the question of peace, no man of good will can be neutral."

64. *U Thant the wisdom-bestower*

U Thant the wisdom-bestower is unique in presenting us with his soul's largesse: "We have already begun to realise that in modern war there is no such thing as victor and vanquished: that there is only a loser, and that loser is mankind."

We are all aware of the undeniable fact that war results in victory and defeat. But this is a surface experience that covers our human mind and our human life. The inner experience is totally different. In the inner world, war is an immediate experience of separativity, and separativity is nothing short of tremendous loss in the world of oneness. Oneness alone can feed humanity's eternal hunger and bring about satisfaction. Those who cherish the body-reality's separation-consciousness are deplorable losers in the process of God's evolution in and through mankind.

65. *U Thant the reality-dreamer of tomorrow's dawn*

Before the dawn of civilisation and after the dawn of civilisation, what the world saw and has always seen has been an endless series of fights, battles and wars. Humanity could have easily avoided the destructive experiences of the hoary past if it had longed for a higher vision and a deeper reality.

U Thant the reality-dreamer says to us: "In the wake of the most catastrophic war in the history of mankind, humanity had a new vision: it saw the glimmer of dawn of a warless world."

Humanity's preparation depends on humanity's willingness. Humanity's willingness depends on humanity's consecrated surrender to God's Will. A oneness-world either in the near or in the distant future is not only possible and practicable, but inevitable. A oneness-world expedites God's Hour, and it is only in God's Hour that humanity's age-long hunger drinks in Divinity's Nectar-Delight.

Undoubtedly, the fruit of the Immortals is for mortals, too, for God the finite reality and God the Reality infinite are inseparable. Together they are heading towards one goal: satisfaction in perfection.

66. *U Thant the miracle-embodiment and exponent of an integral life*

Happiness: where is it, if not in the core of an integral life?
Happiness: what is it, if not an expansion-vision of an integral life?

U Thant, the exponent and embodiment of an integral life, affirms: "Pure intellectual development unaccompanied by a corresponding moral and spiritual development will lead mankind from one crisis to another. Moral qualities of friendship, humility and the desire to understand the other point of view are as important as intellectual excellence."

On the earth plane, an integral life is the glad unification of intellectual, moral and spiritual fulfilment. An intellectual life need not be an expansion of a dry, aloof and superior feeling. Love of intellect, in its purest sense, is a life that desires to see the reality in its minute and subtle details. In the skies of the mind, this yearning itself is a higher step towards the ultimate heights of the Beyond.

Morality does not mean a life-torturing needle. Morality does not mean a constant vigil over the animal in us. Morality is an illumining reality that takes us from a lesser goal of confusion-bondage to a greater goal of perfection-freedom. Morality is not the rope that strangles us; it is the rope that saves us.

Spirituality is not an act of withdrawal from world activities. Spirituality is not hallucination-reality. Spirituality is not something that has a liking for Heaven and a constant dislike of earth. No! Real spirituality is the conscious awareness of God the Creator and God the creation. It is the feeling of constant oneness with God the One and God the many. It is the continuous transcendence of the animal into the human, of the human into the divine and of the divine into the supreme Reality.

If we view life as a unified experience of an intellectual reality, moral reality and spiritual reality, then this world of ours can be nothing but satisfaction-happiness in God's cosmic Play.

67. U Thant the task-giver

U Thant the task-giver asks two questions that can not only keep us on the alert constantly but also fulfil us eventually: "Every man or woman should not only ask himself or herself what he or she is going to do in the world, but also ask, 'Will there be a world in which I can live?'"

Satisfaction of the individual is undoubtedly a most significant achievement. No doubt it is a form of perfection. But the individual has to ask himself whether, with this perfection, he can remain outside the world-boundary. The answer will always be in the negative. Therefore, it is of utmost importance that the world in which we live also be perfect.

As we strive for our individual perfection, even so we shall strive for the collective perfection and the perfection of the world-body. Perfection has to loom large simultaneously in the individual soul, in the collective soul and in the world-soul. This is the only thing that we are supposed to accomplish here on earth and we shall, without fail, accomplish it.

68. *U Thant the freedom-revolutionary*

Revolution, inner and outer. The outer revolution quite often leads to destruction. The inner revolution is our constant cry for illumining progress, which is derived from the heart of freedom.

Freedom is humanity's choice. Freedom is Divinity's choice. With freedom, humanity ultimately grows into God the transcendental Vision. With freedom, Divinity ultimately grows into the universal Reality.

U Thant the freedom-revolutionary tells us: "The revolution brought by science and technology to the developed nations is a revolutionary extension of human freedom. Freedom is choice. Freedom is the ability to act...."

Science and technology help us walk along a particular road of freedom. Spirituality helps us walk along a different road of freedom. But before we walk along the freedom-road of science and technology, science and technology advise us to look around and grasp the secrets of the world's beauty-reality. Before we walk along the freedom-road of spirituality, spirituality advises us to dive deep within and unveil the world's soul-reality. If we abide by their wise advice, we please the science and technology world with our dedication-service and we satisfy the spirituality world with our aspiration-cry. Dedication-service leads us to the Reality that we are supposed to grow into. Aspiration-cry leads us to the Reality which we eternally are.

69. *U Thant the education-lover*

Teacher and student. The teacher prepares; the student completes. The teacher begins; the student ends. The teacher is the vision in reality; the student is the reality in vision. The teacher helps the student climb; the student helps the teacher spread.

"Self-giving is delight." So says the teacher. "Receiving is delight." So says the student.

When giving and receiving can be accomplished cheerfully and unconditionally, seed the teacher and fruit the student fulfil each other.

U Thant the education-lover sees student and teacher as two eternal friends: "....the teachers are the true architects of minds, and the students are the true builders of peace. If the teachers instruct the younger generation in the ways of peace, not only will their work succeed, but the basic idea of peace in our time will triumph."

70. *U Thant the education-seer*

Education is cultivation of knowledge. The outer world feels that world-information is enough for cultivation of knowledge. The inner world feels that there is only one kind of knowledge that can cure the ignorance-night which is humanity's malady of millennia. The cure is called wisdom-light.

U Thant the education-seer illumines us about education, outer and inner: "In Asia, if I may say so, the traditional aim of education is to impress on the young the importance of the mind rather than the body, and even more basically, the importance of the spirit rather than the mind. Education thus becomes inward looking, and the aim of education is the discovery of one's self rather than the discovery of things external to us."

There are two aspects to reality: the body-reality and the soul-reality. The body-reality looks around for its satisfaction. The soul-reality looks within for its satisfaction. The Eastern approach or, let us say, the Asian approach to reality is to dive deep within and discover the soul and, thus, know everything and become everything. The other approach, which we may call the Western approach, instructs us to look inside the body-reality and around the body-reality to see what it really is and what it can contribute to world-success.

71. *U Thant the friend of the mass media*

U Thant, ever a friend to the mass media, wrote in the September 1955 issue of *Guardian Magazine*: "One of the impressions I have gained.... is the essential similarity of national characters on which a world-wide understanding can be built and global solidarity can rest. Everywhere men and women, young and old, love peace, enjoy a good joke and lead affectionate family lives. No doubt mass media.... have bred in the minds of people certain prejudices and bias.... but I believe that the same mass media.... can turn such people into their real selves."

Individuals can go together, mix together and fulfil themselves together. There is and there will always be an underlying oneness, an essential similarity of human beings, nations and national characters. It is not that each one must discover his goal totally apart from the rest of the world. Together we must strive to achieve the selfsame goal, for it is collective oneness alone that can grant us perfect satisfaction.

Again, we are afraid that the mass media have created tremendous confusion in life, a sense of superiority and inferiority that can ruin human minds. But U Thant's prophetic utterance is that the same mass media can help human beings see, realise and become their true selves.

U THANT: DIVINITY'S SMILE, HUMANITY'S CRY

72. Interview on 21 September 1963

David Sureck: The first United Nations Secretary-General, Trygve Lie has described your job as "the most impossible job in the world". What did you think about it on the day you were sworn in?
U Thant: A feeling of humility and an overwhelming sense of responsibility, to which was added a dawning hope that the unanimous support which has so generously been accorded to me would make "the most impossible job in the world" a little less impossible.

73. U Thant the champion of human dignity

Dignity is not a philosophical dream. Dignity is not an expression of ego's aggrandisement. Dignity is a supreme necessity if we want to touch each other, feel each other and realise each other on a higher level of consciousness.

U Thant the champion of human dignity says: "....The dignity and worth of the human person is not merely a philosophic concept. It is, and should be, a working principle of human existence guiding our daily lives. Every human being, of whatever origin, of whatever station, deserves respect. We must each respect others even as we respect ourselves. This, as the sages of many lands have taught us, is a golden rule in individual and group, as well as international, relations."

When we show our dignity, we bring to the fore our divine capacities. When others show their dignity, they also do the same thing. In the expression of dignity, all of us bring forward our inner, divine, illumining and fulfilling capacities and we triumphantly arrive at a higher goal which has been the aspiration of human beings from time immemorial. The sages of the hoary past offered us this sublime vision, and now we are trying in our own age to transform this vision into concrete reality.

74. *U Thant the teacher of mankind*

U Thant has served the world in various capacities, but he started his career as a schoolteacher. We notice in him a born teacher of mankind. He taught the world how to bring to the fore the capacities of the heart and thus create a oneness-world.

U Thant the teacher of mankind offered this momentous advice in his farewell speech: "In this world, try to be both good and able men. If you do not become able men, at least try to be good men. The country has no use for able but bad men."

According to him, what the world needs is a combination of good men and able men. It is good men and able men combined that can create a new society, new progress, new perfection.

75. *U Thant the world citizen and defender of human rights*

In an address to the General Assembly commemorating the adoption of the Universal Declaration of Human Rights, U Thant the world citizen declared: "In this age of the jet plane and the Telstar, the world is fast becoming a community, a community with common interests and common aspirations. Gone are the days when each nation was an island unto itself. Today, questions of human rights are a matter of international concern."

U Thant not only felt humanity's excruciating pangs but also became one with humanity's astounding progress. This progress gave him abundant joy and a true sense of satisfaction. He saw that mind-division is surrendering to heart-oneness and national pride is yielding to international light, creating a new and illumining world-society.

76. U Thant the exemplar of religious tolerance

With his cosmopolitan heart, the unparallelled seeker U Thant climbed up the aspiration-tree to a surprisingly lofty height. From there he illumined the votaries of the world-illumining religious faiths.

At the opening of the African Summit Conference in Cairo on 19 July 1964, U Thant the exemplar of religious tolerance said: "How are we to practise tolerance? What states of mind are necessary for all of us to live together in peace with one another as good neighbours? How are we to unite our strength to maintain international peace and security? The answers to these questions lie, it seems to me, in our ability to bring out the best in us and to return to the basic moral and ethical principles of all great religions. Let us, therefore, dedicate ourselves anew to a new pledge: to make Muslims better Muslims, Hindus better Hindus, Christians better Christians and Buddhists better Buddhists."

77. U Thant the visionary

U Thant feels that as different religions live in the peace room, even so societies can live in the peace room. There is no hard and fast rule that societies cannot have the same inner growth and the same outer broadness as religions.

U Thant the visionary says: "....As Buddhism, Christianity, Islam, Hinduism and all other religions are existing peacefully in amity, I believe a day will come when these different societies – communist societies, capitalist societies, socialist societies, and any other type of societies – are going to exist peacefully. I believe in these things."

Peace is within, peace is without. The core of society we touch with our inner peace. The body of society we touch with our outer peace. The inner peace unites the heart and the soul of the world. The outer peace unites the body and the mind of the world.

Spirituality has achieved considerable success in casting aside unfortunate and unlit conflicts with regard to religious beliefs that once upon a time dominated the human mind. Likewise, aspiration is going to achieve towering success in different societies. U Thant's belief in these things is nothing short of his infallible vision.

78. *U Thant the prophet of the United Nations*

We have already possessed the body-consciousness but we have not yet possessed the soul-reality. If we know what the United Nations truly is and what it stands for and what it can do to serve, illumine and fulfil mankind, then only we can embody fulfilling hopes for tomorrow's dawn.

U Thant, the United Nations pilot, while most successfully steering the United Nations boat, voiced forth during a United Nations Day address in 1964: "The United Nations.... is simply an Organization, serving all nations but dominated by none, which has the continual obligation to avoid disaster and misery and to provide for a better and more productive future for all peoples. The emergence of such a mechanism is both a great step forward and a historic challenge. This is, indeed, an idea to possess men's souls."

79. *U Thant the soul-voice of the United Nations*

There is a time when we see eye to eye with one another in solving the world problems. Again, there is a time when we totally disagree. There is a time when we have individual goals. Again, there is a time when we have a common goal.

U Thant speaks on behalf of the soul of the United Nations with regard to the common goal: "Here in the United Nations we also have a basic aim in common, which is to preserve the peace and to enhance human happiness and dignity throughout the world in accordance with our Charter."

At the United Nations, many nations with different opinions are working together. Although outwardly they seem to have divergent goals, they are running towards an inner goal which is nothing short of a common goal.

80. *After talks with Indian Prime Minister Shastri*

After talks with Indian Prime Minister Shastri, U Thant expressed his optimism that the India-Pakistan conflict would be solved. Speaking at Delhi airport on 15 September 1965, he declared:

"I would, however, like to say here that even if an end to the fighting has not yet been achieved, that is no reason for any cessation of the efforts of all men of good will to achieve it.

"For myself, I shall continue to work towards a ceasefire and a peaceful solution to this tragic problem in the light of the very frank and useful talks I have had in both countries in the last few days. I look forward to the co-operation and support of both Governments and of public opinion in this effort and I dare to express the hope and the belief that we may soon see better days."

81. *Moral force and inner light*

Former Indian Prime Minister Lal Bahadur Shastri and U Thant were both frail in body and dauntless in spirit. But both of them conquered the world with their moral force and inner light.

82. *Confidence in Kurt Waldheim*

On 22 December 1971, U Thant expressed his boundless confidence in Kurt Waldheim and warmly welcomed him as his worthy successor:

"I was right to insist that I should leave my office at this time. In doing so I am greatly heartened and encouraged by the thought that I shall be leaving this office in such capable hands.

I have known Ambassador Waldheim ever since he first came to New York as Permanent Representative of Austria to the United Nations in 1964. Subsequently he has been Foreign Minister of his own country, and I was personally very pleased when he was reappointed as Permanent Representative of Austria to the United Nations last year. I know that he is held in very high esteem by all of those who have come to know him during his many years in New York. Apart from his well-known diplomatic ability, he has shown a special talent for conciliation in his work as Chairman of the Outer Space Committee and in other United Nations bodies. I wish him every success in his new and high responsibilities."

83. *From Mrs Aye Aye Myint-U, 15 January 1977*

Dear Sri Chinmoy,

On behalf of my mother, Mrs Thant and my family may I take this opportunity to express our profound gratitude to you for your kind sentiments and love for my father. Father had always cherished the time he spent with you for he found in you love and tranquillity. He shared with you the importance of morality and spirituality in this complex and troubled world, and he was always inspired by your humility and dedication for the enlightenment of innerself.

We are deeply proud to share father's life, and are most fortunate to have received his unselfish love and care.

We pray and hope that your continued effort may bring forth the dreams of my father, peace, happiness and prosperity for all mankind.

With our esteem admiration and respect,

— Aye Aye Myint-U

84. *To Aye Aye Myint-U, 16 January 1977*

Dear Aye Aye,

Your beloved Father and my beloved spiritual Brother, U Thant, will always triumphantly stand in the vanguard of humanity's soulful success and fruitful progress.

I liked him. I admired him. I adored him. I loved him. I liked him because in him I saw a sea of simplicity, humility and purity. I admired him because I saw a wisdom-sun upon him constantly radiating its unhorizoned effulgence. I adored him because his heart's Illumination lovingly covered the length and breadth of the entire world. I loved him because his life of self-giving to humanity's cry and Divinity's Smile made him the supremely perfect instrument of the Lord Buddha.

Your unparallelled oneness-heart with your Father's vastness-heart and your Father's soul-concern for you have touched the very depth of my heart. The human in us misses him badly. The divine in us tells us that he is with the Lord Buddha here on earth, there in Heaven, inside all human beings and all divine souls.

He is at once with the Creator's ever-transcending Vision and ever-manifesting Reality.

As the Creator and the creation are inseparable, even so his unconditionally surrendered will to the Will of the Lord Buddha are eternally inseparable. Infinity's greatness he has. Immortality's goodness he is.

I wish to offer my most respectful salutation to your mother, my loving regards to your kind and good husband, Dr Myint-U, and my soulful love to your divinely sweet children.

I pray to the Lord Buddha to bless you and your whole family with His infinite Compassion-Light and His eternal Satisfaction-Delight.

Affectionately yours,

— Sri Chinmoy

85.

Only a highly advanced soul like U Thant can achieve detachment-light. Most illumining was U Thant's intrepid detachment from the fruitless trivialities of human life. To our deep sorrow, some unlit human beings took his detachment-light for insouciance-night. Again, to our deep joy and satisfaction, they eventually realised their grave folly.

86. *A man of silence*

The human mind, like the wind, is uncontrollable. By virtue of scientific development, we have discovered the ways and means of controlling the restless wind to a considerable degree. But alas, control of the human mind is still a far cry to millions and billions. It just baffles human understanding.

But U Thant was endowed with preternatural qualities. He was adept in the divine art of controlling the mind. Therefore, with aplomb and purity in his heart he was able to throw himself into the tornado of world-activities while maintaining silence soulful and fruitful.

87. *Faithful son and fruitful father of the third world*

U Thant had a cosmopolitan heart. Impartiality was one of his names. His modesty, kindness, sacrifice and oneness have made him Eternity's treasure.

What he wanted for mankind was happiness. From where? From a self-disciplined oneness-heart.

He was an emblem of the ideals of justice. Sublime was his spiritual message to the world at large: "Give totally what you have; become what Truth-satisfaction eternally is."

His heart made him feel that he was of all and for all. Most sincere was his effort to bridge the gap between the rich and the poor, between the strong and the weak, between the unlit human beings and the illumined human beings.

It is most astonishing how God played in and through him the role of an untiring and faithful son of the third world and, at the same time, unfailing and fruitful father.

88. Colossal soul

Four are the most special gifts that humanity received from U Thant's colossal soul: concern-sun, sympathy-sea, dedication-realisation and compassion-perfection.

Unlike U Thant, we wrap ourselves in the cocoons of self-concern, self-sympathy, self-dedication and self-compassion.

U Thant's soul knew that he was of all. U Thant's heart felt that he was for all.

89.

U Thant gave us his soul's glorious leadership. U Thant gave us his heart's precious friendship. U Thant gave us his Lord Buddha-worship.

90. A heart of pole-star purity

U Thant was more than successful in veiling his minds stupendous brilliance with his heart's pole-star purity and humility.

The great seeker in him discovered the truth that the fastest way to become part and parcel of humanity is the way of the heart and not that of the mind.

He also discovered that it is the heart that has infinitely more capacity than the mind to establish an abiding oneness with the world community.

He further realised the supreme fact that the mind has to be illumined by the soul, for this is the only way to bring about a radical transformation of human nature and the world family.

91. *A life of self-transcendence*

His was the life of conscience. His was the heart of compassion. His was the mind of serenity. His was the vital of determination. His was the body of sanctity.

To him, an outer life of violation indicated an inner life of imminent destruction.

His single-minded service to the United Nations for ten long years showed the world what mental equanimity and psychic luminosity can do for mankind.

He showed the world that a life of self-transcendence, a life of truth-discovery and a life of light-manifestation must not remain always a far cry.

In him the United Nations quite astonishingly discovered a faithful servant, a soulful friend and a fruitful leader.

3. *(p.323)* Sri Chinmoy delivered this lecture in the Dag Hammarskjöld Auditorium, United Nations, New York, on 12 December 1974, as part of the continuing Dag Hammarskjöld monthly Lecture Series sponsored by the United Nations Meditation Group.

4. *(p.325)* United Nations, New York, NY, 29 February 1972.

5. *(p.327)* During a meeting of the United Nations Meditation Group on 14 May 1976, various persons offered reminiscences about their most significant experiences at the United Nations. Sri Chinmoy spoke about his first meeting with U Thant.

37–39. *(p.344)* On the evening of 25 May 1973, U Thant attended the first performance of *Siddhartha becomes the Buddha,* a series of one-act plays based on incidents in the life of the Lord Buddha, written by Sri Chinmoy and performed by his disciples on an outdoor stage built for the occasion at Old Mill Farm in Harrison, New York. U Thant was accompanied by his daughter, son-in-law and young grandson.

40. *(p.348)* On two separate occasions when U Thant was hospitalised, Sri Chinmoy requested the members of the United Nations Meditation Group to pray for his recovery. The first time was on 4 November 1971, following a lecture Sri Chinmoy delivered as part of his monthly Dag Hammarskjöld Series. The second occasion was on 8 March 1974. This is what Sri Chinmoy said at that time.

53. *(p.354)* On 26 November 1974, the United Nations Meditation Group held a special meditation in the Chapel of the Church Center for the United Nations in tribute to U Thant, who had passed away the previous day.

54–60. *(p. 356)* U Thant's death left the whole world deeply bereaved. These are some reminiscences about the late Secretary-General.

72. *(p. 367)* From an interview in *The Saturday Evening Post* of 21 September 1963.

PART VIII

THE SEEKER'S MIND:
TALKS DELIVERED AT THE UNITED NATIONS

I – TALKS DELIVERED AT THE UNITED NATIONS

1. *Sri Chinmoy Meditation at the United Nations*

UNITED NATIONS:
THE HEART-HOME OF THE WORLD-BODY

We believe and we hold that each man has the potentiality of reaching the Ultimate Truth. We also believe that man cannot and will not remain imperfect forever. Each man is an instrument of God. When the hour strikes, each individual soul listens to the inner dictates of God. When man listens to God, his imperfections are turned into perfections, his ignorance into knowledge, his searching mind into revealing light and his uncertain reality into all-fulfilling Divinity.

2. *The General Assembly*

The General Assembly begins today. It is a most significant event. The General Assembly is a family gathering of a very special family. Unlike most families, this family knows what to say, what to do and what to become. It knows how to love, how to serve and how to fulfil. What to say? The members of this family say that they wish to live together forever. What to do? They try to understand one another; they try to share with one another their teeming ideas and glowing ideals. What to become? They try to become a cry; they try to become a hope; they try to become a promise; they try to become a smile – a cry that elevates them, a hope that feeds them, a promise that reveals them, a smile that immortalises them. How to love? They try to love with their illumining souls. How to serve? They try to serve with their searching minds and their striving vitals. How to fulfil? They try to fulfil by steering God's Dream-boat towards the Golden Shore.

The General Assembly signifies interdependence. It represents a song of the community of nations, a song of group-souls. While singing this song, these souls will climb high, higher, highest until they one day reach the transcendental Vision of world union. While singing this song, these souls will march far, farther, farthest until they one day reach the transcendental Reality of universal Peace. There is also another reason why this time of year is most significant. Thirteen years ago tomorrow, one of the great pilots of the United Nations passed behind the curtain of Eternity: Dag Hammarskjöld died in a plane crash. But before his soul flew to the highest realm of consciousness, it left behind the quintessence of its love for humanity, its wish for peace within humanity and its feeling of oneness with humanity. Dag Hammarskjöld was a man of God and servant of humanity. The body and soul of the United Nations treasure the quintessence of his love of truth, light, peace and universal oneness.

Here we are all seekers. We, too, belong to a family, a spiritual family. We are all praying for world peace, world harmony and world union in a divine and supreme way. Today the General Assembly begins with new hope, new determination and new aspiration to discover something more illumining and more fulfilling. We, too, the seekers of infinite Truth and Light, can begin today with new hope, new determination and new aspiration as we try to become more spiritual, more sincere, more dedicated. In this way we can serve the Inner Pilot of the United Nations and the Inner Pilot of the entire world-family in a most illumining and fulfilling way.

3. Comments about the Secretaries-General

I have also served the UN, for six years. But unlike you, who have served officially, I have served unofficially. With your kind permission I wish to offer two most striking experiences of mine. The first was when I met with Secretary-General U Thant in his office. His simplicity, sincerity, humility, purity and divinity made me immediately feel that I had found in him a true and genuine spiritual brother. In him I also discovered a heart of universal oneness. Then, a few years ago, I had the golden opportunity to pay my most soulful respects to the soul of Secretary-General Dag Hammarskjöld at his grave in Uppsala. While I was offering my most soulful love, appreciation and adoration to this divinely great soul, I discovered immediately the luminosity of his mind. In his mind I found the most illumining and fulfilling vastness. Two supremely giant souls – Dag Hammarskjöld and U Thant, U Thant and Dag Hammarskjöld. Inside the vastness of Dag Hammarskjöld my heart felt the love of oneness, and inside the oneness of U Thant my soul envisioned the vastness. Their oneness and vastness and vastness and oneness make me feel and realise that this UN – their dream-fulfilling reality and reality-transcending dream – will forever and ever be cherished and treasured by the aspiring, self-giving and truth-loving humanity.

4. Meditation for Dag Hammarskjöld

This is the first time that all the members of the Meditation Group have gone to the Meditation Room and meditated together. This is a significant occasion for us. But something infinitely more important, this is our soulful tribute to the immortal memory of the UN Pilot, Dag Hammarskjöld. We went to the Meditation Room to observe the anniversary of his death.

According to human wisdom, death is a halt, where all movements cease for good. But according to divine wisdom, death is a step we take while walking along Eternity's road.

We went there to observe the passing, or the extinction, of Dag Hammarskjöld's body-consciousness. This is what the outer world will say. But the inner world tells us that we did not go there to observe the extinction of anything. We went to observe the illumination of a great soul, a sublime soul. His mind was illumined, his heart was totally awakened and his soul was fulfilled.

When we think of the Secretary-General Dag Hammarskjöld, we come to realise that in him the great battle, the age-long battle between mind and heart, had come to an end. In him, the mind and the heart became good, intimate friends. We all know that when there are two friends, both friends walk together towards the same destination. But in his case, we observe something extraordinary. The mind went along the road of illumination and the heart marched along the road of liberation. However, they were in perfect conformity to one another, in perfect understanding. We think that if two persons are true friends, then they must walk together. But this is not necessary. If there are two goals that eventually merge into one goal, then these subordinate goals must be reached before we reach the ultimate goal. Illumination was the first goal, which his mind wanted to attain, and liberation of the aspiring heart was the second goal, which his heart wanted to achieve. So his mind went to the illumination-shore and his heart went to the liberation-shore. Then from the liberation-shore and the illumination-shore, the mind and the heart together went to the Perfection-shore. The Perfection-shore is the ultimate goal of each human being.

When we observe a thing with our physical eyes, with our naked eyes, we see a loss and gain, failure and success. But when we use our inner eye, our third eye, we see that there is no such thing as loss or gain, failure or success. On the physical plane, definitely it is a terrible loss for such a great soul, such a good soul, to leave the body in a plane crash. What an unfortunate experience for humanity to have. But from the spiritual point of view, it was not an accident, but a glowing reality that was entering into the ever-glowing, illumining and fulfilling Reality. Here we are all seekers. Dag Hammarskjöld was a seeker in the purest sense of the term. He was a seeker of the highest order. His heart cried for the satisfaction of mankind. His mind cried for the illumination of mankind. His body, his physical consciousness, is nowhere to be found – it is all in the elemental sheaths. But his soul is not only in Heaven, it is also on earth. The soul-bird flies from Heaven to earth, from earth to Heaven. When it comes to earth, it comes with new hope, new light, new illumination, new compassion and new consolation. Then it becomes one with us. And when it flies to Heaven, it carries our inner cry, inner thirst and inner hunger. It also carries our insufficiencies, our weaknesses, our misunderstanding, our lack of sympathy and oneness. It carries to Heaven all the darkness of the unlit, strangling world that we live in or have created for ourselves. Each time the soul of this great seeker, Dag Hammarskjöld, comes down, it brings down for us at the United Nations and for seekers all over the world the hope that awakens mankind, the consolation that sustains mankind and the compassion that eventually lifts up humanity's fate to the golden Heights of Tomorrow's Dawn.

5. *Inner flames at the United Nations*

Inner Flames signify aspiration. Aspiration illumines the undivine in us and fulfils the divine in us. Our doubting mind is the undivine in us. Our loving heart is the divine in us. The doubting mind unconsciously and consciously tries to destroy the whole world. The loving heart consciously and unreservedly creates a new world: a world of hope, a world of light, a world of delight.

Aspiration is the inner cry. Both God and man have this inner cry. With His inner Cry, God claims us. With our inner cry, we follow God. God's inner Cry is for our perfection and our outer cry is for God's satisfaction.

We, the members of the United Nations Meditation Group, are each inner flames, and we are each trying with utmost humility and sincerity to be of service to each member of the United Nations, to the dream of the United Nations, to the pristine purity of the United Nations. Our capacity is very limited, but our willingness, our eagerness to be of service to each member, to each ideal of the United Nations, is sincere. And this sincerity will one day be proved and marked.

Here at the United Nations, all are inner flames. No matter what an individual's post is, whether he holds the highest post or the lowest, he is undoubtedly an inner flame, for his is the cry which is genuine. Each individual server of the United Nations, irrespective of his nationality or religious and cultural background, is undoubtedly an inner flame. And each flame serves the community of nations according to its capacity and according to its receptivity.

The original and pioneer flame was President Wilson. His dream of the League of Nations has blossomed into the United Nations. Once it was a tiny plant, but now it has grown into a huge banyan tree. It was the plant that embodied the inner flame and now, as a huge banyan tree, it has countless flames.

God and Truth are one and inseparable. Truth and Light are also one and inseparable. Truth, when it starts manifesting itself, takes the form of Light and this Light illumines and fulfils the seeker in us.

The seeker in us always wants to satisfy the little world and the big world. The world that we claim at the beginning of our life – our home, our parents, our brothers and sisters, our relatives – is the little world. But as our vision increases, as we look around and see a bigger world, an unhorizoned world awaiting us, at that time we claim the big world as our very own.

Each individual who has come to serve the United Nations represents his own country, his small world. But when he becomes part and parcel of the United Nations, the big world, at that time he is for all, for the entire humanity. He started his journey with his own country and then he arrived at the goal of goals: universal oneness.

The United Nations wants to solve all the world problems. It is more than eager to solve all the problems that the world could ever imagine. In various ways it is trying to solve the world's problems lovingly, devotedly, soulfully and unreservedly. A problem indicates confusion, a problem indicates the dance of ego, a problem indicates human weakness. Each problem can be solved and will be solved by only one thing and that is the message of union. This union comes to the fore only when we kindle the inner flame. We, as seekers, know perfectly well that it is the inner flames that are burning inside all the members of the United Nations that are inspiring the members to solve all the problems of the world.

Today's meeting is honouring the General Assembly. At the General Assembly each individual nation comes to offer its light, truth, willingness-capacity and sense of oneness. Each country embodies truth and light in its own way. But each country feels and knows in the inmost recesses of its heart that the light and truth it embodies cannot be sufficient. Therefore, it tries to accept and receive light from other countries. Similarly, each flame that each individual embodies cannot be sufficient to solve any world problem or to illumine world-ignorance. What is needed is the unification of all the flames that are here, there and everywhere. So all the flames that are here have to be collected so that they can muster their joint strength. At that time, the ignorance-dream that separates one country from another, one man from another, can no longer last. It will be replaced by Wisdom-Reality. And what is Wisdom-Reality? Wisdom-Reality is the song of oneness. This song of oneness is founded only on self-giving, which is nothing short of truth-becoming. And truth-becoming is oneness with the all-embracing, all-loving, all-illumining and all-fulfilling Reality.

The higher reality is the soul in us; the lower reality is the body-consciousness, which we are right now. The lower reality aspires to grow into the higher reality. The higher reality inspires us. A great many individuals think only of the lower reality, the body-reality, as the United Nations building, where thousands of human beings are serving the one cause. The building-reality, the body-reality, of the United Nations immediately captures their minds. The outside world does not easily think of the soul-reality, which is the real reality of the United Nations. But it is the loving souls, the illumining souls of the United Nations that guide the body-reality, or try to guide it. The day will come when the outer world will realise that looming large inside the body-reality is the soul-reality.

We the seekers and members of the United Nations Meditation Group are trying to serve both the soul-reality and the body-reality according to our very limited capacity. Our capacity is very, very limited, but our sincere efforts we place at the Feet of the Inner Pilot of the United Nations. This Inner Pilot is our fate-maker, the Author of all Good, God. It is the Creator in God and the creation-fruit that is all light and life and perfection.

6. *The face of truth*

A seeker wishes to see the face of truth in spirituality, in religion, in love, in brotherhood, in every field of reality, in every branch of the reality-tree. But unfortunately, the face of truth is not to be found there. The face of truth is found only in longing, in the longing for truth. Not only the face of truth, but the very heart of truth, is to be found only in the longing itself. What is truth? Truth is the longing, the birthless and deathless longing which we have and which we are. This is the only truth – nothing more, nothing less.

Some seekers are of the opinion that truth is not to be found here on earth, that truth belongs to the hoary past, that it is a memory of the past which we are carrying and dragging. But this is not true. Truth was there before, truth is here now and truth will also be present in the future.

The truth of the past is the truth-beauty in God's cosmic Vision. The truth of the present is the truth-duty in God's cosmic Realisation. The truth of the future is the truth-infallibility in God's cosmic Manifestation.

Here on earth, a seeker notices three kinds of truth: peripheral truth, median truth and core truth. Peripheral truth says that there is no love. "Love is the essence of life, but there is no love on earth."

Median truth says love and be loved. "I have mankind. Therefore it is obligatory on the part of all human beings to love me."

Core truth, the truth of the inmost reality, says, "I love God the Creator, for He is none other than Love. I love God the Creation because it is nothing other than love."

Truth needs a possessor, a revealer and a fulfiller. The truth-possessor is he who is at least a few centuries in advance of his time. The truth-revealer is he who stands in front of humanity, facing humanity. He enters into humanity's countless needs and transforms humanity's needs into deeds. The truth-fulfiller is he who lives only for humanity, for humanity's sake. Unless and until each human being becomes a perfect instrument of the Absolute Supreme, the task of the truth-fulfiller is not complete.

A seeker of the highest, ultimate Truth, a seeker who has established his constant oneness with the Absolute, can at once be a truth-possessor, truth-revealer and truth-fulfiller on the strength of his oneness with the perennial Source, his oneness with the Transcendental Light, the ever-transcending Transcendental Light.

Here we are all seekers, seekers of the United Nations, for the United Nations. The United Nations itself is both the seeker and the truth. When we look at the body-reality of the United Nations, we see that the United Nations plays the role of the seeker. But when we look at the soul-reality of the United Nations, then we see that the United Nations is nothing short of Truth and Light and Delight.

The seeker in the United Nations is becoming and growing into the truth-reality, and the truth-reality is constantly unveiling its hidden treasures – its immortalising, all-illumining and all-fulfilling treasures. These treasures are concern, sympathy, union, oneness, justice-light, perfection and, finally, satisfaction in all that the United Nations does and all that the United Nations is going to do. The United Nations is growing into the perfection-tree that will offer its branches of concern, sympathy and oneness to humanity.

When we seek, we long for a reality. When we long for a reality which is other than our true self, this reality will always remain a far cry. If we live in the body-reality and, from the body-reality, if we want to reach the soul-reality, then we shall never succeed. But if we can dare to say and feel there is only one reality – the soul-reality – which is founded upon our oneness-reality, our universal oneness-reality, our transcendental oneness-reality, then only can we safely say that inside our longing itself is the birthless and the deathless Truth. Then we can say that our longing itself is the everlasting Truth, the immortal Truth, the eternally transcending Truth, the infinitely fulfilling Truth.

7. *They say and we say*

They say that the United Nations is a mere dream. We say that it is a dream that can grow into reality. Dream is the seed-essence. Reality is the fruit-substance.

They say that the United Nations is not independent. We say that there is no necessity for the United Nations to be independent, for the United Nations lives in the illumining heart of humanity and lives for the aspiring life of humanity.

They say that the United Nations is not powerful. We say that unless the world has given the United Nations the opportunity to show all its strength, outer and inner strength – but especially inner – how can it say that the United Nations is not powerful? The world knows what the outer strength is. But what is the inner strength? The inner strength is revolution. The possessor of inner strength revolts against disappointment-bondage. He revolts against ignorance-night. He revolts against imperfection-mortality.

They say that the United Nations is not stable, that it is constantly changing its policies. We say that if a new policy embodies more light, more perfection and more satisfaction, then naturally it is the bounden duty of the United Nations to adopt the new policy instead of unwisely clinging to the old policy.

They say that the United Nations is losing its moral authority. We say that if it is true, then the world is losing its sanity very rapidly and heading towards an explosion of a devastating character.

8. *The way ahead*

> The way ahead may be difficult, but the future of mankind is bright.

I wish to offer some soulful comments on this divinely illumining and fulfilling utterance made by our dear seeker-friend John from Portugal's Permanent Mission to the United Nations [Mr Joao Teixeira da Motta, Second Secretary of Embassy, Permanent Mission of Portugal to the United Nations], before the Second Committee of the 31st General Assembly on 14 October 1976.

Our John – I cannot pronounce his Portuguese given name, but I have taken his kind permission to call him John – is young in terms of earthly years, but old in terms of heavenly years – young in body, old in soul, ancient in spirit. He is short; that is his physical height. But he is tall, very tall in his spiritual height.

From the strict spiritual point of view, "the way" signifies aspiration-flame. Aspiration is the inner flame which ever ascends and transcends, and while ascending and transcending, it illumines our earthly life. The aspiration-flame shows us how to see the Truth, how to feel the Truth and how to grow into the

THE SEEKER'S MIND

Truth. It helps us see, feel and grow into God's transcendental Vision and God's universal Reality.

There are two ways: the human way and the divine way. The human approach is the approach of separativity; the divine approach is the approach of unity in multiplicity and multiplicity in unity. There the Eternal can grow in the fleeting reality and the Infinite can grow in the finite.

The human way leads us to our destination. In this case the way and the destination are two separate realities. But in the divine way, the destination and the way are the same. Here there is no sense of separativity. Two thousand years ago the Saviour, Christ, taught us, "I am the Way, I am the Goal." He also declared, "I and my Father are One." In these two most significant utterances, we can easily see and feel that the way and the destination are inseparably one.

Again, on the strength of his boundless compassion, when he identified himself totally with earth's ignorance, it was he who said, "Father, why hast Thou forsaken me?"

When we speak about "the way ahead", we have to know that the starting point and the journey's goal, or the journey's close, are two different points. When we say that something is ahead, it means that the starting point is here and the reality that we are seeking, the culmination, is elsewhere. This is what our human eyes and our human mind teach us.

But there is another teacher that we can claim as our own, our very own, and that is our inner eye, the third eye, the eye of God-Light. This eye, which is between our eyebrows and a little above, has a different story to tell us. It tells us that God the cosmic Vision and God the cosmic Reality are one and the same, one and inseparable. When we think of God the Vision, we must realise that we are talking about the cosmic Vision, which embodies Reality itself. And when we think of God the cosmic Reality, we must feel that inside the cosmic Reality is nothing but God the cosmic Vision. The cosmic Vision is the Reality within us in seed form. And cosmic Reality is the Vision in its fruit form, which is for us. The cosmic seed is within us and the cosmic fruit is for us.

"The way ahead may be difficult." Anything that is as yet unachieved may appear difficult. Difficulty is an experience which we go through before the realisation-sun dawns on our devoted and illumined heads and aspiring and surrendering hearts.

"But the future of mankind is bright." The future is something that grows in the immediacy of today. The past has given us the capacity to become great. The present is giving us the capacity to become good. The future will give us the capacity to become perfect. Greatness, goodness and perfection. When we are great, consciously or unconsciously we want to rule the world and lord it over the world. When we are good, consciously or unconsciously we love the world according to the power of our willingness and our receptivity. When we are perfect, we try to love and serve God the Creator in His entire creation, in His own Way. Two thousand years ago, the Christ said, "Let Thy Will be done." This is the supreme prayer; this is the supreme message that humanity has received from above through the Christ consciousness.

"The future of mankind." – Who is man? Man is God yet unrealised. Who is God? God is man yet unmanifested. When it is a matter of realisation, man has not yet realised who he eternally is. When it is a matter of manifestation, unfortunately God remains unmanifested. Therefore, man and God are two complementary entities. Man manifests God through his self-giving and God helps man realise who he eternally is through His own Self-giving.

"The future of mankind is bright." What is bright in our outer life? Inspiration is the only thing that is bright in our outer life. There is nothing else in our outer life that can claim to be bright. Inspiration is the only thing that has the light, so he who has inspiration is bright and nobody else. The possessor of inspiration is the only bright person in the outer life.

What is bright in our inner life? Aspiration is the only bright thing in our inner life. As inspiration is bright in our outer life, so aspiration is bright in our inner life. Without inspiration, the outer life is worse than meaningless; without aspiration, the inner life is worse than useless.

When we have inspiration, we feel that there shall come a day when our inspiration will show us God's Face. And when we have aspiration, we discover that a day shall dawn, at God's choice Hour, when our aspiration will show us God's Heart. God's Face is Infinity's Beauty and God's Heart is Eternity's Duty.

9. *Prayer for the New Year*

This will be our last meeting for this year. May we most soulfully invoke the presence of the soul of the United Nations to bless us and to guide us, and to illumine the road to world peace, world harmony and oneness-world, where God's Truth God's Light and God's Bliss shall reign supreme.

10. *A visit to the United Nations Gift Center*

As far as I know, I was not scheduled to give a talk today, but with your souls' kind permission I wish to say a few words.

Dear friends, dear sisters and brothers, dear seekers, when I use the term "seeker", please do not be scared to death. Some of you are afraid of the term "seeker", while others may be attracted to it out of sheer curiosity. Still others may feel something haunting or illumining in the term.

A seeker may be aware of what he is doing, or he may be totally unaware of it. There are conscious seekers and unconscious seekers, but we are all seekers here. This world of ours is quite vast. There are many, many places on earth where you could have worked for your living and gained earthly and heavenly experiences, but you have chosen this particular place. Why? Some of you or even all of you may give outer reasons, but actually it is your souls that have brought you to the United Nations. Some of you may outwardly convince your minds that because of this or because of that you wanted to work at the United Nations. But I wish to say there is only one inner reason and that is that your heart cares for union and oneness with the world at large. Your heart of aspiration wants to be inseparably one with the rest of the world. Therefore, you found a job here or your soul decided on your behalf to accept a job at the United Nations. You represent not only this beautiful, meaningful and soulful gift shop; you represent not only the United Nations, but you represent also the Almighty Father's Oneness-Heart here, there and everywhere.

Every day people come to this shop from various parts of the world. They come here to identify themselves with the large, larger and largest world. Let me give you an example. I come from a tiny, obscure village in Bengal, India. If I buy something from this place and take it back to my little home and show it to my friends, immediately a new world dawns before them – a world of vastness, a world of oneness, a world of satisfaction. The tiniest possible world is my village, Shakpura, in Bengal, India. The tiniest world comes into this shop and gets a gift which comes from another part of the world. Perhaps that part of the world where the gift was made may also be a small village. But my coming to this shop from one tiny place and your offering this gift from another tiny place makes a happy union between the two places.

We come to the United Nations to be united and to serve humanity with one heart, with one soul and with one body. In this way the little, little worlds become one with the big world; and again, the big world gives to the little worlds what it has and what it is. There are countless drops in the ocean. Each drop is a world of its own, by virtue of its very existence. When all the drops are together inside the ocean, they represent the world itself. So the ocean is the largest world and each tiny drop is also a world, but a little world. This moment the union of countless drops makes the vast ocean and the next moment the vast ocean feeds and nourishes the tiny little drops.

Here in this shop at the United Nations you have ample opportunity to unite the little worlds with the big world, the finite with the Infinite. Each little gift that you sell represents the beauty of the finite and, at the same time, welcomes the Blessings of the Infinite. By welcoming, by invoking and by imploring the Blessings of the Infinite, the little beautiful gift becomes immortal. Then it flies from one part of the world to another, from here to the so-called most insignificant village on earth; it covers the length and breadth of the entire world. The United Nations is extremely fortunate to have you and you are also extremely fortunate to have the United Nations, for from here you offer your heart's magnanimity and your mind's luminosity to the world at large.

In conclusion, I wish to say a few soulful words about your leader-boss, June. She has been with our little spiritual family for about a year. With all my heart's sincerity and my soul's effulgence, I wish to say that she is an extremely sincere, devoted and earnest seeker. In her there is a very rare and unusual combination of the aspiring heart and the illumining mind. There are many, many, many good qualities of hers which I am sure all of you know, for you work with her. But the thing that strikes me most is that she practises what she preaches. Her life of illumining discipline is at once the embodiment of what she has and is and the revelation of what she has and is. Some of you may think that she is a strict disciplinarian, but I wish to say that this very discipline she practises in her own life for the betterment of her own life and the world-body.

The word "discipline" frightens the physical mind and the human in us. But the divine in us knows that inside the so-called earthly discipline there is boundless joy and boundless satisfaction. Punctuality is discipline. We know that our goal, let us say, is three metres ahead of us. If we are punctual, then we go towards our goal. By virtue of the regularity of our course we cover one metre, two metres, three metres. Then we reach our destination. Until we reach our goal there is no satisfaction at all. When we reach our goal we get tremendous satisfaction. So satisfaction looms large inside discipline.

Punctuality is severe punishment if we remain in the mental world. But if we remain in the heart-world, then immediately we will feel that punctuality is just an outer means to reach our goal. It is like our legs. If we are supposed to walk, we desperately need our legs in order to reach our destination. So discipline is the way to reach our destination there can be no other way.

June's heart of aspiration and her life of dedication both are exemplary. In the union of her aspiring heart and dedicated life, she has been contributing something very soulful, meaningful and fruitful, both to the tiniest possible world, the tiniest village in a corner of the globe, and also to the largest possible world, to this earth-planet. Her dedicated service is undoubtedly satisfaction to the soul of the United Nations. All those who are working with her are sailing in the same boat. They are doing the same thing, pleasing the soul of the United Nations in a most significant manner. By pleasing the soul of the United Nations you are pleasing the Real in you, and this satisfaction is the supreme satisfaction of God, our Heavenly Father. Satisfaction He infinitely has and satisfaction He eternally is, and this Existence-Oneness-Reality of His He wants to share with us.

[To Ms Henneberger] My heart's boundless light and my soul's infinite blessing I am offering to you. What I said about you is all from the very depth of my heart. You are uniting the little world and the big world, the finite and the Infinite. It is a most significant achievement of your soul, far beyond your imagination, which we are placing at the Feet of our Eternity's Beloved Supreme.

11. *Meditation*

Exactly five years ago I was extremely fortunate to see U Thant. It was a most memorable day for all the members of the Meditation Group. His blessing and his concern we have been carrying from the day I met with him. Today in silence I am offering and I am requesting all the United Nations Meditation Group members to offer their soulful gratitude to this great lover of truth and brother of humanity.

Aum.

Every Tuesday and Friday we come here to pray and meditate on various planes of consciousness: physical, vital, mental, psychic and so forth. Then we offer the fruits of our prayer and meditation to the soul and the body of the United Nations. I wish to say a few words about meditation.

What is meditation? Meditation is not a kind of prayer of the mind and it is not a prayer in the mind. But it can easily serve the purpose of a soulful prayer *for* the mind.

We meditate for various reasons. Peace of mind we all badly need. Therefore, when we meditate, either consciously or unconsciously we aim at peace of mind. Meditation gives us peace of mind without a tranquilliser. And unlike a tranquilliser, the peace of mind that we get from meditation does not fade away. It lasts for good in some corner of the inmost recesses of our aspiring heart.

Meditation gives us purity. There are various ways to achieve purity. Some people advocate the traditional Indian system of breathing. By breathing systematically and also through some occult techniques of breathing in and out, one can definitely purify one's internal system to some extent. But this purity does not last permanently. However, when one prays and meditates soulfully and, at the same time, brings the soul to the fore, one is bound to achieve lasting purity. The purity that we get from our soulful meditation lasts forever in our aspiring consciousness.

When we pray, we feel either that we have done something wrong or that something can be invoked from above so that we do not do anything wrong. When we pray, we feel that the mistake-world is looming large. Either we have made a mistake by having done something or we have made a mistake by not having done something. Then our sincerity compels us to confess our mistake. So, prayer and confession very often go together.

But meditation does not believe in that kind of confession. Meditation says, "Why do you have to make a mistake and then confess it? Do not remain near mistakes. Remain millions and billions and trillions of miles away from mistakes. Then you won't have to confess anything." Meditation is not an escape exercise. When we pray, we try to bring down into us a higher reality or enter into a higher reality that will separate us from the world of suffering. We try to escape from the suffering of the world. But when we meditate, we do not try to escape. The seeker who meditates is a warrior, divine warrior. He faces suffering, ignorance and darkness, and inside the very life and breath of suffering he tries to establish the kingdom of Wisdom-Light.

The true seeker who meditates also knows that whatever he is doing is not for his own personal salvation. If everything that he is doing is only for his own salvation, then he and the world will always remain two different entities with two different ideals or goals. So, sincere seekers always try to assimilate world-truth, world-light and world-capacity and meditate for world transformation, illumination and perfection.

Real meditation never forces us to do something, to say something or to become something. It is the desiring vital or the desiring mind that enters into our meditation and forces us to try to achieve something. But meditation proper will never compel us to do something, to say something or to become something, for it knows that everything has to be natural and spontaneous. It only helps us enter cheerfully into the current of spiritual life.

Human life is beset with difficulties, dangers and so forth, but we can overcome these difficulties. We can take each difficulty as a powerful warning and we can take each warning as a blessing-light in disguise. The meditation-world invites us and leads us to the highest Reality. We see ahead a light, perfection-light. But as soon as we see this light that perfects us, we are frustrated. A red traffic light is frustration to us, especially when we are in a hurry to reach our destination. But we forget that it is the red light that saves our precious life from destruction. The red traffic light is regular and punctual. Regularly and punctually it is warning us, saving us. Similarly, regularity in meditation saves us, illumines us and fulfils us. The life of our outer smile is strengthened by the regularity of our prayer, and the light of our inner cry is increased by the regularity of our meditation.

When we meditate, we discover something and we invent something. From our regular meditation we discover faith inside us. This discovery we do not get from anything else. Immense, continuous, illumining and fulfilling faith we get only from our pure and sure meditation.

During our daily meditation we also invent. What do we invent? We invent gratitude. Our heart becomes the possessor of something which it did not possess previously, and that something is boundless gratitude. Each meditation creates a gratitude-flower inside our heart, and petal by petal this flower blossoms in worship of our beloved Lord Supreme. So we invent gratitude and discover faith from our meditation.

Meditation helps us hear the Voice of God. It not only helps us hear the Voice of God, but it also helps us listen to the Voice of God and the Choice of His Hour. After hearing the Voice of God, either we can stop or continue further and actually listen to the Voice. If we listen to the Voice of God, if we listen to the inner dictates at every moment, then the world of confusion that baffles us or that we ourselves create will no longer exist for us. The confusion-world we will no longer create for ourselves if we listen to the Voice of God.

There is a special way to listen to the Voice of God, and that special way is to meditate in silence. Silent meditation is the strongest force that can ever be seen, felt and executed. So silent meditation we must learn.

How do we meditate silently? Just by not talking, just by not using outer words, we are not doing silent meditation. Silent meditation is totally different. When we start meditating in silence, right from the beginning we feel the bottom of a sea within us and without. The life of activity, movement and restlessness is on the surface, but deep below, underneath our human life, there is poise and silence. So, either we shall imagine this sea of silence within us or we shall feel that we are nothing but a sea of poise itself.

Then, if we start meditating, we are bound to hear the Voice of God and we are bound to listen to the Voice of God. Once we become accustomed to listening to the Voice of God, at that time we feel that there is no tomorrow. There is no such thing as the future, there is no such thing even as today; it is all now. God is now; His Vision is now. The eternal Now is the only reality. In the eternal Now we grow and glow; in the eternal Now we please God, fulfil God and become perfect instruments of God.

12. *The seeker's mind*

O mind, what are you doing to me? You are destroying all my divine possibilities. You are delaying indefinitely my supreme inevitabilities.

O mind, what are you doing to me? I thought that you would teach my vital and my body – the younger members of our family – how to enjoy the strength of vastness. Alas, instead of doing that, you are teaching them how to enjoy the weakness of meanness.

O mind, look, what are you doing to yourself? I thought that you were wise enough to see and feel the happiness that my heart enjoys by becoming inseparably one with the soul and its unfathomable ecstasy. Alas, instead of doing that, you are enjoying base jealousy towards the heart.

O mind, what are you doing to me? What have I done to you? My life – human life – is for happiness. The moment you think of me, all my happiness disappears. The moment I think of you, I suffer the same fate.

O mind, why, why on earth do you have to become so cruel to me? You torture me ruthlessly. I forgive you unreservedly.

But alas, I fail to forget you, your jealousy, your meanness, your destructiveness. Deathless have become my excruciating pangs.

O mind, cruelty incarnate, you have bound me taut to your pitch-dark, tenebrous and wee world. As if that is not enough, you are strangling me there. Death is undoubtedly preferable to the untold torture that you continuously inflict upon me.

Truth to tell, you have been punishing me since you have known me with your doubt-dart and suspicion-gun. In you meanness has reached its zenith height. In you jealousy plays with the darkest night. In you insecurity fails to see the face of purity's beauty.

O mind, you are nothing but your own unparallelled stupidity. Even when God Himself with His infinite Compassion-Light enters into your sordid existence-hole for its radical transformation and perfect perfection, you suspect God openly, strongly and unreservedly. Your fertile, nay, to be precise, futile imagination instigates you to think that God has an ulterior motive. Not only do you know what a suspicion-snake is, but you are nothing but that and that alone.

Helpless, God enters into His own two birthless and deathless Realities – Transcendental Height and Universal Delight – to hear all at once one solitary message: "Endless patience, endless patience."

God the Compassion is not enough. God the Patience is needed, too.

O mind, you need some retribution which you so richly deserve. I give you my word of honour. And who is the witness? God the Pilot Supreme. Do you know what I am going to do? I shall compel you to be eternally one with my heart that enjoys inseparable oneness-delight with Infinity's Light, Eternity's Peace and Immortality's Love.

13. World Gratitude Day

The United Nations Meditation Group celebrated World Gratitude Day twice in 1977 — once on 12 September in a special programme in the United Nations Secretariat for delegates and staff; and again on 21 September in World Gratitude Days New York Headquarters when the Group's Director, Sri Chinmoy, was honoured at official ceremonies. The plaque, presented to him by Mrs Edna Lemle, president and founder of the organisation, dedicated to promoting the cause of world-wide gratitude, cited Sri Chinmoy for having "enhanced the spirit of globalism with his compassion, his creativity and nobility of spirit." The first 21 September World Gratitude Day celebration was held thirteen years ago. In 1977, citations were presented to nine religious leaders and representatives of organisations. Among others recognised were the Mormon Tabernacle Choir, whose Director, Dr J Ottley, came from Salt Lake City for the ceremony; Judith Hollister, founder of the Interfaith Temple of Understanding; Dr Russell Barber, producer of the NBC television programme The First Estate, *and Rabbi Sally Prisend, the first woman in American Judaism to attain the ranks of the clergy. Past awards have been given to UNICEF (as an organisation) and to former General Assembly President Angie Brooks Randolph. These are the texts from both programmes, which included music and the performance by the United Nations Meditation Group singers of a song by Sri Chinmoy dedicated to World Gratitude Day.*

Mrs Edna Lemle, President, World Gratitude Day: Welcome, Sri Chinmoy, Mr Muller, Mrs de Sola Pool, Kevin Keefe, the United Nations Meditation Group and all you good people who have come here to help us herald World Gratitude Day. I will begin by asking Sri Chinmoy to stand here as he did before and get everyone into the mood which is the absolute essence of Gratitude Day.

[Sri Chinmoy meditates facing the audience.]

Now look inward and find something to be grateful for and remember this feeling. Now open yourself up and share this emotion with everyone here. Know that everyone in this room is sharing the same emotion.... I feel it! It surges though the room.... Thank you. This is the basis of the day.

On 21 September gather together some friends and observe Gratitude Day by repeating this with them, it can be a simple gathering or an elaborate party, depending upon how you would like to do it. The important part is that each one gives thanks in his own way. To whom and for what is for each personal and private. It is the essential emotion that should be universally shared.

The official beginning of this world holiday was in 1965 at the East-West Center in Hawaii where a Thanksgiving Dinner was held for ninety Grantees who came for the most part from Oriental countries. We discussed the need for a globally unifying holiday and everyone was thrilled with my idea of Gratitude Day. Each person in the room pledged, therefore, to hold a Gratitude Gathering the following 21 September, when they returned to their own countries. That was the beginning. And since then Gratitude Day has been observed all over the world.

Each year the Board of Directors of World Gratitude Day presents an award to someone who we feel has done something outstanding in the spirit of globalism. In the past we have honoured such distinguished individuals as Angie Brooks Randolph, first woman president of the United Nations General Assembly, Maurice Strong of Canada and the Nobel Prize Laureate, Rene Cassin. In addition we have honoured UNICEF and Japan, which, incidentally, was the first country to declare World Gratitude Day a national day of thanksgiving.

And so, I am most pleased to present this year's World Gratitude Day Award to Sri Chinmoy, who is most deserving of this honour:

WORLD GRATITUDE DAY is pleased to honour SRI CHINMOY who has enhanced the spirit of globalism with his compassion, his creativity and his great nobility;

Whose being and achievements reflect the spirit of our Proclamation:

WHEREAS, humanity has come to recognise devotion and allegiance to immediate family, to clan, to city, to state, and to nation, and now must experience the concept of globalism; and

WHEREAS, words of praise and positive thoughts generate dynamic harmony, and

WHEREAS, decisions made from a grateful heart are endowed with intrinsic wisdom and engender prosperity; and

WHEREAS, gratitude, the opposite of "taking for granted", is a positive emotion which generates good will, is a basic emotion which is indigenous to all people, is a peace-engendering feeling;

AND WHEREAS, 21 September is a special day. It is an equinox: one of the two times of the year when the sun passes over the equator and night and day are everywhere of equal length and everyone is equal under the sun;

THEREFORE let us proclaim World Gratitude Day, a holiday for all peoples, a day of meditation for all religions, a day of celebration for all humanity, united by knowledge of simultaneously shared emotion, a day when triumph of the spirit can make a world community.

Mrs Edna Lemle: Sri Chinmoy, I think the world should be grateful to people like you. I am honoured to give you this award.

Sri Chinmoy: I am accepting this with my heart's boundless gratitude, and this gratitude is something that is glowing and growing within me. Every day I offer to the Beloved Supreme only one thing: gratitude.

Man's greatest gift to God is gratitude. Man's self-giving and his gratitude are one and the same.

I am extremely grateful to you, Mrs Lemle, for you are opening a new chapter in humanity's evolution. The world is in the process of evolution. You know the utmost significance of gratitude, and the awakened soul in you is awakening others. Gratitude is man's conscious oneness with his Beloved Supreme. I am sure that your soul has felt this supreme oneness with the Beloved Supreme and your soul has come to the fore to urge your illumined mind to offer this loftiest message to the world at large.

Gratitude in the inner world is nothing but self-expansion. It is through self-expansion that we become aware of our true reality, which is Infinity itself. Your contribution to the world at large, to the inner world especially, is momentous. As a seeker, I know that there is nothing on earth as valuable and significant as gratitude. In God's Eye there is nothing more meaningful and precious than man's gratitude. Therefore, to you, to the illumining soul in you, I wish to offer my boundless and ever-growing gratitude.

14. *Mrs Lemle's remarks when presenting the official award to Sri Chinmoy, and Sri Chinmoy's reply*

Mrs Edna Lemle: Now we're going to conclude with an extremely special, unusual man. Sri Chinmoy comes from India. He makes everything seem possible. He is the head of the United Nations Meditation Group and he has people from the different United Nations countries meditating together. By golly, if you can do that, I guess you can do anything. And he is also a very creative man. He is a painter; he is a writer. I met Sri Chinmoy just last week when, Heaven-sent, he offered to have a programme to herald World Gratitude Day at the United Nations. Sri Chinmoy stood there and just meditated, and everybody felt it. He does, of course, so much; I have to strain to reach it.

He is currently having an art exhibit at Grand Central Station with his magnificent paintings. He has written 300 books. There are Sri Chinmoy Centres in fifty or sixty countries or places around the world. We're grateful for your presence, Sri Chinmoy.

[Reading from the plaque] World Gratitude Day is pleased to honour Sri Chinmoy who has enhanced the spirit of globalism with his compassion, his creativity and nobility of spirit, whose being and achievements reflect the spirit of our proclamation.
Sri Chinmoy: Dear Mrs Lemle, dear sister in the Universal Compassion-Heart of the Supreme, your searching mind's World-Gratitude dream is astonishingly beautiful. Your aspiring heart's World-Gratitude reality is supremely fruitful. I am extremely grateful to you and to the Board of Directors for bestowing upon me, upon my devoted heart, this signal honour. You have discovered in me a world-server. A world-server is he who is a God-lover. A God-lover and a world-server are one and the same. Just because God, out of His infinite Bounty, has granted me the opportunity and capacity to love Him, today I am in a position to be of service to humanity, His creation. Your discovery will be a great asset in my service to mankind. I shall try to serve more devotedly, more soulfully and more unconditionally this creation of our Beloved Supreme.

Here many religious faiths are proclaiming the oneness, absolute oneness of our absolute Pilot Supreme. An hour ago when I arrived here, my dear friend and seeker-brother, Dr Russell Barber [producer of NBC's *The First Estate*] and my dear seeker-sister, Pat Parker, greeted me at the entrance. During our conversation, Dr Barber said to me that he was very pleased that he and I were getting the award together on the same day. I said to him, "So, we are sailing in the same boat." He immediately and lovingly corrected me. He said, "Not exactly so. We are sailing towards the same destination but in different boats." Many roads lead to Rome. But here we are arriving at the same destination.

God is the gardener. In His garden there are many beautiful flowers. One flower cannot make a beautiful garden. Many flowers are needed in order to make a beautiful garden. Again, it is the garden that embodies the many flowers and the flowers' fragrance. So the one became many and, finally, the many are reaching the self-same goal and becoming one. We all came from the One, and now the one Tree is having many branches. But each branch knows that there is a trunk, a Source. God is evolving in and through us in various ways, in many forms and many colours and then He is returning to the one destination. So the One became many in order to enrich and fulfil and finally to reach one Goal.

During his short but momentous speech, dear Dr Barber has told us that the United States is next to India in spirituality. With his soul's permission I wish to correct his experience or his pronouncement. It is not because I am here in America that I feel bound to extol America to the skies where spirituality is concerned, but it is because I happen to be a seeker of the Absolute Supreme. Our Beloved Supreme has two most illumining and most fulfilling qualities or attributes: Peace and Power. They are inseparable. They are mutually illumining and fulfilling each other. India embodies and represents the Peace aspect of our Beloved Supreme and America embodies and represents the Power aspect of our Beloved Supreme.

Peace and power we can take as two legs of an eternal runner, who is eternally running along Eternity's Road to reach an endless destination an ever-fulfilling destination. At any moment when we observe the runner running, we will see one particular leg ahead. That doesn't mean that that leg is actually leading or winning the battle. No, sometimes the right leg is in front and sometimes the left leg is in front. We need two legs in order to run properly towards our destination. So peace is one leg and power is another leg. Neither of them is slower, or behind the other. Both of them are equally important. Each one is needed and each one is helping the other to run fast, faster, fastest towards the destination.

My gratitude-heart is my thoughtful inspiration. My gratitude-heart is my prayerful aspiration. My gratitude-heart is my soulful meditation. This inspiration, aspiration and meditation of mine have been helping me to become a devoted instrument of my Beloved Supreme. Today you are honouring me for what I have done to serve the world at large. My contribution is an infinitesimal iota of self-giving. Again, I have to say that there is Someone who is celebrating in the inmost recesses of my heart not only what I have done but also what I have not done. Out of His boundless Bounty God has helped me not to dine any more with ignorance-night, and He is very pleased that I have not done so. So not for what we do but also for what we do not do, God is equally pleased with us.

My inspiration-wings, my aspiration-bird and my soulful life I am offering to each seeker present here, especially to you, Mrs Lemle. You are the head of this organisation, World Gratitude Day. Gratitude is our self-expansion. It is the liberation of the finite reality inside the infinite Divinity. When we offer gratitude to someone, in no way are we showing insufficiency, inadequacy or an inferior existence-reality to that person. He has given us what he has and what he is and we are giving him what we have and what we are. Let us take God, for example. He gives to us what He is: infinite Compassion. This is by far the best Reality that He embodies. For us our best achievement is our gratitude-heart. Our gratitude heart will make us inseparably one with our Beloved Supreme. There is no other way. Consciously, soulfully and unreservedly we become one with Him only by the expansion of our aspiring heart.

Gratitude is what at every moment we must try to grow into in order to fulfil the divine in us. Gratitude is an earth-born and earth-grown fruit which not only nourishes the Heaven-born cosmic gods but also pleases most the Heavenly Creator, our Eternity's Beloved Supreme.

Finally, I wish to invoke the presence of an immortal poet, Shakespeare, whose soulful prayer I wish to share with you all: "O Lord who lends me life, lend me a heart replete with thankfulness."

15. *Mayor Beame honoured*

Mayor Beame: How are you? [Shaking Sri Chinmoy's hand as Sri Chinmoy greets him outside the Gallery.]
Sri Chinmoy: I am extremely grateful to you. It is so kind of you to come. I wish to offer you my deepest gratitude.
Mayor Beame: Thank you.

[Sri Chinmoy welcomes the Mayor into the Gallery.]
Sri Chinmoy: May I play for a couple of minutes on an Indian instrument, the esraj?
Mayor Beame: Yes.

[Sri Chinmoy plays several of his own compositions on the esraj. Then, he presents a plaque to the Mayor and reads out the inscription.]
Sri Chinmoy: To Mayor Beame, the unparallelled champion pilot of New York. Mayor Beame, the soul of New York will eternally

treasure your matchless contributions to change the face and fate of each and every New Yorker. With deepest appreciation and admiration, the United Nations Meditation Group and Fountain-Art.

Mayor Beame: Thank you. May I say something? I'm very deeply moved by this presentation and I want to say that I could have used a lot of these moments of meditation during these last months and years. And I certainly didn't think, the first day I met you, that I'd ever have the pleasure of meeting you again tonight. I want to thank you very much for your kindness and your warmth and your expressions. I appreciate it and I want to thank everybody here as well. [Applause]

Sri Chinmoy: Now we have something else to offer you. Just two hours ago I composed a song in your honour and my students now are going to sing this song. I wish to offer this soulful song to your soul.

Mayor Beame: Thank you.

[The singers sing *O Great Pilot, Mayor Beame*.]

Mayor Beame: What are you doing next week? [Laughter] Thank you very much. I really enjoyed it; I appreciate it. I wish Mrs Beame were here so she could hear it.

Sri Chinmoy: Now, with your kind permission, I wish to paint something. It will take only a few minutes. Right here, in front of you, I would like to paint one painting, and then I wish to offer it to you.

Mayor Beame: All right, fine.

Sri Chinmoy: This will be our third soulful offering to you.

[In a matter of minutes, Sri Chinmoy paints a 16 x 20" original with acrylics.]

Sri Chinmoy: This is my humble offering. [Presenting the painting]

Mayor Beame: Thank you. Thank you very much. If I knew I was going to get so much, I would have brought a valise or something. This is more than I've received in a long, long time, and I not only appreciate it for its material good, but more particularly for your sentiments. I very much appreciate it. Thank you. [Applause]

I wanted to thank the singers. Could I do that?
Sri Chinmoy: Yes, please.
Mayor Beame: I just want to thank you. It was wonderful. Thank you. [Shaking hands with all the singers]

[To everyone] Thank you, you've made my evening wonderful.
Woman from the audience: You made New York great! [Applause]

16. *The United Nations Meditation Group with Muhammad Ali*

On the morning of his championship fight with Earnie Shavers on 29 September, Muhammad Ali met with Sri Chinmoy and members of the United Nations Meditation Group for an hour of prayer, meditation and discussion. Sri Chinmoy garlanded the champion and presented him with a trophy, saying, "Along with this is my heart. My heart is inside this." Later, some thirty United Nations Meditation Group singers sang a song which Sri Chinmoy had composed in the fighter's honour, and the group meditated together in silence for about twenty minutes. Afterwards, Ali told Sri Chinmoy, "I was so deeply absorbed, I couldn't do anything." As the group was leaving, he added, "This really got my spirits high. It might end in one round now. God bless you." This is a short excerpt from the conversation, as well as a commentary about the meeting which Sri Chinmoy gave at the United Nations the next day.
Sri Chinmoy: Yesterday it was our strong desire to honour you at the United Nations. Unfortunately, you could not be at the United Nations.
Muhammad Ali: I was so obligated; I couldn't make it. I appreciated it. I was real honoured to get that invitation, but we couldn't make it. What do you do there?

Sri Chinmoy: We pray and meditate twice a week. On Tuesdays and Fridays we pray together with the delegates and staff. There I was going to offer you my deepest gratitude for what you are doing – not only for the black Muslims but also for mankind. You are changing the face and fate of mankind. Your very name encourages and inspires. As soon as people hear "Muhammad Ali", they are inspired. They get tremendous joy. They get such dynamism to be brave and face ignorance. Your very name does that. That is why I am so grateful to you, so proud of you.

Muhammad Ali: My goal is to be like you one day – to be peaceful and out of this sport working for humanity and for God. I was telling Jeremiah that after we finish boxing I want to learn how to get out of this life and use my popularity and my intelligence for humanity – to help people in whatever way I can. I don't know how, but I want to do something – bring people together, work for God and help people. I know there is something I am supposed to do, but I don't know really exactly what its purpose is; but it's something.

Sri Chinmoy: You know the purpose. It is only a question of Allah's Hour. You are the supreme instrument of Allah. Today He is utilising you as the greatest boxer. One day He will utilise you as the greatest preacher. The other day I was reading in the newspaper about you as a preacher and minister. So, now your heart of love you are using for a special purpose.

Muhammad Ali: I'll only say one thing, Brother, not to cut you off. But I don't want and I never wanted the image of being the greatest preacher. Boxing is all publicity. In this country this is how we promote: "I'm the greatest. I'll get him in round seven." But this is not really my heart. This is just outer appearance to promote fights. I don't really feel this way. Ministry is so serious, and there everybody is equal before God. Therefore, I don't want to get the image of being the greatest preacher, because that's boastful; it is not humble, it is not spiritual. So I don't want to go into the thing that I am the greatest preacher: just a minister, just a lecturer or helper.

There are so many people who are great but only God, Allah, is really great. Therefore, I want to get out of this brashness, this image. We've got to stop that "I'm the greatest" thing and forget it. I am just a humble servant and I have a lot to learn. I need people like yourself to teach me what to say and what to do and how to approach certain things. So I don't want to talk that "I am the greatest" attitude and preach it. Do you understand what I mean? I don't want that.
Sri Chinmoy: You don't have to say that you are the greatest, but your heart of oneness with all humanity makes you the greatest.

17.

Sri Chinmoy: I wish to say a few words about the world-champion, Muhammad Ali. Yesterday was a most significant day both for the members of the United Nations Meditation Group and for the champion, Muhammad Ali. [Pointing to the two photographs] This is Muhammad Ali in his physical consciousness and this is Muhammad Ali in his soulful consciousness. Each individual has two aspects: the physical aspect and the spiritual aspect. This moment he expresses himself or reveals his capacities through physical means; the next moment he expresses his reality's divinity through spiritual means. In this picture we see Muhammad Ali in a devoted, soulful, cheerful and powerful consciousness. Right beside it is another picture which brings forward his other aspect: physical strength. We believe in evolution. From the stone life we go to the plant life, then to the animal life, then to the human life and finally to the divine life, where we are striving for perfection. From the physical and vital consciousness, slowly and steadily we have to evolve to the psychic consciousness, the supreme consciousness.

THE SEEKER'S MIND

The very name "Muhammad Ali" inspires millions of people on the vital plane. We cannot say that the vital plane is not good, that only the spiritual plane is good. No, all the planes are good; only some planes have to be elevated to a higher consciousness. Some planes need more purity, more determination, more awareness and more acceptance of light. The physical, the vital, the mind and the heart are all members of the same family. They must be amalgamated; they must be illumined and perfected.

What can achieve this perfection? It is our inner cry, our aspiration. And what carries the greatest responsibility for elevating the consciousness of human beings all over the world? What place carries the utmost responsibility for elevating, illumining, perfecting and fulfilling the length and breadth of the world? The answer is the United Nations. The United Nations carries the heaviest burden of human problems and the United Nations is responsible for bringing light into these problems.

Right now the physical is wallowing in the pleasures of ignorance-sleep; therefore, the physical needs to be awakened. The vital is aggressive quite often; therefore, the vital needs dynamism. The mind is full of doubt and uncertainty; therefore, the mind needs faith and certainty. The heart is full of insecurity; therefore, the heart needs confidence. When the wakefulness of the body, the dynamism of the vital, the faith and certainty of the mind and the confidence of the heart come forward and become one, then only does the individual become perfect.

Each individual as well as each nation has these good qualities. Since it is the individuals who form the country, it is always advisable for the individuals to bring these qualities forward first; then, whatever the country has will also come forward. When the individual brings forward his good qualities, it becomes easier for the country to bring forward its qualities.

Who is giving us the capacities, the inexhaustible capacities, that are needed to bring these qualities forward and illumine our imperfections? It is the soul of the United Nations. The deeper reality in the United Nations is blessing us at every moment. If we think that we are glorifying the United Nations by working here, then we are making a mistake. It is the United Nations, the soul of the United Nations, that has blessed us by giving us the golden opportunity to be of service to it.

Right now, in the political world, the mental aspect is predominant. In political ways the countries are trying to establish oneness, peace, harmony and so forth. But in our Meditation Group we are trying to bring to the fore the psychic qualities, the inner qualities, which are peace, light, love, harmony and the feeling of oneness. The Meditation Group is aspiring soulfully and devotedly and, according to our inner capacity, each individual member here is receiving light directly from the soul of the United Nations. The soul of the United Nations has given us ample opportunity, out of its boundless bounty, to share with the rest of the world the peace that we get from it.

All religious faiths, all countries, are one on the inner plane. Outwardly they are still not seeing eye to eye with one another, but in the inner world, definitely they have got the message of the United Nations. Therefore, they have all come together here. They see that they are from one Source, and that only in the One will they get their ultimate satisfaction.

When Muhammad Ali accepted our invitation to be with him, it proved in abundant measure that the physical and the vital in him wanted illumination. The interview lasted for about an hour and for about twenty minutes we meditated together soulfully and devotedly in pin-drop silence. If he had not been spiritual, he would not have granted the interview; nor would he have meditated with us and accepted the fruits of our prayer and meditation. But he did meditate with us and receive what we offered to him, so we know definitely that he is spiritual in the purest sense of the term. He prayed with us and meditated with us and he shared with us wholeheartedly his inner divinity.

Many times I have been misunderstood when I see famous people. Some people think that I am going out of my spiritual domain, that I am entering into another world for name and fame. But those who have faith in me do not misunderstand me. Here I wish to say that each individual, no matter in which field he shines, has received some light from above. Since I am a seeker of the Absolute, the Supreme, out of his infinite Bounty, has also given me some light. This light I want to share with others who have received light from above and who are sharing it with the rest of the world in different fields and in different ways. We are all God's children. One son of His has achieved something. The other one comes to soulfully congratulate him and, while congratulating him, he brings with him his appreciation, admiration, good will, love and oneness. This is the exchange of our light.

To be with Muhammad Ali is not just a coincidence; nor is it a display of our vital emotion or exuberance in order to get name and fame. No, here the soul of the United Nations has given us a golden opportunity to spread its light and its message of universal oneness. We are all seekers; we are all in the same boat. Therefore, I can safely say that this morning, while I was running from my house to the playground where we practise sports, I vividly saw – not with my third eye but with my human eyes – the soul of the United Nations. It was extremely happy and delighted at what we have achieved. As a matter of fact, it is the meaningful and fruitful blessing of the soul of the United Nations that has manifested in a tangible form in the divinely inspired meeting between Muhammad Ali and our Meditation Group.

Millions of people will see what we are doing. The heart of each individual who sees this picture in *The New York Times* will definitely feel that the United Nations is the only answer for humanity's oneness and divinity's satisfaction in human life, which is aspiring to be totally transformed and illumined. So this meeting with Muhammad Ali is a supreme achievement for the United Nations which each member of the United Nations can embody and treasure and this achievement is nothing short of a supreme gift from the soul of the United Nations.

18. *Miss Lillian welcomes the Meditation Group*

Mrs Lillian Carter met with Sri Chinmoy and the members of the Meditation Group in Americus, Georgia, on 7 October, charming them with tales of her experiences in India and vignettes about what it is like to be the President's mother. The group, in turn, meditated with Miss Lillian and sang a song composed by Sri Chinmoy in her honour, which brought tears to her eyes. This is a brief part of their conversation. Here Miss Lillian was talking about the United Nations Meditation Group's public concert that evening.

Mrs Lillian: Well, this is going to be a lovely night. I hope you have a crowd. People don't understand this. I don't know whether many people will be here or not. Have you heard?

Mr Steven Hein: We really don't know if a lot of people will come or not. There was a little article in the newspaper.

Mrs Lillian: Yes, and weren't you in Plains this afternoon?

Mr Steven Hein: Yes. There are a few posters up there.

Mrs Lillian: But here they don't understand I am the only one who does, and I wouldn't miss it but I hope you are going to have a nice crowd.

Sri Chinmoy: With your kind permission, may I meditate for a minute?

Mrs Lillian: Oh yes. [To the group] He wants me to be quiet!

Sri Chinmoy: Not in the least! Far from it. Please forgive me. My students had informed me that you would like me to meditate for a minute that is why.

Mrs Lillian: Y'all better be quiet now, we're going to meditate. [Silent meditation for four or five minutes]

Sri Chinmoy: Thank you.

Mrs Lillian: Thank you. Very nice.

Sri Chinmoy: Now I wish to offer a soulful song to you, which I composed yesterday. It is about you. First I would like to sing it and then my students will sing it for you. Could my students come in now, please?

[They open the door and additional members of the United Nations Meditation Group come in.]

Sri Chinmoy: Just yesterday I composed it in honour of you.

Mrs Lillian: Wonderful! Y'all come in! [Turning to the Secret Service agent accompanying her] Ray, you should see the little piano, little organ, or what-do-you-call-it! [To the members of the Meditation Group] Good afternoon.

Sri Chinmoy: These are the members of the United Nations Meditation Group.

Mrs Lillian: Beautiful, beautiful. The saris are gorgeous. I never could wear one because I couldn't put it on. Hello! Hello! How many are there?

Sri Chinmoy: Here there are about forty.

Mrs Lillian: Wonderful.

[Sri Chinmoy sings the song *Compassion-Ocean, Mother Lillian,* accompanying himself on the tote-a-tune.]

Mrs Lillian: That's beautiful.

Sri Chinmoy: Now they will sing.

[The members of the United Nations Meditation Group sing *Compassion-Ocean, Mother Lillian.*]

Mrs Lillian: You just don't know me. I'm not that good! Oh boy, this is wonderful! But I just really don't deserve all this.

Sri Chinmoy: You deserve all this and much, much more.
Mrs Lillian: Oh, no, no, no, I don't. This is just beautiful.
Sri Chinmoy: And we mean it. What we have sung, we literally mean it.
Mrs Lillian: Thank you, thank you, Sir.
Sri Chinmoy: ....It is all of our hearts' feelings.
Mrs Lillian: Thank you very much. It is a great honour that you are doing this for me. But you don't know me. Ray knows me, though. He knows that I'm not that good. Don't you, Ray? It's beautiful. Let me ask you something. Do you go everywhere with....I call him Mr Chinmoy.... all together all the time?
United Nations Meditation Group member: As often as we can.
Sri Chinmoy: We have many more students. We have about eight hundred or so.
Mrs Lillian: I envy you your calmness. It took my best to sit still, much less meditate. I'm not much of a meditator. I did go to the meeting every Thursday night and I did meditate with them.
Sri Chinmoy: But you have meditated with me extremely well.
Mrs Lillian: Do you want me to tell you the truth? I don't know what I was thinking about, but I had a thousand thoughts. I can't get everything out of my head like you can. When you meditate, you completely bare your mind, don't you?
Sri Chinmoy: At that time, we do not have a mind at all. When we meditate, we only live in the heart and we become the heart itself.
Mrs Lillian: I have heard that and I think it is beautiful. But the only way I can meditate is to go somewhere by myself. I go to what I call my Pond House. I can go out and sit and look out over the pond, and then I can meditate.
Sri Chinmoy: We belong to the United Nations Meditation Group. This is for you, Mother, this is our offering. [Sri

Chinmoy presents Mrs Lillian with the United Nations Meditation Group banner]

Mrs Lillian: Oh, this is beautiful. Thank you. Oh it is beautiful.

[At the concert that the United Nations Meditation Group presented later that evening, Sri Chinmoy played the Indian esraj and members of the Group sang several Bengali and American songs, including India's National Anthem and *America the Beautiful.*]

[During the concert Sri Chinmoy commented:]

Sri Chinmoy: I am a seeker. I have been here for six or seven hours. On the strength of my aspiration, I wish to say what I feel about Plains. Simplicity, sincerity, spontaneity, humility and self-giving are the birthright of this town. This is what my inner aspiration tells me and I wish to offer my soulful gratitude to the soul of this town where our dear President was born.

19. *Inspirational talk at the beginning of the New Year*

O soul of the United Nations, we wish to serve you more soulfully and more devotedly, and for that what we need is more peace. Do tell us where peace is in abundant measure.

"Where is peace? Peace is in joy."

Where is joy?

"Joy? Joy is in love."

Where is love?

"Love? Love is in oneness."

Where is oneness?

"Oneness? Oneness is in vision."

Where is vision?

"Vision? Vision is in aspiration."

Where is aspiration?

"Aspiration? Aspiration is in self-giving. Aspiration is in truth-becoming, in light-becoming, in life-becoming and, finally, in God-becoming."

O soul of the United Nations, from the very dawn of this New Year, we wish to serve you more soulfully, more devotedly and more unconditionally.

PART II – WORLD LEADERS

20. *Swami Vivekananda*

Yesterday was the birthday of Swami Vivekananda. Swami Vivekananda was a supreme seeker and supreme lover of mankind. He was also the preserver of the universal vision. I am invoking his presence.

Was Swami Vivekananda a man? Yes, he was. Something else he also was: a lover-hero.

Did Swami Vivekananda really conquer America? Yes, he did. Truth to tell, it was a mutual conquest. Vivekananda conquered America's seeker-heart. America conquered Vivekananda's vision-eye.

What did Swami Vivekananda preach in the West? The Vedantic philosophy. Something he also did. In supreme secrecy, soulfully and lovingly on the vital plane, persistently and unconditionally on the mental plane and compassionately and unreservedly on the physical plane, he distributed Sri Ramakrishna's universal oneness-heart and blessingful joy.

Sri Ramakrishna loved at once Vivekananda's silence-heart and his sound-life. To his Naren what he gave was his own realisation-ocean. In his Naren what he found was his own vision-manifestation. Where? Here, there and all-where.

To the weak, Vivekananda had only one thing to say: "Fear not."

To the strong, he had only one thing to say: "Stop not."

To God, he had only one thing to say: "Delay not."

And to himself, he had only one thing to say: "Ask not."

21. *President Roosevelt*

Yesterday was President Roosevelt's birthday. We wish to observe it today.

President Roosevelt, we, the members of the United Nations, salute you! O man of lofty ideals, O hero-warrior, O prophet of the world-illumining dawn, we soulfully salute you!

Admiration you received in abundant measure; condemnation too. One more thing your soul rightfully deserved – your dear countrymen should have seen life clearer and should have seen it as a whole, as you so surprisingly did.

The supremacy of your soul's will-power over your body's revolt, your physical paralysis, was unparalleled. Your very existence was a stranger to fear. Your indomitable courage was far beyond the flight of our wildest imagination. It was your heart's wisdom-light that so lovingly and convincingly taught the entire world: "The only thing we have to fear is fear itself." Indeed, the vision-light of this loftiest message can illumine the length and breadth of the world.

The embodiment of your vision-height and action-power will always be treasured by the freedom-loving and peace-spreading world. It was your own aspiration-mind and dedication-heart that planned for this organisational conference of the United Nations. Therefore, today's flowering United Nations to you bows with its gratitude-heart.

Peace and faith: these two divine qualities abide in each other. Your last message to the American nation can most unmistakably and most profitably be accepted and treasured by the vast world: "To all Americans who dedicate themselves to the making of an abiding peace, I say the only limit to our realisation of tomorrow will be our doubt of today. Let us move forward with strength and active faith."

O great good illumining, inspiring fulfilling soul, Franklin Roosevelt, to you we bow.

22. *Do we have the capacity to help others?*

Do we have the capacity to help others? Yes, we do. Do we have the capacity to help others in words? Yes, we do. Do we have the capacity to help others in deeds? Yes, we do. Then how is it that we do not help others? We do not help others for various reasons. I wish to cite a few deplorable and painful reasons.

The most deplorable reason is a very simple one. We do not want to see happiness in others; we want only our own happiness. By nature, we human beings are cruel to one another. By nature, we do not want to see others happy. When we see that others are happy, we feel that our own little world is totally shattered and destroyed. The animal in us gets happiness from destruction. The human in us gets happiness from division and a sense of separativity. But the divine in us gets satisfaction only from oneness. The divine in us knows nothing else save and except oneness.

So the main reason that we do not help others is because we do not want to see others happy. This is the root cause. This root cause branches into several subsidiary causes. One of the subsidiary causes is that we want the rest of the world to see how important we are. When others come to us for help, we feel that we are indispensable. But when we come to learn that the same people have gone to others for help, we feel that we were right in not helping them. We feel that since the other party did not feel that we were indispensable, since the party went to others, we did the right thing in not helping. In this way we justify our unwillingness to help.

There is human friendship and divine friendship. Human friendship says, "Give me; I need." Divine friendship says,

"Take me, for I am all yours." When we exercise our human friendship, we tell the world, "Give us; we need." When we exercise our divine friendship, we tell the world, "Take us, for we are all yours." The human in us has not only failed us time and again, but it will always fail us. The divine in us has always succeeded and will always succeed. This divine success is nothing short of world harmony and universal harmony, world peace and universal peace, world satisfaction and universal satisfaction.

Divine friendship is founded upon oneness. The source of divine friendship, divine love and divine concern is oneness. For this reason, divine friendship is lasting. On the other hand, human friendship on earth is nothing but a rope of sand. We shall not be an inch from truth if we say that most human beings are fair-weather friends. When we are desperate and facing inclement weather, our so-called friends desert us in a twinkling. We come out in the street and see an individual and ask him, "Are you my friend?" He says, "Of course, I am your friend, but on one condition: that you never ask me for a favour." Then we see another individual and ask him, "Are you my friend?" He says, "Of course I am, but on one condition: that I shall be at least one inch superior to you. You have to be under me. If you are ready to be at my beck and call, if you are ready to be at my feet, then I will accept you as my friend."

We see a third individual and say, "Are you my friend?" He answers, "Of course I am, but on one condition: whenever I am in need, you have to come to my rescue. But if ever you are in need, you must not count on me, for I have many, many things to do on earth other than helping you. So, if you want to be my friend, then let your acceptance of me be unconditional."

So, when we are looking for a friend, we are like a helpless beggar. At that time, God our supreme Source is playing the role of the eternal beggar in and through us. He wants to play the role of a veritable beggar and we are extremely grateful to Him that He has chosen us for this; in and through us He will fulfil His begging task. Then God goes to some other individuals and asks them to assist others. He wants to play another role in and through them: the role of the eternal giver, the divine friend. But to His wide surprise He gets no response. But since God is compassionate to the needy, He continues trying to find some individuals who will allow Him to play this role in and through them. He is looking for some individuals in and through whom He can fulfil the aspiration-life and the desire-life of those in whom He is playing the role of a beggar. Finally, He finds some souls that are receptive. They are more than willing to abide by His express request, and they come to the rescue of those who are desperately in need of help.

When the seeker needs help, he can only do one thing. He has to dive deep within and bring to the fore his adamantine will. This adamantine will he will place at the Feet of the Absolute Supreme. Then the Absolute Supreme grants His all-fulfilling Compassion-light to the adamantine will of the seeker. When the seeker's will and the Supreme Grace become one and are ready to work together, man's aspiration-world and God's Satisfaction-World make God the Beggar and God the Giver totally fulfilled both in the aspiration-world of earth and the satisfaction-world of Heaven.

23. *A soulful promise*

Dear brothers and sisters, while walking along Eternity's Road, I shall love and serve you. Just because you have given me the opportunity to love and serve you, I shall constantly and eternally offer you my life of concern here on earth and my soul of oneness in Heaven.

We are all of the One, our Beloved Supreme. We came into the world to fulfil one soulful promise which we made to Him before we entered into this world arena. This promise was to please Him in His own Way through our aspiration-heart and dedication-life. We shall without fail fulfil our solemn promise, for we know that our Inner Pilot, our fate-maker, will never allow us to remain unfulfilled.

As we said, Him to please in His own Way we came into the world. Even so, our Beloved Supreme is always ready to please the real in us, the soul, which is inseparably one with Him. The soul is a blue bird which flies in the firmament of Consciousness, Light and Bliss, eternally singing only one song – the song of our Beloved Supreme's constant Victory here on earth and there in Heaven.

III

24. *A meeting with Indian Prime Minister Desai*

Sri Chinmoy: Dear Prime Minister, with you India is great and good; in you India is safe and happy.
Prime Minister Desai: India can't be saved by one man. India can be saved only if people do their thing properly.

★

Prime Minister Desai: All of you work at the United Nations? So I hope you will unite the United Nations. The United Nations is called "United Nations", but they are not yet united. So you have to unite them.

★

Prime Minister Desai: I have written a commentary on the Bhagavad-Gita because I could not find the meaning of some verses satisfactorily in all the commentaries that I read. Therefore, only when I committed the Gita to memory, when I was in jail in 1934, and I began to recite it every day and to apply it to myself, then the meaning became very clear, because I had complete confidence and faith in the Gita, that what it says is right. If I don't understand it, it is my fault. And that is why I wrote the commentary, because when a friend asked me questions about two or three verses, I couldn't give him a satisfactory reply. I thought I would put down on paper what I understand. That is my sole writing. The Gita gives a solution to every problem. At any rate, when there is a conflict of duty, it gives the right answer.

*

Sri Chinmoy: Right at the very beginning Arjuna had that problem.

Prime Minister Desai: It is a problem everywhere. In everyone there is a problem of good and evil. It goes on all the time. So one must accept the Gita's guidance. The gist of it is that you must be at peace with yourself. There should be no tension, no excitement, no anger.

Sri Chinmoy: And for that you have all along taught us to lead a disciplined life.

Prime Minister Desai: To have discipline is not enough. It must be self-discipline.

Sri Chinmoy: That is what you have been teaching us for so many years. A life of discipline is of paramount importance.

Prime Minister Desai: Without that you can get nothing.

IV – EXPRESSIONS OF GRATITUDE

25.

Today you are celebrating my birthday. I wish to offer my gratitude to each of you, and to say that every day I observe my birthday in the hearts of my dear and near ones, in the hearts of those who are seated in the Boat of the Supreme, the Boat that is destined to carry us to the Shores of the Golden Beyond. I observe my birthday every day in your hearts with my deepest gratitude, and at the same time I observe your birthdays every day in the inmost recesses of my heart with deepest love and pride divine.

I came into the world to be of service to the Supreme in mankind. By forming this United Nations Meditation Group you have given me the golden opportunity to be of service to the United Nations and to the world at large, and for that I am immensely grateful to each member of this group. On Tuesdays in this Chapel and on Fridays in the conference room when we hold meditations, what do we actually do? We try to bring down Peace, Light and Bliss from above. In the outer world we are not in a position to show what we bring down from above, but in the inner world I wish to assure each of you that we do bring down these and other divine qualities. The Supreme out of His infinite Bounty showers His Blessings on us and on the United Nations as a whole. We are the chosen devoted instruments of the Supreme.

Again I wish to offer my deepest gratitude to all the members of the United Nations Meditation Group and to all the seekers who come and regularly, faithfully, devotedly, soulfully meditate for Peace. History will bear witness to the fact that we have tried and we are trying and we shall continue to try with utmost sincerity to bring Peace into our lives and into the life of the

United Nations. In the name of the Supreme I wish to assure you that we shall succeed. Our Pilot Supreme is the Absolute Supreme Himself. He will manifest and fulfil Himself in and through all aspiring hearts at His own choice Hour.

26.

Today we are celebrating the fifth anniversary of our Meditation Group at the United Nations. The number "five" has a most special significance. We have five senses. Each sense is of paramount importance. I pray to the Lord Supreme to grant us, out of His infinite Bounty, the capacity and receptivity to perfect our five senses so that we can be of better dedicated, devoted and unconditional service to the illumining soul and serving body of the United Nations. From today on, with our eyes we shall see only the divine Truth in God's creation; with our ears we shall hear only the divine Truth; with our tongue we shall speak only the Truth. From today on, we shall breathe in inner truth; from today on our physical bodies shall be the torch-bearers of the Supreme's infinite Truth. This is the prayer that I wish to offer to our Inner Pilot, the Absolute Supreme, on this auspicious occasion, the fifth anniversary of our Meditation Group at the United Nations.

Finally, I wish to offer my deepest gratitude to Sumedha, the secretary of our Meditation Group, for her constant dedicated service. Also, I offer my sincere gratitude to all the members of the Meditation Group who have been coming here faithfully and devotedly and serving this great body, the United Nations. The delegates and members of the Secretariat are trying to bring about peace. We are also trying to bring about peace in our own way through our prayer and meditation which is equally powerful, soulful and meaningful. The goal is the same, the destination is the same, only we are travelling along two different roads. Once we reach our destination we shall see that whatever is done with real sincerity is true, real and effective. Since the delegates and the members of the staff of the United Nations are also doing the right thing, absolutely the right thing, I wish to offer, on behalf of our Meditation Group, most sincere gratitude to them.

*

Sweet members of the United Nations Meditation Group, dear seekers, I wish to tell you with my heart's utmost sincerity that I was nothing, I am nothing and I shall be nothing. But there is Someone who was everything, who is everything, and who forever shall be everything, and I know Him. Him I have seen and Him I invoke to bless us out of His unconditional Compassion. He is our Eternity's All, our Beloved Supreme. I pray to Him to bless our devoted heads and our surrendered hearts so that we can be His perfect instruments on earth. Once we become His perfect instruments we shall be able to claim Him as our Eternity's own, very own. Beginning today, let us convince our body, vital, mind and heart that we are not only of Him from time immemorial – from before the very birth of creation – but also that we are for Him, that our purpose is to fulfil Him by accepting Him, claiming Him as our very own and playing our respective roles in His cosmic Game. What we all want is a world with a new heart and a new face. To achieve this what we need is constant self-giving to the Inner Pilot, who in silence is guiding every nation slowly, silently, unerringly. His success will be our progress in our life of aspiration, and our progress will be His success in His total and complete manifestation on earth.

From today on, let us claim the Tree, the Supreme, as our own, as He constantly claims us, the leaves, as His very own. If we claim Him as our very own, then our service will be more soulful, more meaningful and more fruitful.

27.

My life is a life of gratitude which I wish to offer to the seekers here and all over the world. This year and all the years that I will be on earth I will have only one purpose, and that is to offer my dedication, my dedicated service. Today there are about fifty seekers in this room. But I wish to tell all of you that when we pray and meditate here, the soul of the United Nations observes us with deepest joy, gratitude and pride. What we do here is recorded in the soul of the United Nations, imprinted in letters of gold. And the appreciation that you have offered now on behalf of the Meditation Group, I wish to place at the Feet of our Beloved Supreme, the Inner Pilot, for it is He who is acting in and through me; it is He who is acting in and through all of us.

What we call dedicated service is nothing but His Compassion-fulfilment in and through us. What we do has already been done by Him. He just allows us to act on the physical plane to convince us that we are participating in His divine Game. Otherwise, there is nothing on earth that we do which has not been done by our beloved Pilot Supreme. Out of His infinite Compassion He makes us feel that we have done it, for when we feel that we have done it we get greater glory and we feel that life is more fruitful. But to be absolutely honest with you, what we do here soulfully is actually being done by our Inner Pilot.

Our service to the United Nations will one day be felt by each and every individual who serves the United Nations. Right now their physical minds may not know what we are doing with our prayer and meditation. But every day their souls do feel what we are doing and their hearts at times also feel it. A day will come when all parts of their being will realise that what we are doing is not for ourselves but for the body, vital, mind, heart and soul of the United Nations. We do not need appreciation now, we do not need recognition. What we need is our own constant feeling of oneness with the body, vital, mind, heart and soul of the United Nations. Our feeling of oneness is what we want from our lives. To all of you, only one thing I can offer and that is my ever-growing and ever-glowing gratitude-flower in the heart of the Universal Reality which you are, which we all are.

28.

This evening you are honouring the seeker in me. I am not a teacher; I am just a seeker and I shall always remain a seeker. Now here in the United Nations Meditation Group we are all seekers; we meditate on God, we pray to God to grant us out of His infinite Bounty peace in the outer world and peace in the inner world. I wanted to give a talk in response to the most inspiring offering that you have rendered to the Supreme in me. The singers have sung with their souls' aspiration and delight; the singers have conveyed my feelings about the United Nations infinitely better than I could have ever imagined. Therefore, I wish to offer to each seeker here something else which I consider to be the best in me, and that thing is my prayerful meditation. Just before I offer my prayerful meditation, I wish to say just a few words.

Greatness, goodness and oneness. Here at the United Nations, what the seeker in me observes right now is the message of greatness. Inside greatness there shall come a time when we shall hear the song of goodness, and there shall come a time without fail when inside goodness we shall see the dance of oneness.

Greatness, goodness, oneness. We have started our journey with our inner cry, which we call aspiration, to become great. This is the first rung of our evolving ladder, which will ultimately reach the highest heights. The second rung is goodness. The third and ultimate rung is oneness. God, the Author of all good, will shower His devoted Blessings upon our surrendered heads and hearts, and at His Choice Hour He will teach us the significance of goodness. He has already taught us the message of greatness; now, at His Choice Hour, He will teach us the significance of goodness. Then finally He will teach us the dance of oneness. At that time, each aspiring soul in God's creation will fulfil God the absolute Truth, the transcendental Light, the universal Peace in His own Way. On behalf of the United Nations Meditation Group, to each seeker present here I wish to offer my prayerful meditation, which is the only thing that I have and that I am in God's ever-fulfilling and ever-illumining Vision.

29.

I wish to offer to each member of the Meditation Group a blessing. From today on we, as members of the Meditation Group and as members of the United Nations staff, shall serve the world body and soul with our heart's soulful gratitude. At times people who are serving the United Nations are assailed with fear, insecurity, worry, doubt and other undivine qualities. But from today on we shall use our best quality: we shall use our soulful gratitude. We shall offer our soulful gratitude to the soul and body of the United Nations every day, every hour, every minute, every second. To serve the United Nations is to serve God's Oneness-Vision, God's ever-transcending, ever-fulfilling Vision of the ever-transcending Reality.

2. *(p.383)* On Tuesday, 17 September 1974, the United Nations Meditation Group held a special meeting at which Sri Chinmoy paid tribute to the two significant events which marked the day: the opening of the twenty-ninth session of the General Assembly and the commemoration of the death of former Secretary-General Dag Hammarskjöld.

3. *(p.385)* On 11 May 1976, during a meeting of the United Nations Meditation Group, Sri Chinmoy asked members to relate briefly some of their significant experiences while working at the United Nations. This is what Sri Chinmoy afterwards commented.

4. *(p.385)* On 17 September 1976, the anniversary of Dag Hammarskjöld's death, the members of the United Nations Meditation Group gathered for a few minutes of silence in the Meditation Room of the United Nations. Afterwards Sri Chinmoy spoke about the experience.

5. *(p.388)* On 20 September 1976, Sri Chinmoy opened the United Nations Meditation Group's Second International Conference for the Opening of the General Assembly with this lecture.

6. *(p.391)* 24 September 1976.

7. *(p.393)* 15 October 1976.

8. *(p.394)* 9 November 1976.

9. *(p.397)* 14 December 1976.

10. *(p.397)* On 11 February 1977, Sri Chinmoy visited the United Nations Gift Center, which was managed by Ms June Henneberger, a member of the United Nations Meditation Group (Ms Henneberger is now Director, Greeting Card Programme, US Committee for UNICEF). Sri Chinmoy meditated with

the staff of the shop before their working day began and then gave a short talk. This is the transcript of his talk.

11. *(p.401)* On 29 February 1977, Sri Chinmoy gave this talk on meditation, prefacing it with remarks about his first meeting with the late Secretary-General U Thant.

12. *(p.405)* 26 April 1977.

13. *(p.407)* World Gratitude Day, New York Headquarters, Dag Hammarskjöld Auditorium, 12 September 1977.

15. *(p.414)* On 28 September 1977, Mayor Beame was the special guest at the Jharna-Kala Gallery, where he was honoured with a song, which Sri Chinmoy had composed about him, as well as a plaque praising him for his life of public service. Sri Chinmoy, who had met the Mayor on two previous occasions, also painted an original Jharna-Kala while the Mayor watched and presented it to him as a gift. This is a transcript of the occasion.

17. *(p.418)* The next day at the United Nations Meditation Group meeting at UN Headquarters Sri Chinmoy spoke about the meeting with Muhammad Ali. Sri Chinmoy referred to the two photographs of Muhammad Ali which had appeared in that morning's *New York Times*. One photograph shows Ali and Sri Chinmoy meditating together the morning of the world championship fight with Earnie Shavers; the other photograph shows Ali in the ring with Shavers.

19. *(p.425)* 6 January 1978.

20–21. *(p.427)* During January of 1978 Sri Chinmoy gave these short inspirational talks as part of a series of lectures on world leaders.

20. *(p.427)* 13 January 1978.

21. *(p.428)* 31 January 1978.

22. *(p.429)* 14 March 1978.

23. *(p.431)* 14 April 1978.

24. *(p.433)* During his visit to the United Nations for the special session on disarmament, Indian Prime Minister Desai received

members of the Meditation Group in a private meeting on 12 June 1978. The Group sang a Bengali song composed by Sri Chinmoy in honour of the Prime Minister, and Sri Chinmoy presented him with a plaque of appreciation with an inscription of the song. Sri Chinmoy and Prime Minister Desai spoke about the Bhagavad-Gita and the need for spiritual discipline in man's efforts towards world peace.

25–29. *(p. 435)* These expressions of gratitude are taken from remarks made by Sri Chinmoy at special meetings of the Meditation Group.

25. *(p. 435)* 4 September 1973.

26. *(p. 436)* 15 April 1975.

27. *(p. 438)* 9 January 1976.

28. *(p. 439)* On 30 April 1976, the United Nations Meditation Group welcomed members of the United Nations community to a special showing of Sri Chinmoy's art at the Jharna-Kala Gallery in New York's Soho art district. This is Sri Chinmoy's reply to a special presentation by members of the Group.

29. *(p. 440)* 14 April 1976.

PART IX

A SOULFUL TRIBUTE TO
THE SECRETARY-GENERAL:
THE PILOT SUPREME OF
THE UNITED NATIONS

I – A SOULFUL TRIBUTE

1. *Kurt Waldheim*

O Kurt Waldheim .... your mind-heart's concern-flames constantly feed this world of fearful cry and tearful sigh, to see a peaceful earth and blessingful sky.

2. *The Pilot Supreme*

To the truth-seeker, peace-lover, oneness-dreamer, perfection-builder, satisfaction-harbinger; to the supreme Pilot in the Secretary-General, Kurt Waldheim, we offer our soulful gratitude-heart.

When the seeker in me concentrates on the illumination-mind, meditates on the oneness-heart and contemplates on the satisfaction-soul of the Secretary-General, he gets three most earth-liberating and Heaven-fulfilling messages. These messages primarily deal with divine necessity and human responsibility in connection with the cry of the world-body – the United Nations – and the smile of the world-soul – United Nations.

*

The message of the illumination-mind of the Secretary-General runs thus: When a human being goes deep within and wants to make friends with necessity, necessity immediately wants to become his friend. Necessity and he become close friends. They have one ideal, one goal, and that ideal is satisfaction, that goal is perfection.

Then a human being goes without and as soon as he comes out, responsibility wants to make friends with him. He does not want responsibility to be his friend, but responsibility compels him to become its friend. Unwillingly, with great reluctance, he condescends to become responsibility's friend. Responsibility's ideal and responsibility's goal he does not sincerely like, but he is compelled to love responsibility's ideal and goal just because he has agreed to accept responsibility as his friend. Responsibility's ideal is to work for others and to be satisfied in others' satisfaction. Responsibility's goal is to work for others' perfection and to find one's own perfection in their perfection.

In the human world, necessity inspires a human being, educates him and prepares him. In the human world, responsibility frustrates him, tortures him and weakens him. In the divine world there is no such thing as compelled responsibility or self-styled responsibility. There is no responsibility whatsoever. There is only one necessity and that necessity is at once illumining and fulfilling. Again, there is a third world, which is God's own self-transcendence world. In God's own self-transcendence world there is neither responsibility; there is not even necessity. In God's world there is only one thing: satisfaction-reality.

Countless wants each individual has; but there can be only one necessity if that individual is sincere to himself, sincere to the world and sincere to God, and that necessity is God's Smile. Countless obligations each individual has; but there is and there can be only one true responsibility, and that responsibility lies in our sincere effort to fulfil the real need of the world and not its wants or demands.

Necessity is self-enquiry for God-discovery. Responsibility is world-education for world-perfection.

Necessity is a one-way street. Here the doer and the action go together. Here the dream of the individual seeker and the reality of the individual seeker live together in perfect harmony, complementing and fulfilling each other.

Responsibility is a two-way street. Here the giver is an individual and the receiver is another individual, and there comes a time when they meet together. When the receiver receives, at times he may be grateful; at times he may not be grateful at all. When the giver gives, at times he may be soulful and at times he may be anything but soulful. But the giver and the receiver meet together at a particular point, at a particular place. The giver either willingly or unwillingly gives and the receiver either gratefully or ungratefully receives. In responsibility there is always a division: two entities, two realities – giver and receiver. In necessity there is only the song of oneness. Here two become one, three become one, four become one; for all of them have one soul and one goal.

*

The message of the Secretary-General's oneness-heart runs thus: the demanding world tells us that it is the responsibility of the United Nations to bring about world peace since it bears the name "United Nations". The demanding world always claims that in order to prove its worth, the United Nations must bring about world peace. This is the truth that the demanding world offers us. But the loving world has something else to tell. The loving world tells us that it is the necessity of the world at large, of the entire world, to have peace, to have love, to have harmony. The United Nations is a member of the world family. The world houses the United Nations. In the case of the United Nations, a member of the world family is most sincerely willing to try to bring peace to all the other members of the family. It is the world-necessity that the United Nations has accepted as its own necessity. This is not responsibility, it is necessity. So the loving world feels a most prominent, qualified member of its family has accepted the world-necessity as its own necessity and is trying its utmost to bring about world peace according to the world's willingness.

In a family there are parents and children. The United Nations can be called a strong young man in the family. The parents or, let us say, the oldest members of the family or the old nations – these the United Nations can keep on its shoulders perfectly safe. And the new nations, the young children, its younger brothers and sisters – these the United Nations can keep beside itself. The parents are satisfied when their strong young boy places them on his shoulders and takes them to the destination, and the little members of the family are also satisfied when they can go alongside their strong brother and reach the destination with him. And what is their destination? World-progress is their destination, world-satisfaction is their destination. So the old nations and the young nations can perfectly be carried to their destination with love, sympathy and inner capacity, provided they claim the United Nations as a real, true, genuine member of their family. The capacity of the United Nations is nothing short of its world-embracing and world-illumining vision.

*

The message of the Secretary-General's satisfaction-soul runs thus: compromise is not and cannot be the real answer to the world's problems. Compromise, the breath of compromise, is very short-lived. It is like a fleeting second. What is needed, what is of paramount importance, is oneness, not compromise. What is compromise? If you don't speak ill of me, I shall not speak ill of you. If you keep silent, then I shall also keep silent; or if you do this, I shall do this and if you don't do that, then I won't do that. This is compromise.

But in oneness we notice something else. In oneness we see that two individuals become absolutely inseparably one for their oneness-satisfaction, even though they are performing two different tasks. One can remain silent and the other can talk. One speaks what he has to say and the other listens devotedly and soulfully; then they change their respective roles. In oneness, each can play the role of multiplicity. With one hand I can do something to please my mind and with the other hand I can do something to please my body. I can please my eyes and, at the same time, I can please my ears. I can look at you and appreciate your beauty and, at the same time, I can hear what you have to say. The soul of the United Nations teaches us the most sublime truth that two individuals or all individuals can do something according to their own capacity, their own willingness, their own receptivity, and still please all the members of their spiritual family. It is like an orchestra. There are many players and each player is playing a different instrument. But each player is needed. On the piano, each key is needed. We cannot say that one is enough, for then there will be no music. All the keys are necessary. Similarly, all the members of the United Nations are necessary. They will produce different notes, but they have to go together if there is to be a musical symphony. In this way there can be real oneness in variety; in this way the world can achieve peace in multiplicity.

Again, each nation need not play the same note all the time. Silence and sound: this is what God eternally is. When it is necessary for some nation to see the face of reality-silence, that nation has to remain silent. When a particular nation feels it is necessary to see the face of reality-sound, it will enter into the life of action. Action and inaction, sound and silence, must go together. On one level these two things are diametrically opposite – action and inaction, sound and silence – but in the deepest reality-existence they are one. Dream-world and reality-world, sound-world and silence-world complement each other and fulfil each other.

The United Nations is playing a most important role in seeking to establish world harmony, world peace, world oneness, world divinity, world perfection and God-satisfaction. The outer world says that the United Nations is not strong enough, but the inner world has something else to say. The inner world says that the real capacity of the United Nations is its willingness, its inner cry. The United Nations is crying for world peace; and this very act of crying is its real capacity. It has no other capacity. The way of oneness that cries to lead us to the ultimate destination: this is the United Nations. The cry itself is its capacity and this capacity is of supreme importance.

True, this capacity cannot or does not meet with satisfaction-reality all at once. I have the capacity to run, let us say, but I am not at the destination. I have just left the starting point; my goal is still ahead. Capacity does not mean immediate success or immediate victory. Capacity is a continuous movement that eventually leads us to our destined goal. So right now the United Nations, which is the supreme human and divine necessity – God's necessity on earth to bring about world peace – is a cry, a movement, a forward march, a forward adventure. A runner is running. Just because the runner has not reached the goal, this does not mean that the runner will fail. There is an appointed hour and at that appointed hour, which is God's choice Hour, the inner dream – the real dream – of the United Nations will be transformed into reality. This is necessity, the inner necessity of the soul of the United Nations and also its God-ordained responsibility. Self-imposed responsibility, self-styled responsibility, does not last more than a few minutes, a few hours, a few days, a few months, a few years. But God-ordained responsibility is like Eternity's own necessity.

What the United Nations has for the world is a dream. In the outer world it is running slowly, steadily and unerringly. But in the inner world it is running fast, faster, fastest. No matter how fast it runs in the inner world, it will not lose its balance. And in the outer world, no matter how slowly it is running, it is bound to reach its destination, for it is running steadily and unerringly. The outer goal it will one day reach, and at the same time the world will notice it. It may take a very short time or it may take a very long time; it all depends on world-receptivity. But in the inner world it will reach its destination very soon, because the inner progress of the United Nations is most satisfactory. In the inner world the dream of the United Nations, like a deer, has the fastest speed. But the necessity that the United Nations has accepted as its own will ultimately be fulfilled in both the inner world and the outer world, for this necessity is nothing short of God-ordained responsibility. And this is every day being engraved in the hearts of the world-loving nations at the United Nations and the hearts of the world-seekers who want only truth-reality to be manifested in individual souls, in individual nations, in collective souls, in collective nations. Peace, which is real satisfaction, will loom large one day, for it is the only choice which the individual and the collective body have, the only choice that God wants, that humanity wants, that the real existence in us wants. All want the same thing: satisfaction-peace, peace-satisfaction; oneness in multiplicity and multiplicity in oneness. There is no conflict; there are only different branches, millions of flowers, leaves and fruits on the everlasting Life-Tree.

3. *Patriotism and world-vision*

When the seeker in me sees the striking physical frame of the Secretary-General, his eyes are at once divine silence-energy, silence-nourishment and divine sound-revelation, sound-expansion. When the seeker in me feels the dynamic inner frame, the vital, of the Secretary-General, his soulful bird with two hopeful wings flies to cover the length and breadth of the world.

What for? To sow the immortal seed of the United Nations for world-union, world-salvation and world-perfection.

The human in our Secretary-General is from Austria. The divine in him is not only for Austria but for the entire world-thirst, world-hunger and world-cry.

Kurt Waldheim's life offers dramatic proof that national patriotism and world citizenship are not necessarily at odds. To be a world citizen does not mean that one has to renounce one's own country, for each country has something special to offer to the family of nations. One country may be lacking in one particular aspect of life but may excel in another aspect. Thus, the fragrance of each nation-flower can inspire and illumine its brother and sister nations.

When his own beloved country is accused, the great patriot in Kurt Waldheim comes to the fore and not only defends his country but throws considerable light on the confusing and confused world-mind:

> From time to time, Austria's foreign policy is accused of lacking glamour. We cannot reject such a criticism strongly enough. It would indeed be a grave mistake for a neutral country to try to attract world attention through dramatic declarations or actions. It might mean a temporary appearance of the country's name in the headlines of world news, but the political consequences would be disastrous. Many such declarations by well-known politicians have in the past aroused much publicity and created a host of misunderstandings that contributed to international unrest. The foreign offices of the countries concerned then had the difficult task of repairing the damage by correcting, redressing or explaining the statement that had been made. A

foreign policy of sensationalism is contrary to the interests of a neutral country. Reason, cool-headedness and continuity are infinitely more necessary than dramatisation.

*

During Kurt Waldheim's term of office as Permanent Representative of Austria to the United Nations, undoubtedly there was a special significance to why he was divinely honoured as Chairman of the Committee on the Peaceful Uses of Outer Space, and later supremely honoured as President of the First United Nations Conference on the Exploration and Peaceful Uses of Outer Space. The peace-lover in our present Secretary-General voices forth:

> The progress achieved has also provided the international community with an eloquent testimony of a historical process, that given the political will, an area of potential rivalry and conflict in international politics can be turned into a fruitful cooperative endeavour for the benefit of mankind.

Man invents war. Man discovers peace. He invents war from without. He discovers peace from within. War man throws. Peace man sows. The smile of war is the flood of human blood. The smile of peace is the love, below, above.

Peace is the whole truth that wishes to enrapture humanity. War is the whole falsehood that wants to capture humanity. Peace begins in the soul and ends in the heart. War begins in the mind and ends in the body.

War forgets peace. Peace forgives war. War is the death of the life human. Peace is the birth of the Life Divine. Our vital passions want war. Our psychic emotions desire peace.

*

Commenting on how the pioneers of outer space have enlightened the world's vision of peace, Kurt Waldheim affirms:

> Man's sense of world community has been sharpened by the dramatic vision of the earth as revealed to us by the pioneers of space. From this perspective the differences which have divided men in the past tend to recede before the reality of common sense.

In April, 1971, Kurt Waldheim was one of two candidates for the Federal Presidency of Austria. But after being appointed Secretary-General of the United Nations, the heart-home of the world-body, this son of Austria proved himself to be first and foremost a lover of mankind. Him to quote:

> .... There is no conflict between citizenship of one's own country and a wider concern for mankind as a whole. The interdependence of mankind is not a rhetorical cliche – it represents a profound reality.

Again he says:

> In my opinion, there should be no fundamental conflict between national self-interest and the goals of the international community and of mankind as a whole.... That is the real function of the United

Nations: to be available to the countries of the world, not as a utopian substitute for traditional international relations, but as a mechanism, an instrument, by means of which national policies can be shaped and harmonised to take into account the legitimate hopes and aspirations of all countries.

*

With regard to his beloved country, Kurt Waldheim has become one with the wisdom of Socrates, the great wise man of the past who taught us: "I am not an Athenian, nor am I a Greek. I am a citizen of the world."

The United Nations message of love and brotherhood can easily be understood and spread by all of humanity if each person can claim the message of Socrates as his own and feel that he belongs to the larger world-family. In this respect, the Secretary-General sees eye to eye with his predecessor, U Thant, whose lofty vision affirms:

> A new quality of planetary imagination is demanded from all of us as the price of human survival. I am not decrying that form of nationalism that prompts the individual citizen to appreciate and praise the achievements and values that his native land has contributed to the well-being and happiness of the whole human race. Nor am I calling for international homogenization, for I rejoice in cultural and national uniqueness. But I am making a plea – a plea based on these ten years of looking at the human condition from my unique vantage point – for a dual allegiance. This implies

an open acceptance of belonging — as in fact we all do — to the human race as well as to our local community or nation. I even believe that the mark of the truly educated and imaginative person facing the twenty-first century is that he feels himself to be a planetary citizen.

No longer can any country dare to live the life of isolation as the vision of a oneness-world grows ever brighter on the horizon. Kurt Waldheim saw this clearly in the case of his own beloved country:

> Living contact with the world outside has become more necessary than ever if the correct decisions are to be made at the right moment. Austria's membership in the United Nations makes this kind of contact possible and therefore is of great help to Austria's foreign policy. In this way Austria has managed to shake off the isolation into which she had been thrust by the tragic events of 1938 and their consequences, and to regain her rightful position on the world scene in view of her noble past and present achievements.

Kurt Waldheim's world-vision encompasses all nations, both large and small. Although the pragmatist in him sees clearly the influential role of the big powers in world affairs, he is firmly convinced that only with the help of the smaller brother and sister nations can a new great alliance be established among all the countries in the United Nations. Him to quote:

> The destiny of the United Nations will ultimately depend on a satisfactory solution of the problem of

relations between the industrialised countries and the far more numerous developing countries. It will also depend very much on whether the United Nations can be made truly representative, truly "universal".

To unite all countries and all men: this is the ultimate goal of the United Nations. To see all human hearts and minds striving for one highest cause: what else is true spirituality if not this? Spirituality is the union of all human aspirations for a better and more illumining life in a world of harmony and oneness.

O Kurt Waldheim, ... your life of duty-tree and beauty-flower awakens the sleeping world and its oneness-power.

4. *The necessity-height of the United Nations*

"I know that the world cannot do without the United Nations." This soulful and fruitful declaration of the Secretary-General inspires and illumines our searching minds and aspiring hearts. Again he affirms: "I firmly believe that, for all its shortcomings and frustrations, the United Nations is an indispensable institution."

The Secretary-General sees the United Nations as essentially a great and unique human experiment. As such, it is open to all the human shortcomings and weaknesses. But it is because it is a human organisation, served by individual human beings from every continent, that its strength and relevance derives.

*

Change of nature, either in human life or in any phase of life itself, has proved to be a most difficult task. When the ascending aspiration-flames from below and the descending Compassion-

Sun from above meet together, the seemingly impossible task of nature's change, either in an individual life or in a country's life, can both surprisingly and satisfactorily take place. Nature's change has always been slow, steady, but unerring. With regard to the nature's transformation of a State, what the United Nations can unmistakably and will convincingly do is most illuminingly expressed by its supreme Pilot, Kurt Waldheim:

> When States become members of the United Nations, they do not suddenly and miraculously change their nature.... But if the United Nations was not meant to initiate a fundamental transformation of the nature of world politics, the Organisation does provide the framework and the machinery for channelling national actions into more constructive directions....

Each dedicated action of the United Nations is not only an experiment of man but an experience of God in the world and for the world. Truth to tell, the United Nations aspiration for brotherhood and peace is divinely indispensable in the eternal march of world-evolution. What could be greater than the hope that the heart and soul of this world family offer mankind? The all-seeing hope and vision of the United Nations will lead humanity to the highest Peace, Light and Bliss for the manifestation of the Kingdom of Heaven here on earth.

To quote the late Secretary-General U Thant, who was one with his successor Kurt Waldheim in his realisation of the indispensability of this world institution:

> Humanity has reached the point of no return. Acceptance of the community of interest has become a requirement of human survival on this planet. It

can no longer be dismissed as an idealistic concept, unrelated to realities. The traditional sovereign state is no longer a viable guarantee of a nation's security or economic prosperity, nor even a guarantee of national survival. More and more men of science and scholarship, as well as business leaders and public administrators, have come to grasp this underlying fact of interdependence today.

To our Secretary-General, the divine reason and purpose of the world organisation are supremely self-evident.

> The world does not need a new political cataclysm to provoke such an alliance. Poverty, hunger, the lack of proper education, health and shelter, and the new problems of the environment and of our endangered seas, waters and atmosphere are big enough problems to justify the co-operation of all forces in the United Nations.

Countless are the problems when we live in the unlit and doubting mind. But there is only one problem – absolutely one and not two – when we live in the awakened life and the oneness-loving heart, and that problem is the problem of survival and prosperity of all men. How do we divinely survive and supremely prosper? Here is the irrevocable proclamation offered to the world by our Secretary-General:

> As we now consider the choices before us, we must realise we are not faced with many separate problems, but with different aspects of a single overall problem: the survival and prosperity of all men and women and their harmonious development,

physical as well as spiritual, in peace, with each other and with nature. This is the solution we must seek. It is within our power to find it.

*

The United Nations offers to seekers and lovers of the world a divine hope and promise, as the truth-seeker and harmony-seeker in Kurt Waldheim so clearly sees:

> The instrument is here, created under the impact of the horrors of the Second World War. It is universal in scope and almost universal in membership. All that is needed is for the leaders of today to use it, support it and meet on the solid basis of its charter.

5. *The message of practical idealism*

Through the United Nations the Creator is offering His illumining Love and Service to His creation. As head and heart of the world-family, the Secretary-General must be constantly and consciously aware of the inner oneness-cry and outer dedication-smile of the United Nations. And the world-server in the Secretary-General must constantly offer inner love and outer service to humanity.

Speaking of the challenges of the secretary-generalship, Kurt Waldheim says:

> The secretary-generalship is at the same time one of the most fascinating and one of the most frustrating jobs in the world, encompassing, as it does, the height of human aspiration and the depth of

human frailty. No one is so exposed to that bitter contrast as the Secretary-General, and it requires a constant effort of will on his part to continue day after day and night after night to face up to the problems of the world and of the United Nations in the full knowledge that, while he cannot hope to solve them, it is absolutely vital that the effort continue.

As supreme Pilot of the United Nations Boat, the Secretary-General must needs constantly inspire and encourage his fellow men. To those fellow travellers who have become too tired along the way to continue the journey to the oneness-world, the Secretary-General Waldheim has a special message:

> Only the vision of a better world, a world of peace, justice and progress for all, can sustain us in the daily struggle to meet the dangers, the challenges and the great problems of our time. I am more convinced than ever that our greatest danger will come if we lose that vision and relapse into defeatism and cynicism.

False hopes often lead to this kind of defeatism and cynicism. The Secretary-General's deep insight tells us:

> All too often in the minds of the public the United Nations is mistaken for a world government with legislative and executive powers, and is expected to solve directly every problem on earth, from peace and security to economic development, the environment and the drug problem. This is not the case and it must be made clear to the public that

the United Nations is based on the co-operation of sovereign member states.

The world needs the faith that evolves slowly and steadily from the Creator to the creation and then back to the Source. To those brothers and sisters who have become disillusioned or who have lost faith in the United Nations' efforts towards world peace, the Secretary-General offers his encouragement:

> Perhaps, there were those whose expectations were too high. But although we may have fewer illusions today, there is no need to be disillusioned. We must not throw away all the advances of the past twenty-five years. We must face the future with realism, but with a renewed dedication to the task of the maintenance of peace and the provision of a better life for all the peoples of the world.

This stoic server of mankind inspires the highest determination and will-power in each individual and each nation to manifest the inner divine opportunities of the United Nations. The divine qualities and potentialities of this world organisation are not wishful imagination but solid inner realities crying to come to the fore. The Secretary-General's one-pointed faith in this divine reality speaks thus:

> If progress is slow, that, in the nature of things, is hardly surprising. But if the will is there, and the talent and the dedication, we should not be dismayed by the difficulties. If we believe that by human actions wisely directed the world can be made a better place, then the United Nations presents unrivalled opportunities. I hope that we shall seize them.

A SOULFUL TRIBUTE TO THE SECRETARY-GENERAL

All the nations are like divine pilgrims proceeding slowly, steadily and unerringly towards the same goal. The divine pilgrim in the Secretary General is "convinced that we are embarked on the right road to objectives of vital importance for the future".

To those who may feel that undertaking this journey on the path to peace and progress is like building castles in the sky, the practical idealist in Kurt Waldheim affirms:

> It is sometimes thought that idealism is unrealistic. In the United Nations, I believe that idealism and practical, far-sighted common sense lead in the same direction. They lead us over a difficult and steep path towards the great objectives of peace, justice, human dignity and equity to which mankind has aspired for centuries. In the United Nations we dare to believe that we can make real progress up this steep path, if we work together with courage and persistence.

The oneness-soul of our United Nations Pilot supreme knows the true truth that this world-body sings the song not only of possibility but also of inevitability. The inner vision and outer reality of the United Nations and the dreams that abide in the hearts of all lovers and servers of mankind are destined to found the Kingdom of Heaven on this very earth. At that time the aspiring soul of the United Nations will sing the song of oneness-world.

O Kurt Waldheim, I always see you as God's lightning-speed. Today you are here, tomorrow there and the day after tomorrow elsewhere. Your penetrating vision not only enters into the world problems, but also solves the problems of the world most miraculously.

6. World ignorance and universal light

To our sorrow, most human beings are satisfied with a life of darkness, limitation and bondage. They aspire not to see a higher existence-reality and to live a more fulfilling life. Yet these very individuals find fault with the United Nations day in and day out, in season and out of season. But they must remember that as they themselves are not perfect, neither are the human beings who are offering their service-light to the United Nations. Again, it is the human in us that sees imperfections in others. The divine in us sees only the perfection of the Creator in His creation.

The wisdom-light of the Pilot supreme of the United Nations knows the necessity of world understanding for and world support of the UN's vision and reality. The capacities and potentialities, as well as the limitations of the world organisation, must be brought into the full view of individuals and their nations.

But to the eyeless critics of the world organisation, the Secretary-General says:

> Critics of the United Nations often demand, "What do we get out of it?" The answer is a great deal, but I would prefer that you should ask the questions, "What can we put into it?" and "What can we do to make the world organisation more effective as a guarantor of peace and human advancement?"

It is an unfortunate mistake to try to judge the United Nations by what the United Nations has or has not achieved. What is of paramount importance is whether we claim the United Nations as our very own. Indeed, if we can feel that we are part and parcel of this world-body, and if we can increase our own aspiration and

A SOULFUL TRIBUTE TO THE SECRETARY-GENERAL

dedication in abundant measure, then we can one day illumine the mind and heart of the entire world.

Clearly the Secretary-General sees the urgency and necessity of illumining the world-mind and world-heart:

> Governments may be more inclined to support and to use the United Nations and to implement its recommendations if there is strong public opinion in favour of the Organisation. The people themselves therefore have a crucial say in world affairs. Support and realistic appraisal by the public could be the razor's edge between war and peace.

Ignorance is man's worst enemy, yet surprisingly man has formed a long-standing friendship with ignorance. The peerless Pilot of the United Nations speaks out against world-ignorance:

> Of all the evils which have beset mankind in its recent history, that of ignorance is perhaps the worst. For out of ignorance there comes intolerance; out of intolerance there comes hostility; and out of hostility there comes conflict. In our interdependent world it is dangerous to be ignorant of other nations, other faiths, other ideologies, other interests, other ambitions, other hopes. From knowledge of these you will learn how it may be possible for the world – your world – to practise tolerance and live together in peace.

The Light of the Supreme can alone disperse our age-old darkness. Here our best friend, according to Waldheim, is the universal light offered by education:

> Every school and every university has the duty to ensure that young people are trained to comprehend the new realities, and to realise that, of all the curses of the past, ignorance has been the most terrible of all. With knowledge comes tolerance; and tolerance is the essential basis not only for detente, but for the much wider peace and security which we are seeking for ourselves and for future generations.

Never must we surrender to ignorance, fear, doubt, anxieties and worries. Each obstacle we face is a divine opportunity to muster and strengthen our inner resources. We must know that if the United Nations reflects the human qualities of mankind, so also it reflects the divine potentialities of man. Our Secretary-General sees the divine as far outshining the human in this comity of nations:

> At root, the United Nations represents a striving after great human goals which are common to all peoples.... The United Nations certainly reflects many human deficiencies, and it is as capable of error and misjudgement as any other human institution. But I also know that it reflects the great human qualities, of which integrity, perseverance, patience, and compassion are, I believe, the most important.

As fate would have it, ignorance quite often doubts God's Compassion-Light that operates in and through the service-light of the United Nations, in spite of the Himalayan efforts of world-lovers to serve humanity. Here the Secretary-General voices the emotions that often fill the hearts of world-servers:

A SOULFUL TRIBUTE TO THE SECRETARY-GENERAL

> There are occasions, looking at the world as it is, and conscious of what it should be, when a compassionate person is dominated by emotions of despair. The problems are so vast, so intractable, so profound! How can we hope to resolve them, to fulfil the noble ideals of the Charter and the Universal Declaration?

Yet man must always reach for the transcendental Peace and Harmony. "While admitting failures and disappointments," continues Mr Waldheim, "we must never lose sight of the ideal. If we abandon that ideal – a world living in harmony, in which true equality exists – we will all lose something in ourselves, we will have abandoned our faith, and we will have betrayed our trust. For we are Trustees for all humanity."

7. Success and progress

Success belongs to the outer world. Progress belongs to the inner world. Success engenders vital gratification. Progress augments psychic satisfaction. Success claims to be the matchless friend of human life, whereas progress is at once the divine and eternal friend. Success is what we, in the march of time, become and progress is what we sempiternally are. The human in us dies for success and ultimately dies in success. When we live in the world of success, the human reality, which is goodness – our God-life in God-Vision's Reality – surrenders itself to the lower reality, which is greatness, world-acclaim and the dance of individuality's supremacy. The divine in us longs for progress, which is the song of gradual self-transcendence in the one for the many and in the many for the one. The soul of the United Nations dreams only of progress in the aspiration-life and dedication-life of each individual and each country.

The oft-quoted adage, "Nothing succeeds like success," has been interpreted with an amazingly broad vision by the Secretary-General:

> There has been some slight progress here and there: certain situations which had been frozen by the cold war are beginning to show some signs of thaw as a result of the over-all detente. We must keep trying. As you say in business: "Nothing succeeds like success." Well, we need progress and success in order to achieve other successes and to create a new climate in the world.

The Soul of the United Nations has granted her beloved son, our Secretary-General, Kurt Waldheim, beckoning hands to invite ignorance-world for a global progress in the life of universal brotherhood and in the heart of perfection's height. His inner courage often inspires him to speak out and offer his guidance and help to the member States, when his conscience dictates that the United Nations, under its Charter, should offer its assistance. "Governments may decide not to make use of these offers, but they will realise in the end that the United Nations, despite its limitations, which we must correct, is still the most advanced instrument ever devised by humanity for its collective security."

The realist in Kurt Waldheim acknowledges that the efforts of the United Nations have not always proved successful:

> The desire for instant success and a disproportionate disillusionment when it is not achieved, is a conspicuous feature of our time. I believe, however – at the risk of being accused of optimism – that we should not resign ourselves to despair

so easily. The fact that we know more about our condition than any previous generation in history is an enormous advantage if it is put to good use. It should certainly not be allowed to lead us to defeatism. But to make use of our self-knowledge we must also accept the necessity of change, of new imperatives and of new patterns of activity.

Nonetheless, the United Nations has succeeded most significantly and progressed most fruitfully. As the Secretary-General points out:

It is only fair to say that it has been of incalculable value to international political progress over the last few decades: it has kept the dialogue between East and West going; it has shown a great many new Afro-Asian states the way into the community of nations; and last but not least, it represents the world's conscience on the basis of the Charter. It has thus become an irreplaceable moral force in the constellation of forces in international politics. In spite of the new crises that confront it and are threatening to drag it down to one of the lowest points in its history, the member States do seem to be moving towards the realisation of what Dag Hammarskjöld once so strikingly formulated: "We should recognise the United Nations for what it is – an admittedly imperfect but indispensable instrument for the nations, designed to ensure a more just and secure world order through peaceful evolution."

Again, he declares:

> Steady, detailed effort is hard to dramatise, and it seldom makes headlines, but who can doubt that the transformations and crises of the past thirty years would have been infinitely more painful and far less subject to peaceful resolution without the United Nations?

The United Nations has progressed to the point where it has much to give in every aspect of human endeavour. Humanity must needs follow its illumining and continuous guidance. Humanity must needs have faith in the United Nations' dedication and service. To quote Secretary-General Waldheim:

> Slowly and painfully mankind has created machinery for international co-operation in almost every area of human activity, from the prevention of disease to the settlement of international disputes, which never existed before in the history of our planet. Tragically that machinery is not always used, but it has, time and time again, demonstrated its unique value when it has been employed. And, increasingly it is being used – not out of idealism, but because it works. In this, we may record a definite advance.

We may ask why the world often does not recognise the true progress and success of the United Nations? Here we can view the United Nations as a mother who is expected to do everything for her child, the world. Unfortunately, the child very often forgets to offer gratitude to the mother for the mother's countless inner and outer gifts. But if the child does something for the mother that may be most unimportant, then that very thing receives undue attention. True, the United Nations receives all kinds of help from the world, but the world is not fully aware of the ideals and service that the United Nations is consciously and constantly offering. The Secretary-General throws considerable light on this deplorable situation:

> Many of the activities of the United Nations are so much taken for granted that they are scarcely reported any more. This is probably not a bad development, but it should not cause us to lose sight of the value of the multiple activities of our Organisation or the dangerous vacuum in international life that would be created if, for any reason, they were to cease.
> We now take for granted that virtually all the Governments of the world can meet in the United Nations to discuss almost any subject under the sun. We take for granted that, when a conflict threatens, the Security Council will meet and sometimes, by that simple fact alone, will provide a breathing space and an opportunity for reflection, reassessment and clarification. We take for granted that in the United Nations there can be meetings and communication between representatives of contending parties who can meet virtually nowhere else in the world. We take peace-keeping and good offices for granted. We assume that the humanitarian agencies of the United Nations will be there in emergency or dire need to take care of the afflicted or the refugees. We have become completely used to the unprecedented idea that the nations of the world, almost as a matter of course can discuss

as far-reaching a concept as the new international economic order.

The time will come when the inner eye of the world will unmistakably show blind humanity the greatness and goodness of the United Nations. The blind world will then receive illumination-vision from the United Nations; the unsatisfied world will receive satisfaction-peace, and the aspiring world will receive the answer to its heart's soulful cry. At that time, the world will sing the gratitude-song for what the United Nations is offering to it. Again, the gratitude-song must echo in the hearts of each member of the United Nations for what the world is doing for the Organisation. In the gratitude-song of the United Nations and in the gratitude-song of the world will be heard the soulful song of oneness-expansion.

8. *World-service*

As the United Nations is indispensable to the world community, so also is each individual nation a necessary part of this world organisation. We can view each nation as a unique branch of the world-tree. Each branch is needed to complete the fulness-beauty of the all-spreading tree, and each branch offers special protection and a special oneness-fruit to aspiring mankind. Similarly, each individual world seeker and world server is needed in the United Nations striving for universal peace and progress. In the words of our Secretary-General:

> We are men and women from many lands, representing a rich variety of cultures. And we have been brought together to work in a great common cause:

the survival and progress of mankind. The concept of unity in diversity .... underlies our various pursuits at the United Nations.

The dedication-life of each individual in the United Nations Boat is of utmost importance. As the supreme Pilots of the United Nations serve the world, we can also do the same, according to our capacity. Our capacities – however limited – and our prayerful inner devotion to humanity are our solid support that we can offer inwardly and outwardly to the United Nations Boat and its supreme Pilots. According to Secretary-General Waldheim:

> I am deeply convinced that all of us who work for the United Nations must maintain our sense of dedication and idealism. We are, after all, privileged to serve an Organisation whose Charter embodies the highest aims of humanity. I know very well that it is easy to talk about dedication and idealism but much harder to maintain them in all the wearisome difficulties of everyday life. However, from my own experience in the past five years, I am convinced that the vast majority of the members of the Secretariat are moved primarily by their devotion to the principles of the Charter and are proud of the opportunity they have been given to serve in the United Nations, whatever their sphere or level of activity.

Supreme perfection is not the necessity of only one individual or even of all the individuals working in the United Nations. This perfection is the true necessity of all human beings on earth. The dedication of all human beings must go hand in hand with that of all who work for the United Nations. All of us must love and serve our larger world-family. Here the role of the international civil servant is of paramount importance. To quote the Secretary-General:

> If the United Nations reflects much that is tragic, it also reflects much that is good and encouraging in the human spirit. And perhaps the most remarkable of all has been the development of the ideal of international service into a practical reality. There were many at Dumbarton Oaks and San Francisco who were sceptical about the practicality of the concept of men and women from all nations voluntarily serving an international cause, but we have seen in the lives of people .... that it can be, and has been, achieved. We see it today in the selfless dedication of people all over the world working for the United Nations in social and humanitarian relief programmes. We see it in the peace-keeping forces who risk their lives in the quest for peace. We see it in those who work in the United Nations refugee camps, in our health, education, and agricultural programmes, and in the provision of food to those most desperately in need through the World Food Programme.

The international civil servant must needs always dive deep within to strengthen his dedication and increase his oneness with his universal brothers and sisters. To see how the United Nations is serving the world, we must know how we ourselves are serving the world and the United Nations. Let us identify with the United Nations ideals and strive ever to manifest these ideals, to transform the United Nations vision-light into a reality of concern and dedication. There is never a moment to lose in this race against ignorance, and each one of us must needs guard against the dangers of complacency. Says the Secretary-General:

> The fact is that our Organisation has come into middle age and is no longer a young prodigy – or a young problem. This is in one way comforting and in another way dangerous. It is comforting that the United Nations is a firmly established and recognised world institution. It is dangerous if the Organisation becomes complacent, set in its ways, unresponsive to new ideas or irrelevant to contemporary issues. We must constantly be on guard to preserve the institution from such tendencies.

Never before has the practical Wisdom-Light of God been so accessible to us as it is today in the United Nations. Inwardly and outwardly we are being illumined by the United Nations, although we may not be fully aware of it. Similarly, those human beings who are striving to offer the Wisdom-Light of God through the United Nations may not be completely conscious of their God-ordained task, and they may see all too clearly their own limitations and the world's imperfections. They may feel frustrated that the unaspiring world is not opening up its heart to the wisdom of the United Nations. But the soul of each individual and of each country in the United Nations knows that it has made the right choice.

The Secretary-General envisions the work ahead for the United Nations:

> The coming years promise us greater challenges, more complex problems and doubtless some very

difficult times. They also promise us very great opportunities for developing the machinery of international co-operation in many areas, into some of which the international community has scarcely ventured before. I am sure that the Secretariat will be inspired rather than discouraged by these challenges and will continue and develop its service to the international community in accordance with the great traditions which it has already established.

When we offer our devotion to the United Nations, we can do so on the physical, mental, psychic and spiritual levels. Each type of devoted service is of paramount importance, and each international civil servant offers a special dedication to the inner and outer United Nations. Truth to tell, each human being holds the key to the progress and success of the United Nations. Indeed, each of us, and the service that each of us renders on all planes, is the key to the fulfilment of the glorious role and goal of the United Nations in mankind and for mankind.

9. The new ethics: the UN Charter and the Universal Declaration of Human Rights

The Charter of the United Nations and the Universal Declaration of Human Rights are the true manifestations of humanity's spiritual values and inner oneness. In these lofty principles we find a divine code of ethics for our time and times to come. To quote our Secretary-General:

> The United Nations has proposed to all Governments and to all peoples standards of respect for individuals and for groups, derived from the best

in the spiritual heritage of mankind as well as from the realities of our rapidly developing societies.

When the Secretary-General met with the head of his own church, Pope Paul VI, in July of 1977, the Pope eloquently spoke about the spirituality of the United Nations:

> Above all, we want the United Nations to be par excellence, the expression and the bulwark of those human rights, which it so solemnly proclaimed almost thirty years ago. A heightened consciousness is needed to make these rights the touchstone of a really humane civilisation and truly to achieve, without excluding any race or any people, the solidarity which is essential between brothers all created in God's Image.

As part of his message of condolence upon hearing about the sudden death of the Holy Father in August 1978, the Secretary-General declared:

> In the United Nations we specially recall Pope Paul's historic visit to our Headquarters in New York and his powerful but simple message, "Never again war." This visit not only set a unique precedent; it also foreshadowed a much closer contact between the leadership of one of the great churches and congregations of the world and the leadership of the world organisation. It forged a new link between the spiritual and the temporal world which has time and again proved its value.

There is only one religion and one truth: man. All peoples can unite to raise an inner temple where all nations can worship the highest ideals and principles of man. And within this temple of man shall shine the benevolent Smile of God. According to the Pilot of the United Nations Boat:

> The United Nations contains many different faiths, ideologies, and beliefs. It embraces all the doctrines and attitudes of mankind, and it was the genius of the founders to create a Charter to whose principles all nations could freely and willingly subscribe.

The Secretary-General's fervent request runs thus:

> The United Nations needs the help and the support of all the leaders and of all the great religions of the world, if it is to succeed in solving the very complex problems of peace.

The divine ideals of the United Nations will eventually save and free mankind from ignorance, turning man's vision of peace into true reality. To the Secretary-General, the Charter is supremely instrumental in manifesting the United Nations ideas and ideals:

> The greatest strength of the United Nations is the enduring power of the great and necessary ideas expressed in its Charter-ideas great enough to encompass the complexities, rivalries and differences of all the nations in the co-operative pursuit of certain common aims.

Now what is needed is co-operation and faithfulness to these ideals by all members of the world family. According to our Secretary-General:

A SOULFUL TRIBUTE TO THE SECRETARY-GENERAL

> The United Nations Charter opens with the words "We the peoples of the United Nations". Thus, every man and woman has a profound personal stake in the future of the United Nations. If we work together in a spirit of friendship and understanding, we will have little to fear. Let that be our personal commitment.

Again, he affirms:

> We must always remember that the United Nations was built upon reason, and not emotion. It was built upon the realisation that the true self-interest of sovereign nations lies in international co-operation. The fact of our physical and political interdependence, and the common dangers which all mankind faces, demand that we continue in our task, together, so that we may move closer to the goals of the Charter, and the hopes of mankind which gave them birth.

His predecessor, U Thant, shared Kurt Waldheim's soulful commitment to the UN Charter. To quote U Thant:

> Tolerance is the principal foundation on which the United Nations Charter rests. Without the spirit of tolerance, one cannot understand, much less appreciate, the Charter. "To practise tolerance and live together in peace with one another as good neighbours" is the actual language of the Charter, and one of the primary functions of the Secretary-General is not only to practise tolerance in his personal dealings, but also to extend this concept of

tolerance to international relations. In other words, my conception of the Secretary-General's role is to build bridges between peoples, governments and states. This is why my main preoccupation during my tenure of office was not only to bring about a *détente* between differing nations, but also to eliminate the obstacles to such a *détente*.

Without a doubt, the UN Charter and the American Declaration of Independence are proceeding to the same destination — two trailblazers on the path to human freedom and world peace. True, one started the journey before the other, but the two are now marching together confidently and unerringly. Comparing the UN Charter with the Declaration of Independence, our Secretary-General says:

> There are many parallels between the work of the founding fathers of this Republic in Philadelphia nearly two centuries ago, and the task of the founders of the United Nations nearly thirty years ago in San Francisco.... Both have evolved far beyond the expectations of their founders. Both have continued to derive inspiration and direction from the declarations of principles and aims drawn up by their founders.
>
> The spirit which inspired Thomas Jefferson in Philadelphia in 1776 was also present at San Francisco in 1945 and in the creation of the Universal Declaration of Human Rights in Paris in 1948. For above all, the belief that "all men are created equal" is the same faith which made the founders of the United Nations declare their resolution to

> "reaffirm faith in fundamental human rights, in the dignity and worth of the human person, in the equal rights of men and women, and of nations large and small".

About the Universal Declaration of Human Rights Secretary-General Waldheim comments:

> The Universal Declaration was the first occasion in history when the inalienable rights of all individuals were formally established. It was an expression, in simple and clear language, of the principles which should govern human relations. It represented faith in the value of the individual, and in the conviction that politics is about people.

Such a Declaration, believes Mr Waldheim, can serve to form an inner and outer world conscience which will raise humanity's level of existence from the human to the divine in a practical way:

> The link between human rights and international politics is fundamental. The concept of "the international conscience" is a reality, and we often underestimate the effectiveness of agreed international standards of conduct.

Unfortunate it is that the manifestation of the ideals of the United Nations into concrete world action and achievement is still a far cry. But let us not forget that Rome was not built in a day; vision cannot turn into reality overnight. As our Secretary-General points out, the Declaration of Human Rights "created standards by which all must be judged. It represented, it is true, an ideal. It pointed towards a goal, and did not establish a fact. The authors knew that mankind would not be transformed overnight and that the achievement of their purpose would be a long, difficult, and often frustrating process."

With the guiding light that shines through the UN Charter and the UN Universal Declaration of Human Rights, the world is destined to attain harmony and peace, for inside the United Nations vision, reality looms large. The fulfilment of the United Nations ideals is an inevitability, but that hour will dawn only when humanity wholeheartedly and unreservedly accepts the message of the United Nations soul. The Secretary-General offers his encouragement to those who have committed themselves to the United Nations cause:

> We can never relax in pursuit of the human rights goals of the Charter and of the Universal Declaration. Nothing could be more worthy of our continuing labours than a steady expansion of the realm in which the dignity and worth of the human person are firmly secured and fully honoured.

When the seeker in me feels the dynamic inner frame or vital of the Secretary-General, the Secretary-General's soulful bird, with two hopeful wings, flies to cover the length and breadth of the world. What for? To sow the immortal seed of the United Nations for world-union, world-salvation and world perfection.

10. *O Kurt Waldheim*

O Kurt Waldheim,.... in you I always see a divinely inspired miracle-man. You see, you touch and you cure the suffering heart of humanity.

II – MEETINGS WITH SECRETARY-GENERAL KURT WALDHEIM

11. Meeting with Secretary-General Kurt Waldheim on 16 July 1976

On 16 July 1976 Sri Chinmoy met with Secretary-General Kurt Waldheim in the Secretary-General's Office. Sri Chinmoy presented Mr Waldheim with a plaque engraved with the United Nations Meditation Group motto and a song he had written, *O Kurt Waldheim.* The Secretary-General thanked Sri Chinmoy for the plaque, which was decorated with the Secretary-General's picture and the United Nations and Austrian flags and, pointing to his desk, said, "I will keep this here." Sri Chinmoy also presented the UN leader with an article he had written about him, and the Secretary-General said he would read it with great enthusiasm and interest. While looking through the *Meditation Group Songbook,* which had also been give which had also been given to him, the Secretary-General saw U Thant's picture and remarked, "Ah, here is my dear friend."

At Sri Chinmoy's request, the Secretary-General then invited the members of the Meditation Group to come upstairs into his conference room to sing the song, *O Kurt Waldheim.* When the group entered the room, the Secretary-General greeted them warmly. "Welcome to the 38th floor," he said. "I am pleased to meet all of you and I want to thank you for your work and dedication to the UN. I know how hard your Group is working for the United Nations. I thank you for the gift that your leader has presented me and I look forward to hearing the beautiful song that you have prepared."

After the song was sung the Secretary-General said, "It is a very beautiful, very thoughtful song, which is deeply interesting and unique. Thank you very much. I wish you all the best for the future: good health and happiness, and especially happiness of the soul, which is perhaps the most important thing for our life."

Ms France Vacher presented the Secretary-General with the banner of the United Nations Meditation Group. The Group also gave him a framed message: "With deepest appreciation and admiration for piloting the United Nations Boat untiringly, soulfully and fruitfully." It was signed by "Sri Chinmoy and the Members of the United Nations Meditation Group." Included alongside the message were the names and departments of the more than sixty members of the Meditation Group.

The Secretary-General expressed his appreciation for these gifts and read the motto several times. Then he said, "You must be from many different countries. That is very good; the world is getting smaller." Then, smiling graciously and warmly, he began to walk around the room shaking everyone's hand, occasionally asking where a person was from, speaking in English, French and German and joking lightly. When he came to the last member, Richard Howard, who was the official UN photographer for the day, he said, "Now you have a big responsibility to see that the pictures all come out. I certainly hope they turn out."

Sri Chinmoy said, "We, the members of the United Nations Meditation Group, soulfully pray to the Absolute Supreme for your re-election," and everyone laughed in appreciation. The Secretary-General thanked the Group again and Sri Chinmoy responded, "We shall remain eternally grateful to you."

After the interview was over and the Group had begun to leave, the guard called Sri Chinmoy and Richard Howard back into the Secretary-General's office.

The Secretary-General wanted to have some more pictures taken. Later, Sri Chinmoy described the incident: "We stood next to the UN flag; he stood on one side and I stood on the other. He was all joy. He grabbed my hands and was clasping them strongly and affectionately with such love and joy. At first he didn't speak. He placed his hand on my shoulder, clasping my arm and elbow to show his joy and appreciation. Then he said, 'It is a great challenge to bring about peace, but we are trying.' I answered, 'We shall succeed.' The Secretary-General continued, 'We want only peace, peace. You are praying, praying for peace. I know what you and the Group are doing for us. I know it, I can feel it.' He said that he would read the article about him with greatest joy and thanked us for our prayers for his re-election.

Sri Chinmoy commented on the meeting: "It does not belong to me, it is also yours. It belongs to all of us. This significant and historical meeting we offer to the soul of the United Nations and to the soul of the peace-loving world with all our hearts' love and gratitude. Right now we may not value it fully, but in years to come we shall give proper value to this momentous achievement."

12. *A meeting with the Secretary-General on 7 March 1977*

As soon as I entered into his office, the Secretary-General came to the door. With a smiling face and a warm heart he said, "Good morning."

I said to him also, "Good morning." Then we shook hands and, for a few seconds, both of us remained in a contemplative mood. Then he signalled me to sit down. He also sat. He was in a very deep and, at the same time, benevolent mood. I offered the book to him and he looked at the cover and said, "Ah, here is my dear friend, my humane friend. I had the greatest admiration for him. In simple and genuine modesty he surpassed us all. Nobody knew how he sacrificed his life to bring about world peace, world understanding, practically to the end of his life. He carried a tremendous load on his shoulders. He suffered and suffered for humanity. His vision was so clear and, at the same time, so broad."

At this point I turned to page thirteen where his own comment on U Thant was. He read the whole page very carefully, completely absorbed, and then said, "He was really great. I talked to him many, many times while I was serving my country as Ambassador. He inspired me in so many ways. His heart never wanted to compromise to the wrong and destructive forces of the world. Slowly and steadily he did everything. His great responsibilities at the United Nations did affect his health. His death was a tragic end. We all dearly miss him. His steady vision for the world community is still inspiring us. I personally am extremely, extremely grateful to him."

Then I said to him, "As you know, everything has a divine sanction. We are extremely grateful to God, for He has given us you to steer the Boat of the United Nations so devotedly, speedily, surprisingly and successfully. I always see you as God's lightning speed. Today you are here, tomorrow you are there and the day after tomorrow elsewhere. Your penetrating vision not only enters into the world problems, but also solves the problems of the world most miraculously. In you I always see a divinely inspired miracle-man. You see, you touch and you cure the suffering heart of humanity."

Then he said to me, "I am so sincerely grateful to you for your encouraging words. This world needs only one thing: co-operation. U Thant gave his all to bring about world co-operation. I am trying to do the same with all my heart's concern and love for humanity. You are also doing the same with your prayer and meditation at the United Nations. I am sincerely grateful to you, for you are offering your depth and vision to the United Nations through the Meditation Group."

Then I told him, "Every day I pray for you, for your success; I pray that the world will accept your most illumining light. On Tuesdays and Fridays, in the special meditations we hold here at the United Nations, I regularly offer my gratitude-heart to your world-illumining soul. I have started writing a book about you and I hope to be able to offer it to you the way I am offering you this book on U Thant."

He said, "You know, in the coming few months I shall be extremely busy, but I am sure I will be able to set aside some time for you as I have done today."

I said, "I know. I know how extremely busy you are with the world problems. My mind knows it and my heart feels it. It is your heart's magnanimity that has granted me this rare opportunity to offer you this book."

Then he said, "Oh no, I am extremely happy to see you and to have you here with me. It is very nice and kind of you to write something about me. By the way, please be in touch with Mr Rohan. He will be able to assist you, if you need any special information about me. Again, I wish to say it was extremely thoughtful of you to present to me my best friend. I miss him; we all miss him. Indeed, he was our true friend."

At this time he stood up and I stood up. I folded my hands and his eyes were extremely soulful. Then I shook hands with him. He came to the door and, placing his left hand on my right shoulder and holding my right hand, he said to me, "Please tell the members of your Meditation Group that I am sending them my greetings."

I said to him, "I shall do that. I am offering you on behalf of our Meditation Group our heart's deepest gratitude."

13. *To the truth-seeker*

To the truth-seeker, peace-lover, oneness-dreamer, perfection-builder, satisfaction-harbinger and the supreme Pilot in the Secretary-General, Kurt Waldheim, we offer our soulful gratitude-heart.

III – APPENDIX

14. *Honorary degrees*

In addition to the degree of Doctor of Jurisprudence awarded by Vienna University in 1944, the Secretary-General has received the honorary degree of Doctor of Laws (LLD) from the following colleges and universities:

- Fordham University (1972)
- Carleton University, Ottawa, Canada (1972)
- University of Chile, Santiago (1972)
- Rutgers University (1972)
- Jawaharlal Nehru University, New Delhi (1973)
- University of Bucharest (1973)
- Wagner College, New York (1973)
- Catholic University of America (1974)
- Wilfred Laurier University, Waterloo, Can. (1974)
- Catholic University, Leuven, Belgium (1975)
- Charles University, Prague, Czechoslovakia (1975)
- Hamilton College, Clinton, NY (1975)
- University of Denver (1976)
- University of the Philippines (1976)
- University of Nice (1976)
- Vanderbilt University (1976)
- American University, Washington, DC (1977)
- Kent State University, Kent, Ohio (1977)
- Moscow State University (1977)
- Warsaw University (1977)

NOTES TO A SOULFUL TRIBUTE TO THE SECRETARY-GENERAL:
THE PILOT SUPREME OF THE UNITED NATIONS

11–12. *(p.485)* Sri Chinmoy and the members of the United Nations Meditation Group met with Secretary-General Kurt Waldheim on 16 July 1976. Sri Chinmoy again met privately with the Secretary-General on 7 March 1977 to present him with a copy of his book, *U Thant: Divinity's Smile and humanity's cry*. These are the accounts of these meetings.

PART X

UNITED NATIONS
MEDITATION-FLOWERS AND
TO-MORROW'S NOON

1. *Sri Chinmoy Meditation at the United Nations*

UNITED NATIONS:
THE HEART-HOME OF THE WORLD-BODY

We believe and we hold that each man has the potentiality of reaching the Ultimate Truth. We also believe that man cannot and will not remain imperfect forever. Each man is an instrument of God. When the hour strikes, each individual soul listens to the inner dictates of God. When man listens to God, his imperfections are turned into perfections, his ignorance into knowledge, his searching mind into revealing light and his uncertain reality into all-fulfilling Divinity.

2. *The seeker in me*

The seeker in me says, "I wish to see God." But do I not know that God is continually looking at me?

The seeker in me says, "I wish to love God." But do I not know that God is continually loving me?

The seeker in me says, "I wish to give God my life's best achievement: surrender." But do I not know that God has already given me His Eternity's best achievement: oneness?

Seeing is a two-way experience. Loving is a two-way realisation. Giving is a two-way perfection.

Experience makes us infinite. Realisation makes us eternal. Perfection makes us immortal.

Infinite is dream. Eternal is reality. Immortal is progress.

Dream is God the cosmic Seed. Reality is God the cosmic Fruit. Progress is God the universal and transcendental Tree.

3. Possibility-seed

O my heart's possibility-seed,
In you I see my mind's hopeful plant,
My life's soulful flower and
My soul's fruitful food.

O my heart's possibility-seed,
You embody my promise-dawn,
You reveal my success-sun,
You manifest my progress-light.

O my heart's possibility-seed,
This moment you are my caterpillar-dream,
The next moment you are my butterfly-reality.
This moment you are my rainbow-beauty,
The next moment you are my satisfaction-prosperity.

O my heart's possibility-seed,
In God's entire creation
I have only one possession
And that is you, only you.

O my heart's possibility-seed,
With you, my journey's Eternity;
In you, my goal's Infinity.

O my heart's possibility-seed,
You gave me my inspiration-capacity,
You are giving me my aspiration-Divinity,
And you will give me my realisation-Immortality.

O my heart's possibility-seed,
You are at once unveiling the universal art
of my life's mystery
And granting me the transcendental picture
of my soul's victory.

4. *Sorrow*

Sorrow, my sorrow, my world-sorrow,
You have given me a pure heart.
Sorrow, my sorrow, my world-sorrow,
You have granted me a wise mind.
Sorrow, my sorrow, my world-sorrow,
You have given me a brave vital and a sleepless body.
Sorrow, my sorrow, my world-sorrow,
You have given me two most precious gifts:
Patience-seed and perseverance-fruit.
Sorrow, my sorrow, my world-sorrow,
You warn me timely, you correct me soulfully
And you perfect me unreservedly.
Sorrow, my sorrow, my world-sorrow,
You have taught me how to walk along the road of Truth.
You have taught me the secret of self-giving.
You have given me universal Love
So that I can become the Transcendental Soul.
Sorrow, my sorrow, my world-sorrow,
It is from your infinite bounty
That I have developed an eternal hunger to devour
The infinite Light and Delight of my Beloved Supreme.

5. *Now is the only time*

I hear a still small voice in the depth of my heart.
It tells me that now is the only time for me
To become great in the outer world,
And that now is the only time for me
To become good in the inner world.
My greatness is from God the omnipotent Creator.
My goodness is from God the omnipresent Liberator.

Now is the only time to do God's Will.
What is God's Will?
God's Will is that I should never try to earn anything from God.

I cannot earn anything from God.
Indeed, that is an impossible task.
Indeed, that is an absurd notion.
I can only cheerfully accept from God
What God unconditionally gives me.
Needless to say, God grants me at every moment
What He has and what He is.
But alas, where is my receptivity?
I know God has a special Will for me.
He always wants to take the initiative.
He wants me to follow Him.
He tells me that I am not going to lose my personal freedom.
On the contrary, I shall increase my freedom,
For His Freedom-Vision is carrying me to my destination
Which is flooded with Perfection-Delight.
In this connection, I have also discovered something very important.
There is a great difference between these two realisations:
I am one with God's Will and God is one with my will.

I am one with God's Will. What does it mean?
It means that I am swimming in the ocean of God's Wisdom-
    Delight.
God is one with my will. What does it mean?
It means that God is more than willing to be with me in my
    ignorance-night
With His infinite Compassion-Light.
To know God's Will, surrender is the real way.
Indeed, that is the road for me.
I can weather all the storms of my inner life and outer life
When my existence becomes unmistakably and unreservedly
A surrendered flower-heart.
God tells me, "True, you do not know Me, but your surrender-
    life knows.
True, you do not love Me, but your gratitude-heart loves.
Your surrender-life is my cosmic Vision-Seed.
Your gratitude-heart is my cosmic Reality-Fruit."

II – APHORISMS

6.

To love is to see man in God. To serve is to see God in man.

7.

Ungratefulness strengthens the animal in us, weakens the human in us and shortens the divine in us.

8.

Do you want to be happy? If so, then either push your desire-life aside or pull your aspiration-life inside.

9.

To err is human, but only a special person has the God-given capacity to forgive.

10.

We shall eventually give to God what He has already given to us: Eternity's soulful cry and Infinity's fruitful smile.

11.

To have cheerfulness in utter helplessness is to start climbing up the Realisation-tree and to start climbing down the Manifestation-tree.

12.

I have discovered two places where God is not. He is not in my ingratitude-heart and He is not in my non-acceptance of life. No matter how hard I try, I simply cannot be where God is not.

13.

Yesterday my cheerfulness was my unparallelled achievement. Today my soulfulness is my unparallelled achievement. Tomorrow my willingness will be my unparallelled achievement.

14.

No two friends are as intimate as cheerfulness and confidence.

15.

A spiritual Master was once asked: "Why do you talk so much?" His immediate answer: "It satisfies. It satisfies the human in me and it satisfies the divine in my spiritual children."

16.

Our best performance on earth is to employ God's Compassion. God's best performance is to destroy our imperfections.

17. *Like me*

>Like me, do you dare to believe
>That the finite has taken full responsibility
>For revealing the Infinite?
>
>Like me, do you dare to believe
>That the life of duality has taken full responsibility
>For revealing the sole Absolute Supreme?
>
>Like me, do you dare to believe
>That the life of sorrow has taken full responsibility
>For revealing the life of Delight?

18. *How do I know?*

>How do I know
>That I shall have a better opportunity tomorrow
>To pray to God and to meditate on God?
>
>How do I know
>That I shall have the same opportunity tomorrow
>To pray to God and to meditate on God?
>
>How do I know
>That I shall have any opportunity tomorrow
>To pray to God and meditate on God?
>
>How do I know
>That God will stay with me tomorrow
>In spite of my lengthening lethargy?

How do I know
That God will stay with me tomorrow
In spite of my increasing insecurity?

How do I know
That God will stay with me tomorrow
In spite of my staggering impurity?

Such being the case,
I shall have to depend only on today.

Even today is too much.
Stark temptation and wild frustration
May kill me if I wait for God-realisation
Until the end of the day.

To be sure, there is no tomorrow, not even a today.
All I have is now.
All I can ever have is now.

With now, my preparation begins.
In now, my realisation dawns.
For now, my perfection glows.

19. *I am happy*

I am happy because I always choose the right moment.
I am happy because I am a good listener.
I am happy because I keep my voice down.
I am happy because I do not try to convince others.
I am happy because I do not complain.
I am happy because I do not do two things at the same time.
I am happy because I never think of two objects at the same time.
I am happy because I have realised the truth that the most important thing in my life is self-improvement.
I am happy because I unreservedly accentuate the good in others.
I am happy because I have considerably cut down on my desiring needs.
I am happy because I follow my thought-control programme every day.
I am happy because I never quit.
I am happy because every day I purify my heart by offering my heart of gratitude to the Absolute Supreme.
I am happy because I know that my love of purity works wonders.
I am happy because of a soulful daily prayer of mine, and that prayer is:

> "O Beloved Supreme,
> O Eternity's Pilot Supreme,
> Do transform the world
> Starting with me, my life, my all."

I am happy because every day I cry and cry to see the Real in me. The Real in me is my oneness divine, unreserved and unconditional, with the Will of my Beloved Supreme.

I am happy not because I am for my Supreme Pilot, not because my Supreme Pilot is for me, but because my Supreme Pilot eternally is. His very existence here on earth, there in Heaven, is my satisfaction. When I try to have Him for myself, I pull Him into my desire-life. But when I am for Him, I carry my desire-life into Him. In no way do I want to bind my Beloved Supreme. From now on my satisfaction, my supreme satisfaction, will lie only in my discovery of the fact that He alone eternally is.

20. *Spirituality speaks to simplicity*

Simplicity, you have been for long years my soulful guide. It has always been my valued privilege to work with you.

Simplicity, you tell me that I do not need any mental equipment. I do not need a degree of erudition. What I need, according to you, is a vast wealth of experience. Although this wealth is *of* the inner world, it is unreservedly *for* the outer world.

The world of crying aspiration needs you. The world of smiling dedication needs you. The world of prayerful humanity needs you. The world of meditative divinity needs you.

Simplicity, you have been serving God the Creator in God the creation through the long millennia.

Simplicity, alert you are, dynamic you are. In you there is always an inner urge for new and illumining realisations. In your heart there is no place for the static, stagnant, barren and dead realities. Your heart is unreservedly involved in determining man's soulful success and fruitful progress.

Simplicity, you are great. You do not house mental narrowness, vital laziness or intellectual indifference. Simplicity, you are good. Your very existence on earth grants the Truth-seeker, the God-lover, the rare capacity to combine in his life beauty with power, duty with delight and expectation with satisfaction.

21. *Courage versus humility*

Courage challenges the world. Humility illumines the world. Courage strongly urges us to stand up for our own rights. Humility soulfully inspires us to stand up for God's rights alone.

Courage is not aggression. Aggression is man's destruction-force. Humility is not humiliation. Humiliation is man's rejection-force. Courage is man's self-determination. Humility is man's oneness-distribution. Self-determination eventually succeeds. Oneness-distribution constantly proceeds.

Courage is man's conquering force. Humility is man's unifying force. Courage feeds the divine human in us. Humility feeds the unifying and immortal divine in us.

The seeker in us uses courage to conquer the teeming doubts in the mental world. The seeker in us uses humility to constantly gain faith, to increase faith in God's universal Oneness and Light.

Courage is the struggle, birthless and deathless, between man's victory and defeat, between man's joy and sorrow, between man's smiles and tears, between man's acceptance and rejection, between what man has and what man is. What man has is sound-satisfaction and what man is is silence-perfection.

Humility is man's divine and supreme Glory-bird that flies from God's Infinity-Dawn to God's Eternity-Day and from God's Eternity-Day to God's Infinity-Dawn.

With courage we manifest God in our own way. With humility, God manifests Himself in and through us in His own Way.

22. *We must not give up!*

Let us keep going. We must not give up. Although the dragon-thoughts of frustration assail us, we must not give up! There is definitely a goal, and this goal must needs be ours. We must not give up!

Although Heaven does not feed our heart's cry regularly, although earth does not entirely support our spiritual journey, still we must not give up!

Let us invoke the presence of our indomitable courage-fount to help us conquer the feelings of loneliness and unworthiness. We must not give up!

Although the world does not appreciate us, although the world does not see the beauty and the light in us, we must not give up appreciating the world. Indeed, this world of ours is also an instrument of God. Like us, it considers God-realisation, God-revelation and God-manifestation as its bounden duty. Therefore, we must appreciate the world. After all, what is appreciation? Appreciation is self-expansion. Self-expansion is oneness-awareness, and oneness-awareness is truth-distribution. We must not give up!

Although we do not have a sunny present, although we had a foggy past, although we suspect inclement weather in the near future, we must not give up!

With our mind's resolution, our heart's determination and our soul's illumination, we shall eventually succeed in life. Success is our choice. Progress is God's choice. Man chooses to become. He becomes confidence-lion within and confidence-elephant without. God chooses to give. He gives us His universal Light constantly, unreservedly and unconditionally. He gives us His transcendental Delight constantly, unreservedly and unconditionally.

We must not give up! Let us prepare ourselves for God's choice Hour. We must not give up!

23. *What is my next duty?*

What is my duty? I have stopped dining with ignorance-sea. I have stabbed darkness-night. I have given a smart slap to frustration-giant. I have boxed the ears of anxiety-twinges. I have broken the nose of jealousy-impurity. I have kicked off my insecurity-world.

What is my next duty? I have literally taken the life-breath out of pride-autocracy. I have soulfully embraced humility-light.

What is my next duty? I have unlearned everything that I have learned from this insufficiency-world.

What is my next duty? Simplicity's life I have become. Sincerity's heart I have become. Purity's soul I have become.

What is my next duty? I have seen God face to face. I have loved God's Earth-Body and God's Heaven-Soul all at once.

What is my next duty? My vision has inseparably become one with God the Silence in Heaven. My mission has inseparably become one with God the Sound on earth.

What is my next duty? My next duty, my only duty, is to beg the present God the Creator to transform Himself into a new Creator. I shall then urge the new Creator to create a new world which will be known as Infinity's Satisfaction-Delight, founded upon Immortality's Perfection-Light.

24. *On a birthday*

On our birthday the Absolute Supreme reminds our soul about the promise that it has made to Him. On our birthday the soul reminds the body, the physical consciousness, about the promise that the physical has made to it.

The soul's promise to the Absolute Supreme is God-manifestation through conscious and constant cooperation with the body-consciousness. The body's promise to the soul is cooperation and unreserved and unconditional manifestation of the Supreme. When these two promises are fulfilled, the human being becomes a perfect instrument and perfect representative both of Heaven and of earth.

25. *A special meditation*

[To seekers below thirty years of age.] Today we shall do a special type of meditation. We shall focus our attention on various places. When we concentrate on the top of our head, we shall imagine a conch. And when we focus our concentration inside the mind, inside the head, we shall imagine a beautiful rose. Then, when our concentration is inside the heart, we shall imagine a beautiful lotus. And when it is around the navel area or below the navel area, we shall imagine a few jasmine flowers.

A conch signifies divine victory. When we meditate on the top of our head, on the crown centre, then it will help us to blow the conch, to sound the divine victory. Then, when we meditate on the head proper, on the mind, the beauty and fragrance of the rose will help us to illumine our unlit human life. When we meditate inside the heart, the beauty and the fragrance of the lotus will help us identify ourselves with the soul. Then, when we meditate around the navel area, the jasmine flowers will help us purify our impure body-reality.

It will be safe and wise to start with the navel area. So for a few seconds please meditate on the navel area and imagine a jasmine flower and establish purity. The jasmine signifies purity. Then come to the heart centre and there imagine a lotus. Imagine a lotus and identify yourself with the soul. When you come to the head, kindly imagine a rose and then illumine your unlit human life. Then come to the top of the head and imagine a conch, the divine victory. Imagine that it is announcing the divine victory, your victory.

[To seekers over thirty years of age.] Now let us do a different type of meditation. We shall focus our concentration first on the heart, then on the third eye, and then on the head. While concentrating inside the heart we shall imagine a boat, a golden boat. While concentrating on the third eye we shall imagine the sky. And while concentrating on the top of the head, on the crown centre we shall imagine the sun. The boat is your own Eternity's boat, the sky is your own Infinity's self-expansion and the sun is your own Immortality's new creation.

So let us start with the boat. We shall imagine the boat inside the heart. This boat will be our Eternity's boat, our own Eternity's boat which is sailing inside us. And then, when we meditate on the third eye, we shall imagine the sky and our own Infinity. Our own Infinity's expansion we shall observe. Then we shall meditate on the crown centre and imagine the sun, which is our own Immortality's new creation.

26. *My lifelong friends*

Simplicity is my lifelong friend. My simplicity-friend has cut down my desire-tree.

Sincerity is my lifelong friend. My sincerity-friend has snapped my guilt-conscience-chain.

Purity is my lifelong friend. My purity-friend has secretly told me that love is the only force, the illumining force, fulfilling force, the supreme force.

Divinity is my lifelong friend. My friend divinity teaches me how to live always inside the Source and how to live only for the Source, the perennial Source.

Immortality is my lifelong friend. My friend Immortality tells me that here on earth my heart's inner cry is the only thing immortal, and there in Heaven my soul's smile is the only thing immortal.

My Beloved Supreme is my lifelong Friend. My Friend, my Beloved Supreme, tells me that here on earth His Grace is my only salvation, and there in Heaven His Face is my only satisfaction.

O my simplicity, sincerity, purity, divinity, Immortality and Beloved Supreme friends, to each of you I offer my own Eternity's gratitude-heart, my own Infinity's oneness-source, my own Immortality's perfection-delight.

27. *Expectation*

Expectation is frustration, especially when I want to possess the world. Expectation is frustration, especially when I want to lord it over the world. Expectation is frustration, especially when I want the world to surrender to my will.

Expectation has its justification when I love the world and want the world to offer me a gratitude-heart. Expectation has its justification when I pray to God for the betterment, for the transformation, for the illumination of the world and want the world to offer me a gratitude-heart. Expectation has its justification when I sincerely, devotedly and unreservedly try to elevate the earth-consciousness according to my capacity and want the world to offer me a gratitude-heart.

Expectation is nothing short of satisfaction when I wait devotedly, soulfully and unconditionally for God's choice Hour to arrive to liberate, illumine, transform, perfect and fulfil me. Expectation is satisfaction when I feel in the inmost recesses of my heart that God is not only my sovereign Lord, the Absolute Supreme, but also my Friend, my eternal Friend and only Friend. Expectation is satisfaction, especially when I know that God has done everything for me in the inner world. This discovery of mine is founded on my faith, my inner faith in Him, not because He has done everything for me, not because He is all Love for me, but because I have realised something else that is infinitely more significant than all this. My realisation is this: my God, my Lord Supreme, my eternal Friend, is everything in and through me. He is expanding and enlarging His own cosmic Vision in and through me. When I realise my expectation of what He has done for me and what He is to me, my life has its soulful purpose and fruitful delight.

When I use the human in me to serve any purpose, my expectation becomes frustration. When I use the divine in me to serve any purpose, my expectation has its justification. At that time expectation itself is justification. But when I use my Lord Supreme, my eternal Friend, to fulfil something, my expectation is satisfaction, for the expectation is the Vision-Light, and the satisfaction is the Reality-Delight. They are one and inseparable.

III – TO-MORROW'S NOON

28.

Altruism is good, but to know what God's Will is and act accordingly is infinitely better.

29.

If you feel ambivalence towards humanity, I assure you, God will forgive you, humanity's soul will forgive you, but your own inner oneness-heart, which wants constant divine fulfilment on earth, will not forgive you.

30.

It seems that we are in an absurd situation: on the one hand we desperately try to ameliorate our life of aspiration; on the other hand we cherish our teeming doubts and our darkening frustrations.

31.

If you are amenable to the reasoning mind, then your life will be a fruitless, continuous start; but if you are amenable to the aspiring heart, then yours will be the life of immediate start, immediate progress, immediate finish and immediate satisfaction.

32.

Although you are amoral, you have a fair chance for your nature's transformation, for you strongly believe in God's all-forgiving, all-illumining Compassion.

33.

To have aplomb is to compel success to come and touch your feet instead of your running after success.

34.

O ascetic soul, I did love you once upon a time, but now I love to live with and die for life's acceptance-soul.

35.

As God's unconditional Compassion permeates humanity's entire being, even so, humanity's gratitude-heart can permeate God's entire creation.

36.

The study of etymology will undoubtedly make you a learned and great man. But if you know how to climb up the aspiration-tree in the inner world, then you become a wise man, which is infinitely more important than to become a learned man or a great man.

37.

A prevaricator is he who not only exploits God's Transcendental Truth, but also squanders God's Universal Bliss.

38.

A nefarious person is he who has destroyed his heart's beauty long before he has made his nefarious attempt to destroy God's Reality-Beauty in others.

39.

If you are spontaneously gregarious, that means you have already taken a long stride to see the heart of oneness on the face of multiplicity.

40.

A simple and sincere seeker finds it extremely difficult to mix with either the intelligentsia or stark fools.

41.

When there is a fight between impurity and purity, humility's role as the intercessor is of tremendous importance.

42.

An intransigent person can never have peace of mind.

43.

In the inner world, there is but one intrepid hero and that hero is our sterling faith.

44.

Only a true and genuine seeker will not and cannot foment trouble for any human being on earth.

45.

If you get a thing in a fortuitous manner, your happiness will not or cannot last for good.

46.

With aplomb, you entered into the world. With aplomb, you can easily return to the Source.

47.

Do not speak ill of humanity. Humanity will ostracise you. But if you speak ill of divinity, divinity will not only forgive you but also illumine you and fulfil the Supreme in you at His choice Hour.

48.

The human way is bound to remain stereotyped, unless the divine way liberates the human way. The human way is to catch the reality and smile at the reality. The divine way is to feel the reality as one's very own and to dance with the reality in eternal oneness.

49.

A stilted life casts a slur on humanity's inner progress and divinity's pride inside human beings.

50.

Since God's Will is inscrutable, the best thing for us is to pray to become one with God's Will and derive joy from it rather than try to understand God's inscrutable ways.

51.

To say that God is only for others and not for you is the height of your insidious and unbecoming attitude towards God the all-loving and all-nourishing Source.

52.

A life of insouciance indicates an abrupt end of oneness-beauty inside the universal heart.

53.

The maudlin sentiments of humanity are the cause of the world's downfall in Reality's oneness-height.

54.

You will realise God only when your aspiration carries all its appurtenances – belief, simplicity, generosity, sincerity, humility and purity – to the highest height.

55.

The outer laughter creates pandemonium when the inner cry is totally dead.

56.

If you deliver a panegyric and don't mean it, then your insincerity-dog will always follow you.

57.

Needless to say, each human life is fraught with teeming dangers; but the brave will always win in the battlefield of life.

58.

To do the wrong thing and to try to escape nemesis is nothing short of futility.

59.

If you want to claim the whole world, then become a perfect stranger to nepotism and offer yourself only to those who deserve you.

60.

God-realisation will always remain a far cry if you are niggardly at every moment in your self-giving to God.

61.

An insincere and impure person carries with him a noisome odour.

62.

The nominal president of our life is the mind. The actual president of our life is the will-power.

63.

The cosmic gods were nonplussed when they saw our faith-warrior losing to the doubt-warrior in the battlefield of life.

64.

His life is nothing but a hackneyed expression of his self-styled pious and complacent ideas.

65.

The inner life of aspiration is more than willing to constantly give and make the outer life a breath-taking panoramic view.

66.

If you follow verbatim the Master's instructions, then your goal can never remain a far cry.

67.

The real fool is he who thinks that the act of surrender is an exorbitant price for God-realisation.

68.

Do not yield to frustration, for God-Compassion is running very fast towards you in order to save you, please you and fulfil you.

69.

Neither your aridity nor your austerity can bring God closer to you, for that task is meant only for your surrender-heart.

70.

A sophisticated life is not only a divine failure but also a human failure.

71.

Our doubting mind is usually distraught by the absence of its brood: frustration and destruction.

72.

Nothing is so hard as to dissuade the mind from doubting the reality's Existence-Bliss.

73.

A seeker of all-illumining and all-fulfilling harmony must have a discerning ear for any dissonance either in the vital world or in the mental world.

74.

Love and serve humanity sincerely. Your name will be disseminated constantly over God's special Radio.

75.

If you have a solicitous heart, then rest assured that God has a blessingful Eye.

76.

Sobriety in all things may not always be attainable, but it is always desirable.

77.

A sincere seeker must never be afraid of the doubting mind. On the contrary, he should take the doubting mind as a skittish animal.

78.

A sceptical person has to remain always a stranger to the bliss of oneness-reality.

79.

It is the height of stupidity to attempt to dissemble fear, doubt, anxiety and frustration in the spiritual life. Fear, doubt, anxiety and frustration must be brought to the fore before they can be transformed.

80.

Insincerity and impurity are undoubtedly sinister forces in the life of a seeker.

81.

It is a deplorable mistake to think that faith's position as the chief leader is a sinecure in the spiritual life, for it is faith that functions, performs, illumines and fulfils us more than anything else.

NOTES TO UNITED NATIONS MEDITATION-FLOWERS
AND TO-MORROW'S NOON

2–5. *(p.496)* Sri Chinmoy delivered these talks during meditations that he held at the United Nations.
2. *(p.496)* 18 January 1977.
3. *(p.497)* 28 January 1977.
4. *(p.498)* 28 January 1977.
5. *(p.499)* 1 February 1977.
6–16. *(p.501)* 4 February 1977.
17. *(p.503)* 8 February 1977.
18. *(p.503)* 11 February 1977.
19. *(p.505)* 15 February 1977.
20. *(p.506)* 22 March 1977.
21. *(p.507)* 19 April 1977.
22. *(p.508)* 22 April 1977.
23. *(p.509)* 3 May 1977.
24. *(p.510)* 20 May 1977.
25. *(p.510)* 10 June 1977.
26. *(p.511)* 8 July 1977.
27. *(p.512)* 12 July 1977.

PART XI

PÉREZ DE CUÉLLAR:
IMMORTALITY'S RAINBOW-PEACE

I – COMMENTARIES ON QUOTATIONS BY SECRETARY-GENERAL
PÉREZ DE CUÉLLAR

1. *Humanity's cherished dream*

> Peace – the word evokes the simplest and most cherished dream of humanity. Peace is, and has always been, the ultimate human aspiration.

With these soulful words, the reality-dreamer in our Secretary-General reminds us that the age-old dream of peace is not merely a human dream but a divine vision, which is slowly, steadily and unerringly moulding and shaping the world's destiny.

2. *Speech versus action*

But the pragmatic realist in our Secretary-General immediately alerts us:

> And yet our history overwhelmingly shows that while we speak incessantly of peace, our actions tell a very different story.

3. *A new age of world peace*

The world has ceaselessly struggled, immeasurably suffered and significantly achieved things meaningful and fruitful. Nevertheless, the dream of peace is still a far cry. The supreme Pilot of the United Nations offers us abundant encouragement:

> To say that we have perhaps entered a new age of world peace does not sound half as fanciful today as

it would have a year ago. In their respective idioms, the leaders of the two most powerful States in the world have said it at the United Nations. People all around the globe have greeted our progress in moving regional conflicts towards their solution with a new mood of optimism and of faith in the workings of multilateral diplomacy.

The world is steadily progressing, although not always to our great satisfaction. Therefore, the human in us at times may be sadly discouraged. But on the strength of our progress-loving oneness with the world-evolution, we unmistakably see the turtle-progress-speed of the world.

4. *The price of peace*

Peace is humanity's sleepless and breathless need. Needless to say, no earthly human sacrifice can ever be too great to make for the Heavenly divine peace. According to the seer-statesman Mr Pérez de Cuéllar:

> Peace has its price. In terms of political compromise, of accommodation, even of short-term disadvantage for the sake of the longer gain, the price may be considerable. It requires courage and statesmanship. In terms of finances, the price is negligible. In a pragmatic sense, war's devastation dwarfs the costs of peace. And in a moral sense, there is no price to place on a single human life.

5. Peace requires effort

We are badly mistaken if we think that peace will miraculously enter into our lives unconditionally. The Secretary-General's guiding eye tells us that to achieve peace we need both fearless persistence and endless faith:

> Let us not forget that peace does not come accidentally or automatically. The impressive progress we are making to end a number of conflicts is the result of hard effort, in some cases over many years. The United Nations has been at the forefront of that effort.

6. A humane peace

The absence of war is not and cannot be the real peace. Real peace is the unmistakable establishment of celestial harmony and universal love. The head of the United Nations family graciously tells us:

> The peace that we desire is not the peace of the cemeteries, the peace of the concentration camps or the prisons. It is a profoundly humane peace, free from all physical or spiritual violence and founded on two indissociable values which are none the less difficult to reconcile: justice and freedom. The feeling of world solidarity which I mentioned earlier as a force for peace can inspire only men who are free and aspire to equality.

7. The Charter

The UN Pilot tells us that the United Nations Charter is humanity's unparallelled friend, confidently leading us towards the supreme destination of immortal satisfaction: world-peace. The Charter embodies the vast dignity of illumining vision and awakens us to the fundamental human needs:

> The United Nations Charter and the Universal Declaration of Human Rights proclaim that peace can grow only from justice. It demands respect for the human rights and fundamental freedoms of every individual.

8. A universal undertaking

The great player of the universal peace-game in the Secretary-General lovingly teaches us that peace is a game to be played by all – a game that needs the conscious and self-giving participation of all human beings and nations, large and small, powerful and week, illumined and unillumined:

> In awarding their Peace Prize to the peace-keeping forces of the United Nations, the Nobel Committee recognises that the quest for peace is a universal undertaking involving all the nations and peoples of the world.

9. The common good of mankind

Division is cast aside, suspicion is buried in oblivion, faith in all human beings is restored when all nations scrupulously, devotedly and untiringly work together. Then only can they proudly invoke and reveal the peace-sun of eternal love and universal oneness. In the words of the universal statesman:

> Nowadays, the State's morality has to be in keeping with the morality of mankind, and all political decisions are the outcome of a compromise between purely national interests and the interests of the international community. It is on this world ethic that peace, the supreme universal good, is based. To build peace is in fact to abolish frontiers, to transcend private interests and pursue the common good of all mankind.

10. Sustaining momentum towards peace

True, the world's recent achievements are significant encouragements, but these achievements are shockingly insignificant when we measure them against our quenchless thirst for ultimate achievements. "Never give up, never give up" is the birthless and deathless motto of aspiring humanity. Here the great worshipper of the all-embracing and all-illumining temple of the world tells us:

> We cannot rest on our laurels. It is of the utmost importance that the positive trends which have recently emerged are strengthened and extended to other issues – some of them of major importance

– which still remain unresolved. The present historic moment calls for a firm resolve on the part of all Member States to sustain the momentum for peace, to consolidate the recent improvements in international relations and to expand the areas of agreement on issues of common concern. The climate of conciliation should not be allowed to prove transitory.

11. *The answer to injustice and despair*

At the moment unfortunate humanity has not discovered an effective answer to the untold world-despair, but we do know that self-giving will be the eventual answer, the only answer. And for that we are awaiting God's choice Hour. The momentous utterance of the Secretary-General runs:

> Since injustice and despair find expression in violence, everything that the United Nations does to give assistance to the countries that suffer the most, economically and financially, contributes to world-peace.

12. *The builders of peace*

Peace is not the sole monopoly of the elite. Peace is not the sole monopoly of the chosen few. Peace is for all human beings who are walking along the world-path. Peace is nothing other than a spontaneous flow of humanity's life-river. How beautiful and fruitful are the revelations of the UN architect:

> Peace is not a matter only for statesmen, soldiers and diplomats, but also for peoples themselves.

> Peace is not just the outcome of Government decisions. Peace is a dynamic process which each individual can impede or promote. As a French philosopher once said: "Peace is built from day to day," and we, my dear friends, are the builders.

13. *Children and peace*

A childlike heart is of supreme importance if we sincerely want to fulfil the beautiful dream of the child's world. And who are the ones unmistakably qualified to perform this momentous task? It is the peace-lovers and the truth-servers who are singularly qualified. The Secretary-General says:

> Our task is to plant the seeds of peace in the mind of every child. Young people must be brought up in the spirit of peace, justice, freedom, mutual respect and understanding. We must heed the Declaration of the Rights of the Child which insists that each child must be able to develop normally in health and with freedom and dignity. We must never forget that children everywhere are entitled to our special protection and care.

14. *A time of opportunities*

Individuals and nations alike are receiving powerful glimpses of the peace-fulfilling reality-body, the United Nations. The Secretary-General's confidence-surcharged message is that the United Nations is at once earth's colossal hope and Himalayan promise:

It is now a time of opportunities which we must seize. Nations are talking to one another again, and more openly. They have reached important new agreements such as on disarmament, arms control and the protection of the ozone layer. They are more willing to use the techniques and institutions the Charter provides. Nations now recognise yet again that only the purposes and principles of the Charter can guide us to a peaceful and prosperous world. They understand once more that, ultimately, they can end some of the world's most stubborn threats to peace only by using the United Nations.

15. *Soldiers of peace*

Yes, humanity's heart should be surcharged with aspiration, humanity's eyes with inspiration and humanity's arms with power. What for? Not for destruction, but for the correction of the mind, the perfection of the life and the satisfaction of the heart. It is the bounden duty of each world-citizen to be a soldier of peace. Beautifully, powerfully and convincingly the Secretary-General states:

> These soldiers of peace are military forces interposed to prevent the use of force. They carry arms only to forestall shooting and conflict. In their composition, they reflect an aspiration for peace, stability and security that knows no frontiers.

16. The Nobel Peace Prize

Each member of the United Nations is a force, and the source of this force is either a human desire or a divine will. The human desire cherishes the love of power. The divine will cherishes the power of love. The Nobel Peace award to the United Nations gloriously declares the victory of the power of soulful love and fruitful oneness. Let us learn from the Secretary-General what the higher will accomplishes in and through us for the world-family:

> Peace-keeping operations symbolise the world-community's will to peace and represent the impartial, practical expression of that will. The award of the Nobel Peace Prize to these operations illuminates the hope and strengthens the promise of this extraordinary concept.

17. Military non-violence

The real power does not conquer. The real power illumines. The real power liberates. The real power fulfils. The UN Pilot's glowing revelation:

> The technique which has come to be called peace-keeping uses soldiers as the servants of peace rather than as the instruments of war. It introduces to the military sphere the principle of non-violence. It provides an honourable alternative to conflict and a means of reducing strife and tension, so that a solution can be sought through negotiation. Never before in history have military forces been employed internationally not to wage war, not to establish

domination and not to serve the interests of any Power or group of Powers, but rather to prevent conflict between peoples.

18. *Every day devoted to peace*

Sacrifice, sacrifice, sacrifice within, sacrifice without – sacrifice, the secret and sacred achievement above all others. To the brave self-givers, the Secretary-General's mind is all appreciation and his heart is all admiration:

> No day of peace should pass without a special salute to the brave men and women of our international peace-keeping forces. For them, every day is devoted to peace. For this, they have earned the respect, the admiration and the gratitude of the international community.

19. *Setting a course for the future*

I give, you take. You give, I take. It is this reciprocal self-giving that we all immediately and eternally need. As the individuals, even so the nations must play this inevitable, nourishing and fulfilling role. Our Secretary-General is all praise for those who cheerfully give and soulfully receive:

> The men and women serving in the peace-keeping forces, and the troop-contributing countries that provide them, have set a course for the future, a course full of promise and exemplifying a vision and courage far out of the ordinary.

20. *Indispensability of the United Nations*

The genuine self-giving of the United Nations has already become a tangible reality in the inner world. Now slowly and steadily it is being manifested in the outer world. Before long there shall come a time when the entire humanity will fully realise the indispensable peace-contribution that the United Nations has been making right from its very birth. No awakened human being will fail to subscribe to the Secretary-General's self-evident utterance:

> All supporters of the United Nations have been greatly encouraged by the fact that many of the confrontations and conflicts in the world are giving way to dialogue. Their belief in the indispensability of the Organisation has been fully justified. Multilateral efforts towards peace as stimulated, directed or channelled by the United Nations have been seen to bring results.

21. *Fulfilling the United Nations mission*

We are not obliged to see eye-to-eye with those cynics who propagate the faulty and absurd idea that the United Nations has not fulfilled its promises. Let us soulfully and powerfully sing in unison with those who feel that the United Nations has been given neither the well-deserved authority nor the adequate opportunity to reveal and manifest its world-embracing, world-illumining and world-fulfilling vision. The Pilot of the UN Boat tells the world:

> If the United Nations is subject to so many legal, political and practical constraints when it wishes

to intervene in current conflicts, can it really fulfil its primary mission of maintaining peace? I will answer that, in the context in which it has to operate, it can contribute, and it does contribute to a considerable extent to a reduction of violence and the promotion of peace. It works to prevent conflicts by attacking their underlying causes. It tries to bring them before the international community as soon as they begin to emerge. It helps, in short, to contain them and settle them by peaceful means.

22. *Nations must work together*

United we must see the reality. United we must feel the reality. United we must grow into the reality. There is no other way – none. Little brothers and big brothers in strong harmony and perfect peace must live. If not, danger shall threaten and devour the world. The divine words of the Secretary-General are indeed of supreme value:

> It is in the equal interest of all nations, large or small, to work towards a world where nations, like individuals, will operate within a complete, coherent and viable system of law, impartially administered and enforced. Any movement away from this goal holds equal danger for all.

23. *The United Nations and the future*

Division and separation will not and cannot appease the inner hunger of the comity of nations. It is the unity in multiplicity that can and will fulfil this hunger. And our Secretary-General tells us that the hour has struck and the world is ready for a new truth – the truth of world-union:

> The main issues of the time we are about to enter are multilateral in their essence. They can only be tackled and solved by nations working together. And that collective action will inevitably require international organisations. Thus, the United Nations fits the future. Its Members know they need it. They will certainly use it.

24. *The necessity of the United Nations*

The Secretary-General reminds us that more than ever before, the lovers of world-peace cannot hope to achieve a oneness-life in a oneness-world without the supreme assistance of the world-body:

> Assuming rationality on the part of the world's political leadership and also assuming that international anarchy is not to be countenanced and a nuclear disaster to be avoided, it is hard to see how nations can manage the vast areas of their joint concern except through the world-organisation.

25. *An instrument of peace*

The United Nations as a divine instrument is undoubtedly the embodiment of God's Dream. And we must serve this world-organisation devotedly and untiringly in order to transform this dream into reality. Let us be illumined by the supreme message of the great instrument of the United Nations:

> We will not be misreading the historical process we are going through if we believe that what previously happened domestically is now happening on the global plane. The United Nations provides nations with an instrument designed precisely to bring about the accommodation of legitimate national interests in the wider international interest. But this demands a sense of purpose, a clear idea of the direction that needs to be given to international affairs and the stamina to pursue that course.

26. *To search for peace is an honour*

To search for peace is a supreme honour. By no manner of means is it abject humiliation. High idealism the United Nations has within. Vast reality it will reveal without. Indeed, this is the glorious vision of the Secretary-General:

> The United Nations has advantages which are, first, its permanence, all the more necessary because wars are more protracted, second, its neutrality, which it must jealously preserve, and lastly its idealism, which makes the search for peace an honour and not a humiliation.

27. *The door to peace*

Satisfaction we want? Then we needs must have peace. To achieve this peace, the Secretary-General invites the world-citizens to cheerfully and lovingly proceed with a oneness-heart:

> Let us work together for a peace of harmony, of justice, of human welfare and of human rights that expresses the best we know and feel from all our cultures. The door to that peace is open wide – let us walk through it together.

II – SONGS DEDICATED TO THE SECRETARY-GENERAL

28. *UN Pilot*

> O UN Pilot, Javier Pérez de Cuéllar!
> Yours is the silver journey
> To the Oneness-Fulness-Harbour.
> Calmness-mind, softness-heart,
> Boldness-life and brightness-soul.
> Wisdom within, wisdom without:
> A splendid role!

29. *We take the United Nations seriously*

We take the United Nations seriously when we desperately need it. I would urge that we also seriously consider the practical ways in which it should develop its capacity and be used as an essential institution in a stormy, uncertain world.
– Javier Pérez de Cuéllar

30. *Peru*

> Peru, Peru, Peru, Peru!
> Pabitar shashi ekatar meru.
> Tomar lagiya urdher kripa sopan.
> Tumije tomar nimner trisha bagan.
> Tomar parane swapanir dak.
> Tomar nayane ushashir shankh.
> Gaurab shir saurabh nir.
> Kulu kulu swane nadi anadir.

Peru, Peru, Peru, Peru!
You are purity-moon and unity-mount.
For you, the compassion-flights
Of the higher worlds.
And you are the quenchless thirst
Of your heart-garden.
The supreme Dreamer is beckoning you.
Your eyes blow the dawn's victory-conch.
You are your lofty glory's height.
You are your fragrance-affection-nest.
Murmuring, through you is flowing
The birthless and deathless life-river.

31. *O United Nations*

O United Nations, O UN,
You are the world-body
Crying for the world-soul.
And you are the earth-life
Longing for oneness-goal.
In the heart of your glowing dream,
Big brothers and brothers small
Shall smile, sing and dance,
O Vision-Perfection in all!

32. *O body of the world*

>O body of the world,
>O soul of the world,
>In you the silence-nest
>Of cosmic oneness-rest.
>Yours is the nectar-role
>To end earth's sombre dole.
>Our souls desire to flow
>In your duty's vision-glow.

33. *UNESCO*

>O UNESCO, needed you are
>Within, without, from near and far.
>Knowledge, science, culture-light
>You bestow on ignorance-night.
>You are your heart's hope-fragrance-flower.
>You are your soul's promise-hour-power.

34. *A moment's peace*

>A moment's truth
>Can and shall make the world beautiful.
>
>A moment's peace
>Can and shall save the world.
>
>A moment's love
>Can and shall make the world perfect.

35. *UNICEF*

> UNICEF,
> O mother and child,
> O sweetness-sea,
> O beauty-flower and duty-tree!
> You are your glowing eyes of light,
> You are your loving oneness-height,
> You are your soaring fulfilment-dream,
> A true triumph of the Lord Supreme.

III – A CHRONOLOGY OF GOOD WILL: MEETINGS AND CORRESPONDENCE WITH THE SECRETARIES-GENERAL

During the nearly twenty years that Sri Chinmoy and the Peace Meditation group have been offering programmes at United Nations headquarters, many messages of good will and mutual appreciation have been exchanged with the United Nations Secretaries-General and their office. The following selection of quotations and correspondence illustrates this relationship founded on mutual respect for service to the cause of peace.

36.

During a meeting on 29 February 1972, Secretary-General U Thant remarked: "Whoever speaks to me about you is all appreciation and admiration, and I personally feel that you have been doing a most significant task for the United Nations."

37.

At a meeting on 16 July 1976, Secretary-General Waldheim presented Sri Chinmoy with a silver medallion in appreciation of his work at the United Nations. The two met again on 7 March 1977 and on 24 October 1978. During their first meeting Mr Waldheim remarked: "You are praying for peace. I know what you are doing for us. I know it. I can feel it."

38.

Secretary-General Pérez de Cuéllar meditated with Sri Chinmoy on 13 January 1983, remarking later in the meeting: "I am indeed touched by your sincere expression of support for my efforts in the cause of peace and international understanding.

"In your meditation you see beyond the superficial distinctions of race, sex, language or religion, as the Charter encourages us to do. You concentrate on the truths and ideals which unite all mankind: the longing for peace, the need for compassion, the search for tolerance and understanding among men and women of all nations.

"We must never forget that all our activities are aimed at fulfilling the lofty principles of the Charter. We must not lose sight of these objectives despite the frequent difficulties we encounter along the way. In recalling the fundamental goals which inspire our work, you are helping to re-affirm our commitment to the Organisation and its purposes."

39. *From Giandomenico Picco, 20 January 1982*

Dear Sri Chinmoy,

On behalf of the Secretary-General, I should like to thank you for your letter of 28 December 1981.

The Secretary-General was indeed grateful for your good wishes for his endeavours in the service of the international community. He also appreciated your kind invitation to participate in a special meditation programme this month, but I am sure you will understand that his many commitments in connexion with his very recent assumption of office will prevent him from joining you on this occasion.

May I also take this opportunity to convey to you the Secretary-General's sincere appreciation for the kind birthday wishes you expressed at your meeting on 18 January.

Yours sincerely,

— Giandomenico Picco
– First Officer

40. *From M'Hamed Essaafi, 3 May 1982*

Dear Sri Chinmoy,

On behalf of the Secretary-General, I should like to thank you for your letter of 29 April 1982. You may be sure that the kind words you addressed to the Secretary-General with regard to his efforts in the cause of peace and international understanding were indeed appreciated.

With regard to your request for an appointment with the Secretary-General, I am certain you will understand that his very busy schedule will unfortunately prevent him from meeting with you at present, but I should like to take this opportunity to convey to you our thanks for your prayers on behalf of the work of the United Nations.

Yours sincerely,

— M'Hamed Essaafi
– Chef de Cabinet

PÉREZ DE CUÉLLAR: IMMORTALITY'S RAINBOW-PEACE

41. From Javier Pérez de Cuéllar, 28 January 1983

Dear Sri Chinmoy,

I should like to thank you for your thoughtful letter of 26 January.

It was indeed a pleasure to receive you earlier this month and I warmly appreciated your kind expression of support for my endeavours in the cause of peace and international understanding. Let me also thank you for the photographs and tape you sent to me, which I shall certainly treasure as a memento of our meeting.

With best wishes,

Yours sincerely,

— Javier Pérez de Cuéllar

42. From J Paul Kavanagh to Mr Davidson, 24 January 1986

Dear Mr Davidson,

I have been asked by the Secretary-General to thank you for your letter of 16 January apprising him of your intrepid endeavours in support of the International Year of Peace.

He read with gratification of the admirable commitment, so widely recognised, which you and your colleagues in the Meditation Group share for the principles which underlie both the United Nations Organisation and its International Year of Peace. There could be no more fitting venue than Hiroshima and Nagasaki to make such a demonstration.

He has asked me particularly to send to you and your colleagues in the Group his very good wishes for the year ahead.
Yours sincerely,

— J Paul Kavanagh
– Second Officer

43. *From Alvaro de Soto, 3 September 1986*

The Secretary-General has learned with interest of Sri Chinmoy's remarkable accomplishment in raising a 303 lbs weight overhead with one arm. He would be grateful if you could convey to Sri Chinmoy his hearty congratulations.
Yours sincerely,

— Alvaro de Soto
– Special Assistant to the Secretary-General

44. *From Alvaro de Soto, 5 November 1986*

I write on behalf of the Secretary-General to thank you for your letter of 3 November by which you invite him to the ceremonies for the U Thant Award which will be presented to Dr Russell Barber on 6 November.

I am afraid that the Secretary-General is unable at such short notice to envisage the possibility of joining you. He has nonetheless asked me to convey to you and to all the participants in tomorrow's ceremonies the attached message together with his very good wishes.
Yours sincerely,

— Alvaro de Soto
– Special Assistant to the Secretary-General

PÉREZ DE CUÉLLAR: IMMORTALITY'S RAINBOW-PEACE

45. Message of the Secretary-General, 1986 U Thant Peace Award Ceremony

My sincere congratulations go to Dr Russell Barber, the 1986 recipient of the U Thant Peace Award.

The promotion of mutual human respect across religious, ideological, political and economic boundaries is at the very root of the United Nations and imbued the life's work of my distinguished predecessor, U Thant. As we remember him therefore we should also bear in mind that the ideals of tolerance and mutual accommodation, which he espoused so dearly, retain today all their power and relevance. They should inspire all our endeavours.

My good wishes to you all.

— Javier Pérez de Cuéllar

46. From Alvaro de Soto, 5 February 1987

Dear Sri Chinmoy,

The Secretary-General, who as you know is at present away from headquarters on an official mission, has asked me to thank you on his behalf for the good wishes and lovely flowers which you so kindly sent him on the recent occasion of his birthday.

With kind regards,

Yours sincerely,

— Alvaro de Soto
– Special Assistant to the Secretary-General

47. *Message of the Secretary-General to the world Peace Run*

It is my pleasure to greet the organisers and participants in this remarkable event.

Your aim is to foster harmony and peaceful co-operation among nations through increased human contacts. Your essential message is that we, the members of the human family, despite our many differences, have infinitely much more to unite and bond us together. Nothing could be more in consonance with the essential purpose of the United Nations Organisation.

Accordingly, as United Nations Secretary-General, I wish you every success in this endeavour, for you are all ambassadors in the cause of peace.

— Javier Pérez de Cuéllar

48. *From Javier Pérez de Cuéllar*

Dear Sri Chinmoy,

Your energetic efforts in the cause of peace have again been brought to my attention. The current Peace Run '89 is a case in point.

This is but a brief note to express appreciation for all your support of the United Nations and its work.

— Javier Pérez de Cuéllar

49. *From Alvaro de Soto, 20 June 1989*

I write on behalf of the Secretary-General to thank you for your kind letter of 9 June inviting him to participate in the Peace Walk's finale on 26 June. I am afraid that the Secretary-General will be prevented by a very full programme from joining you and your colleagues for this important event.

The Secretary-General has nonetheless asked me to convey to you his best wishes in your endeavours.

Yours sincerely,

— Alvaro de Soto
– Executive Assistant to the Secretary-General

NOTES TO PÉREZ DE CUÉLLAR: IMMORTALITY'S RAINBOW-PEACE

29. *(p. 542)* Words by Javier Pérez de Cuéllar put to music by Sri Chinmoy.

30. *(p. 542)* This song is dedicated to Secretary-General Javier Pérez de Cuéllar, the beloved son of Peru. Sri Chinmoy composed it during a visit to the country in January 1987.

36–38. *(p. 546)* The first edition of *Pérez de Cuéllar: immortality's rainbow-peace* presented these quotes as captions to photographs of those events.

47. *(p. 552)* This message was offered by the Secretary-General on the occasion of the 1987 Oneness-Home Peace Run, a global relay for peace inspired by Sri Chinmoy.

PART XII

A REAL MEMBER OF THE UNITED NATIONS

1. *O body of the world*

    O body of the world,
    O soul of the world,
    In you the silence-nest
    Of cosmic oneness-rest.
    Yours is the nectar-role
    To end earth's sombre dole.
    Our souls desire to flow
    In your duty's vision-glow.

2.

A real member of the United Nations
Is his country's powerful choice.

3.

A real member of the United Nations
Is the world's fruitful voice.

4.

A real member of the United Nations
Is the ascending earth's aspiration-cry.

5.

A real member of the United Nations
Is the descending Heaven's satisfaction-smile.

6.

A real member of the United Nations
Asks his division-mind to be quiet.

7.

A real member of the United Nations
Tells his oneness-heart to voice forth.

8.

A real member of the United Nations
Must needs care for the continuous success of his own country.

9.

A real member of the United Nations
Must needs dare to dream of the precious progress of the entire world.

10.

A real member of the United Nations
Tells the other countries that he is not here at the United Nations to speak ill of their sad incapacities and bad blunders.

A REAL MEMBER OF THE UNITED NATIONS

11.

A real member of the United Nations
Tells the other countries that he is here at the United Nations to appreciate their great achievements and admire their good promises.

12.

A real member of the United Nations
Prays in the morning for his self-giving preparation of a oneness-world-family.

13.

A real member of the United Nations
Prays in the evening for the perfection-becoming completion of a oneness-world-family.

14.

A real member of the United Nations
Is he whose mind flies infinitely higher than the dividing and intimidating world-thought-clouds.

15.

A real member of the United Nations
Is he whose mind-pocket will never be empty of a global understanding and whose heart-pocket will never be empty of a universal concern.

16.

A real member of the United Nations
Is he who claims the United Nations to be his own, very own. Unless and until he claims the United Nations to be his own, he will not be richly inspired to change its face and fate lovingly and surprisingly for the better.

17.

A real member of the United Nations
Is he whose heart and mind will at once respond to the inner and outer world-concern-duties.

18.

A real member of the United Nations
Is he who does not forget that his is the supreme responsibility to bring to the fore the inspiring capacities and aspiring qualities of his own nation so that other nations can faithfully and gloriously do the same. Needless to say, the combined divine capacities and supreme qualities of all the nations will expedite the zenith-climbing longings of mankind.

19.

A real member of the United Nations
Is he who is no longer a prisoner of selfishness-demands.

20.

A real member of the United Nations
Knows that if he dreams only of his own country's benefit and neglects and ignores other countries, then his self-chosen limits will eventually disappoint him, for a happy oneness-world will remain a far cry.

21.

A real member of the United Nations
Does not wait for other countries to accept his country; he goes forward carrying his own country's life-breath to meet them, accept them and thus create a new world harmony.

22.

A real member of the United Nations
Is he who has surmounted the doubt-hurdle and now is climbing safely and proudly while flying the victory-banner of universal faith.

23.

A real member of the United Nations
Every morning without fail wears the armour of patience-light.

24.

A real member of the United Nations
Is always most sincerely desperate for a moment's peace among the community of nations.

25.

A real member of the United Nations
Does not believe in the permanent life of thorny uncertainties. He believes in his and others' ever-blossoming and everlasting heart-roses and their world-pleasing fragrance.

26.

A real member of the United Nations
Is he who in his silent meditation and dedication-life offers his soulful obedience-heart and his cheerful willingness-mind to the Inner Pilot of the United Nations.

27.

A real member of the United Nations
Knows that only genuine truth-seekers are entitled to be the most perfect world leaders.

28.

A real member of the United Nations
Is he who offers every day his own heart's blossoming receptivity to all nations.

29.

A real member of the United Nations
Offers his heart's gratitude-flames to his own country, for being asked to represent its lofty aspiration and dedication to the world community. He is also grateful to all the nations for making him fully acquainted with their teeming wants and needs.

30.

A real member of the United Nations
Never allows himself to be buffeted by the winds of self-doubt and world-suspicion.

31.

A real member of the United Nations
If asked what he is doing, will immediately say: "I am accelerating my self-transcendence and world-acceptance-pace."

32.

A real member of the United Nations
Carries in his heart-pocket a valid visa to humanity's oneness-heart.

33.

A real member of the United Nations
Is he whose self-offering-joy surprises the entire world.

34.

A real member of the United Nations
Is he who sings only aspiration-perfection-song and never wants to watch desire-possession-dance.

35.

A real member of the United Nations
Is he who sends every morning beauty's peace around the world.

36.

A real member of the United Nations
Is he who knows that his wisdom-knowledge-light of other nations will never lose on the battlefields of misunderstanding.

37.

A real member of the United Nations
Is a true lover of the United Nations soul and a true server of the United Nations body.

38.

A real member of the United Nations
Makes very clear his soulful request to all the nations: "Please, please the truth; thus only can you fulfil the countless needs of all the countries."

39.

A real member of the United Nations
Never uses doubt-brakes on his world-elevating inspiration.

40.

A real member of the United Nations
Has a most rare peace-passport to safely and successfully cross any heart-border.

41.

A real member of the United Nations
Prepares himself for the perfection of his own life and his own country, and at the same time, has given up his own expectation-frustration from other countries.

42.

A real member of the United Nations
Will never allow himself to be blinded by the glare of suspicion. He likes to establish an illumining and nourishing faith not only in his own heart but also in others' hearts.

43.

A real member of the United Nations
Knows perfectly well that if he makes one serious blunder, then this blunder can easily be multiplied, not only by his foes but also by his friends.

44.

A real member of the United Nations
Is a genuine truth-defender and the distributor of the heart's happiness-flames.

45.

A real member of the United Nations
Must feel the necessity of his life's humility and his mind's self-esteem.

46.

A real member of the United Nations
Knows that a higher force is operating in and through him. He knows that he is a mere instrument. He also knows that his own inner faith will bring him progress-perfection-victory.

47.

A real member of the United Nations
Is a stranger to unwillingness. He is his willingness, inner and outer, to change the outer fate and inner face of mankind.

48.

A real member of the United Nations
Knows that he is not dealing with an old generation of frustrations but with a new generation of promises.

49.

A real member of the United Nations
Bravely fights against two things: his own ego-thunder and his own insecurity-violin.

50.

A real member of the United Nations
Does not have any time to mix with the transformation-unwillingness representatives.

51.

A real member of the United Nations
Does not expect the complete cure of world maladies by a forty-four-year-old United Nations. Countless problems were born long before it was born. Slow and steady wins the race. Let us hope for the best. Let us fervently hope that the world of peace the United Nations envisages will without fail be manifested on earth.

52.

A real member of the United Nations
Knows that to see each member of the United Nations happy, cheerful and hopeful is by no means a luxury, but a supreme necessity.

53.

A real member of the United Nations
Knows that the small-minded workers will eventually surrender to the large-hearted world-servants.

54.

A real member of the United Nations
Needs only two things: capacity-tower and tenacity-wisdom.

55.

A real member of the United Nations
Says to the United Nations: "Who has told you that your golden hopes are all at stake? No, they are not. Every day a new, illumining and fulfilling hope-flower is blossoming in your heart-garden."

56.

A real member of the United Nations
Has fired his superior mind and has hired his auspicious heart.

57.

A real member of the United Nations
Forgives the United Nations mistakes, for he knows that the United Nations has been in existence for only forty-four years. He hopes that in the forthcoming endless days the United Nations will not only rectify all its mistakes but also become the embodiment of truth-perfection.

NOTES TO A REAL MEMBER OF THE UNITED NATIONS

1. *(p. 557)* This poem was also set to music by Sri Chinmoy.

PART XIII

THE INNER ROLE OF THE UNITED NATIONS

I – INTERVIEW WITH UNITED PRESS INTERNATIONAL

1. UPI: *You said once that honesty and frankness are the birthright of the West, humility and devotion are the birthright of the East, and the combination of these four powers should be the ideal of a human being. What do you mean by this?*

Sri Chinmoy: When these qualities, the good qualities of the East and the good qualities of the West, are all combined, a human being can be perfect. Right now the good qualities that the East has are not enough. Similarly, the good qualities that the West has are not enough. But when we can amalgamate, when we can have the qualities of both worlds, then an individual can become perfect. Right now the West wants to proceed with only honesty and frankness, but this is insufficient. Humility is also required. The East has humility, but honesty is also required if it wants to become perfect.

2. UPI: *What is it that you do at your meditation sessions?*

Sri Chinmoy: We pray and meditate, plus I give short talks and answer questions. The inner world embodies peace, light and bliss. The outer world, unfortunately, does not embody these qualities right now, whereas the inner world has them in boundless measure. So we try to establish a free access to the inner world by virtue of our inner cry and our soulful meditation. We call this our aspiration.

3. UPI: *So you don't sit down and talk about the boundaries in the Middle East; you talk about other things?*

Sri Chinmoy: Yes. I am quite ignorant of politics as such. My forte is spirituality. There are two approaches to every problem. One is the inner approach; the other is the outer approach. Those who come to meditate want to try to walk along the inner road. But ultimately both the roads can lead to the same destination.

4. UPI: *What is the inner road?*

Sri Chinmoy: The inner road is the road of sincere dedication to the highest Cause. In the outer world one can aim at a particular goal without having sincere dedication to the goal. But the inner road represents the attitude of the seeker. The seeker tries in every way to lead a more illumining and more fulfilling life, to find and follow the way that is right from the highest point of view.

5. UPI: *Do you envision the day when your goals will be achieved?*

Sri Chinmoy: In the outer world it is a very, very slow process. In the process of time, definitely we will reach the destined Goal. No sincere cry will meet with frustration, disappointment or failure. If we have a sincere cry, the day is bound to dawn when our sincere cry will meet with satisfaction, supreme satisfaction, which is illumination within and without.

THE INNER ROLE OF THE UNITED NATIONS

6. UPI: *But you don't ever see the day when your work will be done, do you?*

Sri Chinmoy: No, my work is not like that. It is a slow and steady process. We have to sow the seed, which has to germinate, then become a sapling and gradually become a huge banyan tree. We are now in the process of consciously becoming that which we always were in the inner world. But this process of growth is an ever-transcending process. We can grow eternally. We need never stop.

7. UPI: *Where are you now? Have you dropped the seed? Do we have a seedling?*

Sri Chinmoy: This is a most inspiring, encouraging question. I have been asked thousands and thousands of questions all over the world, but this last question of yours so far nobody has asked me, not even my disciples. We have sown the seed. Now we have a tiny plant. This tiny plant will grow and become a strong tree. If storms of doubt and hurricanes of jealousy and other undivine things enter, then naturally the progress can be very slow. But if there is implicit faith and devoted oneness, then naturally the plant will very soon grow into a tree. Now we are in the plant stage; we have sown the seed, and it is no longer a seedling. It has germinated properly. Previously it was only a seedling, but now it has become a tiny but healthy plant. So there is every hope that it will weather all the buffets and blows of human doubts and weaknesses and grow into a huge tree.
UPI: Thank you very much.

8. *United Nations Day*

Today is UN Day. What does UN Day signify? It signifies a day of universal hope, a day of universal promise, a day of universal peace and a day of universal oneness. Hope brightens humanity's present deplorable fate. Promise encourages humanity's speed, which embodies success and progress. Peace enlightens humanity's age-old ignorance. And satisfaction, which is founded upon oneness, the oneness-family that we would like to live in, will one day dawn in our aspiring heart and our dedicated life.

To us, the United Nations is not a mere building, it is not a mere concept, it is not wishful thinking or even a dream. It is a reality which is growing, glowing and manifesting its radiance here, there, all-where, throughout the length and breadth of the world. All those who are sincerely crying for a oneness-family, according to their receptivity, are receiving light from the soul of the United Nations.

9. *Norman Rockwell: artist of Americana*

Let us for a minute offer our prayerful meditation so that the artist of Americana, Norman Rockwell, may receive the universal peace and transcendental bliss which his soul so rightly and richly deserves.

He not only saw America's simplicity-life and America's happiness-heart, but he also became simplicity and happiness in the purest sense of the term.

No matter what ultra-modern science has made of America, no matter what the modern intellectual giants have made of America, in the depths of America's heart and life there shall always dwell three virtues: simplicity – a childlike simplicity; happiness – a child's happiness; and satisfaction – a child's constantly blossoming satisfaction that comes when America becomes and offers to the world what the child in it has. No virtue that America has can ever diminish or vanish, for virtue is an immortal gift which God Himself grants to aspiring souls and aspiring nations.

America's vastness the world knows. America's oneness only a soul like Norman Rockwell could feel. We the seekers shall always feel in him America's oneness-loving life and America's satisfaction-distributing heart. Norman Rockwell embodies the Reality's revealed dream.

10. *Divine friends and undivine foes*

As a beginner in the spiritual life, you have to feel that you are standing inside your room behind a door. It is up to you whom to accept as your friends and whom not to accept. Faith, love, devotion, surrender, courage, will-power: these are your friends. You will allow these persons to come into your room and then bolt the door from inside to keep out your enemies. If you allow your enemies – fear, doubt, anxiety and worry – to enter into you, they will come into your room most gladly. As a matter of fact, they are always there waiting to come in, but you do not allow them.

Once your friends have entered your room and you have bolted the door, you will start conversing with your friends. Each time a devoted friend of yours speaks to you, immediately the particular power or capacity that he has increases inside you. When your friend who is embodying love speaks of love, immediately your love for God increases. You also have another friend sitting beside you: courage. He speaks of inner courage and immediately your own inner courage comes to the fore.

When your friend surrender speaks to you, you will see that spiritual surrender becomes easy, spontaneous. Previously you thought that surrender meant self-extinction. You were afraid of surrender because you thought that your individuality would disappear. But when this friend of yours who embodies surrender tells you what divine surrender is, immediately you are eager to throw yourself into the surrender-sea. In this surrender you are not losing anything. On the contrary, you are becoming the vast Infinite. So when these friends tell you about their own qualities and what these qualities actually represent on earth, immediately you will make the fastest progress.

So a beginner should always make a selection as to whom he is going to establish his friendship with, for a beginner's progress entirely depends on the friendship he has made with divine or undivine qualities. Establishing a friendship with divine qualities is the easiest and the most effective way for a beginner to make the fastest progress. Then, when he becomes advanced, the so-called friends that wanted to enter into him – fear, doubt, anxiety and worry – feel that it is a hopeless case. Once the seeker is advanced, he will never, never make a mistake and allow fear, doubt or other undivine elements to enter into him. And these qualities will feel this.

But right now you are a beginner, so at any moment doubt can assail you. Doubt may make you feel doubting is good, but don't be fooled. If you doubt as much as you can, eventually doubt will fail you. Then, doubt sends its best friend, the reasoning mind. The reasoning mind will come and tell you, "All right, doubt has failed. But if you do this, perhaps you will get this. If you don't do this, you won't get it." The reasoning mind will create all darkness and confusion. But in the spiritual life you have come to know that doubt is only poison and the reasoning mind also is useless.

A spiritual person does not reason; he just gives. A beginner especially should always act like a child. A child, when he comes to his mother, does not use the reasoning mind. He acts as if he has no mind. He just runs to her and gives everything that he has found on his way, whether it is divine or undivine. He gives to his mother gladly, cheerfully and devotedly what he has, and the mother gives him what she has. Naturally, the mother has infinitely more than the child. Then, when the seeker becomes advanced, fear, doubt and other undivine forces come to realise that they are knocking at the wrong door.

So beginners have to feel always that they are standing at their door and that divine forces or undivine forces are all the time trying to enter into their room. You should only allow the divine forces to enter into you. Each time a divine force operates, you gain or achieve that divine quality in yourself. Then gradually, gradually all the divine qualities blossom as a flower, petal by petal; they blossom slowly, steadily and perfectly. Then the beginner seeker will be fully ready to offer himself at the Feet of the Lord Supreme.

There are some forces that will attack you and there are some that will help you. You must always be on the alert; you have to open your eyes and allow only those forces to come in that will elevate your consciousness. When you become advanced, wrong forces will not dare to come near you. Now they dare because you are a beginner, but you won't remain a beginner forever. Once you continue walking along the right path, you become advanced. You make progress and reach your destined goal.

11. *Food and God*

> Food has God. God is food.
> Food has life. God is life.
> Food has reality. God is reality.
> Food has sound-success.
> God is sound-success.
> Food has silence-progress.
> God is silence-progress.

I eat. I eat to survive. From my very birth I have been seeking nourishment. Food saves my life from starvation. Food saves my life from extinction.

Mine is the hunger that does not permit me to think soulfully.
Mine is the hunger that does not permit me to act selflessly.
Mine is the hunger that does not permit me to pray to God constantly.
Mine is the hunger that does not permit me to meditate spontaneously.
Mine is the hunger that does not permit me to love God unconditionally.

I know my food-hunger is reasonable and inevitable. But my power-hunger is unreasonable and unpardonable. Finally, my God-hunger is incomparable and insurmountable.

To my great sorrow, poverty attacks plenty. To my widest astonishment, plenty invades poverty. One of the lofty principles of the United Nations is: "Poverty anywhere in the world is a threat to prosperity everywhere." Indeed, this is a heart-unifying and life-fulfilling message. The United Nations was founded upon the vision-hunger for world peace. I am sure there shall come a time when that vision will be transformed into reality in spite of today's teeming, threatening and frightening clouds over the firmament of the United Nations.

O body, I tell you a supreme secret:
"Shortage is poverty."
O vital, I tell you a supreme secret:
"Rivalry is poverty."
O mind, I tell you a supreme secret:
"Doubt is poverty."
O heart, I tell you a supreme secret:
"Insecurity is poverty."
O life, I tell you a supreme secret:
"Impurity is poverty."
O truth-seeker, I tell you a supreme secret:
"Disobedience is poverty."
O God-lover, I tell you a supreme secret:
"Ingratitude is poverty."

    I eat to live.
    Indeed, this is my wisdom-light.
    I live to eat.
    Indeed, this is my ignorance-night.

    God says to my desire-life:
    "Love to live."
    God says to my aspiration-life:
    "Live to love."
    God says to my realisation-life:
    "Love to become a oneness-heart.
    Live to be a perfection-life."

12. *What is it?*

> Meditation: what is it?
> Peace of mind.
>
> Peace of mind: what is it?
> Self-giving.
>
> Self-giving: what is it?
> God-becoming.
>
> God-becoming: what is it?
> The beginning of a new journey.
>
> The beginning of a new journey: what is it?
> A transcending Eternity.
>
> A transcending Eternity: what is it?
> An increasing Infinity.
>
> An increasing Infinity: what is it;
> A fulfilling Immortality.
>
> A fulfilling Immortality: what is it?
> It is something that I have and I am.
>
> What have I?
> A birthless and deathless smile.
>
> What am I?
> A sleepless and breathless cry.

13. *Success-march and progress-flight*

Indeed, the power of helplessness in human beings is remarkable. Do we dare to believe this?

Indeed, the power of hopelessness in human beings is staggering. Do we dare to believe this?

Indeed, the power of uselessness in human beings is frightening. Do we dare to believe this?

What is this power? This power is self-oblivion. Self-oblivion has blighted man's aspiration and blinded man's vision.

Here at the United Nations, each man is a representative soul of his nation. It is in and through him that his nation gives and receives. It is in and through him that his nation thirsts for world-acceptance, world-recognition, world-appreciation and world-admiration.

His willingness to hoist the banner of truth in order to bring about national and international victory determines his life's success-march and his heart's progress-flight. Indeed, his life's success-march and his heart's progress-flight are the success-march and the progress-flight of his nation as well. This success-march and progress-flight can be founded only on his and his nation's self-giving to the United Nations, which is the world's peace-envisioning home – the world's oneness-home and a fulness-vision-manifestation.

14. Hope

> Hope is my mind's secret fear.
> Hope is my heart's sacred courage.
> Hope is my life's daring experience.
> Hope is my soul's illumining success
> And fulfilling progress.
> Hope is my Lord's ascending Perfection
> And my Lord's transcending Satisfaction.

We, the members of the Meditation Group at the United Nations, have only one friend – a soulful friend, a oneness-friend – and that friend is hope. We started with hope-friend. Hope-friend and hope-life were synonymous in our case. This hope-life was firmly established on 29 February in 1972, when I had the golden opportunity to meet with former Secretary-General U Thant, who embodied colossal hope for the entire world. U Thant's life itself became the grandiose flowering of hope. A simple schoolteacher from Burma became the principal teacher of the comity of nations. Here his teaching life did not come to an end. He went one step ahead to serve divinity in humanity with the message of the all-illumining and all-fulfilling Truth, the Truth that has no alternative. The message of his soulful heart was: "No compromise, no compromise with falsehood. Truth is paramount; Truth alone can save, illumine, perfect and fulfil the world."

Hope-vision he discovered. Hope-realisation he became. Hope-illumination he offered to the world at large. This is our beloved brother, U Thant, the Pilot who will ever be remembered for his simplicity-life, kindness-heart and oneness-soul. In him we observe that the finite hope of today does not have to remain with the finite and fleeting forever. It can slowly, steadily and unerringly grow into infinite, life-saving and life-illumining Reality.

U Thant's compassion was at times misunderstood by human souls. But his oneness with all nations big and small, his oneness with all and sundry was never, never misunderstood. For what he was, what he is and what he will remain forever is simplicity's oneness, purity's oneness and divinity's oneness.

15. *Because I need*

>Because I need God's Love,
>God's Compassion saves me.
>
>Because I need God's Compassion,
>God's Forgiveness illumines me.
>
>Because I need God's Forgiveness,
>God's Satisfaction inspires me.
>
>Because I need God's Satisfaction,
>God's Oneness liberates me.
>
>Because I need God's Oneness,
>God gives me His Eternity's Boat,
>His Infinity's Sea
>And
>His Immortality's Shore.
>
>Because I need God's Boat, God's Sea
>And God's Shore,
>God gives me two things that He loves most
>In His entire creation:
>A sleepless cry and a deathless smile.

16. *My body wants to sleep*

My body wants to sleep.
My vital wants to run.
My mind wants to know.
My heart wants to grow.
My soul wants to glow.
My Lord Supreme wants to flow.

My body cries.
My vital sighs.
My mind fears.
My heart hesitates.
My soul wanders.
My Lord Supreme wonders.

My body likes to sleep.
My vital likes to conquer.
My mind likes to prosper.
My heart likes to surrender.
My soul likes to discover.
My Lord Supreme likes to remember.

My body will see.
My vital will feel.
My mind will believe.
My heart will realise.
My soul will smile.
My Lord Supreme will rest.

17. *Man's inner inspiration*

Man's inner inspiration
Is his outer success.

Man's inner aspiration
Is his outer progress.

Man's inner dedication
Is his outer manifestation.

Man's inner realisation
Is his outer perfection.

Man's divine hunger
Is his deepest depth.

Man's divine duty
Is his brightest beauty.

Man's divine love
Is his highest height.

Man's divine oneness
Is his purest satisfaction.

The man in God
Is the birthless Knower.

The God in man
Is the deathless Doer.

Man the God discovers within.
God the man uncovers without.

18. The inner role of the United Nations

The US State Department invited Sri Chinmoy to come to Washington on 6 June 1980 to address its "Open Forum", a policy discussion group inaugurated during the Viet Nam War to acquaint policy-makers with different points of view on critical issues of the day. Sri Chinmoy was asked to speak on the inner role of the United Nations. Sri Chinmoy also delivered this same talk at United Nations Headquarters on 13 June 1980 as part of his Dag Hammarskjöld Lecture Series.

When I speak of the United Nations, my mind, heart and soul immediately compel me to speak of the United States in the same breath. When I speak for the United Nations, my mind, heart and soul are immediately blessed by the prosperous and generous soul of the host state – the Empire State – New York.

The term "united" has always had a special appeal to all human souls, and this transcendent idea has remained in vogue down the sweep of centuries. There was a time when America was under the repressive yoke of Great Britain. Then America fought dauntlessly and sleeplessly for its rightful independence. At first, the newly liberated Americans and their beautiful, vast land were sadly wanting in oneness. But there came a time when a new dawn of oneness-glory broke upon the glowing and illumining horizon. Americans felt the supreme necessity of a "united" country, and the thirteen colonies gradually, steadily, unerringly and selflessly became unified. Similarly, although at the present time peace is not reigning supreme in the United Nations, there shall definitely come a time when peace-flood will inundate the "united" nations around the globe.

Who could have envisaged that the thirteen colonies would one day develop into such a powerful country – fifty states standing indivisible, united by none other than the Hand of the Supreme Being? For the United States, the heart-throbbing and life-illumining song "united" had its birthless and deathless origin in the hearts of the great Americans whose names are synonymous with the lofty principles of liberty, justice and oneness. The founder of the nation, George Washington; the vision-luminary, Thomas Jefferson; the wisdom-sun, Benjamin Franklin; and the tireless fighter, John Adams: these powerful luminaries, along with others, bravely dreamt of unity for the thirteen colonies.

Again, it was a great son of the United States, Woodrow Wilson, who had the pioneer-vision of the League of Nations – the hallowed source of the United Nations. Some people are of the opinion that the League of Nations totally collapsed and failed, but I cannot see eye to eye with them. The League of Nations did not fail. We must view the League of Nations as the loving mother and the United Nations as her most promising child. When parents leave the earth-planet, their children often manifest more aspiration-light, more vision-power and more manifestation-delight than the parents themselves were able to do. Unmistakably, it is from the dying parents that a bright new light comes to the fore. When the children successfully offer much more than their parents to the world at large, we never think that the parents were hopeless and useless in comparison. On the contrary, we perceive a most significant inner connection, inner link and inner growth between them. We see that the children are marching and progressing in their parents' footsteps. Here we can safely say that Woodrow Wilson's League of Nations actually offered its wisdom-light to its future child, the United Nations.

As I said before, to me, the United States and the United Nations are divinely destined to run abreast. Not in vain is the headquarters of the United Nations in the United States – in New York, the capital of the world. This dynamic and fascinating world capital draws the world's attention at every moment. Is there any place that can be more appropriate than New York City to house the vision of universal oneness, which is in the process of being realised and manifested in the heart and soul of humanity?

True, at times the United States and the United Nations are not on good terms. But each knows perfectly well that the one adds tremendous value to the other in terms of prestige, recognition, self-awareness and oneness-perfection. Inwardly they know that they truly need and deserve each other. In silence, unreservedly the United States gives the United Nations confidence-light. In silence, unreservedly the United Nations gives the United States oneness-height. Being a seeker, in my silence-heart I feel that the concept of the United Nations has verily come from the United States, unconsciously if not consciously, for the United States had this united feeling two hundred years ago, whereas the United Nations is only thirty-five years old.

At the present moment of evolution, the United States says to the United Nations, "If you take my help, you have to use it in my own way."

The United Nations says to the United States, "I am ready to take your help and I shall remain most grateful to you. But if I use your help in your own way, then I will be totally lost in the comity of nations. Whatever you can afford to give me, please give me unconditionally."

The United States immediately responds, "Oh no, I do not want to give you my help unconditionally. I have a right to know whether or not my momentous and generous offering is being utilised properly. As it is my bounden duty to help your supreme cause, O United Nations, I feel that it is also your bounden duty to accept my wisdom-sun on rare occasions."

The United Nations says, "Sorry to stand firm in my belief, O United States. One day you will be blessed with the real joy of unconditional self-giving, which is always without a second."

THE INNER ROLE OF THE UNITED NATIONS

The inner role of the United Nations amuses the intelligentsia, inspires the world-peace-lovers and nourishes the world-oneness-servers. God has showered His choicest Blessings upon the inner role of the United Nations. When we contemplate on the idea of "role", we immediately think of either responsibility or challenge. But when it is a matter of inner role, there is no such thing as responsibility or challenge; there is only one self-giving Divinity which is breathlessly growing into a self-becoming reality.

The United Nations is often misunderstood. Perhaps its fate will always remain the same. But is there anybody who is not misunderstood, including poor God? Misunderstanding is the order of the day. But that does not and cannot prevent the United Nations from making its soulful self-offering in the creation of a oneness-home for all.

The United Nations has been marching resolutely and triumphantly towards its inner goal. Indeed, the remarkable leadership of its four Secretaries-General has made its outer success and inner progress not only convincing but also fulfilling. Our present Secretary-General, Kurt Waldheim, throws considerable light on the inner role of the world organisation: "We are not faced with many separate problems, but with different aspects of a single over-all problem: the survival and prosperity of all men and women, and their harmonious development, physical as well as spiritual, in peace with each other and with nature. This is the solution we must seek. It is within our power to find it."

Secretary-General Waldheim's predecessor – the Supreme Pilot of the United Nations, U Thant – valued unreservedly the inner or spiritual obligations of the United Nations. Him to quote: "I have certain priorities in regard to virtues and human values.... I would attach greater importance to moral qualities or moral virtues over intellectual qualities or intellectual virtues –

moral qualities, like love, compassion, understanding, tolerance, the philosophy of live and let live, the ability to understand the other man's point of view, which is the key to all great religions.... And above all, I would attach the greatest importance to spiritual values, spiritual qualities."

Secretary-General Dag Hammarskjöld offered the hallowed message-light that each individual has a responsibility to his own inner role. According to him, each individual must strive inwardly as well as outwardly to achieve abiding peace: "Our work for peace must begin within the private world of each one of us. To build for man a world without fear, we must be without fear. To build a world of justice, we must be just. And how can we fight for liberty if we are not free in our own minds?"

Illumining leaders from all over the world who are serving the United Nations remind us of the undeniable fact that the earth cannot exist without the world body – the United Nations – in spite of its apparent failings and problems. Secretary-General Trygve Lie's precious message ran: "The one common undertaking and universal instrument of the great majority of the human race is the United Nations. A patient, constructive, long-term use of its potentialities can bring a real and secure peace to the world."

The outer role of the United Nations is greatness remarkable. The inner role of the United Nations is goodness admirable. The supreme role of the United Nations is fulness adorable.

Greatness our mind desperately needs. Goodness our heart sleeplessly needs. Fulness our life breathlessly needs.

Greatness surprises the curious world. Goodness inspires the aspiring world. Fulness fulfils the serving world.

Greatness is blessed with an outer challenge. Goodness is blessed with an inner promise. Fulness is blessed with an integral perfection. Challenge awakens, promise expedites and perfection immortalises our varied capacities.

THE INNER ROLE OF THE UNITED NATIONS

Greatness is sound-amplification. Goodness is silence-enlightenment. Fulness is God-Satisfaction.

The pillars of the United States, its Presidents, call upon us to dedicate ourselves to the most significant cause that the United Nations embodies. Needless to say, the world organisation is God's gracious experiment and precious experience. Such being the case, we must feel an inner obligation to participate in this aspect of God's cosmic Drama. The late President John F Kennedy spoke not only to his fellow Americans but to all his fellow beings when he proclaimed: "My fellow inhabitants of this planet, let us take our stand here in this assembly of nations. And let us see if we, in our own time, can move the world towards a just and lasting peace."

President Carter has also powerfully encouraged his country to remain part and parcel of the United Nations. He tells us the true truth that real leadership and continuous service to mankind are inseparable: "There is no possible means of isolating ourselves from the rest of the world, so we must provide leadership. But this leadership need not depend on our inherent military force, or economic power, or political persuasion. It should derive from the fact that we try to be right and honest and truthful and decent."

The favourite son of New York, Senator Daniel Moynihan, former United States Ambassador to the United Nations, expresses his country's sincere awareness of the sublime necessity of the United Nations: "While there have been some calls to boycott the General Assembly, or not to vote in it, there have been but few calls for withdrawal from the United Nations. It is almost as if American opinion now acknowledged that there was no escaping involvement in the emergent world society."

The United States' Special Ambassador to the United Nations Law of the Sea Conference, Elliot Richardson – a heart of peace and a life of light – encourages, strengthens and spreads a global viewpoint: "The interdependence of the world is an increasingly visible fact, and I believe that out of that fact is bound to emerge in due course a compelling – and comparably inspiring – concept of the opportunities for global cooperation."

A staunch supporter of the United Nations – indeed, the donor of the land upon which the UN stands – Nelson Rockefeller vividly draws the parallel between the roots of the United States and the roots of the United Nations: "The federal idea, which our Founding Fathers applied in their historic act of political creation in the eighteenth century, can be applied in this twentieth century in the larger context of the world of free nations – if we will but match our forefathers in courage and vision. The first historic instance secured freedom and order to this new nation. The second can decisively serve to guard freedom and to promote order in a free world."

As the Declaration of Independence of the United States is an unparallelled discovery, even so is the Charter of the United Nations. The US Declaration of Independence and the UN Charter are humanity's two aspiration-dedication-realities. The beacon-light of the Declaration of Independence shows countless human souls the way to their destined goal: "We hold these truths to be self-evident: that all men are created equal, that they are endowed by their Creator with certain inalienable rights, that among these are life, liberty and the pursuit of happiness, that to secure these rights, Governments are instituted among men, deriving their just powers from the consent of the governed."

The United Nations Charter bravely and heroically proclaims these rights for all of humanity and seeks "to reaffirm faith in fundamental human rights, in the dignity and worth of the human person, in the equal rights of men and women and of nations large and small, and to establish conditions under which justice and respect for the obligations arising from treaties and

THE INNER ROLE OF THE UNITED NATIONS

other sources of international law can be maintained, and to promote social progress and better standards of life in larger freedom."

Concern for and satisfaction in the towering achievements of the United Nations may be a confidence-trip into the unknown, but never into the unknowable. The greatest messenger of the Catholic world, Pope Paul VI, during his visit to the United Nations in 1964, eloquently expressed the inner role of the United Nations: "The Church considers the United Nations to be the fruit of a civilisation to which the Catholic religion.... gave the vital principles. It considers it an instrument of brotherhood between nations which the Holy See has always desired and promoted.... The convergence of so many peoples, of so many races, so many States, in a single organisation intended to avert the evils of war and to favour the good things of peace, is a fact which the Holy See considers as corresponding to its concept of humanity and included within the area of its spiritual mission to the world."

When Pope John Paul II visited the United Nations in October 1979 and spoke to the General Assembly, Secretary-General Waldheim introduced him thus: "Your presence among us on this historic occasion is particularly encouraging since it dramatically reaffirms the great spiritual values which you represent and which inspire the Charter."

Pope John Paul II indeed reaffirmed the value of the inner United Nations and the spiritual dimension of world politics when he told the General Assembly: "An analysis of the history of mankind, especially at its present stage, shows how important is the duty of revealing more fully the range of the goods that are linked with the spiritual dimension of human existence. It shows how important this task is for building peace and how serious is any threat to human rights."

The composer of the immortal *Hymn to the United Nations*, the late Maestro Don Pablo Casals, reminds us that individuals and their countries undeniably need the United Nations. He gives an inspired call for us to selflessly play our parts in the inner and outer roles of the United Nations: "Those who believe in the dignity of man should act at this time to bring about a deeper understanding among people and a sincere rapprochement between conflicting forces. The United Nations today represents the most important hope for peace. Let us give it all power to act for our benefit. And let us fervently pray that the near future will disperse the clouds that darken our days now."

The outer role of the United Nations is a colossal hope. The inner role of the United Nations is a generous assurance. The supreme role of the United Nations is a prosperous satisfaction.

Hope is a growing plant. Assurance is a blossoming tree. Satisfaction is a delicious fruit.

At the present stage, the United Nations is a growing plant which is only thirty-five years old. Is it not absurd for us to expect the United Nations to solve the overwhelming problems of centuries? Let the child-plant grow and glow, smile and cry. Then there shall come a time when this tiny plant will grow into a huge tree, with countless leaves, sleepless flowers and spotless fruits – sheltering, inspiring and nourishing all those who desperately need its protection-shelter, rejuvenation-inspiration and satisfaction-nourishment.

19. *Philosophy, religion and yoga*

Philosophy is man's close association with God. Religion is man's conscious and close union with God. Yoga is man's conscious, close and constant oneness with God.

Philosophy sees the wisdom in truth. Religion realises the code of life with truth. Yoga becomes the delight for truth.

Philosophy is often the mind-capacity. Religion is often the heart-capacity. Yoga is always the God-capacity.

Philosophy ascends from the searching mind. Religion ascends from the crying heart. Yoga ascends and descends: ascends for the discovery of the silence-world and descends for the mastery of the sound-world.

Philosophy unmistakably tells the world about its stupendous victory. Religion unreservedly tells the world about its momentous mission. Yoga unconditionally tells the world about its auspicious perfection.

Philosophy is brave. It tries to understand the higher world. Religion is wise. It tries to acknowledge the outer world. Yoga is pure. It tries to accept the higher, the outer and the inner world.

Philosophy inspires us to become great. Religion inspires us to become good. Yoga inspires us to become perfect.

Philosophy teaches and teaches. Religion preaches and then praises. Yoga praises and praises.

Philosophy gets untold joy in guiding the world. Religion gets boundless joy in conquering the world. Yoga gets spontaneous joy in serving the world.

The United Nations philosophy is to sincerely please all the countries. The United Nations religion is to generously help all the countries that are abiding by the truth principles. The United Nations yoga is to sleeplessly turn the entire world into a peaceful and soulful oneness-home.

20. *The inner role of the United Nations*

You have just observed me praying and meditating. Prayer and meditation are of supreme importance if we are to execute the inner role of the United Nations. Perhaps some of you know that twice a week we pray and meditate at the United Nations in New York. And from time to time I give spiritual talks, soulful talks, which are perfectly in tune with our prayer and meditation.

The inner role of the United Nations is a shadowless dream.

The inner role of the United Nations is a relentless determination.

The inner role of the United Nations is a breathless promise.

The inner role of the United Nations is a sleepless struggle.

The inner role of the United Nations is a faultless progress.

The inner role of the United Nations is a deathless satisfaction.

The inner role of the United Nations is a cry and a smile – an inner cry and an outer smile – and this inner cry and outer smile have to be improved. The inner cry has to be genuine and the outer smile has to be soulful. The inner cry has to climb up to reach the highest pinnacle. The outer smile has to be illumined and fulfilled at the same time, and it has to reach the length and the breadth of the world.

The inner role of the United Nations is the link with the immortal power of infinite peace that spans the universe. This is the power that builds, not breaks. This is the power of peace that inundates our inner beings and, at the same time, our outer lives. This peace is also delight; it evolves slowly, steadily and unerringly towards the great and ultimate destination.

The inner role of the United Nations tells us that duty and responsibility have to be seen in a different light. Each member of the United Nations has a significant duty and responsibility. Here, by virtue of our prayer and meditation, we have come to realise that duty is nothing other than opportunity, and that responsibility is another name for privilege. Therefore, to serve the United Nations unique capacity is to be blessed with a golden opportunity and fruitful privilege.

The inner role of the United Nations tells us success is fleeting, whereas progress is everlasting. It tells us that success on the physical plane, vital plane or mental plane cannot lead us to the final Goal; it is only progress that slowly and unmistakably leads us to our ultimate Goal. Again, when we reach the ultimate Goal, we get the message to go farther, for the ultimate Goal is not a fixed place; it is always in the process of transcending its own reality.

The inner role of the United Nations helps us discover a unique prayer which is the prayer of prayers. At each moment, we have to pray not to conquer but to serve and, while serving, to free the oneness-reality in and around the world. We have to pray not to lead and, again, not to only follow, but to become inseparably one with the comity of nations. Together, all the nations will dive the deepest, fly the highest and march the farthest.

21. *Prayer and meditation*

>Prayer is man's soulful cry for God.
>Meditation is man's fruitful smile in God.
>
>Prayer is personal; also, universal.
>Meditation is impersonal; also, transcendental.
>
>Prayer is petition; also, adoration.
>Meditation is absorption; also, perfection.
>
>Prayer needs God's Compassion-Shower.
>Meditation needs God's Illumination-Tower.
>
>I pray for Immortality.
>I meditate on Infinity and Eternity.
>
>Prayer is night crying for light.
>Meditation is light searching for delight.
>
>Prayer reminds us of our hidden sins.
>Meditation reminds us of our forgotten sun.
>
>To prayer God says:
>"My child, I am waiting for you.
>Come and see Me."
>
>To meditation God says:
>"My child, wait for Me.
>I am coming to see you."
>
>Prayer is the purity that counts.
>Meditation is the luminosity that mounts.

THE INNER ROLE OF THE UNITED NATIONS

My prayer-teacher shows me
The beauty of soulfulness.
My meditation-teacher blesses me
With the duty of oneness.

Prayer soulfully reveals man's faith in God.
Meditation smilingly reveals God's faith in man.

God; who, you? No!
God; who, me? No!

Who then is God?
God is my prayer-purity's guest.
God is my meditation-divinity's nest.

My God is mad because nowadays
I do not pray
Either in the morning or in the evening.

My God is sad because nowadays
I do not meditate
Sleeplessly and unconditionally.

22. *Prayer for Gratitude Day*

My Lord Supreme, this is a special day, Gratitude Day. Alas, I do not have even an iota of gratitude to offer You. Since I have no gratitude, please tell me what I can offer You instead.

"My child, then give Me a soulful promise."

My Lord Supreme, I do not know what a soulful promise is. I always break my promise. I promise in season and out of season. But never do I fulfil my promises. Such being the case, my Lord Supreme, please tell me what I can offer You instead of a soulful promise.

"My child, then tell Me that you love Me divinely."

My Lord Supreme, I do not know what divine Love is. How can I offer You divine Love when I do not know what divine Love feels like?

"My child, then give Me a fruitful cry. Cry for Me once, only once in your life."

Alas, my Lord Supreme, I do not cry even for myself. How do You expect me to cry for You?

"My child, let Me tell you one thing. Both of us deserve two special names. Each of us will have a new name. Your new name will be a secret and clever unwillingness, and My new Name will be an unreservedly open and compassionately stupid Forgiveness."

23. *Women's liberation and oneness-satisfaction*

Women have one common name: sacrifice. They can sacrifice everything that they have and that they are, either for their dear ones or for an unknown, if not an unknowable, supreme Reality. From time immemorial, Indian women have been revealing the supernal beauty of sacrifice. An Indian wife is synonymous with an Indian sacrifice-heart. The Indian goddess Sati could not bear the unending insults which her father Yaksha lavished upon her husband Shiva. Her love for her husband could only be felt and never described. Finally, she destroyed her life, for she felt that death was unquestionably preferable to enduring her husband's humiliation-life.

In the hoary past, Maitreyi, wife of the great sage Yagnavalka, received a call from the Absolute Reality. Therefore, she found it impossible to be satisfied with earthly riches and fleeting happiness. Easily she could have wallowed in the pleasures of earthly prosperity, but she chose the path of renunciation. Her immortal utterance will forever and ever reverberate in the Indian firmament: "What shall I do with the things that will not and cannot make me immortal?"

In the Ramayana, Sita became an incarnation of sacrifice. She cheerfully and unconditionally accepted the life of exile for fourteen years in order to be with her beloved Rama. Urmila, the wife of Rama's younger brother, Laksmana, made a similar and ever-memorable sacrifice. She allowed her beloved husband Laksmana to follow his eldest brother into exile, although she could not go with him. She sacrificed the company of her dearest husband by cheerfully letting him fulfil his desire to be with his brother Rama.

Savitri's love for Prince Satyavan touched the very depth of Immortality. When death snatched him away, Savitri continued following the spirit of her husband until she proved to death that nothing in God's entire creation could stand between her and her husband. Finally, death had to return Satyavan to the world of the living, for the power of Savitri's oneness-love for her husband far surpassed the division-power of death.

Even an ordinary Indian woman can be an emblem of sacrifice. A certain Rajput king was killed in battle by another king, and the enemy's soldiers entered into the palace to kill the king's family. The maid Panna, seeing the grave situation, carried away the infant prince and put her own child in the prince's place. She said to herself: "I am an ordinary human being, and my son will always remain an ordinary human being. But this infant will one day be a king. The king and queen were always kind to me. Can I not do them a favour now? If God takes care of this infant prince through me, he will grow up and someday may be able to regain his kingdom. My sacrifice is no sacrifice when I am doing something for a noble cause."

The soldiers came and killed Panna's infant immediately, but in the course of time the real prince did regain his father's kingdom.

Satisfaction can be achieved in various ways. These women, by their matchless sacrifice, got satisfaction. Some present-day women, especially in the West, try to achieve satisfaction in another way. They try to achieve satisfaction by equalling or transcending men. Achieving satisfaction by sacrificing or serving is the Indian way. Achieving satisfaction by equalling or surpassing is the Western way.

To get satisfaction, you can stand on someone's head, you can be at his feet or you can be inside his heart. Some women want to compete with men and defeat them. If these women want to get satisfaction by surpassing others, then they can, provided they are not affected by others' jealousy. Some want to get satisfaction by becoming equal with others. This is another way.

Again, by remaining at the foot of the tree, a woman can also get satisfaction. When she remains at the foot of the tree and serves others, no one is jealous of her. Those she is serving show her all love. At that time, she does not feel that she is inferior. In a family, if the youngest thinks that he is inferior, he feels miserable. But if he feels that God wanted him to play the role of the youngest, and that the older children are not superior to him but merely have a different role to play, then he will get satisfaction. Similarly, these women get satisfaction by fulfilling the role of serving and sacrificing.

Satisfaction can come by serving others, by equalling others or by surpassing others. But the satisfaction that comes in these ways will not last. In India they tell about three kinds of disciples. An absolutely useless disciple will try to stand on top of his Master's head. A foolish disciple will feel that he is one person and his Master is someone else, and that they are equal. A devoted disciple will try always to be at the feet of the Master. But if someone is a devoted disciple and, at the same time, wants to conquer insecurity forever and live all the time in oneness-joy, then he will try to live in the heart of the Master.

The satisfaction that one gets by serving, equalling or surpassing others will not last. Only oneness-satisfaction will forever last. In the heart's oneness, there is no superiority or inferiority; there is not even equality. There is only oneness-joy. Here it is not a competition-game but a oneness-game.

Today we hear a lot about women's liberation. Many women are trying to equal or surpass men. But I wish to say that real liberation does not lie in equalling or surpassing others, but in becoming one with them. Liberation is satisfaction, and satisfaction is found only in oneness.

Man's inner strength is his poise. Woman's inner strength is her love. When poise and love blend together in oneness-game, at that time true satisfaction, constant satisfaction, perfect satisfaction, infinite and immortal Satisfaction will dawn on earth.

1–7. *(p. 573)* On 15 June 1977 Sri Chinmoy was interviewed at the United Nations by a reporter from the worldwide news service United Press International. These are excerpts from that interview.

8. *(p. 576)* On 24 October 1978 the Peace Meditation at the United Nations observed United Nations Day with a programme in the Dag Hammarskjöld Auditorium. Sri Chinmoy made these remarks on that occasion.

9. *(p. 576)* On 10 November 1978 Sri Chinmoy paid this memorial tribute to the American artist Norman Rockwell during a meeting of the Meditation Group.

10. *(p. 577)* 9 January 1979.

11. *(p. 580)* 1 February 1980.

12. *(p. 582)* 26 February 1980.

13. *(p. 583)* 27 February 1980.

14. *(p. 584)* On 29 February 1980, Sri Chinmoy gave this inspirational talk on the anniversary of his first meeting with the late Secretary-General U Thant which took place on 29 February 1972.

15. *(p. 585)* On 21 March 1980, Sri Chinmoy gave this inspirational talk at a memorial service for former Ambassador Allard Lowenstein held at the United Nations.

16. *(p. 586)* 3 June 1980.

17. *(p. 587)* 3 June 1980.

19. *(p. 596)* 10 June 1980.

20. *(p. 598)* Sri Chinmoy gave this talk at United Nations Headquarters in Geneva on 16 June 1980.

21. *(p. 600)* 1 August 1980.

23. *(p. 602)* 2 March 1981.

APPENDIX

NOTES TO THE PRESENT EDITION

Additional writings

Additional writings related to the United Nations are also published in *The works of Sri Chinmoy, vol. 5** (2016), which includes the original *Flame-Waves* series. From its preface:

> The United Nations Meditation Group is a group of United Nations staff members, delegates and representatives from non-governmental organisations accredited to the United Nations who believe that there is a spiritual way to work for world peace as well as a political way. Twice a week the Group meets at the U.N. for non-sectarian meditations and spiritual discussions on brotherhood and world union.
> The United Nations Meditation Group functions under the inner guidance of its Spiritual Director, Sri Chinmoy, who conducts the Group's meetings and also delivers the continuing Dag Hammarskjold monthly lecture series at the U.N.

---

* SRI CHINMOY, *The works of Sri Chinmoy: questions & answers II*, Ganapati Press, Lyon and Oxford, 2016.

Sri Chinmoy Meditation at the United Nations

Sri Chinmoy Meditation at the United Nations, originally named United Nations Meditation Group, was created on 14 April 1970. Its credo, as expressed by Sri Chinmoy in 1970:

> We believe that each man has the potentiality of reaching the Ultimate Truth. We also believe that man cannot and will not remain imperfect forever. Each man is an instrument of God. When the hour strikes, each individual soul listens to the inner dictates of God. When man listens to God, his imperfections are turned into perfections, his ignorance into knowledge, his searching mind into revealing light and his uncertain reality into all-fulfilling Divinity.

Later on it was slightly changed, to read:

UNITED NATIONS:
THE HEART-HOME OF THE WORLD-BODY

> We believe and we hold that each man has the potentiality of reaching the Ultimate Truth. We also believe that man cannot and will not remain imperfect forever. Each man is an instrument of God. When the hour strikes, each individual soul listens to the inner dictates of God. When man listens to God, his imperfections are turned into perfections, his ignorance into knowledge, his searching mind into revealing light and his uncertain reality into all-fulfilling Divinity.

FOREWORDS TO FIRST EDITIONS

Foreword to first edition of Pérez de Cuéllar: immortality's rainbow-peace

United Nations Secretary-General Pérez de Cuéllar has offered his most illumined stewardship to the world-body since 1982. During these highly significant years, humanity has seen unprecedented progress in the fulfilment of its ancient and soul-stirring cry for peace in the world. Through the Secretary-General's unparalleled contributions as both a far-sighted visionary and a fully determined realist, the goals outlined in the Charter of the United Nations are coming to fruition as never before. As a small token of his deepest appreciation and admiration, Sri Chinmoy has selected some excerpts from the Secretary-General's most recent speeches and added his humble comments to each. As leader of the Peace Meditation at the United Nations since 1970, Sri Chinmoy wishes to offer the group's most heartfelt gratitude to the Secretary-General, as well as its sincerest prayers for the world-body's continued victories for peace.

Foreword to first edition of United Nations meditation-flowers and to-morrow's noon

Since the spring of 1970, Sri Chinmoy has been conduction meditations and lecturing at the United Nations as spiritual leader of the United Nations Meditation Group, recently renamed Sri Chinmoy Meditation at the United Nations. This book is a collection of some of Sri Chinmoy's inspirational talks, essays and aphorisms published during 1977 in the monthly bulletin of the meditation group under the titles *United Nations meditation-flowers and to-morrow's noon*.

Other volumes of Sri Chinmoy's lectures and answers to questions which he was asked at the United Nations include *The Garland of Nation-Souls, The tears of Nation-Hearts, Reality-Dream, Union-Vision, Bicentennial flames at the United Nations*, and *Flame-Waves*.

BIBLIOGRAPHY

SRI CHINMOY:

– *The Garland of Nation-Souls*, New York, Sri Chinmoy Lighthouse, 1972 [GNS]
– *The tears of Nation-Hearts*, New York, Agni Press, 1974 [TNH]
– *The bicentennial flames at the United Nations*, New York, Agni Press, 1976 [BF]
– *Reality-Dream*, New York, Agni Press, 1976 [RD]
– *Union-Vision*, New York, Agni Press, 1976 [UV]
– *Two God-servers and man-lovers*, New York, Aum Publications, 1977 [TGS]
– *U Thant: Divinity's Smile, humanity's cry*, New York, Agni Press, 1977 [UT]
– *The seeker's mind: talks delivered at the United Nations*, New York, Agni Press, 1978 [SM]
– *A soulful tribute to the Secretary-General: the Pilot Supreme of the United Nations*, New York, Agni Press, 1978 [TSG]
– *United Nations meditation-flowers and to-morrow's noon*, New York, Agni Press, 1978 [UNM]
– *Pérez de Cuéllar: immortality's rainbow-peace*, New York, Aum Publications, 1989 [PDC]
– *A real member of the United Nations*, New York, Agni Press, 1989 [RUN]
– *The inner role of the United Nations*, New York, Agni Press, 1993 [IR]

[Suggested cite key is in square brackets.]

POSTFACE

Publishing principles

The works of Sri Chinmoy series aims to obey the Author's wish: scrupulous fidelity to his original words, use of typographical style by him selected, specific spelling choices, end placement of any editorial content (i.e. not written by Sri Chinmoy himself), particular treatment of some personal nouns in special cases, etc.

Textual accuracy

The series has been checked to ensure faithful accuracy to the originals. Although much effort has been put in proofreading and comparing different versions of the text, this print may still present lingering errors. The Publisher would be grateful to be apprised of any mistypes via postal mail or facsimile, possibly with scan of the original page where the text is different. Please use original books only, specifying the year of publication, as no online version can be considered authoritative.

Ongoing reprints will include any revised text from these errata.

Acknowledgements

The Publisher is very grateful to the late Professor Lambert and his équipe for his invaluable advice. For many decades Prof. Lambert conducted a small publishing house specialising in hand-made prints of philological edition of the classics. The standard of this edition would not have been the same without his scholarly advice.

The Publisher is also grateful to the international team of collaborators that spent countless hours proofreading and checking the current text against the originals.

Our deepest gratitude to Sri Chinmoy. His living presence can be felt breathing throughout his writings. It is a privilege to be involved with his works, in any form.

Citation keys

Citation keys can be used throughout *The works of Sri Chinmoy* to allow accurate cross-reference of texts across titles and editions. Examples: EA 13, ST 50000, UPA 7. Suggested citation keys can be found in the bibliography at the end of each volume.

Sri Chinmoy Canon

We could not use better words than Professor Lambert's, who kindly offered the name *Sri Chinmoy Canon*:

«By defining Sri Chinmoy's first editions as *editio princeps* we chose to follow classical scholarship criteria, not because we consider Sri Chinmoy's work antique, but because we believe it is among the few post ‹classical antiquity› works to rightly deserve to be considered a *classicus*, designating by that term *superiority, authority* and *perfection*.
«The monumental work Sri Chinmoy is offering to mankind is awe-inspiring and supremely pre-eminent in proportions and quality. It is manifest that Sri Chinmoy's work — which we feel right to call *The Sri Chinmoy Canon* — will be of profound help and source of enlightenment to anyone seeking a higher wisdom, truth and reality supreme.»

[Translated from French by M. G.S.]

TABLE OF CONTENTS

1. THE GARLAND OF NATION-SOULS
I – THE GARLAND OF NATION-SOULS 4
II – TALKS FROM THE PEACE ROOM 11
III – MEDITATIONS FROM THE UNITED NATIONS 62
2. THE TEARS OF NATION-HEARTS
3. THE BICENTENNIAL FLAMES AT THE UNITED NATIONS
QUESTIONS AND ANSWERS 154
4. REALITY-DREAM
I – TALKS 173
II – SERIES ON GREAT MEN AND WOMEN 190
III – TALKS 202
5. UNION-VISION
I – TALKS 242
II – SPIRITUAL WORDS 275
III – TALKS 288
6. TWO GOD-SERVERS AND MAN-LOVERS
QUESTIONS BY MR ROBERT MULLER 305
7. U THANT: DIVINITY'S SMILE, HUMANITY'S CRY
I – DEDICATION TO U THANT, PART 1 323
II – KIND WORDS FROM WORLD LEADERS 330
III – DEDICATION TO U THANT, PART 2 341
IV – PERFORMANCE OF SIDDHARTHA BECOMES THE BUDDHA 344
PART V – PRAYERS FOR U THANT'S RECOVERY 348
VI – LETTERS FROM U THANT 349
VII – PRAYERS AND TRIBUTES 354
VIII – REMINISCENCES ABOUT U THANT 356
IX – DEDICATION TO U THANT, PART 3 360
8. THE SEEKER'S MIND
I – TALKS DELIVERED AT THE UNITED NATIONS 383
PART II – WORLD LEADERS 427
III 433
IV – EXPRESSIONS OF GRATITUDE 435

9. A SOULFUL TRIBUTE TO THE SECRETARY-GENERAL: THE PILOT SUPREME OF THE UNITED NATIONS
I – A SOULFUL TRIBUTE   447
II – MEETINGS WITH SECRETARY-GENERAL KURT WALDHEIM 485
III – APPENDIX   490
10. UNITED NATIONS MEDITATION-FLOWERS AND TO-MORROW'S NOON
I – UNITED NATIONS MEDITATION-FLOWERS   496
II – APHORISMS   501
III – TO-MORROW'S NOON   514
11. PÉREZ DE CUÉLLAR: IMMORTALITY'S RAINBOW-PEACE
I – COMMENTARIES ON QUOTATIONS BY SECRETARY-GENERAL PÉREZ DE CUÉLLAR   527
II – SONGS DEDICATED TO THE SECRETARY-GENERAL   542
III – A CHRONOLOGY OF GOOD WILL: MEETINGS AND CORRESPONDENCE WITH THE SECRETARIES-GENERAL   546
12. A REAL MEMBER OF THE UNITED NATIONS
13. THE INNER ROLE OF THE UNITED NATIONS
I – INTERVIEW WITH UNITED PRESS INTERNATIONAL   573
II – TALKS AND POEMS   576
APPENDIX
NOTES TO THE PRESENT EDITION
FOREWORDS TO FIRST EDITIONS
BIBLIOGRAPHY
POSTFACE
TABLE OF CONTENTS

*Composition typographique par imprimerie
Ab Academia Aoidon, Paris & Lyon.*

*Un grand merci à Prof Knuth pour
l'utilisation avancée de T_EX.*

A LYON, LE 13 MARS XC Æ.G.

www.ingramcontent.com/pod-product-compliance
Lightning Source LLC
Chambersburg PA
CBHW030110240426
43661CB00031B/1359/J